20TH CENTURY

CERAMIC
DESIGNERS

IN BRITAIN

Andrew Casey

December 2002

20TH CENTURY

CERAMIC
DESIGNERS

IN BRITAIN

ANDREW CASEY

ANTIQUE COLLECTORS' CLUB

British Library Cataloguing-in-Publication Data
A catalogue record for this book is available from the British Library

This book is dedicated to my father
Dennis Casey, 1925-1999

Frontispiece illustration: see page 145
Title page illustration: see page 181
Endpapers: A lithographic sheet for the *Variations* pattern,
designed by Susan Williams-Ellis in 1964.

Origination by Antique Collectors' Club
Woodbridge, England
Printed and bound in Italy

CONTENTS

ACKNOWLEDGEMENTS

During my research I have come into contact with several important authors, researchers and recognised authorities who have written about twentieth century designers and ceramics. Not only have they answered my many questions, but they have also allowed me access to their original research. More importantly, they were willing to examine the many drafts as the book developed. I would particularly like to thank Leslie Hayward for his constant support and advice, and for the research material on the history of the Poole Pottery that he has allowed me to use for this publication. I am also indebted to Jennifer Hawkins for kindly granting me access to archive material from the Ceramics and Glass Department of the Victoria and Albert Museum, not only on Poole Pottery but also on designers that she has researched. I am indebted to Alun Graves from the Ceramics and Glass Department, Susan Bennett from the Royal Society of Arts and Eugene Rae from the Royal College of Art. Rodney Hampson's research and his book on the history of James Broadhurst and Sons Ltd. and Kathie Winkle have greatly assisted my understanding of the company's history. Stella Beddoe of the Brighton Museum and Art Gallery kindly gave me permission to reproduce her research material on the work of Truda Carter, as did Dr. James King with his invaluable research on the influences of this designer. Robert Prescott-Walker granted me access to his research material on the Burslem School of Art and the transcript of an interview with Jessie Tait from 1985. Cheryl Buckley generously allowed me to use some research material from her work on this subject area, providing invaluable help with the development of this book. The pioneering research undertaken by Una des Fontaines for her comprehensive book on Daisy Makeig-Jones was a vital resource, as was the research by Bernard Bumpus who kindly let me use his material on the work of Charlotte Rhead and her family. I am grateful for the support and generosity of Anne Ullmann who granted me access to correspondence, archive material and examples of the work of Eric Ravilious. Constance Messenger kindly let me examine the private papers and press cuttings of Keith Murray. I wish to gratefully acknowledge the kind support and generosity of Anwyl Cooper-Willis and Euan Cooper-Willis for allowing me unrivalled access to their collection of Portmeirion papers, archives and pottery and for the photographs that they have kindly loaned for this publication.

I am fortunate to have met a number of the designers featured in this book. They were so willing to talk to me about their lives and work. These were Susan Williams-Ellis, Kathie Winkle, Jessie Tait, Eve Midwinter, John Clappison and the late Susie Cooper. Furthermore family members, working colleagues and associates of all the designers generously gave me the benefit of their experiences and an insight into the subject. These include Louise Blackwall, Ronald and Joan Bailey, Philip and Peter Barnes, Terry Corn, Rene Dale, May Doorbar, John Evans, the late Richard Fletcher, John Hayward, Rena Jefferson, David Johnson, Barry Leigh, Anne Makeig-Jones, Richard Midwinter, Ray Reynolds, Michael Roper, John Ryan, Eddie Sambrook, Joanna Thomas, Michael Walker and Alison and Michael Wright. A special thanks must be given to Norman Tempest for guiding me through the history of both Midwinter and Royal Stafford and advising on dates, designs and shapes.

I acknowledge the help I have received from the Wedgwood Museum during the preparation of this book and the kind permission of the Trustees to reproduce various items of archive material. Certain material owned by Josiah Wedgwood and Sons Ltd. also appears with their consent. They allowed me access to the archives and pattern books and also patiently put me in touch with several designers and pottery workers who were willing to speak to me about the period. I would like to give particular thanks to Gaye Blake Roberts (Curator of the Wedgwood Museum), Lynn Miller, Information Officer, Sharon Gater, Martin Chaplin, Joanne Riley, Jo Nutt and Sue Houndle. In particular Lynn Miller has kindly organised the many images from the Museum's collection for the book. I am indebted to Sharon Gater for new information and her suggestions during our many interesting and informative discussions on the work of Millicent Taplin, Victor Skellern and Daisy Makeig-Jones. Without these people's contributions this book would not have been possible.

The Potteries Museum in Stoke-on-Trent has been so willing to allow me to examine archive materials and grant me access to the Charlotte Rhead archives, a special thank you to Miranda Goodby and Kathy Niblett. I would like to thank Julie McKeown of Royal Doulton Ltd., Joan Jones and Margaret Sargeant for their advice and support. Over the last four years I have corresponded with many people. Collectors, designers or researchers, they have all willingly given me the benefit of their knowledge. I would like to thank the following: Sue and Bob Anderson, Angela Atkinson, Mary Babb, Clive Bailey, John Barter, Colette Bishop, Tom Bloor, Lynn Boyd, Stuart Breeze, Margaret and Derek Brindley, John and Jean Broadbent, Jon Brown, Simon Carter, John Clark, Chris Davenport, Richard Dennis, Sally Dummer, Ann Eatwell, Helene Elder, Mavis Ellerton, Linda Ellis, Janet Fishwick, Peter Goodfellow, Julian Gooding, Millicent Green, Christine Haines, Ann Hartnet, Julie Holland, Irene and Gordon Hopwood, Peter Hulbert, Michael Jeffrey, Steven Jenkins, David Johnson, Francis Joseph, Sue Kennedy, Carole Lovatt, Harry Lyons, Steve McKay, Peter Mills, Ivan Monty, Elizabeth Moody, Simon Moss, Tracey Parker, Julie Pople, David Redman, Peter Rimmer, Peter Robertson, Michael Roper, Stephen Roper, John Runiff-Nuttman, Mike and Maz Sharman, Dora Shaw, Gerrard Shaw, Brian and Briar Shepard, Pascal Skrimshire, Victoria Stanton, Greg Stevenson, Ian and Anne Strover, Linda Taylor, Julian Teed, Stuart Walker, David Walton, Ian and Jane Watson, Robin Welch, Alex Werner, Mark Wilkinson, Ron Willer, David V. Williams, Harold Woodward, Brian Wooley, Wendy Wort and Celeste Yap.

With regard to getting my research into some form of order, I would like to thank Gael and Bob Shipshank, who encouraged me throughout the development of the book and read and corrected my many proofs. During my research I have used several libraries and archives and wish to acknowledge their kind co-operation. These are; Leeds City Art Library, Hanley Library in Stoke-on-Trent, the British Library in Wetherby, West Yorkshire and the New York Public Library, New York City.

To illustrate this book, the publishers are grateful to those who have been willing lend examples of pottery: Pat Adams, Andrew Casey, John Clark of art deco etc, Brighton, the Keithmurray.net website, Anila Mamujee, Christine Norman, the Ravilious family, John Runniff-Nuttman, Ian and Anne Strover and Steve Tallowin.

The author would like to thank the following newspapers and periodicals for granting permission to reproduce extracts from articles: *The Daily Telegraph*, Daily Mail Newspapers Ltd., *The Guardian*, *Pottery Gazette and Glass Trade Review* courtesy of Tableware International Ltd. and the Chartered Society of Designers.

Lance Cooper, Jan Edwards and Tim Ferguson photographed ceramics from private collections.

1. The *Bubbles* pattern (Z5257), part of the Fairyland Lustre range, decorated on a bone china Malfrey pot (shape 2303). Designed by Daisy Makeig-Jones for Josiah Wedgwood and Sons Ltd., 1920 to about 1929. (Special orders for this pattern were taken until 1941.)

DESIGN IN THE TWENTIETH CENTURY
CERAMICS INDUSTRY
A BRIEF OUTLINE

Throughout the twentieth century in Great Britain efforts were made to improve the quality of pottery design and production, for commercial and social reasons. In the early part of the century, concerns about the country's poor industrial performance needed to be addressed and the quality of life of the British people needed improvement. Several independent organisations, Government initiatives and reports were set up alongside individual responses to the crusade to improve quality. British pottery designers were presented with the challenge of improving design and during the course of the century they worked in various capacities, either as art directors for large companies with total responsibility for patterns and shapes, or as part of a team designing patterns only, or working to a strict brief from the management. Only a small number of innovative designers were able to meet the demands of this challenge and their impact is discussed in this book.

The Design and Industries Association (DIA) was set up in 1915, with the intention of promoting good design through a series of exhibitions and publications. The founder members, including Ambrose Heal, Harry Peach and Frank Pick, promoted the concept of 'Fitness for Purpose'. Despite all their efforts a general lack of interest was shown by the majority of pottery manufacturers and more importantly the general public. However, their work prompted the Government to set up the British Institute of Industrial Design (BIID) in 1920. It was given a budget to organise a number of exhibitions, such as the 'Industrial Art for the Slender Purse'. However, before this organisation could make any impact on British society it was closed down.[1]

In 1921 the pottery trade press reported: 'When approaching the question of the vital importance of art in relation to the pottery industry, it was necessary to point out that, whether one liked it or not, quality in design was becoming the chief factor in the competition for trade, both at home and in foreign markets, the latter more especially.'[2]

Throughout the twentieth century these designers were united by the desire to produce innovative, quality designs using new decorative techniques and contemporary shapes. Moreover, they wanted to produce well designed inexpensive pottery that would be available to a larger market, yet still be allied to aesthetic considerations. In retrospect this was not achieved until the introduction of mass production during the post-war period, made possible by the arrival of superior and faster printing machines. In the pursuit of raising standards in the pottery industry, chiefly situated in Stoke-on-Trent, Staffordshire,

2. A lesser known stylised abstract design decorated on a red earthenware vase shape 916 (no pattern code recorded). Designed by Truda Carter for Carter, Stabler and Adams Ltd., from about 1928-34. Height 14½in. (36cm).

many pioneering designers were hampered by a number of factors. In particular, the industry had historically been cautious of change, not least on the introduction of innovative designs. To many manufacturers, reliance on the familiar tried and tested patterns and shapes was commercially the best option. Furthermore, some of the smaller manufacturers were not able to invest in the development of new shape ranges. Customers preferred, and to some extent still do, the printed blue and white conventional patterns typified by Spode's *Old English Castles*. This attitude has, in many respects, dogged most development throughout the past hundred years. Fortunately, larger companies such as Josiah Wedgwood and Sons Ltd. and Royal Doulton Ltd. always had a strong tradition of employing designers and artists to develop new patterns and shapes in order to maintain their individual share of the market. During the early twenties Wedgwood introduced their first commercial lustres, created by Daisy Makeig-Jones. Her Fairyland Lustres proved very popular and were much copied by other manufacturers (Plate 1). At the same time some of the smaller companies, such as Carter, Stabler and Adams, based in Poole, Dorset, and A. E. Gray & Co. Ltd. in Stoke-on-Trent, were doing their utmost to promote a new pioneering approach to both patterns and shapes.

One of the most influential events of the twentieth century was the Exposition des Arts Décoratifs et Industriels Modernes that took place in Paris in 1925. This special event showcased the work of European designers in many areas of design such as interiors, furniture, textiles, ceramics, glass and silverware. A number of British companies, including Wood and Sons Ltd. and Josiah Wedgwood and Sons Ltd., displayed selections of their current products. However, many British pottery manufacturers felt that there was little point in showing at this event as their main markets were in North America and not in Europe. Gordon Forsyth, reporting on the exposition, found the British section staid and commented that: 'If British potters are to lead in the various markets of the world, they must be creative artists and not complacent tools of retailers. They must have the courage of their convictions and belief in the artistic possibilities of their material.'[3] Clearly, the British pottery industry was way behind Europe in terms of innovative design. However, the exhibition made British designers aware of Art Deco, a style that was to have a long-lasting effect on all areas of industrial design.

The most outstanding European ceramic designers made an enduring impression on British designers such as Susie Cooper, Truda Carter and Clarice Cliff. This is demonstrated in many of Truda Carter's creations for Carter, Stabler and Adams Ltd. (Plate 2). In different ways, they all later incorporated some of the decorative themes and colours that had inspired them into their own wares, whilst others looked more to the modernist approach. Furthermore, as Gordon Forsyth commented in his report, there was 'an overwhelming preponderance of hand-painted work'.[4]

The move to hand-painted decoration was welcomed by many manufacturers, especially some of the smaller companies who found it easier to respond quickly to changes in fashion. If a pattern proved unpopular it could be withdrawn immediately, which the larger

companies, producing great quantities of certain patterns for their many markets, could not do as easily. A.E. Gray and Co. Ltd., for instance, was one of the first companies to meet the new demand for hand-painted pottery during the early twenties. In retrospect, the stimulation to improve or change production was purely economic, as the country was threatened with a flood of imported peasant pottery from Europe during the twenties. Furthermore, hand-painted decoration was far superior to lithographic decoration, that was on the whole very poor and was also expensive to produce. Manufacturers were required to buy over 2,000 sheets of the same pattern at the same time from the specialist suppliers.

3. A bone china coffee set decorated with the *Blocks* pattern, printed in black with hand painted decoration on the Vogue shape. Designed by Eric Slater for Shelley Potteries Ltd., about 1932.

11

Nikolaus Pevsner, writing about transfer-printed patterns, commented that 'unless a pottery manufacturer buys it up [the pattern], he is not safe from competitors. Therefore, it pays to use lithographs if about 50,000 to 60,000 pieces of one design are going to be produced. This means, of course, considerable initial expense.'[5] Hence, many smaller firms tended to misuse the transfers by applying them without consideration to the size and proportion of the ware.

The return to hand-painted decoration also created employment for many decorators, mainly women who were recruited directly from the various Schools of Art and were paid on a piecework basis. In the late twenties Wedgwood set up a handcraft studio for the production of hand-painted tablewares and fancies designed by Alfred and Louise Powell.

This trend for hand-painted decoration was promoted by several designers, including Susie Cooper and Clarice Cliff, who both used the cheaper earthenware body rather than fine bone china. However, Eric Slater was able to produce fashionable patterns successfully on bone china for Shelley's, a commercial risk which brought the company to the forefront of modern design (Plate 3). These stylish wares were promoted in artistically presented sales catalogues (Plate 4). The increased employment of decorators brought opportunities for one or two to become designers, such as Millicent Taplin who started out as a paintress for Josiah Wedgwood and Sons Ltd.

Important commentators of the period, such as Gordon Forsyth, did much to encourage serious debate on the many issues and problems facing the pottery industry. In 1920 he was appointed as Superintendent of Art Education in the Stoke-on-Trent area. As well as changing the way that young people in the area were taught, he also forged strong links with industry. Several successful designers have credited this influential man with placing them in positions with pottery companies after leaving art school. Forsyth was also an accomplished designer, who produced a range of lustre wares for Pilkington's Tile and Pottery Co. He believed that good design could help to improve the quality of wares. He made the point that 'it took the same amount of coal to fire bad work as good, and it was the elimination of bad work and the waste of human endeavour, that art stood for.'[6]

Despite the devastating effects of the General Strike and the subsequent economic slump caused by the Wall Street Crash in 1929 the pottery industry managed to survive. The general uncertainty of the trade prompted new initiatives and experiments. For instance Clarice Cliff used unsaleable ware to try out her range of geometric patterns in an experiment that proved successful. Her *Bizarre* wares were an outstanding achievement in such difficult times (Plate 5). When Susie Cooper established her own company she was able to buy blank wares from suppliers who would not have wanted to supply such a small operation in the more prosperous years. The production of new designs by the larger companies was severely curtailed, with many of the more ornate and expensive ranges being discontinued as they were no longer affordable. Even Wedgwood went through a period of financial concern and hardship, relying on the production of cheaper modern lines that could be mass-produced. Keith Murray was one of the designers to be drafted

4. An illustration of one of the new Shelley patterns. Designed by Eric Slater for Shelley Potteries Ltd., about 1933.

in to do this. His first range of modern shapes was hand thrown, therefore not requiring the development of expensive new moulds (Plate 6). In an effort to bring art to industry Wedgwood also employed a number of free-lance designers including Edward Bawden, Clare Leighton and Laurence Whistler. One of the most outstanding contributions was made by Eric Ravilious, whose graphic works proved popular during the thirties and later, in the fifties.

In 1930 the Society of Industrial Artists and Designers was set up to secure the status of designers. In 1932 the North Staffordshire branch of the society was formed, with members including Millicent Taplin, Susie Cooper and Eric Slater, all established designers by this time. This organisation provided a platform for discussion on the many aspects and issues affecting the industry, not least the move towards mass-production. Despite the attempt to promote the important role of the designer, Nikolaus Pevsner reported that: 'The narrow-minded manufacturer does not appreciate the importance of a well-trained and up-to-date designer. I heard from several experts that almost ninety per cent of the firms in Stoke have no full time designer at all.'[7]

In 1931 the Labour Government set up a Committee on Art and Industry under Lord Gorell, that included several artists and designers. The Gorell Report, published in 1932, commented that if the public were to buy good design then they should be shown examples through exhibitions and other forms of display. With this in mind, the Council for Art and Industry was formed in 1934, aiming to educate consumers, raise design standards and especially to improve the training of designers. Several important exhibitions were staged during the thirties, including the British Industrial Art in Relation to the Home exhibition held at the Dorland Hall during the summer of 1933. This was followed two years later by the British Art in Industry exhibition at the Royal Academy.

During the early part of the thirties many British designers, such as Keith Murray, were inspired by Scandinavian industrial design, typified by the ceramic productions of Gustavberg and glass by Orrefors. This interest was consolidated after an influential exhibition of Swedish design in London in 1931. This exhibition promoted a simpler modernistic approach to design, but many designers were still wary of change, fearing that mass-production would result in mass-unemployment in the pottery industry.

In 1937 the National Register of Industrial Art Designers was set up. Concern over the country's poor industrial performance had been growing even before the Second World War. The pottery industry was greatly affected by the restrictions made by the Board of Trade and shortages of labour during wartime hostilities. Restrictions on the sale of new goods on the home market were not lifted until 1952. Therefore British people had to endure years of austerity and rationing. In 1948 bread, jam and potatoes were de-rationed and two years later the rationing of milk ended. The mood of the day was symbolised by three ducks flying towards a sunnier and calmer sky. For the duration of the war, many pottery firms had either been closed or used by the Ministry of Defence. Those continuing in production were responsible for the export market and the production of Utility ware.

In 1943 the Weir Report recommended that an organisation should be set up to promote good design. The report recommended that a central design council should be established without direct responsibility to the British Government. As a result of the Weir Report, the Council of Industrial Design (COID) was formed in 1944. The Council aimed to promote by all practicable means the improvement of the products produced by British industry. It was also keen to educate both the consumer and the industry to be able to differentiate between good and bad design with its motto, 'Good design, Good business'. The Labour Government asked the COID to organise an exhibition of consumer goods which would demonstrate to the world the high quality of British products and assist in reviving the export market. This exhibition, entitled 'Britain Can Make It', was staged at the Victoria and Albert Museum in London in 1946. The show also aimed to introduce the concept of industrial

5. Notable examples from the Bizarre range designed by Clarice Cliff (1929). Top centre and bottom right: the *Diamonds* pattern hand painted on a Lotus jug and Tankard shape coffee pot; centre: an earthenware bowl (shape 356) decorated with the hand-painted *Mondrian* pattern; left: an earthenware plate decorated with the *Fruit* pattern (from the Fantasque range, 1929); bottom left: an abstract pattern hand painted on shape 369 and top right: the *Castellated Circle* pattern, hand painted on a plate.

art to the general public. On show was a selection of pottery by Eric Ravilious, Keith Murray, Susie Cooper and Eric Slater. However, the exhibition was criticised as many of the exhibits were prototypes or items not yet in production. This led to the exhibition being re-named 'Britain Can Make It, But Britain Can't Have It' by the British people, who would have to wait another six years before sales restrictions on the home market were lifted.[8]

Immediately after the war, British designers looked to the United States of America and Scandinavia for inspiration. In many ways, the imposition of rationing enabled Britain to avoid some of the vulgarities of some pre-war styling. Further promotion of good design was forthcoming in magazines such as *Design*, first published in 1949. One of the most discussed subjects of this period was 'What is good design?' This new magazine provided a forum for many of the most important design issues. A new significant style evolved called 'Contemporary', introduced into people's homes mainly through ceramics and glass.[9]

The Festival of Britain in 1951 was one of the most significant events of the post-war period in terms of bringing modern design to the attention of the population. It had first been suggested as early as 1943 by the Royal Society of Arts, which felt that some sort of festival should be organised to commemorate the Great Exhibition of 1851. As the idea grew, so did the scale of the event. Sir Stafford Cripps and the Ramsden Committee wanted an international exhibition to demonstrate to the world that Britain had fully recovered from the effects of the war. However, due to the shortage of materials and financial problems faced by the country, the scale had to be reduced. The Festival of Britain took place on the South Bank in London, with many other events taking place across the country. One of its major achievements was to give the public a glimpse of the future by

6. A footed bowl (shape 3806) decorated with a matt blue glaze. Designed by Keith Murray for Josiah Wedgwood and Sons Ltd. Introduced in 1933. Height 4¼in. (10.8cm).

7. An earthenware Fashion shape coffee set, decorated with the *Zambesi* pattern. Designed by Jessie Tait for W.R. Midwinter Ltd., about 1955.

showing them new technology and science. Many of the pavilions and room settings were designed by young graduates such as Hugh Casson, Ralph Tubbs and James Holland. The Festival had over eight million visitors and featured more than ten thousand examples of British goods selected by the COID. Gordon Russell, a renowned furniture maker and designer, fully aware of the criticisms voiced over the 'Britain Can Make It' exhibition, insisted that all exhibits should be real goods actually available in the shops.

In the 1950s Roy Midwinter produced a range of organic styled shapes for the Midwinter Pottery, inspired by American designer Eva Zeisel's forms. The new Midwinter shapes were hand painted with fresh and innovative patterns designed by Jessie Tait (Plate 7). At the same time Alfred B. Read produced a range of free form vases at Poole Pottery that were outstanding examples of contemporary design (Plate 8). Towards the end of the fifties John Clappison was producing important patterns for the Hornsea Pottery that were clearly influenced by contemporary Swedish style.

In many cases prominent designers of the pre-war period found it rather difficult to adapt to the new style, while others, such as Clarice Cliff, focused on the North American market by producing traditional printed patterns such as *Tonquin* and *Charlotte* (Plate 9). There was no longer a demand for her bold art deco patterns.

The British public had to wait until August 1952, when all restrictions were lifted on the sale of goods on the home market, to be able to buy new pottery. This demand for

8. A selection of hand thrown and hand-painted shapes decorated with contemporary patterns. Designed by Alfred B. Read for Poole Pottery Ltd., about 1955.

fashionable pottery hit the smaller 'family run' businesses hard, as they could not afford to change production methods to compete, resulting in closure or takeovers by larger companies. For those able to survive, many continued to copy current styles by applying new prints to pre-war shapes, thereby missing the point of the contemporary style. Despite the efforts of the prominent designers of the fifties, the British people were so desperate for something new that they were willing to accept anything! The companies coming to the forefront were those that embraced the many changes in lifestyle and the demands of the ordinary customer. For instance, the impact of war on young people had created a new outlook and attitude to life. This generation enjoyed opportunities and choices that had previously only been available to the middle classes. Smaller combinations of sets were introduced as younger people did not want to buy complete dinner services for six. The new starter packs, later available in carry-home packs, consisted of the basics, such as four plates, cups, bowls, etc.

Even though the pottery industry experienced peak production in 1953, within three years financial strains took hold with a gradual loss of trade. In 1956 the Government passed a 'Clean Air' Act forbidding the use of coal in smokeless zones. Many small businesses, unable to convert to oil or gas-fired kilns, went out of business.[10] During the sixties larger companies, including Josiah Wedgwood and Sons Ltd., took over smaller companies such as J. & G. Meakin Ltd., Susie Cooper Ltd. and Johnson Brothers Ltd. The introduction of the Murray Curvex printing machine, with its improved quality of reproduction, had a strong influence on the designers' approach to surface decoration and shape.

The demand for fashionable pottery is typified by some of the earliest work of Susan Williams-Ellis at the Portmeirion Pottery, established during the early sixties. Her outstanding *Totem* range, with its hugely tall coffee-pot, inspired a new phase in the industry and set a

standard in design and manufacture that was heavily copied by other manufacturers. At the same time John Clappison's *Heirloom* range for Hornsea Pottery heralded a new period of high quality printed decoration. Clappison later responded to the demands of the mid-sixties by producing a number of humorous and topical patterns for mugs. Throughout the industry coffee sets were increasingly in demand as coffee-drinking became more popular, with larger coffee cups being produced.

The important influences of fashion and art were never more evident than during the late sixties, better known today as the 'Swinging Sixties'. The music and fashion, coupled with the popularity of Carnaby Street in London, resulted in bold new patterns and colours that also reflected an interest in the art nouveau style. Some of the more innovative designers produced ranges of topical patterns inspired by art nouveau, including Susie Cooper with *Carnaby Daisy* and Eve Midwinter with *Poppy*. Kathie Winkle's geometric patterns, named after famous holiday resorts of the period such as *Monaco* and *San Marino*, reflected the increased opportunities for the British holidaymaker (Plate 10). Robert Jefferson promoted the studio approach by producing *Delphis*, a dynamic range of vases, bowls and plaques.

The move towards the trend for oven-to-tableware was successfully met by the major companies during the early part of the seventies. In particular the new look of browns, hessians and cheesecloth summed up the period. New standards were set by Eve Midwinter with her distinctive Creation glaze, introduced by Midwinter in 1972. During the same period, Portmeirion changed the industry's approach to pattern with its multi-motif *Botanic Garden* range, which led to the production of a comprehensive range of co-ordinated tableware and associated items such as tablecloths, curtains, tablemats and other such items over a span of twenty years (Plate 11).

The financial difficulties faced by the pottery industry during the late seventies led to over thirty-seven factories being closed, with hundreds of redundancies. As a result cut-backs

10. The *Lorette* pattern on an earthenware dinner plate, printed in black with painted decoration. Designed by Kathie Winkle for James Broadhurst and Sons Ltd.

were made and the role of the full time resident designer was curtailed in favour of the free-lance designer. Many designers, such as Robert Jefferson, worked for several different subsiduary companies owned by Royal Doulton Ltd. During the mid-eighties patterns by featured designers, including Laura Ashley and Mary Quant, were produced by Johnson Brothers Ltd.

The buying public also continued to demand traditional styles during this period. These were particularly popular on the export market. Several manufacturers, including Wedgwood, continued to successfully market patterns and shapes, such as *Edme*, that had been introduced many years earlier. In contrast, Royal Albert launched the new but traditionally styled *Old Country Roses* range of bone china. Since its launch in 1962 over one million items have been sold.[11]

Towards the end of the twentieth century a more widespread interest in period styles and antiques resulted in the production of limited editions, mainly of items produced between the wars. Wedgwood successfully introduced a selection of Clarice Cliff items that proved popular with those unable to afford the 'real thing'. Other manufacturers, fully aware of the demand for popular patterns, made the decision to progress into new styles, with the Portmeirion Pottery taking the lead most recently. Having enjoyed such huge success with their *Botanic Garden* range, they have adopted a new contemporary look with their *Dawn to Dusk* wares.

The motivation to improve the quality of design in the pottery industry in the twentieth century has succeeded against a backdrop of tremendous social, cultural and economic changes. These ceramic designers set standards that today are acknowledged, studied and, more recently, eagerly collected by a new generation.

11. A selection of earthenware dishes decorated with the *Botanic Garden* pattern. Designed by Susan Williams-Ellis for Portmeirion Potteries Ltd., introduced in 1972.

CHAPTER 1

SOME GLIMPSES OF FAIRYLAND

DAISY MAKEIG-JONES (1881-1945)

Daisy Makeig-Jones was one of the first women of the twentieth century to gain recognition as a ceramic designer. She achieved this despite the difficulties imposed on the industry by the effects of the First World War. During her brief, prolific career with Josiah Wedgwood and Sons Ltd., she created some of the most dazzling lustre patterns ever produced by any firm in the industry. In a leaflet to promote Fairyland Lustre she declared: 'In Fairyland All Things are Possible.'[1]

Her family was based in Wath-upon-Dearne, a mining village near Rotherham in South Yorkshire. Her father, William, the son of a Welsh parson, was a doctor and they enjoyed considerable standing in the local community. In 1880 he married Anne Tofield Reeder, the daughter of Thomas Reeder, a local solicitor. Makeig-Jones was born on 31 December 1881 and was christened Susannah Margaretta. She was the oldest of seven

12. Portrait of Daisy Makeig-Jones taken during the Wedgwood Bicentenary celebrations in 1930. Note the 'Portland Vase' costumes that she designed for this special event.

children, with three younger brothers, John, William Totfield and Thomas Geoffrey, and three sisters, Anne, Ethel and Hilda Mary. During her childhood she spent much of her time playing in the garden and in the surrounding countryside. She would often read to her siblings from the popular children's books of the day, such as the *Colour Fairy Books*, edited by Andrew Lang. She was adventurous, which was probably inappropriate for a young girl in those days.[2]

She was taught by governesses at home prior to attending a private boarding school in Rugby. She showed a great flair for painting under the direction of a Mr. Lindsay, who took an interest in her work and became a friend of the family. In 1899 the family moved to Torquay, on the Devonshire coast, where her father was setting up his own doctor's practice. At about this point he hyphenated the Makeig in his name to the Jones in order to avoid confusion with another William Jones in the area and to make his surname sound more distinctive.[3] It was changed by deed poll in October 1913. Makeig-Jones attended classes at the School of Art in Torquay. She was fortunate that her family had the wealth to support her ambitions and the connections to help her to progress further.

Makeig-Jones studied in London for a period, staying with an aunt.[4] Although little is known about this part of her education, it is likely that she would have visited some of the London art galleries and department stores to examine the latest design styles and art movements. Her parents were concerned that she should use her artistic skills in some meaningful direction so they looked for an opportunity for her. Fortunately this presented itself when the Reverend Archibald Sorby, Vicar of Maer in Wales, suggested that she should consider becoming a designer of pottery. The Reverend, a distant relative, offered to use his influence with the Wedgwood family.

Makeig-Jones was fuelled with excitement following this suggestion and wrote to Cecil Wedgwood, Chairman of the Wedgwood Company, in 1909. Cecil was a very sympathetic and eminent man, much respected by the industry and by the company's

14. A pattern book entry illustrating the *Golliwog* pattern. Designed by Daisy Makeig-Jones for Josiah Wedgwood and Sons Ltd., about 1916.

workers. The recent revival of the firm's prospects, restoring Wedgwood as a leader of pottery producers, was largely due to his keen business sense and energy.[5] In his reply he explained that she would have to undertake the same basic training as anyone else on the shop floor, and would need to understand the basic principles and processes of working in a factory, which she may not like. She responded tersely that she had made a straightforward application to join the factory staff, and had not consulted him as to whether she would enjoy it![6] Her mind was set, despite the class difference between a doctor's daughter and the working class paintresses which was, at that time, immense, let alone the fact that she was twice their age. To her this was a mere trifle and with her ambition decided upon she went to the factory to become a designer for Wedgwood.

The prestigious firm Josiah Wedgwood and Sons Ltd. was established by Josiah Wedgwood in 1759, and based at Etruria in Stoke-on-Trent from 1769 (Plate 13). During the 1860s Wedgwood had developed a range of art wares with patterns submitted by outside designers such as Christopher Dresser and Walter Crane. In 1875 Wedgwood had opened a new London showroom, after fifty years without a London base. In about 1875-76, Thomas Allen was appointed to the position of Art Director. Allen made an important contribution to Wedgwood by extending the range of studio

24

and art wares and introducing new free-lance designers to the company. Wedgwood commenced production of decorative tiles in 1875 but when interest declined, the tile department was closed down in 1902.

During the late nineteenth century Wedgwood had experienced considerable difficulties with a loss of artistic direction and some financial problems due to a decline in the export trade. Two of the senior directors had fought in the Boer War of 1899-1902. In 1891 a new partnership was formed between Laurence Wedgwood and his nephews, Cecil and Francis (Frank) Hamilton. Cecil was the great-great-grandson of Josiah Wedgwood. In 1895 the Wedgwood directors removed family control from the company to form a limited company. Recognising that the firm's designs were still deeply rooted in the nineteenth century, Wedgwood appointed John Goodwin, a Company designer since 1892, as Art Director in about 1902. Goodwin ensured that a good balance between the traditional and the modern was maintained. New shapes and patterns were devised to meet the expanding markets in Europe. Goodwin undertook some rationalisation of the current product range by withdrawing certain lines and reviving several early shapes and patterns, adapted for the new markets. New art wares were produced by Alfred and Louise Powell.[7] This was the situation at Wedgwood when

15. Artwork illustrating the *Yellowstone Zoo* nursery pattern designed by Daisy Makeig-Jones for Josiah Wedgwood and Sons Ltd., about 1916.

Daisy Makeig-Jones joined the company in 1909.

Her advancement at the works was rapid. Due to her art education she was able to quickly complete the basic training given to all the workers at the factory. Within one year Cecil agreed to engage her as a trainee paintress. By August 1911 she was placed on the staff and moved to the Goodwin studio and was paid an annual salary of £52 a year. By January 1914 she had become a Wedgwood designer and was given her own studio and a considerable increase in salary. Her studio was situated on the first floor of one of the outbuildings adjacent to the studio of James Hodgkiss, Chief Designer. The room behind his was occupied by a special team of paintresses, who were to decorate the new range of patterns that the Company was developing. The studios were accessible by a set of rickety steps, which proved problematic, considering that the decorated ware had to be carried on boards down these steps to the bottle ovens, just behind the building.[8]

Makeig-Jones was one of several designers working for Wedgwood during the 1920s. A range of designs depicting animals such as white horses against a blue back-drop was not hers, but John Goodwin's. New designs were given many individual prefixes of a letter code denoting the type of ware used. These are as follows: Z for china ornaments, W for bone china dinnerwares, A and C for Queen's Ware tableware and F for Queen's Ware fancies with gold. Her early designs were a series of simple nursery ware from 1912. One of the first was *Thumbelina*, based on the story by Hans Christian Andersen, produced on a variety of shapes including toilet ware and a Queen's Ware octagonal bowl, finished with a stylised border of fish. The design was used some years later for her lustre ranges. A more audacious design, *Brownies*, produced in 1913, depicted goblins cycling, skipping and horse-riding. This range was designed for toy tea ware and toy dinner services. In 1914 a third nursery design was launched called *Noah's Ark*, a pleasing pattern for toy dinner, tea wares, toilet set, basin, chamber pot and soap tray, vase and dish. *Golliwog*, from 1916, featured golliwogs sailing, riding a kangaroo, and sitting on top of a hot air balloon (Plate 14). Her first major designs to be produced in quantity were also nursery ware patterns – *Yellowstone Zoo* (Plate 15) and *Cobble and Zoo* from 1916. The latter was a series of landscapes, painted to resemble children's paintings, with a cobble bead border printed in black on earthenware.

Makeig-Jones was no doubt a keen observer of the experiments undertaken at the Wedgwood factory to imitate the Chinese decoration known in Europe as 'bleu soufflé', which gave the effect of powder blue. Four years later James Hodgkiss was able to create the powder blue glaze, following a request made by Mr A.M. Powell of James Powell & Sons. In order to achieve this distinctive form of decoration the company borrowed a Chinese antique from the Victoria and Albert Museum. To master the technique, John Goodwin, George Adams, the resident chemist and Bernard Moore, the artist potter, all collaborated. The first results of their labours were shown to the public in April 1912.

Makeig-Jones' interest in lustre decoration was furthered by an exhibition held at the King's Hall in Stoke by Ashworth & Co., a pottery manufacturer successfully producing a

16. The *Dragon* pattern (Z4829), from the Ordinary Lustre range, on a bone china vase (shape 2046). Designed by Daisy Makeig-Jones for Josiah Wedgwood and Sons Ltd., about 1915.

lustre called Lustrosa, first shown in London in 1909. These items were viewed by George V and Queen Mary during an official visit to the Potteries in April 1913.[9] These events both inspired and influenced Makeig-Jones, who had already begun to experiment with Far Eastern motifs.

Makeig-Jones wanted to use a variety of decorative techniques using strong lustre colours applied through mottling, staining and sponging on bone china wares.[10] The designer was determined to develop new lustres and enlisted the help of the decorators, and in particular James Hodgkiss, to help her achieve her aim. The first results were approved by the selection committee and then entered into the pattern books in October 1914. They were launched in the autumn of the following year. These Ordinary Lustres, as they were called, used recognisable combinations of lustre colours such as orange and mother-of-pearl with mottling. The first range of printed motifs was taken from examples that had already been used for a number of years. These were categorised into five separate groups: *Fish*, *Butterflies*, *Insects* and *Dragon* (Plate 16) and Oriental motifs, such as *Flying Humming Birds* (Plate 17), and a few years later, *Fruit*. Makeig-Jones would later adapt these printed motifs by adding geometric details and flourishes to the prints. This range was recorded under the Z4823 to Z4832 numbers (the Z prefix indicates bone china ornaments). By 1916 these patterns were selling well and for the most part continued in production throughout the twenties, with one or two patterns such as *Dragon* lustre remaining in production for longer. In April of that year the trade press mentioned: 'This series of ornamentals is one which it seemed to the writer should be largely sought after as portraying the highest technical accomplishment of the times.'[11]

Due the outstanding success of these lustres Frank Thorley, the Wedgwood Representative, suggested that more elaborate designs should be developed to meet the increasing demand. This prompted Makeig-Jones to begin dreaming up dazzling and unusual landscapes combined with characters from children's books. She delved into her childhood, remembering the many stories, myths and fables that were popular at the time. From her inspiration she combined fantastic landscapes that incorporated flamboyant castles, palaces and dense forests. These places were inhabited by elves, pixies and goblins. Many traditional stories and folklore myths were used by her but were mixed together with other stories. One of her more popular designs for instance, *Garden of Paradise*, was based on the popular story by Hans Christian Andersen. This story gave her plenty of ideas for flowers, exotic motifs and archways, etc. She was influenced by several leading illustrators of her day such as Edmund Dulac, Kay Neilsen and in particular the *Colour Fairy Books* she had enjoyed reading as a young girl. The trade press also made reference to her sources, noting that 'the designs belong to the modern bizarre school, connected with the names of Rackham and Dulac'.[12] Makeig-Jones tended to directly copy from these original sources, often quite blatantly. This approach to developing new patterns, based on published sources, prompted Godfrey Hammersley, Decorating Manager at Wedgwood, to state: 'there is nothing new under the sun, but

clever adaptation of old ideas is a refreshing contribution to Art.'[13]

This new range was called Fairyland Lustre, decorated in several types of colour and glazes. Whilst her Ordinary Lustres were limited to a range of patterns, this new line was far more complex. Although Fairyland patterns were given names by the designer, others were sometimes suggested by her decorators. More recently, pattern names have been established by Una des Fontaines in her important book *Wedgwood Fairyland Lustre: The Work of Daisy Makeig-Jones*, published in 1975. The Company records and pattern books, for the most part, do not indicate the exact date when patterns were put into

17. The *Flying Humming Birds* pattern (Z5294), from the Ordinary Lustre range, decorated on a bone china vase (shape 2311). Designed by Daisy Makeig-Jones for Josiah Wedgwood and Sons Ltd., about 1917.

production. Moreover, the numbering system for this range is confusing as the pattern number Z4968 encompassed at least twenty different patterns. To understand this system one must look to the shape. Each size of a particular shape was used for different patterns.

While Makeig-Jones was developing her first lustre patterns she became friendly with the Wedgwood family, in particular with Cecil's two daughters, Phoebe and Audrey.[14] As a result, she enjoyed a privileged position within the company and the family. Her brother married Audrey in 1928. During the First World War Audrey ran the factory, almost single-handedly. She worked in all the departments to gain experience and knowledge of how everything operated. Sadly Cecil Wedgwood was killed on 3 July 1916 whilst leading the 8th Battalion of the North Staffordshire Regiment into action at La Boiselle during the Battle of the Somme. Francis Hamilton Wedgwood succeeded him as Chairman.[15] In 1920 Audrey was appointed Secretary to the company.

Traditionally, the individual designer's name or signature did not feature on the backstamp, or indeed a signature. The only exceptions were the special production pieces by Alfred Powell and Thomas Allen. Of course Makeig-Jones wanted her name on her own ware and was able to get around this restriction by skilfully incorporating her initials into the engraving plate.[16] Her patterns were marked with the standard Wedgwood mark but at some stage during the war, probably in about 1916, some of her nursery ware patterns featured a special mark which read DESIGNED BY S.M. MAKEIG-JONES. It is believed that this was introduced by Audrey, but for a limited period.[17]

With the critical success of her work Makeig-Jones became so engrossed that she often forgot to follow the rules respected by the other Wedgwood designers. For instance, it was unheard of that a designer would make notes in the pattern book, as this was the responsibility of one person. Despite her less than conventional way of working she did care for her team of decorators. Her work was developed in her own studio supported by a small dedicated team whom she looked after at all times, calling them 'her' paintresses. A sketch entitled 'The Colossus' was made by one of these workers.[18] They were required to undertake the laborious processes that included several firings. First, each piece was fitted with a paper transfer which was rubbed on to the body to enable the printed outline to stay on the ware. Once the paper had been removed by immersion in water, underglaze colour was applied within the printed outline by the decorators, then fired at a low temperature. Each piece was dipped in a lead glaze and then passed through a glost kiln. Once this was completed the lustre was painted on to the ware. The final process was the application of the gold printing, over the first printed outline. The item was fired in a low temperature kiln and the gold printing was then polished.[19] Makeig-Jones produced a number of the engravings herself, having attended engraving classes whilst at the Torquay School of Art.

From these ideas the first pattern, *Poplar Trees* (Z4935) was released in 1915 and

shown to the press towards the end of that year. This pattern and its subsequent variations met with a promising reception from the trade, indicating that there was a demand for highly decorative ware of this kind. Fairyland Lustre was first exhibited at the British Industries Fair in 1916. At the following year's event a larger display was put together, alongside the current Wedgwood products. The trade press commented: 'In almost startling contrast to these historic pieces were some thoroughly modern lustred lamps, bowls and vases, one of which, by the way, had been purchased by the Queen. The colours were in rich underglaze colours, representing dragons and other Chinese emblems, but a complete breakaway from the spirit of reproductions is made in the genuine innovation of "Fairyland Ware", on which vivacious imps and fairies are seen disporting themselves among fantastic trees, this topic being particularly well adapted to the variegated and kaleidoscopic colouring of the lustre glazes.'[20]

Fairyland Lustre had a great appeal amongst the fashionable upper classes who were able to afford such expensive items. As popularity increased several other firms, such as Crown Devon and Carlton Ware, copied the style but they could not achieve the same dazzling effects that Makeig-Jones developed in her studio. The trade press reported that:

18. The *Dana, Castle on a Road* pattern (Z5125), from the Fairyland Lustre range, decorated on a bone china vase (shape 2442). Designed by Daisy Makeig-Jones for Josiah Wedgwood and Sons Ltd., about 1917. Height 7⅝in. (19.4cm).

'Now, however, Josiah Wedgwood and Sons Ltd. have taken a long stride beyond the old Chinese masters by producing lustres as fine as theirs in combination with the most up-to-date artistic designs. Vividly depicted pixies, elves, changelings and sprites, mingled with grotesque insects, sport among enormously elongated trunks of fantastic trees or hide behind shapeless masses of bosky bush; the weirdness of the general effect being much enhanced by the variable and elusive colour schemes caused by the play of light and shade on the surface of the lustre glaze.'[21]

Over the next five years she created many outstanding patterns, putting Wedgwood firmly at the forefront of decorative wares. In 1917 Wedgwood launched *Dana, Castle on a Road* (Z5125), featuring pictorial views of hills, rivers and bridges framed by a cobbled bead border (Plate 18). This pattern, featured a few years later in a company sales catalogue, became one of her best sellers. This was followed by *Candlemas*, based on a Roman festival deriving its name from the blessing of candles by the clergy, the candles were then distributed to the people who carried them in procession. At the same time the church bells were rung to keep away the underworld (Plate 19).[22] The design, produced in four different colour variations, was eventually cancelled in 1929. In 1918 her *Firbolgs* pattern was launched, decorated with comical accident-prone imps and produced in several colour variations. The red *Firbolgs* (Z5200) was the version longest in production. More of her notable patterns included *Leapfrogging Elves* (Plate 20), depicting elves jumping over toadstools, and *Fairy Gondola*, a river landscape with exotic follies and flower baskets (Plate 21). Makeig-Jones also revised an early Wedgwood pattern of a toucan design, first issued in 1916, to create the *Amherst Pheasant* (Z5267) with a central bird motif (Plate 22).

By 1920 Makeig-Jones became firmly established as a designer following the success of her new pattern ranges, featured in the national press. To work towards new patterns she looked at Japanese, Scandinavian, Indian and English myths and stories. This is evident in patterns such as *Lahore* (Z5266), featuring a range of Indian motifs and elephants painted in solid black on a mother-of-pearl ground, with swags of curtains and hanging lanterns. This pattern was adapted for the various shapes but was eventually cancelled in December 1929. In 1920 her *Bubbles* pattern was launched, inspired by a combination of two myths from Japanese mythology (see page 8). Two other versions were produced, with one for earthenware plaques, from 1926 (Plate 23). In 1920 the *Ghostly Wood* pattern was released. It was one of the most complex designs and depicted a land of illusion. The pattern was based on the 'Legend of *Croque-Mitaine*', a French fairytale, used to frighten children (Plate 24). With some variations, the pattern was produced on a wide range of shapes.

The popularity of Fairyland Lustre saw the production of a catalogue entitled 'Some Glimpses of Fairyland', in 1920. This was used for promotional material and perhaps to give the dealers some explanation of the stories behind the patterns. It was never sold to the public. The introduction to the booklet read: 'The doors to Fairyland are many, but

hard to find, some are hidden in hollow trees or caves; others in wells or lakes, or at the bottom of the sea. It is possible to get there by climbing up a rainbow, a sunbeam, or a moonbeam, or by getting a leprechaun to make you a pair of fairy shoes.'[22]

Makeig-Jones also developed new patterns based on Celtic designs. She had persuaded Wedgwood to purchase a reproduction copy of the Book of Kells dating from the sixth century. Her Celtic range represented one of the more interesting aspects of her career, lesser known than her lustres (Plate 25). These items were introduced in about 1919, produced mainly on bone china tea ware and a selection of bowls and vases, each allocated the Z5224 pattern number. Whilst some had pattern names, others did not. Bone china tea ware patterns, including *Celt*, *Armagh* and *St. Chad's*, were given a W prefix, with a different number for the various colour variations. Gilded tableware patterns were given a prefix of G, with *Lindisfarne* G5133 and G5134 and *St Chad's*

19. The *Candlemas* pattern, from the Fairyland Lustre range on a bone china vase. Designed by Daisy Makeig-Jones for Josiah Wedgwood and Sons Ltd., about 1917.

20. The *Leapfrogging Elves* pattern (Z4968), from the Fairyland Lustre range decorated on a Persian Cup (shape 3199). Designed by Daisy Makeig-Jones for Josiah Wedgwood and Sons Ltd., about 1916. Height 7in (18cm).

G5005 being good examples. Patterns include *Gothic Circles* and *Tyrone*, that featured a black and red border depicting serpents within a black panel and gilt decoration to edge. Makeig-Jones went on to produce several variations and new patterns for many years, although they were not as popular as Fairyland.

During 1923 several new patterns and colour schemes were launched, including *Coral and Bronze*, used for a number of patterns (Plate 26). A series of bright orange Flame lustres were used on existing patterns, such as *Flame Willow* (Plate 27). Makeig-Jones turned to several sources to conjure up new landscapes, distant lands and imaginary palaces. The *Garden of Paradise* pattern was inspired by the fairy tales of Hans Christian Andersen, translated into English in 1911. This story tells of a Prince who wanted to find the Garden of Paradise but was warned by the Queen of the Fairies that he must not kiss her. Every night his willpower to resist her was weakened and at last he succumbed. As soon as he had kissed her the Garden of Paradise sank into the ground. In a quest for new designs Makeig-Jones returned to the *Thumbelina* motif for a new approach to her series of nursery ware patterns. Other notable patterns include *The Stuff that Dreams are made of*, produced on earthenware plaques (F3078/F3080) (Plate 28).

Throughout her career Makeig-Jones designed many lesser known patterns, which were either in limited production or may have been trial patterns. One such example was *Hares, Dogs and Birds* (Z5448) produced for a limited period of two years from November 1927 (Plate 29). Notable designs include *Mythical Animals* (Plate 30) and *Peacock* Bowl. She also added more nursery ware designs to the range that included *Toy Rabbit*, *Moa* and *Coq du Bois*. Makeig-Jones developed a limited range of shapes including a sugar caster and a salt container that she nicknamed *Emily* and *Dawg*, respectively. At about the same time a range of buttons and badges, each depicting some part of a lustre design, were produced.

Makeig-Jones spent some time developing new ideas with both glazes and motifs.

21. A Chalice bowl decorated with the *Fairy Gondola* pattern (Z5360), from the Fairyland Lustre range designed by Daisy Makeig-Jones for Josiah Wedgwood and Sons Ltd., from about 1920. Diameter 10½in (26.7cm).

Norman Wilson, appointed to the position of Works Manager, later recalled that none of the people on the factory side understood what her designs were about. During one particular experiment Makeig-Jones didn't realise that the majolica glaze that she wanted to use wouldn't stay on the bone china body. However, the resultant effect of the glaze sliding down the ware was liked by both Makeig-Jones and Norman Wilson.[23] In 1923 she experimented with a series of double lustres (one colour superimposed on another).

Sadly, the early part of the twenties saw change for Makeig-Jones. In 1922 her father retired from his practice and the family moved to the small town of Seaton, on the East Devon coast. A year later she spent some time in hospital suffering from diphtheria.[24] When her father became ill Makeig-Jones spent as much time as she could with him, he died in 1925. This probably accounts for the fact that few new patterns were entered into the pattern books between the latter part of August 1924 and the August of the following year.

The Wedgwood company exhibited at the British Empire Exhibition of 1924. Their impressive and monumental stand, featuring a large Adams style archway, was designed by the architect Oliver Hill. Alongside their most famous lines, such as Basalt and Jasper,

22. The *Amherst Pheasant* (Z5267) pattern, decorated on a small bone china bowl. Designed by Daisy Makeig-Jones for Josiah Wedgwood and Sons Ltd., from about 1916.

23. The *Bubbles* pattern (F.3083), part of the Fairyland Lustre range, decorated on an earthenware plaque, height 15⅝in. (40cm). Designed by Daisy Makeig-Jones for Josiah Wedgwood and Sons Ltd., about 1926.

24. A bone china Malfrey Pot (shape 2312) decorated with the *Ghostly Wood* pattern (Z4968), from the Fairyland Lustre range, designed by Daisy Makeig-Jones for Josiah Wedgwood and Sons Ltd., 1916. Height 15in (38cm).

a small range of Makeig-Jones' wares was shown including examples of Celtic designs and Fairyland lustre. The trade noted that the latter was now available in five different colours – ruby, orange, mother-of-pearl, blue and green, that 'seems to be attracting special notice'.[25]

In 1924 Wedgwood launched the *Imps on a Bridge* pattern, partly a direct copy of a cartoon by Rose O'Neill, that first appeared in 1909 (Plate 31). The *Rainbow* pattern, inspired by Scandinavian mythology, was later re-issued in 1923 and in production until the end of 1929. Makeig-Jones continued to introduce new designs during the late 1920s, including *Blue Willow* in 1926 and *Daventry* (Plate 32). The latter was allocated six pattern numbers. In 1929 two new patterns, *Nizami* and *Phoenix* were launched. *Nizami* was the name of the first dramatic poet of Persia (c.1140-1203). In 1928 a new book on the subject inspired Makeig-Jones to produce several designs such as a service plate, released in March 1931.

Unfortunately the Potteries were about to face difficult challenges as a result of the Wall Street Crash in 1929. At the same time the massive trade slump and subsequent rationalisation of Wedgwood's products by the new management team resulted in several Fairyland patterns being withdrawn. In 1929 Wedgwood cancelled twenty-three pattern numbers outright and by the end of 1932 trade had worsened and patterns were cut from thirteen to nine. This was compounded by the loss of the North American market.

In 1930 the Wedgwood company planned a wide range of events to celebrate the bi-centenary of the birth of its founder. As Makeig-Jones had previously staged 'Cinderella' and 'Aladdin' for the works' pantomimes, she soon organised her own tribute to Josiah Wedgwood by creating human Portland Vase costumes (Plate 12), stencilled with copies of bas-relief decorations, worn by one hundred girls.[26] Other celebrations took place in London and several parts of the country. In London the Army and Navy Store organised a display of Fairyland Lustre, alongside examples of Jasper and a bust of the founder of the company.

The production and organisation of the factory changed following the death of Major Frank Wedgwood. Josiah V became Managing Director. James Hodgkiss had already left when in April 1931, due to the imposition of cutbacks and changing taste, Makeig-

26. A bone china cigarette box and cover decorated with the *Coral and Bronze* pattern (Z5406), part of the Fairyland Lustre range. Designed by Daisy Makeig-Jones for Josiah Wedgwood and Sons Ltd., about 1923. Width of box 7in. (17.8cm).

Jones was asked to retire. Having considered herself for many years as a permanent fixture at the works, she ignored the request and continued her job for some time. When she was finally confronted by Josiah V regarding her retirement, Makeig-Jones soon left. She ordered a boy to destroy all her trials and samples, however many were saved.

For a short period following her retirement she continued to live in the area, keeping in touch with her friends. A few years later she moved to live with her family in Seaton. At the same time she decided to abandon the name 'Daisy' and return to her Christian name of Susannah. Gardening became one of her new interests and she undertook doll-making for local charities. The family was very important to her and she helped when needed, driving around the area in her Morris Minor. When her uncle's wife died she did the cooking and Parish work for him.[27]

By 1941, the production of Fairyland Lustre designs was cancelled and the remaining stock sold off. At the same time the Wedgwood Company handed over hundreds of

27. The lesser known *Flame Willow* pattern (Z5360), decorated on a bone china vase (shape 2140), height 9⅞in. (24.7cm), part of the Fairyland Lustre range. Designed by Daisy Makeig-Jones for Josiah Wedgwood and Sons Ltd., about 1923. (Special orders for this pattern were taken until 1941.)

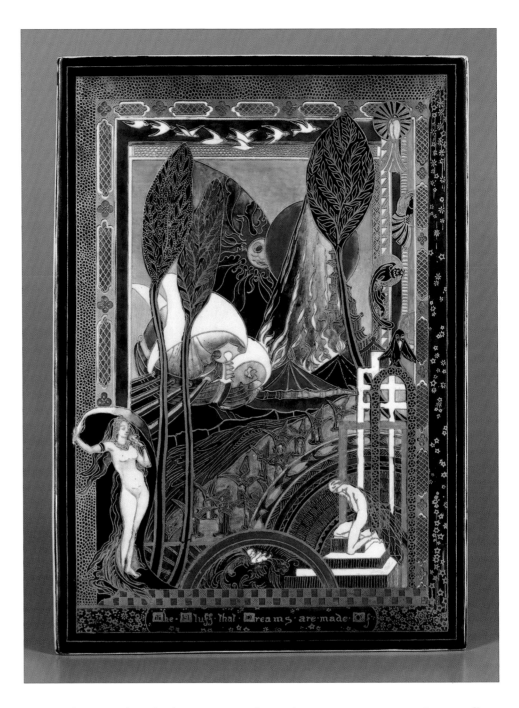

28. An earthenware plaque, 16in. (41cm) by 11in. (27.9cm), decorated with the pattern *The Stuff that Dreams are made of* (F3078). Designed by Daisy Makeig-Jones for Josiah Wedgwood and Sons Ltd., about 1926.

engraved copper plates for the 'Saucepans for Spitfires' campaign to assist the war effort. Many of these included those used by Makeig-Jones for her Fairyland Lustre range.

Her mother died in March 1943 and during that year Makeig-Jones underwent major surgery for a stomach complaint. Sadly, for the last part of her life she was bedridden, dependent upon people going upstairs to talk to her. Members of her family remember that she would always muster up enough energy to entertain the children who visited. Her great-niece spent some time at the family house when her own mother was ill. She recalls sitting on the bed with Makeig-Jones. The bedroom was full of cubby holes, and together they would construct an imaginary world using different sets of props with mirrors for

29. A large bone china bowl decorated with the lesser known *Hares, Dogs and Birds* pattern (Z5448), part of the Fairyland Lustre range. Designed by Daisy Makeig-Jones for Josiah Wedgwood and Sons Ltd., between 1927-29.

30. A large plate decorated with the lesser known *Mythical Animals* pattern, designed by Daisy Makeig-Jones for Josiah Wedgwood and Sons Ltd.

31. A large plate decorated with the *Imps on a Bridge and Tree House* pattern, from the Fairyland Lustre range designed by Daisy Makeig-Jones for Josiah Wedgwood and Sons Ltd., about 1924.

ponds, furniture made of conkers and pins wrapped with wool and people made of wish-bones. Like the mysterious landscapes and faraway lands she had created for Wedgwood pottery, she was now recreating something for her family's children.[28] Maybe she remembered how, as a young girl, she would read stories to her younger brothers and sisters. Makeig-Jones developed peritonitis from a perforated diverticulum and died on 21 July 1945, at the age of sixty-three.

During the late 1960s, as interest in the art nouveau style increased, collectors began to look at the pottery of the period. At the same time Una des Fontaines lectured to the Wedgwood Society on Fairyland Lustre in 1963. Several years later she produced a definitive and comprehensive work on Daisy Makeig-Jones. In 1973 a record £1,600

was reached at Sotheby's Belgravia for a small Fairyland Lustre plaque signed by the designer.[29] Responding to demand, Wedgwood produced two reproductions – a plaque, *Enchanted Place* in 1977 and an octagonal *Poplars* bowl produced in 1979. Not until her lustre wares became sought-after and valuable did her family begin to appreciate what she had achieved. They had been dismissive of her fantasies about fairies.[30]

Inevitably these highly decorative wares attract the higher end of the market, and as a result appeal to both North American and Japanese collectors. In 1998 a large ginger jar sold for over £25,000. It would be fascinating and intriguing to know how this amazing and innovative designer would have felt about her pottery fetching such elevated prices.

32. The *Daventry* pattern (Z5419) decorated on a bone china vase without lid (shape 2311), from the Fairyland Lustre range. Designed by Daisy Makeig-Jones for Josiah Wedgwood and Sons Ltd., about 1926. Height 9in. (23cm).

CHAPTER 2

TUBE-LINED VARIATIONS

CHARLOTTE RHEAD (1885-1947)

33. Portrait of Charlotte Rhead, 1930s.

Charlotte Rhead was one of the most unique among the twentieth century women designers. The Rheads were an old Staffordshire family who made an important contribution to the pottery industry. They were greatly respected both in the fine and applied arts, in Britain and in the United States of America. Significantly Charlotte successfully designed through two twentieth century design styles, from art nouveau to the streamlined art deco period. Despite her reputation for being quiet and shy, she managed to survive within an industry fraught with cut-backs, restrictions and closures. Through these difficult times she produced a striking range of decorative patterns for both fancies and tablewares, working for several major pottery companies.

Charlotte's father Frederick married Adolphine, the daughter of the famous Copeland flower painter C.F. Hürten, who came from Germany. The Rhead family lived in a small house at 12 Newport Street in Burslem, having moved into the area in 1881. Charlotte Antoinette Adolphine Rhead was born on 19 October 1885. From an early age she was affectionately called Lottie, the fourth child of six and the second daughter. Throughout her childhood she benefited from her family's work in design and the applied arts.

Her grandfather, George Woolliscroft Rhead, the well-known art teacher and artist, established the Fenton School of Art in 1899. He obtained a post at the prestigious firm of Minton. Rhead's father, with his two brothers George and Louis John, and her sister

Alice, served their apprenticeships there. Frederick was a pupil of the famous designer Louis Marc Solon at Minton, in about 1872.[1] Solon, who had come to Britain in the 1870s, had developed pâte-sur-pâte decoration. This highly decorative technique was achieved by building up layers of slip, rather than enamel colour, to create relief decoration. Examples by her father were produced in about 1875 and 1877. He later worked for a short period at Josiah Wedgwood and Sons Ltd., who exhibited a selection of his patterns at the Paris Universal Exhibition in 1878.[2]

In 1894 Frederick Rhead became Art Director at the Brownfield Guild Pottery. His two sons, Frederick Hurten and Harry, served their apprenticeships there and also attended evening classes. Charlotte's brothers received a thorough training.

Frederick would often bring work home with him, spending time drawing and painting with his children. He was, without doubt, the most important influence in Charlotte's life. Not only did he teach her the skills of decorating but he also secured employment for her over a number of years. Her family life and formal education were disrupted on a number of occasions, as her father gained new employment in and around the Potteries. At about nine years of age, she attended the Longport School, when the family moved from Burslem to Stoke.

36. Lesser known examples of Lottie Rhead Ware designed by Charlotte Rhead at the Ellgreave Pottery Ltd. The pattern, decorated on an earthenware plate and jug, featuring tube-lined decoration, dates from about 1923. Height of jug 2⅜in. (6cm).

Unfortunately her education was set back after illness and problems with a broken thigh. This resulted in a limp, corrected through a primitive form of traction. She later attended the Hanley Higher Grade School.

In 1896 Frederick was appointed to the position of Art Director at Wileman and Co., based in Longton. This prestigious and respected pottery was established in the 1850s by James Wileman. In 1872 a partnership was formed with Joseph Shelley. Frederick introduced tube-line decoration to the company; this highly decorative technique required accomplished workers to undertake the skilled work. Essentially, a bag containing liquid clay was used to squeeze the clay slip through a narrow glass tube on to the surface of a piece of pottery in order to apply the thin line of tube, very similar to icing a cake. The application of the design was very difficult and usually required the use of a pounce as a guide. The pounce was a sketch of the design on tracing paper produced by the designer, which was then pierced along the guide-lines, with soot rubbed over the pounce, which was then removed to leave a line of dots to make up the guide-line.

Occasionally the pattern was drawn on the ware first by an outliner or decorator for the tube-liner to use as a guide.[3]

During Frederick's employment at Wileman and Co. he introduced several ranges, including one of his most successful lines, Intarsio, launched in about 1898. Examples were exhibited at an important show at Earls Court, London in 1900, over a six month period. Charlotte, who had just left school, and her sister Adolphine, known as Dollie, assisted their mother in the running of the stand at the fair. Other successful lines included the Urbato and Primitif, introduced in about 1898 and 1897 respectively.[4] His innovative patterns were decorated on a variety of elaborate shapes such as elongated coffee-pots and handled vases. His two sons joined him for a period. In about 1903 Frederick left the company and was replaced in 1905 by Walter Slater.

In 1899 Charlotte's brother, Frederick Hurten Rhead, became Art Director of Wardle & Co., established in 1854 by James Wardle, at the Washington Works, Hope Street, Shelton. By 1881 they had moved to a new site in Victoria Road, Hanley. Frederick

37. A flat earthenware bowl decorated with a stylised fruit pattern (735), tube-lined in black with hand-painted decoration on a red lustre ground. Designed by Charlotte Rhead for Wood and Sons Ltd., about 1926.

Hurten introduced tube-line and pâte-sur-pâte decoration. The firm had previously produced relief-moulded art wares, toilet wares, flowerpots and pedestal vases chiefly targeted at the North American market. The firm also displayed its latest productions at its showrooms in London and at leading stores such as Liberty's.[5] In 1903 it was registered as a limited company, with a capital of £10,000. Rhead and Dollie joined Wardle's in about 1901, working as tube-liners. However, in 1902 Frederick Hurten left the country to take up a post as Art Director at Avon Pottery in Tiltonville, Ohio, followed by a brief period at the Weller Pottery and then at the larger Roseville Pottery, both in Zanesville. In 1927 he joined the Homer Laughlin China Group in West Virginia. Of his many achievements, Fiesta Tableware stands out as being one of the most popular ranges ever produced.

When Frederick Hurten left Wardle's, Rhead's other brother, Harry, took the position as Art Director there for a short period, moving to North America in about 1908. For some time her father had supervised the production of new patterns at Wardle's. However when his freelance work increased he stopped assisting the Wardle productions, resulting in the business failing. In 1925 the firm was purchased by the Cauldon Pottery.

Rhead and Dollie undertook an art course at the Fenton Art School, studying a variety of subjects, including enamelling. After they qualified, positions were found for both of them at Keeling and Co., based in Burslem, in about 1905. This small firm started production around 1886 specialising in hotel and hospital ware. It did not produce tube-line decorated items, therefore the two young girls were employed as paintresses, being paid on piecework rates. The work was both demanding and very hard.

38. A view of the Burgess and Leigh Ltd. factory, Burslem, Stoke-on-Trent.

In 1908 Frederick Rhead, in association with Mr. F.H. Barker, formed a tile manufactory called F.H. Barker and Rhead Ltd. This small firm was based at the Atlas Tile Works in Vine Street, Hanley. The site was previously operated by Sherwin and Cotton, who made tiles until about 1890, followed by a number of small organisations until this new association was formed.[6] Both Rhead and her sister worked as decorators for this firm. However, the business failed and went bankrupt in about 1910. The resultant problems put a financial strain on the Rhead family, forcing them to move to a smaller house to save money. The failure of the business forced Frederick to consider his position and look for new opportunities. Eventually he went to North America to join his two sons, intending to move the family over there once he had secured work. However, he was unhappy there and returned within a year. During this difficult time, the two sisters

PLATE 6.

BURGESS & LEIGH, LTD., Middleport Pottery, BURSLEM.

Deco. 3973.

Deco. 3973.

Deco. 4001.

Deco. 4001.

"Rose Bowl"

Vase 42.

Deco. 4001.

"Chinese Bowl"

Vase 50.

Vase 48.

Vase 68.

Deco. 4016.

Deco. 4016.

"Warwick" Flower Pot.

Vase 76.

"Regent" Floating Bowl.

Vase 35.

Vase 69.

Deco. 3961.

Deco. 3934.

"Kew" Floating Bowl. 3990.

Vase 77.

Vase 74.

Vase 73.

Vase 52.

"Beverley" Fruit Bowl Deco. 3934.

Sq. Spill. 3961.

"Avon" Fruit Bowl Deco. 4002.

"Burleigh" Art Ware.

39. An illustration from the Burgess and Leigh Ltd. catalogue of about 1927, illustrating the latest pattern range, including patterns 3973, 4001, 4002 and 4016 by Charlotte Rhead.

worked for a while at T. & R. Boote, one of the leading producers of tube-lined tiles.
When Frederick returned from America he probably worked for a period, with his
daughter, at Birks, Rawlins and Co., at the Vine Pottery in Stoke-upon-Trent, formed in
1894. The Managing Director was an old friend.

At about this time Rhead began to produce her own patterns, albeit on a small scale,
depicting various subjects, one of a boy and girl dressed in Puritan clothes and another
of a young girl wearing a headdress.[7] In 1911 she exhibited two bowls decorated with
a ship motif at the Turin International Exhibition, both produced while working for Birks,
Rawlins and Co.[8]

In 1912 her father become Art Director at Wood and Sons. This highly regarded firm
was established in 1865 at the Trent and New Wharf Potteries, based in Burslem. The
Managing Director was Harry Wood. Wood's had gained a high reputation over the
years for good quality earthenware and ironstone. They also produced a wide range of
blank wares for sale to other companies such as A.E. Gray and Co. Ltd. It was the plan
that Frederick would smarten up the company's range of hotel, badge and tablewares
that were staple goods for the firm. His earliest decorative designs included Elers and
Trellis, from 1913 and 1915 respectively. Underglaze printed patterns for tea and coffee

41. A hexagonal bowl decorated with a stylised fruit pattern (4000), tube-lined with hand-painted decoration, designed by Charlotte Rhead for Burgess and Leigh Ltd., about 1927. Diameter of bowl 10¼in. (26cm).

ware featured the best selling patterns, Yuan and Wincanton, introduced in 1916. Eventually Frederick began to develop a range of art pottery, being given a free hand to devise new patterns in keeping with current tastes. He produced a cheaper range of pâte-sur-pâte, having introduced this form of decoration at Josiah Wedgwood and Sons Ltd in the 1870s.

Around 1913-14 Charlotte joined her father at Wood's. As part of her duties she trained decorators to tube-line. The commercial success of the tube-lined designs required a new studio to be set up to specialise purely in ornamental wares such as vases, bowls and plaques.

One of Rhead's earliest known designs was *Seed Poppy*, a stylised flower pattern, tube-lined in black with hand painted decoration, dating from about 1915. The pattern became such an outstanding success that production was later transferred to Bursley (see below) and at some stage it was given a special backstamp, incorporating a poppy motif. Her *Persian* pattern dates from about 1918 (Plate 35). She also produced a range of tube-lined plaques depicting Japanese women, some playing musical instruments (Plate 34). A few years later Frederick Rhead persuaded Harry Wood to purchase the Crown Pottery, adjacent to the main site, for the production of such items. The new pottery was

42. An earthenware vase, height 8¾in. (22cm), decorated with a stylised pattern of fruit and leaves (4016), tube-lined in black with hand-painted decoration, for Burgess and Leigh Ltd., about 1927.

renamed Bursley Ltd. in 1920. The subsequent pieces were sold as Bursley Ware. Frederick Rhead moved his studio to the Crown Pottery during that year. The acquisition of this site and the subsequent purchase, a year later, of the Ellgreave Pottery indicates that Harry Wood was keen to develop the art ware side of production. During the twenties Frederick Rhead designed several pattern ranges including Baghdad, Sylvan, Amstel, Benares and Merton, each one featuring a special backstamp range. In 1924 his range of patterns was described by the trade press as being 'a very interesting range of toilet ware, trinket sets, and fancies, many of which, although they were extremely smart, were offered at very popular prices'.[9]

In 1922 Rhead joined her father at the Bursley works, becoming increasingly involved in the development of new designs for tea and coffee wares, and a range of small fancies. She was given her own studio. One notable pattern was *Pomona* (456), depicting stylised pomegranates, flowers and grapes on a mottled ground, and dates from 1922. A year later Rhead was directed to revise the products of the Ellgreave Pottery. The designer developed simple patterns for the distinctive body of the clay (Plate 36). The resultant range was named 'Lottie Rhead Ware' marked with a special backstamp. The products of both the Ellgreave and Bursley works were displayed together on the Wood's trade stands at the British Industries Fairs. Her designs for Bursley were produced alongside those of her father. Generally, the printed and painted designs can

be assigned to her father whilst tube-lined designs were hers. There were, however, a few exceptions, as it is thought that Rhead produced a few printed and painted fruit patterns, such as (767).[10] Her fruit motifs were successfully exploited on a range of tube-lined patterns such as (735) on a red lustre ground (Plate 37). Rhead used the same range of ornamental shapes, such as the Greek Hydria vase, Greek Lekythos and a hexagonal vase range, as her father did. She also produced a simple range of border patterns. In highlighting the current products at their showroom the trade press recorded that these items 'embrace many distinctive decorative schemes wrought with the same care. Futurist, cubist, or the more constrained less flamboyant styles, as the case may be'.[11]

By 1926, a wide range of tableware and fancies was displayed at the British Industries Fair alongside toilet wares and trinket sets, with some patterns featuring mottled lustres.[12] A simple trellis pattern (726) of oranges with small green leaves, designed by Rhead, was exhibited. Unfortunately few records have been saved from this period and information is limited on the work that she produced for both the Ellgreave Pottery and Wood's. Attributing patterns without access to the company's pattern books has proved problematic for designs of this period. It has however been established that by the time Rhead left the company in 1926, pattern numbers had reached about 900.[13]

The Crown Pottery was severely damaged by fire in August, 1926. Because of the damage and loss of equipment little further work was undertaken. Shortly afterwards

43. An earthenware hexagonal dessert bowl, diameter 10¼in. (26cm), decorated with a stylised fruit border (4367), tube-lined in black with hand-painted decoration, designed by Charlotte Rhead for Burgess and Leigh Ltd., about 1927-28.

44. A stylised tulip motif (4471) decorated on an earthenware teapot, tube-lined in black with hand-painted decoration. Height 5in. (12.5cm). Designed by Charlotte Rhead for Burgess and Leigh Ltd., about 1928.

Rhead decided, at the age of forty, to leave Wood's. She accepted a position as designer at Burgess and Leigh Ltd. Little is known of her reasons for leaving the Wood's organisation, but possibly she wanted to establish herself as an independent designer, away from her father. It has been suggested that Rhead continued to supply patterns to Wood's, on a free-lance basis, after she had left. Three years later Frederick Rhead also left Wood's to take a position with the firm Cauldon Potteries, based in Stoke. The Crown Works was later occupied, from 1931, by the designer Susie Cooper.

Burgess and Leigh was established in about 1851, initially known as Hulme and Booth. By the 1860s the firm was owned by Frederick Rathbone Burgess, William Leigh and Frederick Lowndes Good. When the latter retired in 1877 the firm became known as Burgess and Leigh.[14] It was initially involved in the production of toilet wares, jugs and basins, sold under the Burleigh Ware name. In 1889 new premises were located at the Middleport Pottery, based in Burslem (Plate 38). Twenty years later the firm was made into a limited company, the first directors being Edmund Leigh and his three sons. By the early 1920s overseas agents were established in North America, New Zealand and Canada, with the London showroom located at 44 Farringdon Street, run by Mr. Barlow. During the twenties the firm was mainly concerned with the production of domestic tablewares in traditional patterns such as Blue Willow.

The firm's Art Director, affectionately known as 'Designer Leigh', but not a relation of the owners, was elderly when Rhead began working for the company. As they had not previously utilised tube-line decoration, she was initially responsible for training a number of free-hand paintresses to undertake the detailed work. In order to develop the more artistic side of production a special studio was set up. The company placed an advertisement in the trade press, declaring: 'We have secured the services of the accomplished lady artist Charlotte Rhead who has produced for us a number of original

45. An earthenware egg set and bowl decorated in the *Sunshine* pattern (4609), with a shaded band in yellow with tube-lined dashes in black. Designed by Charlotte Rhead for Burgess and Leigh Ltd., about 1928-29. Diameter of bowl 6⅜in (16cm).

46. A Nursery Ware pattern, *Who Said Dinner* (3131), tube-lined in black with hand painted decoration on an earthenware mug and beaker. Designed by Charlotte Rhead for Crown Ducal Ltd., about 1932.

47. A notable example of the stitch theme, a utilitarian tube-lined decoration in black and yellow for a range of tea, coffee and dinnerware patterns. Designed by Charlotte Rhead for Crown Ducal Ltd., about 1932-33.

decorations all pure Handcraft combining grace and dignity of design with the most beautiful under glaze colourings.'[15]

For this new association it seemed appropriate to the management that her wares should feature a hand-painted signature, 'Rhead', next to the standard printed mark. A special printed mark was not forthcoming for Rhead, even though the firm must have been aware of the trend to feature named designers on each piece of ware. Perhaps they felt that her decorative items would lose their handcraft quality with a facsimile signature. As soon as the decorators had been trained she concentrated on developing new patterns. Although stylistically similar to her earlier work there was a clear accent towards abstraction. Rhead used a wide range of stylish and functional shapes that were currently in production, including the Warwick flowerpot, Regent floating bowl and Avon fruit bowl. As production increased during subsequent years a limited range of new shapes was produced from her designs, probably modelled by Charles Wilkes and Ernest Bailey. The majority of her patterns were not given names. Her first ranges started at about 3973 and her last designs were around the 4908 when she left the firm in 1931. Rhead was not the only designer working for the company. It is known that a W. Adams was responsible for a number of patterns numbered around the 4400 region.[16]

48. The popular *Stitch* pattern (3274), tube-lined in black with hand-painted decoration on a vase height 8⅝in. (22cm). Designed by Charlotte Rhead for Crown Ducal Ltd., about 1933-34.

49. An earthenware jug decorated with the *Patch* pattern, tube-lined in black with hand-painted decoration. Designed by Charlotte Rhead for Crown Ducal Ltd., 1935.

By March 1927 about fourteen patterns were in production, the earliest being a simple floral border (3973). Patterns such as *Gouda* (4001), featuring stylised Islamic motifs, helped to establish the luxury side of the firm's products (Plate 39). Stylised birds, flowers and fruit motifs were exploited for a range of decorative plaques. A notable pattern was her *Persian* design (Plate 40). In contrast she also devised patterns for a range of moulded wares in the form of embossed leaves, fruit and grapes. A new range of ornamental and decorative patterns, including a stylised fruit design (Plate 42) decorated in lustres ,and a fruit border (Plate 41), proved profitable for the company. The trade press commented that her patterns should be 'recommended to the trade as vigorous conceptions, artistic to a degree, unlike anything offered elsewhere, and fully up to date in style without encroaching upon the futurist'.[17]

In 1929 the trade press illustrated a new design called *Sylvan* (4100) that depicted stylised tree motifs in a landscape, produced in various colourways. The pattern proved popular and repeat orders continued. Towards the late twenties Burgess and Leigh were, according to the trade press, placing more emphasis on suite ware, namely sandwich sets and tea ware, for which they found a ready market. The new crescent Richmond shapes, one set consisting of a single large dish and six smaller plates, were praised by

50. An earthenware vase decorated with the popular *Persian Rose* pattern (4040), tube-lined in black with hand-painted decoration on a green glaze. Many colour variations of this pattern were produced. Designed by Charlotte Rhead for Crown Ducal Ltd., 1935.

the trade, noting that a set would make a respectable gift at a reasonable price. These plain and functional shapes, soon patented, were ideal for Rhead's simple patterns featuring fruit motifs, notable examples including *Garland* (4101) and a version of *Rutland* (4367), that proved popular (Plate 43). These simple and pleasing designs were produced in several colourways. Rhead also designed a number of patterns for general tea ware, such as (4471), depicting a stylised tulip motif (Plate 44). After viewing her latest designs the trade press noted: 'The effects achieved are distinctly pleasing, and there is something here which is quite bright and new without being garish. Such a style of treatment is, perhaps, seen at its best in connection with morning sets, coffee sets, sandwich sets, fruit sets, sugar and cream sets, and a few other special pieces suitable for the present side.'[18]

In about 1929 Rhead produced a few audacious patterns including *Carnival* (4120), boldly painted in red, coral, yellow and black, and *Harlequin* (4132). The patterns were probably produced to compete with the art pottery of the period, typified by the work of Clarice Cliff. In complete contrast to these complex designs Rhead devised simple patterns such as *Sunshine* (4609), featuring simple tube-line dashes (Plate 45). She also

51. An earthenware lamp base decorated with the *Manchu* pattern (4511), tube-lined in black with hand painted decoration. Designed by Charlotte Rhead for Crown Ducal Ltd., 1936.

52. An earthenware vase, height 8⅝in. (22cm), decorated with the *Indian Tree* pattern (4795), tube-lined in brown with hand-painted decoration. Designed by Charlotte Rhead for Crown Ducal Ltd., 1936.

created a number of patterns that were not tube-lined, such as a hand-painted tiger with palm trees painted in silver lustre (4672). A selection of nursery ware patterns including *Dogs* (4419), *Cats* (4420) and *Chickens* (4421), were introduced in about 1929.

The steady flow of new patterns was, by 1930, slowing down. Burgess and Leigh had employed a new designer, Harold Bennett, to work alongside the Art Director, who was at that point in his seventies. Unfortunately Rhead did not enjoy working with Bennett and as a result a difficult situation developed. Barry Leigh, a descendant of the firm, observed that they seemed not to get on with each other to such a point that their working relationship became uncomfortable.[19] Perhaps this explains why she decided to leave, despite having enjoyed considerable success. Rhead left the firm in 1931, after a mere five years, leaving behind the group of highly skilled decorators that she had trained. Some of her last patterns, such as *Orchard* (4767) and *New Florentine* (4908), were probably launched in about 1932. Her final pattern is thought to be (4816), therefore any patterns with numbers above this were probably not hers, although Burgess and Leigh did launch a new range of nursery wares in about 1932, including the amusing *Quack Quack* (4766), *Bunny* and *Baa-Baa*, which probably were Rhead's designs.[20]

The thirties were to be her most prolific period. At the end of 1932 she started work for A.G. Richardson Ltd. This medium-sized pottery successfully traded under the name of Crown Ducal. Production began in 1915 at the Gordon Pottery, Pinnox Street in Tunstall. Following their initial success and expansion a new showroom was opened at 46 Holborn Viaduct in London during the late 1920s. They were represented by Mr. Harry E. Parker with listed agents in the USA, Australia, New Zealand, Belgium, The Netherlands and Norway.[21] During the early twenties their products underwent a distinctive change following the introduction of aerographed plain coloured tea wares and new high class dinnerwares. Some of these wares, including a Happy Days dinner set for £2.12s, were featured in a full page advertisement for the famous department store Harrods in *The Sphere* newspaper.[22] In particular, the Spectria Flambé range by Mr. E. R. Wilkes, for the 'upper class trade', caught the attention of the trade press during the late twenties. During the 1920s the designer Norman Keates had designed several successful patterns such as Cairo and Woodland, the latter better known today as Orange Tree.[23] Crown Ducal also produced a number of chintz patterns. These charming and high quality designs found a ready market overseas and were described by the press as possessing 'the attributes of reliability and distinctiveness without being high priced and exclusive'.[24]

Rhead did not join Crown Ducal as the chief designer. Mr. W.B. Johnson held the position of Art Director, although by that time he was over seventy years old. It is probable that the company used a wide range of sources for new patterns, including bought-in transfer prints from quality suppliers and those submitted by free-lance designers. In her new role, Charlotte returned to her formal name, rejecting Lottie, possibly as it was too familiar and was used by her previous employer. Her patterns were marked with one of the many standard marks, with the larger pieces bearing a facsimile signature applied by the paintress. Her first designs proved to be commercially successful almost straight away, being featured in the trade press. *Byzantine* (2681), a stylised floral pattern, was produced in several colour variations to both body glaze and enamel decoration throughout the thirties. This was followed by *Turin* (2691), consisting of overlapping lotus leaves on a distinctive blue turquoise glaze, and an overtly art deco pattern, *Aztec* (2800). These were typical examples of her work. The trade press noted: 'This is a class of production which no one of cultural taste would hesitate to accept and accord a worthy place in a well furnished household.'[25]

Rhead devised a whole range of patterns during this period. In particular, she introduced some attractive nursery ware patterns that successfully combined hand-painted decoration with tube-lining (Plate 46). The range included *Who said Dinner* (3131), *Little Boy Blue* (3133), *Little Red Riding Hood* (3135) and a lesser known design called *Look at Us*. These novelty items were introduced in about 1933.[26] The designer also developed a simple tube-lined dash border that was inspired by men's tailoring.[27] The *Stitch* pattern, as it became known, was decorated mainly on the standard Crown Ducal

53. A vase decorated with the *Wisteria* pattern (4954), tube-lined in blue with hand-painted decoration on a snow glaze. Designed by Charlotte Rhead. for Crown Ducal Ltd., 1937.

54. An earthenware vase, height 8¾in.(22cm), decorated with the popular *Golden Leaves* pattern (4921), tube-lined in brown with hand-painted decoration. Designed by Charlotte Rhead for Crown Ducal Ltd., 1937.

tea and coffee shapes, such as Cotswold. This simple design, and its many variations, catered for the cheaper end of the market and as it was easy to produce it proved economically successful (Plate 47). The additional decorators brought in to undertake the increasing orders were trained how to space and use tube-lining techniques on this range.[28] From this simple idea she developed *Stitch* (3274), that resembled stylised patchwork in various colours on vases and other decorative items (Plate 48). This pattern inspired many variations, such as *Patch*, exhibited at the British Industries Fair in 1935 (Plate 49). The range demonstrated her ability to design utilitarian patterns as well as the more elaborate ornamental wares. Moreover, they were cheap to produce and priced to be well within the reach of most people. The trade press recorded that every dealer who visited the stand admired the range of wares on display. Rhead also produced a range of patterns including *Breedon* and *Rosemary* for the Victory range of tea and coffee wares.[29]

As production increased, the company purchased the Britannia Pottery in Cobridge in 1933, for the production of earthenware. Rhead's designs were eventually produced at both factories. The success of the firm was no doubt partly due to her successful patterns including *Rhodian* (3272), *Granada* (3321) and *Hydrangea* (3797). Her *Persian Rose* (4040) pattern was launched at the British Industries Fair in 1935 (Plate 50). This outstanding pattern proved to be a commercial success and was praised by the trade press who declared that it 'reveals freedom and vigour'.[30] It is evident that Crown Ducal held their designer in great esteem, promoting her new ranges with full page advertisements. One in particular boasted new shapes and designs in flower jugs, vases and bowls and illustrated amongst others the *Peony* (4016) pattern.[31] Another notable design was *Omar* (4036), an interesting pattern depicting a Persian figure seated under a tree with a quotation around the edge of the piece that read: 'here with a loaf of bread beneath the bough. A flask of wine. A book of verse and thou.' This quotation was taken from the first edition of Edward Fitzgerald's translation of *The Rubaiyat* by Omar Khayyam.

At the British Industries Fair in 1936 the firm launched several new patterns by Rhead, including the outstanding *Manchu* (4511), a stylised dragon motif that the designer used on a number of occasions (Plate 51). The trade press noted that Crown Ducal had made an excellent and distinctive display stand in buff red with a grey effect on the ceiling. The range on display included *Tudor Rose* (4491). *Indian Tree* (4795) was also introduced during that year (Plate 52).

At the following year's Fair, her latest patterns were again given a prominent space on the Crown Ducal stand. The large centrepiece, featuring glass shelving and tasteful back lighting, emphasised two new designs – *Foxglove* and *Wisteria* (Plate 53), These two designs, commercial successes for Crown Ducal, were shown on a range of over twelve different shapes of vases, plaques and bowls, placed underneath the firm's banner. The standard products of the firm were positioned on either side of Rhead's work.[32] Of special interest was the new snow glaze that she had developed a year earlier. Probably as a mark of its success the words 'snow glaze' were incorporated in the backstamp of some patterns using this pleasant glaze. Queen Mary, in particular, was impressed and made several purchases, including a *Wisteria* flower jug. The trade press reported that 'the demand for this new type of decoration outstrips all anticipation.'[33] The trade stand also displayed the *Golden Leaves* pattern (Plate 54), which became a bestseller for the firm.

Rhead designed a pattern for the Coronation souvenir range incorporating the Royal Cypher with a chequered border, launched by the firm in 1937 and produced in at least four colourways (4724-4726). Whilst *Persian Leaf* (Plate 55) and *Fruit Border* (Plate 56) are fairly common, others such as *Tarragona* (5623), *Palermo* (5803) and *Ankara* (5983) are lesser known. In 1939 she introduced the *Trellis* pattern (6016), a simple panelled design with small floral motifs (Plate 57). Some of the last patterns she produced before leaving Crown Ducal included *Mexican* (6198), featured in a 'Britain Can Export' promotion in September 1940.[34]

By 1934, a year after her father's death, Rhead and her mother had moved to a rented semi-detached bungalow in Stoneleigh Road in Chell. They lived a quiet life there for six years, assisted by their live in housekeeper, May Doorbar. May recalled that Rhead would spend her evenings working on engravings at home and in her small studio shed in the garden. Mother and daughter enjoyed the simple pleasures of life such as gardening, listening to music and making rugs, and occasionally visited Charlotte's sister in Somerset. In

55. A large earthenware jug decorated with the *Persian Leaf* pattern (5391), tube-lined in blue with hand-painted decoration. Designed by Charlotte Rhead for Crown Ducal Ltd., about 1938.

56. A stylised fruit border pattern (5802) decorated on an earthenware handled jug. Tube lined in grey with hand-painted decoration. Designed by Charlotte Rhead for Crown Ducal Ltd., about 1938.

1940 Rhead bought a house in Marsh Avenue, Wolstanton. Prior to the move May had left to get married, and although asked to return in a letter from Rhead's mother, she declined.[35]

Throughout her career Rhead, unlike her contemporary Clarice Cliff, avoided contact with the press. However, as she became more successful it was inevitable that the press would want to talk to her. In an interview a reporter explained that 'owing to Miss Rhead's extremely shy disposition, she was rather reticent to say anything about herself, and it was only through the good offices of Mr. Hancock, who is O.C. staff at the Gordon Pottery, that we were able to have a talk'.[36]

By the late 1930s Rhead was at the height of her success, having significantly built up the firm's range of ornamental and decorative wares. Sadly, the disruption in production and the expected restrictions caused by the Second World War necessitated changes within the company. There was no longer significant demand for decorative wares of the sort that Rhead was renowned for. In about 1942 she left Crown Ducal. Several designs, such as stylised floral pattern (6454), were probably by her. After the war, Crown Ducal also produced several patterns based on her style but these lacked the same high quality.

When Rhead became unemployed, Harry Wood came to her assistance. Having always held the family in high regard, he offered her a position as designer at H.J. Wood Ltd., at the Alexandra Pottery, on Amicable Street in Burslem, in 1942. The firm had agents in several countries, including Argentina, Australia, Canada, Cuba, Uruguay and

57. An earthenware handled jug 8⅝n. (22cm) high, decorated with the *Trellis* pattern (6016), tube-lined in brown with hand-painted decoration on a brown glaze. Designed by Charlotte Rhead for Crown Ducal Ltd., 1939.

Peru. For many years it had been run by Percy Wood. Being chiefly involved in the production of teapots, it suffered financial difficulties when the teapot trade went into decline, during the late twenties. The business was sold to Harry Wood. During the forties the main production was Radford Handcraft Ware that included ranges such as Jacobean, Chinese Rose, Butterfly ware and a series of teapots called 'Little Old Ladies'.

Rhead's task was to create a new range of decorative tube-lined designs. She was given an office situated at the New Wharf Pottery, requiring her to walk round the corner in the street to get to the works, until a connecting door was installed.[37] The setting up of her studio, with space for six decorators, took longer than expected, probably due to the lack of materials. Her work was only a small but a significant part of the firm's products. Her tube-lined items represented less than one-tenth of the entire output. The rest of the works continued to be used for the production of Radford ware, which had proved popular during the 1930s.

Harry Wood decided that these wares should be marketed under the Bursley Ware mark that both Rhead and her father had used during the twenties. Wood's had retained the Bursley trade name, even though the original home of Bursley was currently occupied by the Susie Cooper Pottery. The new mark for her productions featured the words 'Bursley Ware, Charlotte Rhead, England'. Her patterns were given a new prefix of T.L., an abbreviation of tubelined, probably to distinguish them from other products produced by the Wood's companies. By 1943 she had developed almost fifty new patterns, from T.L.1 to about T.L.69, though not all of the numbers were used. Some were simple colour variations of earlier patterns. Patterns included *Trellis* (T.L.3), a fruit border in browns (T.L.5) (Plate 58), a stylised floral (T.L.14) (Plate 59) and *Daisy* (T.L.37). Only one pattern, *Arabesque* (T.L.4), was given a special backstamp. Jessie Tait, better known for her designs for W.R. Midwinter Ltd. during the fifties and sixties, recalled that she worked on this pattern during 1947.[38] A later pattern (T.L.76), depicting stylised tulips, was produced in large quantities (Plate 60), whilst a design similar to (T.L.37), decorated on a lamp base, and probably by her, is unknown. Rhead's patterns were decorated on an assortment of shapes, including bowls, nut trays, small baskets, wall pockets, lamp bases, decorative jugs and vases. Pattern numbers after T.L.105 were definitely not by Charlotte, as they date to July 1955 in the pattern books.

In 1946 Eddie Sambrook, Artistic Director for Wood's, returned from the war and began working with Rhead. They enjoyed an excellent working relationship, which proved both creative and fruitful, and they soon became good friends. As a young boy he had worked with Rhead's father. Following discussions, they decided that the designs were beginning to look a little dated. Eddie Sambrook particularly recalled that patterns

such as *Trellis* and *Arabesque* were stylistically too close to her Crown Ducal patterns. As a result they experimented with new glazes to produce designs that could not be linked with the styles of the inter-war period. They both wanted to achieve an effect of lushness through glazes and hand-painted decoration. These experiments took a long time, with hundreds of trials being produced. Unfortunately, these ideas were not fully developed when Rhead became ill, although she made every effort to come into the factory despite her sickness. Besides working on patterns together, Eddie Sambrook produced several designs of his own.[39]

The firm took a stand at the first post-war British Industries Fair in 1947, held in London. Eddie Sambrook recalled that each firm was given a set space and set shelves due to austerity measures of the period. With the intention of making a more attractive display he hung three chargers above the main stand, including one that he had worked on with Rhead. Sadly the organisers did not like the additional contribution and made him take them down.[40]

For some years Wood's had attempted to create decorations for the best-selling Beryl Green tea ware, with little success as the copper came out of the glaze and stained the ware black. However, Rhead ingeniously used tube-lined decoration to create *Woodland* (T.L.82), a simple tube-lined leaf border which became a bestseller. This very simple and utilitarian style, so typical of the period, was available in other colourways. The range, marketed as Wood's Ware, also included lamp bases, gift wares and suite ware, and was promoted for some years in the trade press.[41]

58. An earthenware vase, 11⅜in. (29cm) high, decorated with stylised fruit motifs (T.L.5), tube-lined with hand-painted decoration. Designed by Charlotte Rhead for H.J. Wood Ltd. The date of production is unknown but this pattern was illustrated in a company catalogue of 1954.

59. A small earthenware ginger jar, 6¼in. (16cm) high, decorated with a stylised floral design (T.L.14), tube-lined with hand-painted decoration. Designed by Charlotte Rhead for H.J. Wood Ltd. The date of production is unknown but this pattern was illustrated in a company catalogue of 1954.

60. An earthenware jug, 9in. (23cm) high, decorated with a stylised floral pattern (T.L.76), tube-lined with hand-painted decoration on a grey glaze. Designed by Charlotte Rhead for H.J. Wood Ltd. The date of production is unknown but this pattern was illustrated in a company catalogue of 1954.

Charlotte Rhead died on 8 November 1947 following an eight week illness and the trade press commented: 'The pottery industry has lost one of its most talented designers.'[42]

The majority of her wares were not produced until after war restrictions were lifted in 1952. A catalogue of 1954 lists just over ten of her designs, including *Trellis* (T.L.3) and *Arabesque* (T.L.4). Many were still being marketed until about 1960. A company advertisement from this date illustrated her stylised tulip design (T.L.76), with other designs not by Rhead. The slogan reads: 'Simplified Elegance: pleasing shape, attractive superb craftsmanship, these are the qualities of gift ware by H.J. Wood, to buyers and customers.'[43]

For many years after her death, Charlotte Rhead's original and innovative wares were not regarded as collectable. Perhaps this was due to the low profile she maintained throughout her life. Alongside the growing popularity of Susie Cooper and Clarice Cliff, interest in Rhead's work has increased. Recently, special sales have been held annually in London, chiefly targeted at her early vases and plaques produced for both Bursley and Burgess and Leigh Ltd. Her outstanding contribution to pottery design, in particular her tube-lined decoration, has yet to be surpassed either in terms of originality or quality.

CHAPTER 3

THE ORIGINAL BIZARRE GIRL

Clarice Cliff (1899 -1972)

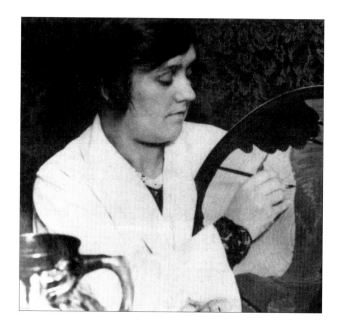

No other designer has come to epitomise the art deco period more than Clarice Cliff, with her fantastic, outrageous and colourful ceramics. She embraced the styles and shapes of European designers and successfully transferred them into pottery for the British housewife. Over a span of ten bright years she produced original and often unique designs that some people considered vulgar. During the post-war period, when tastes changed, she responded to the market by producing more traditional and occasional modern wares until the early 1960s.

Clarice Cliff was born on 20 January 1899 in Tunstall, Stoke-on-Trent. She was the fourth child in a family of seven children, with two brothers, Frank and Harry, and four sisters, Sarah, Hannah, Dolly and Ethel. Her father was an iron moulder by trade and was employed by Messrs. Fuller Ltd. As part of his job he worked on the ornate gates for the local park and the hanging sign for the Tunstall Public Library, the latter dated 1901. The family's terraced house at 19 Meir Street was situated around the corner from her father's place of work.[1] Her mother, Ann, spent most of her time looking after the children and running the family home. When the family increased in size they moved to a house on the corner of Edwards Street. Like most of her family, Clarice took an active part in the local church, working as a Sunday school teacher. Her sister Dolly made dresses and was also

61 Portrait of Clarice Cliff, hand painting one of her designs, about 1932.

a ballroom dancer. In 1909, aged ten, Clarice changed school from the High Street Elementary School in Tunstall to the Summerbank Road School, where she showed some interest in artistic endeavours. Recalling a particular event she said: 'How pleased I was to miss some lessons, and to be entrusted to make large papier mâché maps, built on nails of varying heights, coloured for use in geography.'[2]

Although she had little opportunity at home to develop her artistic skills, her older sister Sarah was in charge of the decorating shop at Johnson Brothers in Tunstall. Clarice would often go there to watch her sister working. Her interest in the pottery trade was no doubt stimulated by these visits, as she was impressed at how quickly the paintresses applied colour to the ware. Like most working girls from the area a job as a paintress in a small, family led company was inevitable. She remarked later that, 'if one must earn one's living there is little to do on leaving school except to work in a factory. I started as most girls do, at the bottom of the ladder.'[3]

Her first post was secured as an apprentice enameller at the firm of Lingard Webster and Co, based at the Swan Pottery in Hunt Street, Tunstall in 1912 (Plate 62), only a few streets away from the family home. They manufactured domestic tableware in a variety of styles suitable for the current market. In particular, the firm's advertisements of that period emphasise that they specialised in the production of teapots. As an apprentice Cliff learned how to paint free-hand on to pottery. During her three year's apprenticeship at the firm she earned two shillings a week.

When Cliff left the firm to join Hollingshead and Kirkham, at the Unicorn Pottery in Tunstall in 1915, her parents were not pleased. They were concerned that her work in the lithography department would not allow her the opportunity to develop her decorating skills, thus limiting her employment prospects. Therefore they decided to fund their daughter to attend evening classes at the Tunstall School of Art in order to compensate. Cliff also studied at the Burslem School of Art, undertaking a good training in art and design, chiefly drawing, as she later recalled, from plaster casts and vases of honesty. Following this, she passed exams to become a teacher at the age of sixteen.[4]

With the advent of the First World War many skilled workers left the pottery industry to fight for the country. New opportunities became available for women. Being determined to progress, Cliff took the decision, in 1916, to leave Hollingshead and Kirkham to work for a much bigger company with an international clientele. The well-appointed and reputable firm of A.J. Wilkinson Ltd. was based in Burslem, trading as Royal Staffordshire (Plate 63). Arthur Wilkinson had established the firm in 1885. Sadly in 1891 he was killed in an accident whilst on holiday in Switzerland. In 1894 the firm was taken over by Arthur Shorter, a member of the Wilkinson family, in collaboration with Edmund Leigh. Arthur Shorter had married Arthur Wilkinson's sister, Henrietta Elizabeth, some years earlier. He had already established a small pottery business, based in Hanley, in 1874. By 1878 he had sold his interest and formed a partnership with James Boulton, selling a range of products including majolica. By the early part of the twentieth century the business was known as Shorter and

62. A view of the entrance to the Lingard Webster and Co. Ltd. factory in Tunstall, Stoke-on-Trent.

Son.[5] Under Arthur Shorter's direction A.J. Wilkinson Ltd. became increasingly profitable before the First World War, due to the export of pottery to the North American market. Business continued to do well and over the next ten years the works expanded. Shorter's two sons, Colley and Guy, joined the company on leaving school and were appointed as Directors in 1916. Two years later their father retired. The trade press recorded that the two brothers had great flair for sales and promotion. A wide range of traditional and contemporary table wares, toilet sets and dinnerware formed the main production. Agents were established in South Africa, North America and London. In 1920 they purchased the Newport Pottery from Edge, Malkin and Co. This small pottery works boasted facilities such as flatware and casting shops, joinery, and maintenance departments.

For the first few years of employment Cliff was involved in free-hand decoration. However, in about 1920 her painting skills were recognised by the Decorating Shop Manager, Jack Walker. Noticing her painting a butterfly design on to a piece of ware, he realised that she could do more than just copy from set patterns and discussed her potential

with Colley Shorter, his brother-in-law.[6] They decided that she should be moved from the general decorating shop to work alongside the designers John Butler and Fred Ridgway, in the design studio. The artistic and expensive wares that they had created, including Tibetan, Rubaiyat and Oriflamme, were not typical of the main Wilkinson's products. The Oriflamme range, designed by John Butler in 1910, was named after 'the heraldic device on the Old French banner with its gold and ribboned tongues of flame'. This range encompassed several patterns, throughout the years of production, including Golden Mean, Medice, Ruby and Opal.[7] Some years later, John Butler produced a wide range of modern patterns, such as Aquatic, possibly inspired by Cliff's use of colour.

Cliff worked closely with these designers, learning about the various forms of pottery decoration. In September 1922 she received her Indentures of Apprenticeship for modelling.[8] This was, however, her second apprenticeship. She was then given a little more responsibility and a wage increase. Eventually she held special responsibilities including maintaining the pattern books, covering imperfections on the expensive pieces and undertaking very fine filigree gilding with a pen. The first mention of her name was when it was placed next to a Fred Ridgway design, featuring a bird and dragon motif on a plaque from February 1923. Cliff noted that during this period she 'gained a very useful knowledge of the making and firing of pottery'.[9]

Whilst working on these expensive ranges, Cliff had the opportunity to develop her modelling skills which were to play a major role in guaranteeing her success in later years. Probably her first commercially produced work was a pair of Dutch figures, *Old Dutch Man* (7482) and *Dutch Woman* (7483), illustrated in the trade press as early as October 1923.[10] These pieces predate the small moulded figures of Arabs, thought to have been her earliest attempts at modelling. Further figures issued under the World's Workers banner included *Collier* (7508), *Oriental Figure* (7509) and *Old Bill* (7511). The trade press noted: 'The person who is chiefly responsible for the production of these figures at the works

is an artist first of all and a modeller as the outcome of being artistically minded. The consequence is that there is an unspoilt directness about some of these figures that is distinctly refreshing.'[11]

For the British Empire Exhibition of 1924 Cliff produced a scale model of the Wilkinson's site, showing the various buildings and bottle ovens in true perspective for the company's stand.[12] She also showed a range of modelled figures that included the Dutch figures and two new ones called *Seville Oranges* (7652) and *Pin Seller* (7653), inspired by Fred Ridgway's 'Old London Cries' decorative plaques. One of her better-known figural pieces was *Lady Candlestick on Cushion* (7567), an elegantly modelled piece, produced to sit in a large low bowl. This piece, of particular interest to Australian buyers, was produced in several colour variations throughout the decade (Plate 64). The British trade press noted that 'the poise of the figure, the features and expression, the hang of the drapery, coupled with the pleasing general point of view one gets at any angle of the object makes us feel disposed to describe it as the piece-de-resistance.'[13] This was soon followed by a new fancy called *Milady* (7701), a small piece featuring a graceful English lady modelled as the knob of a box lid. Moreover she gained recognition when the trade mentioned her by name, noting that 'this firm has a clever lady modeller in Miss Cliff, and at the hands of this lady has just been produced an additional attractive novelty in the form a puff box, to be known as Milady'.[14]

By the spring of 1925 Cliff had produced a further group of figures that included *Dancing Girl* (7939), *Market Day* (7940) and *Girl Figure: Early Victorian* (8022). The latter was stylistically close to those produced by Royal Doulton (Plate 65). During this important year the *Pottery and Glass Record* took a tour of the Burslem showrooms, guided by Colley Shorter. The resultant article illustrated several examples of her modelled figures, noting that they were both cleverly conceived, skilfully modelled and rather striking.[15] With this praise and recognition it was little wonder that Colley wanted to cultivate her artistic abilities

64. An illustration from an article in *The Pottery and Glass Record*, March 1925, showing several modelled works by Clarice Cliff. From left to right (top): *Seville Oranges*, *Old Dutch Man*, *Oriental Figure*, *Collier*, *Pin Seller* and *Lady Candlestick on Cushion*. The two bird figures probably predate Clarice Cliff's period at the factory.

65. A very rare example of Clarice Cliff's modelling work. This *Girl Figure: Early Victorian* (as described in the pattern books) is dated 1925 on the base.

further. Firstly she attended evening classes at the Burslem School of Art, in about 1924 and 1925. She was also given her own studio at the Newport Pottery, situated away from the main production area, so that she could experiment with new ideas. The studio boasted a small photographic studio and a collection of art books. In about 1925 Cliff had moved out of the family home into a one-bedroom flat at 40 Snow Hill in Hanley.

Whilst these experiments were under way, Colley Shorter spent considerable time with her. As a result, speculation began to grow about what form their relationship was taking. Certainly, the relationship was more than that of employer and designer. Moreover, Colley was a married man, his wife was a long term invalid, and they had two daughters. Their love affair created a lot of resentment amongst the workers at the factory and caused a scandal in the industry. Cliff's situation changed as key people at the works, who had done so much to help her, distanced themselves from her. Sadly, this affair has been used to discount her contribution to design, with some recent commentators asserting that it enabled her advancement. However, she had already made a significant contribution to the company's production and reputation. Besides, Colley was an astute businessman and wasn't interested in the idle chat, being determined to see the venture through, especially considering the amount of financial investment he had allocated to developing Cliff as a designer.

At this point in Cliff's career her skills were concentrated in modelling and were not involved in creating patterns. When she was sent to the Royal College of Art in London in early 1927, her formal studies were concerned with modelling, figure composition and life drawing. These two one-month sessions were a valuable experience for her. During the same year she took a trip to Paris. This amazing opportunity for a young working class girl made a great impression on her. In London, she was unimpressed by the many window displays around the city, she found that they lacked any interest. Cliff also examined the latest styles in pottery decoration and shapes noting: 'I thought how drab the old china was and how ugly the few examples of modern ware were and when I got back I persuaded the works to try out some of my designs.'[16]

These trips gave Cliff inspiration to produce colourful and modern patterns. As soon as she returned to the factory she worked closely with Colley to set up an experimental studio to develop new patterns. Cliff had the idea of using the old stock of inferior ware that came with the purchase of the Newport Pottery. As Wilkinson's had no immediate use for the

66. Examples from the Bizarre collection designed by Clarice Cliff, including two earthenware Original Bizarre Lotus jugs and a cigarette box and cover. The hand-painted earthenware bowl, left, is decorated with the *Diamonds* pattern (1929) and the two cups and saucers are decorated with the *New Flag* pattern (1929). Height of twin-handled Lotus jug 11⅞in. (30cm).

67. A selection of *Crocus* items by Clarice Cliff illustrating the various colourways. Top: Several items including an earthenware Bonjour tea for two decorated in the most popular colourway that was in production from 1928 to about 1963. The *Blue Crocus* colour variation, hand painted on an earthenware Bonjour shape preserve pot and cover is lesser known (centre), and dates from about 1935 and a Daffodil shape preserve pot. Height of teapot 5½in. (14cm).

ware it was agreed that Cliff could experiment on these pieces, and if it was a failure no monies would be wasted. This exercise presented a challenge to Cliff. She noted that: 'I was allowed to experiment. First, with one or two of the girls who had learned how to use the decorator's wheel, round shapes were covered from top to bottom with coloured bands. Between guidelines we then drew simple diamonds which in turn were filled in with bright colours by other girls.'[17]

The range was produced in secret over many months, using mainly ornamental wares such as vases, ginger jars and bowls. The first of her bold geometric patterns was completed during the latter part of 1927 and shown to the public in London in August of that year. The paint was applied thickly to cover the defects of the ware and also to give a strong feeling of hand-painted decoration. Cliff named the range 'Bizarre' (Plate 66). The salesmen responsible for selling the range to the shops were used to selling traditional Victorian style wares, and thought that Bizarre was crude and far too advanced for the current market and likely to be short-lived. Cliff noted that, 'after much persuasion the largest car on the factory was filled with an assortment and to their amazement it was quickly sold and within two days they were back for more. So Bizarre by Clarice Cliff was launched'.[18]

The range, comprising sixty dozen pieces, was first revealed for market testing in the spring of 1928. Each piece was marked with the standard Newport Pottery mark with 'Bizarre' hand painted on the base. This was soon replaced with a printed mark. The popularity of Bizarre relied upon novelty and innovative marketing to generate sales that

were so outstanding that part of the Newport factory was devoted to its production. However, some dealers remained sceptical, convinced that it was just a passing fashion. In response to this scepticism the trade press advised 'in viewing this type of pottery decoration one has to remember that there is a demand in the realm of modern furnishing for, shall we say, extravagant colouring'.[19]

Those dealers sceptical of her more adventurous designs warmly accepted the *Crocus* pattern, a simple floral design (Plate 67). The pattern derived from a lithographic floral pattern of crocuses produced by the firm from about 1925. Cliff asked one of her paintresses to work up a hand-painted version for her to create the new design. Once completed, it proved to be one of her most successful patterns spanning thirty years, publicised in several ways, including the distribution of leaflets to retail outlets. As with Bizarre, a special workshop was set up to cope with the demand. A series of interesting colour variations to the basic design were produced, including *Blue Crocus* and *Purple Crocus*, issued in about 1935. The design underwent further modifications throughout the many years of production, eventually phased out in about 1963. The pattern was particularly popular on traditional shapes such as Athens and Globe. Cliff recalled: 'HM Queen Mary bought quite a lot of this pattern every year when she came to the B.I.F. She remembered the prices she had paid in previous years.'[20]

In 1929, Colley relaunched the Joan Shorter Collection of nursery ware that had not proved commercially popular when it was produced a few years earlier. The task of

68. A wide range of Conical sugar shifters designed by Clarice Cliff. Including patterns (top) *Alton* (1933), *Pastel Melon* (1930), *Chintz* (1932), (centre) *Secrets* (1933), *Idyll* (1932), *Orange Roof Cottage* (1932), *Passion Fruit* (1936), (front) *Red Roofs* (1931), *Berries* (1930), *Rudyard* (1933), *Blue Firs* (1933) and *Honolulu* (1933). Height 5½in (14cm).

organising the production was imposed on Cliff. Clarice developed the range from a set of children's drawings by Joan, Colley's nine-year-old daughter. The set comprised a porringer, mug, plate, tea ware and an eggcup set with a yellow duck standing in the centre. The set also included the humorous Bones the Butcher teapot, Boy Blue milk and a Humpty sugar. The muffineer set was called United Service Figures and comprised a sailor, guardsmen and Air Force mustard pot. Clarice modelled all these shapes. At about the same time, two lesser-known Joan Shorter ranges were produced under the 'Joan Shorter's Kiddies Ware' backstamp. One pattern featured giraffes, lions, elephants and monkeys in an African setting, while the other, Huberto, featured various scenes depicting a hippopotamus chasing a young boy around! Further pattern ranges under the Joan Shorter banner were introduced during the early thirties but were probably developed by Clarice Cliff.

From the Bizarre range Cliff soon developed new ideas and patterns, often available in a variety of colourways. These included *Diamonds*, *Mondrian* and *Castellated Circle* (see Plate 5, page 15). Although she gave names to a large number of her patterns, many have been named more recently. The outstanding success of Bizarre established Cliff as a prominent designer in the pottery industry. It also depleted the stock of inferior ware. Re-issuing some of the old Wilkinson's shapes, with some streamlining, initially solved this situation. From the start Cliff knew that modern patterns required modern shapes, so she set about developing more appropriate ones. As early as 1929 she was experimenting with cone shapes, taking her inspiration from the French designer Desny. Cliff's Conical shape was initially a set of bowls, with a teapot being added later that year. In 1932 a range of dinnerware shapes was introduced.[21] Although visually attractive, the teacup and teapot shapes were impractical; the solid triangular handles were prone to gaining heat and thus often dropped and broken. Even Cliff admitted that the handles were problematic, explaining that once they had been opened up they sold especially well. She also produced a coffee-pot, a larger teapot and the Conical sugar sifter, which was decorated with many different patterns (Plate 68).

The Bizarre range was extended to such an extent that separate groups were introduced, such as *Inspiration*, *Archaic* and *Latona*. *Inspiration* was a distinctive and prestigious set of decorative vases, bowls and other items featuring stylised patterns against a bold blue background. Achieving the outstanding finish was difficult both in terms of application of the glazes and also the many firings, which proved costly. The glazes tended to run and get embedded into the kiln, thus creating a high loss factor. *Inspiration* was issued in 1929, but retailed at such a high price that it proved rather hard to sell. The *Archaic* range of vases and architectural columns, modelled by Cliff, were directly copied from the influential book *The Grammar of Ornament* by Owen Jones, both in terms of shape and colour. Publicity material cheekily explained that these items showed the life and tastes of nations, whose civilisations were old at a time when Britain was overrun by savages![22] Unfortunately they were not popular with the public and didn't sell well. The *Latona* range, featuring a very

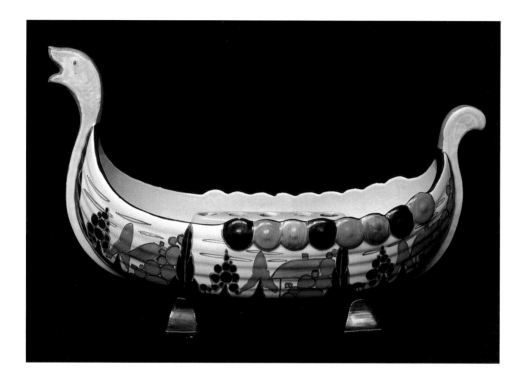

distinctive milky-white glaze, was decorated with specially designed patterns such as *Latona Dahlia* and *Latona Red Roses*.

To maintain the momentum achieved by Bizarre, new patterns were introduced. Cliff used a whole range of source material, drawing heavily from the portfolios of prints she had purchased in Paris. In particular, she was keen on certain French designers and found their work of great inspiration. She also subscribed to *Mobilier et Décoration*, a French monthly magazine. However, sometimes Cliff came too close to the original examples. Her *Butterfly* pattern was a very obvious copy of a design by Edouard Benedictus, whilst her *Carpet* design was an almost direct copy from a design by Ivan DaSilva Bruhns, both from 1930.[23]

Her taste was varied and diverse, and she had the ability to manipulate the images she had collected and transfer them successfully into surface patterns on to pottery of modern form. This enabled her to progress from simple squares to intricate landscapes, featuring the 'cosy cottage' image, so popular during the thirties, often seen on stained glass windows of the period. Her first formal landscape pattern was *Trees and House* (Plate 69), shortly followed by similar patterns that were sold alongside some of her more adventurous designs such as *Melon* and *Sliced Circle* (Plate 70) and *Tennis* (Plate 71). In order to cut down the firm's tax duties a new pattern range called Fantasque was introduced in 1928. The first eight patterns included *Broth, Caprice, Autumn*, soon followed by *Kew*. This diverse range contrasted with *Ravel* (5799), a simple pattern decorated on the Conical range that demonstrated her ability to produce discrete and commercial wares.

Now that the firm had put together a wide range of designs on a range of new shapes it was imperative that they reached a much wider market. From his experience with marketing Bizarre, Colley exploited the press interest to maximum effect by organising special events and promotional trips. Of most significance was the arrangement for the Bizarre Girls, his decorating display team, to decorate pots in the windows of the leading

69. An outstanding modelled work of an earthenware Viking Boat by Clarice Cliff, first produced in 1927. The piece is decorated with the *Trees and House* pattern, from 1929. Length of boat 9⅞in. (25cm).

stores in London and other major cities, to the amusement of the passing crowds (Plate 72). Clarice Cliff's work was sold in all the major department stores such as Harrods, Liberty's, Waring and Gillow and Selfridges. Colley also gained endorsements from film stars and celebrities of the period.[24]

In October 1932 the London department store, Barkers, organised a special Cliff exhibition of thirty table settings that she personally arranged. Few exhibitions of pottery took place without examples of Cliff's work being featured. Each year Wilkinson's took a stand at the British Industries Fair and the Daily Mail Ideal Home Exhibition. Her work sold in such quantities that Clarice became a household name. The press and women's magazines, such as *Home Chat*, began to pick up on this unique designer with her new, vibrant and colourful ware. They placed an emphasis on Cliff as a person, focusing on the rags to riches fairy tale. They also persuaded the average housewife that a vase or tea set by the designer was both practical and modern. As a result of this coverage her work became extremely sought after and fashionable with young people. Of course this meant that new patterns had to be introduced all the time to keep up with the latest trends. These articles also gave Cliff an opportunity to express her tastes and intentions: 'I have always loved vivid, bright colours and think that the modern idea of using them for pottery and china adds such a cheerful note.'[25]

Her achievements were recognised in 1930, when she was made Artistic Director, following the resignation of John Butler, who moved to the Wood's factory in Burslem.[26] This important year proved to be the most productive for Cliff. Several new shapes and patterns were introduced that became popular. However, as she relied on variety and novelty, many of the most popular patterns were phased out after two or three years and those designs that did not attract interest from buyers at the major trade fairs were discontinued. The market that Cliff designed for wanted novelty and variety all the time. Her new ranges included the Stamford shape, which was infinitely more practical and functional than Conical, although the set used conical shape teacups and saucers. The Stamford range, decorated with patterns such as *Berries* (Plate 73) and *Rudyard* (Plate 74), proved successful. A lesser-known shape from this year, produced for a short period of time, was Eton, with its distinctive flat square lids. Cliff also introduced an interesting range of geometric shapes during this period. Notable examples include a vase, 464, decorated with various patterns such as *Gibraltar* and 511, decorated with *Chintz* (Plate 75).

Cliff also expanded her range of the fancies that had proved popular during the early part of the twenties. Some of these, for example Viking Boat, were decorated with current patterns such as *Trees and House*. A wide range of figures, face-masks and novelty items were produced to sell alongside her latest patterns. This diverse range included decorative wall plaques. Bookends incorporated cottages and an assortment of birds. One of the most

70. An unusual earthenware umbrella stand decorated with the hand-painted *Sliced Circle* pattern, from the Bizarre range, 1929. Designed by Clarice Cliff. Height 27⅜in. (69.5cm).

71. An earthenware
Conical teacup, saucer and
side plate decorated with
the *Tennis* pattern, from the
Bizarre range, 1930-31,
designed by Clarice Cliff.

outstanding but short-lived sets was the *Age of Jazz* figures, introduced in 1930, intended
as table decorations. The set consisted of five pieces with three dancing couples, a
drummer and a saxophonist. Further masks were introduced from 1933, including *Marlene*,
who was probably the most popular (Plate 76). During that year she produced a blackbird
pie funnel, inspired by the nursery rhyme and in production until the 1950s.

Cliff's constant experimentation with new decorative techniques, in order to keep ahead
of her competitors, resulted in new pattern ranges such as *Delecia*. A stunning effect was
achieved by allowing thin paint to drip down the ware, with colours blending into each
other. This decorative technique was combined with painted fruit, floral and landscape
motifs to great success with *Delecia Citrus*, from 1932, and *Forest Glen*, incorporating a
cottage with trees, dating from 1935 (Plate 77). Another outstanding range was *Appliqué*,
produced using a concentrated form of hand-painted decoration. The patterns, such as
Appliqué Lugano and *Appliqué Lucerne*, depicted stylised landscapes (Plate 78). As they
were costly to produce the range was short-lived. *Appliqué Idyll* depicted a crinolined lady
in a garden setting. A few years later Cliff experimented with stippling paint on the ware,
to create a base colour that she called Café au Lait. This pleasing effect was used on
several patterns such as *Canterbury Bells* in 1932 and *Cowslip* in 1933.

'Your customers want the best, so look for the original signature', boasted a company
advertisement in the trade press, promoting Cliff's name as a selling point for quality and
originality.[27] During 1931 Wilkinson's shared an exhibition space with Paragon China to
display their latest ranges, with the aim of targeting both the home and overseas markets.
The display of her work featured a large two-dimensional bottle kiln with a cut-out section
in the middle revealing several new patterns.[28] Probably the biggest, and most audacious
creation by Cliff in pottery was the Bizooka, a promotional horse. This was made up from
decorated pottery and used for window displays and exhibitions both in Britain and

abroad. One of the paintresses, Rene Dale, played the role of jockey on Bizooka during one of the Crazy Day Charity events.[29] This approach helped to publicise the pottery and the increased orders required the recruitment of more free-hand paintresses. When other factories in the area were struggling for orders, the Newport Pottery kilns were being operated for twenty-four hours a day to cope with the abundance of orders. This success was noted and shortly afterwards her competitors started copying Cliff's tableware styles.

72. An archive photograph of some of the 'Bizarre Girls'. From left to right: Vera Hollins, Ivy Stringer, Winnie Pound, Elsie Nixon and Florrie Eardley. About 1933.

The popularity of patterns such as *May Avenue*, *Orange Roof Cottage* and *Windbells* further increased Cliff's reputation for innovation. Her *Coral Firs* pattern was also produced in a blue and green colourway on a range of different shapes (Plate 19). However, at the same time one or two of her ranges proved to be unpopular. One such was a tea ware range called Le Bon Dieu, inspired by a tree trunk she had seen. Despite her great belief in the design the range was not popular with the public. Undaunted, a new range, Bonjour, was soon developed, proving an outstanding success when launched in 1933. The shapes for tea, coffee, and dinnerware items were able to take all manner of decoration including banding and transfer printed designs. To complement her new shape, Cliff launched the striking Biarritz plates, that were oblong (Plate 80), proving very popular for some years.[30]

During the early thirties the promotion of good design was initiated by both the Government and independent organisations such as the Design and Industries Association. They wanted to educate the public by exhibiting examples of pottery that they felt demonstrated an understanding of good design. One such exhibition was the British Art in Relation to the Home exhibition at the Dorland Hall in London in 1933. Cliff showed several patterns including *Hello*, decorated on the new Daffodil shape that was soon phased out. The press noted that it was 'a decoration which is modern without being so trying to our patience'.[31]

Simultaneously, there was an attempt to unite art with industry. The idea was to commission leading artists to design tableware patterns to demonstrate how standards could be improved. Thomas Acland Fennemore, Art Director for E. Brain, co-ordinated the project. Artists such as Vanessa Bell, Graham Sutherland, Ben Nicholson and Barbara

Hepworth were invited to submit patterns to be produced on bone china. Cliff became involved with the project when Colley decided to produce the earthenware range for this project. No doubt he felt that it would provide further publicity for his firm and increase Cliff's reputation. However, she was not keen to be involved in the project. Some of the first items received a cool response when exhibited at the Dorland Hall exhibition in 1933. This prompted further artists to become involved, including Freda Beardmore, Allan Walton, Billie Walters and Dame Laura Knight. The finished pieces from twenty-seven artists were shown at Harrods in October 1934. The exhibition generated a considerable amount of press coverage in over thirty newspapers and periodicals. Unfortunately the exhibition was not successful and was criticised. Moreover, the project took a lot of Cliff's time, as she was responsible for adapting the sketches sent to her to be decorated on the Bonjour and Biarritz shapes.[32] Some years later, Cliff recalled: 'I remember what headaches we had over the reproduction… this was the nearest thing to a flop that I have ever been associated with.'[33]

By the mid-thirties, there was a shift away from the more strident, bold colours exploited so magnificently by Cliff. The public's taste had changed and as a consequence sales of many of her Bizarre and Fantasque lines were slowing down to such an extent that some were phased out completely. There was little scope for the more outrageous modern shapes that had made her name. In response to these changes she developed new shapes such as Lynton, launched in 1934, that featured a soft ribbed body to give it a hand-made look. During the same year the *My Garden* range was introduced, that included vases, bowls, trays, candlesticks and fancies featuring moulded flowers and fruits on the handles and base of each piece. These could be easily decorated by the lesser skilled paintress. The range

73. The *Berries* design, hand painted on an earthenware Stamford tea for two, from the Fantasque range, designed by Clarice Cliff, 1930. Height of teapot 5in. (12.5cm).

74. An earthenware Bonjour shape tea for two decorated with the *Rudyard* pattern, from the Fantasque range, 1933. Designed by Clarice Cliff. Height of teapot 5⅛in. (13cm).

proved so popular that Cliff recalled later, 'I had to have help with the modelling'.[34]

The softer and less complicated pattern *Rhodanthe*, issued in 1934, proved very successful, as were the colour variations such as *Aurea* (Plate 80). A similar range of soft coloured patterns includes *Honeydew* and a colour variation, *Sundew*. In 1935 the Trieste shape was released, decorated with patterns including *Killarney* (Plate 81). The decreasing orders required both Colley and Cliff to work very hard to remain competitive in the industry. Popular patterns were updated with softer colours, more in tune with the mid-thirties, whilst some were reduced to simple shoulder motifs. Her selection of fancies was severely limited as well. All the new designs were marked with the simple words, 'Clarice Cliff'. Without the skilled outliners and free-hand paintresses the emphasis was placed on moulded ware. The *Raffia*, *Corncob* and *Celtic Harvest* ranges demonstrated this new shift in style. In particular, *Celtic Harvest*, originally produced with a pink glaze, proved very popular and was produced briefly after the war. A later shape range called *Waterlily* was also launched (Plate 82). In 1937 Cliff employed Aubrey Dunn to undertake modelling for her; he was later promoted to decorating manager after the war to set up the hand-painting department.[35]

As late as 1937, business remained poor, forcing the factory to wait until the salesmen came back with orders before they knew which patterns they would be working on. A limited range of new novelty items was produced in about 1938, including Zodiac plaques, sold with an accompanying horoscope prediction written by a Mr. R.H. Taylor. With the approach of war and the concentration of industries, it became apparent that further production of new ranges was not possible.

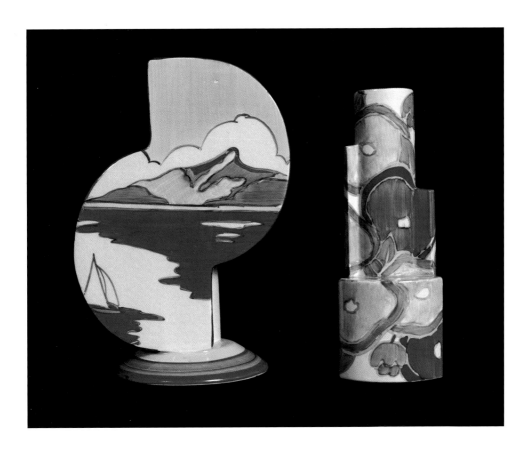

On 2 November 1939 Colley Shorter's wife Annie died, after a long illness. The relationship between Cliff and Colley was now much easier to conduct, although some hostility was still evident towards the couple. In December 1940 they decided to marry, at the Stafford Registry Office. Few people were informed, apart from very close friends. As his new wife, Cliff moved into Chetwynd, the home of Colley Shorter and his family since 1926 (Plate 83). This large arts and crafts house was built in 1899. Shorter was particularly keen on fine arts and antiques and his collection filled his home. Moving from her small flat to a prestigious house must have been both exciting and daunting for Clarice.

In 1940, Cliff had modelled a Winston Churchill Toby jug, as part of the First World War Allied Services set. With the assistance of Betty Silvester, she also created fourteen character jugs based on the Gilbert and Sullivan Operas, under a franchise from the D'Oyly Carte Opera Company. Due to wartime restrictions, these were not produced until the late forties, as was a Teepee teapot, modelled by Betty Silvester.[36] Despite the large number of staff leaving for the war some wares were put into production, albeit simple banded designs on the Georgian shape. Before all production ceased in about 1942, the only ware produced was shipped for export. The Ministry of Defence took over Newport Pottery and used the buildings for the storage of rubber. The pottery was never used again and from 1943, until the end of the war, little was done at Wilkinson's. Despite the production of utility wares there was little to keep Cliff at the factory so she went into semi-retirement at Chetwynd. With the production of goods for the export market there was hardly any opportunity for new designs to be developed.

Once hostilities had ended, Colley began to re-establish some of his pre-war contacts,

75. Two examples of the modern shapes introduced by Clarice Cliff during the early thirties. Left: A 464 vase decorated with the *Gibraltar* pattern from 1931 and a vase 511 decorated with the *Chintz* pattern, from 1932. Both items from the Fantasque range. Tallest vase 9½in. (24cm) high.

76. *Marlene*, one of the many face masks modelled by Clarice Cliff, 1931.

making several journeys to North America. He obviously wanted to get the business back into full capacity as he asked Cliff to return to the factory to examine the old shapes and patterns and to see if something could be done to create a new impetus. In such difficult conditions of austerity, it was surprising that as early as 1946 the firm was promoting the new *Georgian Spray*, on the Georgian shape. Colley had not lost any of his promotional flair, featuring the words, 'Designed by Clarice Cliff'.[37] During that year the trade press reported that the firm was about to introduce two new patterns, *Cotswold* and *Rosemary*, both featuring a distinctive honey glaze.[38] A small display of patterns was put together for the British Industries Fair in 1947. These included *Crocus*, *Chelsea Basket* and *Georgian Spray* and a selection of vases, bowls and beakers designed by R.Y. Goodden, ARIBA, originally launched in 1940. Of particular interest was a pattern called *England* that featured various London scenes. The patriotic backstamp included the words 'There'll always be an England!' alongside an image of a knight on horseback, a motif that Cliff had used during the early thirties.

Eventually, Cliff began to accompany Colley on his trips to North America. As it turned out these visits proved invaluable, as they both had an opportunity to examine the latest trends in tableware, collecting a wide range of leaflets and cuttings for reference. Although some recent commentators assert that Cliff had very little involvement with design after the war, it is unthinkable that she would not contribute to the running of her husband's company. Her tremendous experience and ability to create new designs and shapes was probably

77. The *Forest Glen* pattern, decorated on a large earthenware plate designed by Clarice Cliff, from the Bizarre range, 1935.

78. A rare example of the *Appliqué Lucerne* pattern decorated on a plate, diameter 9½in. (24cm), from 1930. Designed by Clarice Cliff.

the biggest asset the company had. Typically Cliff was fully aware of the changing trends in the industry and the tastes of the North American market. She noted that 'their mode of living is so different from ours. They like these quick, slick, smart styles for their informal living, but for formal as they term it, they must have traditional, or, in other words, the elaborate design and quality achieved only by the skilled craftsman, and that is what they look for and expect from us.'³⁹

One of the first popular designs targeted at the North American market was *Bristol* (7488), introduced in 1948. This was based on a hand-painted floral plate in the collection of Colley Shorter, originally produced by the French artist Duvivier in about 1770. During late 1949, Cliff produced *Lorna Doone*, an all-over chintz design, and *Jenny Lind*, a pink Scottish scene. In 1951 she produced a range of patterns under the banner of the Confederation Series, featuring eight individual Victorian views of the famous sights in Canada, including Niagara Falls,

79. A popular hand painted Clarice Cliff landscape pattern produced in three colourways. Left to right: A candlestick holder decorated with the *Green Firs* pattern, an earthenware Bonjour shape vase decorated with the *Coral Firs* pattern and a Lynton shape coffee set decorated with the *Blue Firs* pattern. All from the Fantasque range, 1933. Height of coffee-pot, 7¼in. (18.5cm).

Toronto and Montreal.[40] Another depicted a Canadian Mountie resplendent on a horse, produced on a plate and mug. In 1953 she designed two sets of Coronation giftwares, the more elaborate items were for the North American market. The backstamp incorporated the words 'Approved by the Council of Industrial Design'.

Following the success of the first range of patterns, Wilkinson's concentrated on producing dinnerware patterns chiefly targeted at the North American market, placing an emphasis on high quality. As the number of patterns expanded, a new formal backstamp read 'Royal Staffordshire, Dinnerware by Clarice Cliff, Made in England'. Patterns such as *Chelsea Basket* and *Ophelia* were typical (Plate 84), the latter pattern was originally produced during the late 1930s.[41] Initially these were produced with some hand-painted decoration, but perhaps due to the lack of skilled paintresses they were issued in one colour, either blue, sepia or pink. Notable examples include *Rural Scenes* (Plate 85), *Davenport* and *Harvest*. Some of these patterns were featured in the Grand Rapids Press in 1953. The *Charlotte* design, an overall underglaze floral pattern, was based on original drawings by F. Cutts from about 1830, and was available in either pink or brown (see Plate 9, page 19). B. Altman and Co., a major store on 5th Avenue in New York, extensively publicised the current patterns in several newspapers, including the *New York Times*. They described Clarice's designs, such as *Rural Scenes*, *Devonshire* and *Sutherland*, as 'Delightful patterns

80. An earthenware vase (shape 14) and a Biarritz plate decorated with hand-painted patterns, left *Rhodanthe* and right *Aurea*, from about 1934. Designed by Clarice Cliff. Height of vase 9in. (23cm).

81. The *Killarney* pattern hand painted on an earthenware Lynton shape milk jug, from the Bizarre range, 1934. Designed by Clarice Cliff.

82. An earthenware milk jug and plate decorated with the moulded *Waterlily* pattern. Designed by Clarice Cliff, about 1935-36.

in rich, traditional colourings ideal for the contemporary table.'[42]

The most popular pattern on the North American market was *Tonquin*, a traditional style landscape print (Plate 87), produced on a wide range of combinations including a sixteen-piece starter set. *Tonquin* proved so popular that special items, such as a three-piece mayonnaise set, a water pitcher and a ceramic baby cradle, were produced! A version of the pattern in vitrified hotel ware was called *Belinda*.

Profitable connections with the overseas markets resulted in the production of other giftwares, such as an ashtray that could hold sixteen cigarettes at one time, decorated with the more traditional *English Game Birds* pattern. Another unusual item was the Gowpens, the Hand of Hospitality, and a rather oddly shaped novelty of two hands, decorated in either *Devonshire* or *Tonquin*. These two special pieces were probably modelled by Cliff.

The modernisation of the factory in the late forties eventually saw the recruitment of new design staff. Eric Elliot joined the firm in 1951, as the Assistant Art Director. Colley gave him a free hand, probably in an attempt to compete in the fashion pottery market. His Sunkissed pattern, depicting large hand-painted fruit motifs, was featured in several company advertisements in about 1954. The backstamp curiously included the words 'Genuinely Handpainted'. He also introduced several large floral patterns, including Magnolia (7797), Paris (7824) and Clematis. Responding to the latest customer needs, several patterns were created for a cup on a large plate, to capitalize on the growing trend for eating whilst watching the television. These included the Memories of the Past series, featuring various vehicles including a hansom cab and a mail coach. Another design, The Good Old Days, depicted various forms of horse-drawn carriages and scenes of people ice-skating. Archival sketches indicate that lesser known patterns featuring Dick Turpin, Robin Hood, Friar Tuck and Long John Silver, were produced.[43] He also developed ideas for new shapes, based on eighteenth century jugs, as fruit and vegetables. Two sets of figures were planned, one set featuring the Queen and Prince Philip and the other Military Figures, but

83. A view of Chetwynd House.

neither went into production. Cliff owned a trial set of the latter range that was later sold at auction in 1973.[44] Throughout his time at the factory Elliot produced many drawings and sketches of contemporary patterns in the firm's pattern books, some of which were commented on by either Cliff or Colley. With one particular abstract design in blues and pinks, a typewritten note was added, stating 'can't see this one at all'.[45]

Despite these designers working on new patterns for the company, all wares continued to be stamped with the Cliff mark. In 1954 Aubrey Dunn left, soon followed by Eric Elliot, a year later.

With the purchase of a Murray Curvex machine in 1955, Wilkinson's attempted to compete with the leading pottery companies such a Midwinter and Johnson Brothers, renowned for their contemporary designs. Most importantly, it allowed them to abandon the need for lithographs, which Cliff was not keen on. As a result she must have taken a more active part in the design work of the company. With this new impetus, it seems that Colley must have convinced Cliff to produce a new range of shapes, launched in about April 1956, called Devon. At the same time, she revived several shapes from the thirties, including Regency and Windsor. In response to the North American taste a coupe plate was introduced. The Georgian shape was used for new patterns, such as *Wild Beauty*, a very simple floral border. In 1957 her Clayton shape was launched and within a year a whole range of simple printed floral borders was issued. The company was still keen to promote its latest patterns by placing a full colour advertisement in the trade press featuring two printed floral designs, *Tit Willow* and *Golden Rain*.[46] Other patterns included *Blossom Time*, *Pink Susan*, *Chestnut* and *Flower Garden*; some of these were printed with hand-painted decoration promoted alongside wares by Shorter and Co.[47] In contrast to these simple designs Cliff designed an unusual set of mugs featuring *Playing Card* motifs, specially developed for a department store in Montreal in Canada in 1957, but they were not produced (Plate 86).

In 1961, Colley became ill and Cliff spent most of her time looking after him. The business had been in decline over a number of years. Despite this, Colley made her promise to never sell the works. However after his death, in 1963, it was clearly not possible for her to continue on her own and without doubt she had no intention of carrying on. The firm of W.R. Midwinter Ltd., which required more capacity to meet increased orders following the success of its Fine shape, made an approach. Following negotiations between the two companies, the factory was sold in December 1964. Up to 300 Wilkinson's staff were kept on by Midwinter. In 1966, Cliff donated several items from her husband's extensive collection of decorative arts to the Museum in Newcastle-under-Lyme.

Contrary to the many assumptions about her life, Cliff did not become a recluse after selling the factory. In fact, she found great comfort and enjoyment amongst her family's children. Her great-niece, Alison, spent most of the summer with her great-aunt during 1965. Although Cliff seemed to be quite bossy, this eight-year-old girl soon realised what a very kind and generous woman she was. They would eat their breakfast of eggs, bacon and mushrooms prepared by Cliff, in the kitchen, even though she had a servant called

84. An earthenware plate, diameter 9¾in (25cm), decorated with the *Ophelia* pattern, printed and with hand-painted additions. Designed by Clarice Cliff, about 1952-54.

85. An earthenware dinner plate, diameter 7⅞in. (20cm), with the *Rural Scenes* pattern printed in pink. Designed by Clarice Cliff, about 1952-54.

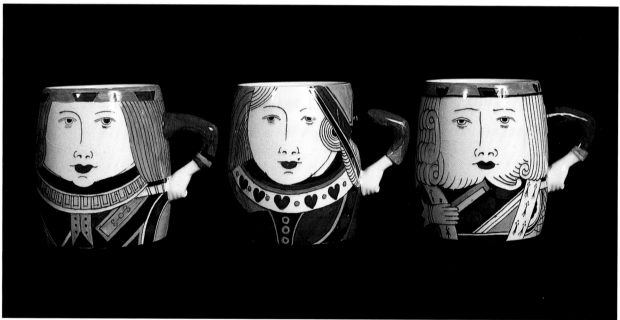

Alice. Most of the day was spent in the garden, undertaking activities such as cleaning up the lily pond and planting new plants. In the evenings they would play games together, often sitting on the floor attempting to complete a jigsaw puzzle. Alison recalled fondly that as a young girl, she was mesmerised by the wooden owl coat hanger on the bathroom door. When a towel or dressing gown was hung on it, the wings would rise up. Alison found it so amusing that Cliff finally gave it to her as a present![48]

As interest developed for the art deco period, the Brighton Museum and Art Gallery

86. This unusual set of mugs, 4in (10cm) high, decorated with *Playing Card* motifs, was not put into production. Designed by Clarice Cliff, about 1957.

87. An earthenware dinner plate, diameter 9¾in. (25cm), decorated with the *Tonquin* pattern. This is probably the first version, printed in brown with hand-painted decoration. Subsequent versions were printed in a single colour such as blue. Designed by Clarice Cliff, about 1952-54.

staged a small exhibition of Clarice Cliff's work during the first few months of 1972. Cliff even wrote an introduction in the catalogue giving a brief account of her life and work. Despite not attending the exhibition, she donated the items that she had loaned for the exhibition to the museum. These pieces included two Frank Brangwyn plaques, a Dame Laura Knight candlestick, a Biarritz plate decorated with *Windbells* and a *Honolulu* vase.[49] Cliff died in October of that year.

New interest in her work began to develop during the late 1960s, culminating in a special sale in London in the early eighties. Since then, her popularity has risen beyond all expectation. Her colourful and audacious pottery continues to influence new designers and artists. In 1999, her centenary was celebrated with a major exhibition at the Wedgwood Visitors Centre and the publication of a new book on her life and work. A commemorative plaque was erected on the canal, opposite the site on which the factory once stood. A fitting tribute to an outstanding and original designer.

CHAPTER 4

THE ART DECO DESIGNER

Truda Carter (1890-1958)

88. A view of the Carter and Co. Ltd. factory, at Poole in Dorset, about 1902.

During the twentieth century, production of decorative pottery was not solely confined to Stoke-on-Trent. Several leading manufacturers elsewhere produced ranges of innovative and influential ceramics. In particular Carter, Stabler and Adams, better known as Poole Pottery, was at the forefront. Over a twenty-year period Truda Carter produced some of the most outstanding patterns in the art deco style. Despite her prolific contribution to pottery design she did not enjoy the same amount coverage or media interest as many of her contemporaries. This may have been her own choice, but as a result very little was written about her in the journals and press of the day. She initially designed under the name Truda Adams, and then Truda Carter; this text will use the latter, for sake of clarity.

Her family enjoyed great status in British society. Her father David Sharp, MD, FRSA (1840-1922) was a distinguished entomologist. In 1875 he married Jessie Margaret Murdoch at Eccles in Dumfries. Gertrude Ellen Sharp was born in Wilmington, near Dartford, Kent in 1890. From an early age she was affectionately known as Truda. She had four sisters, Helen, Edith, Annie and Jessie, and two brothers, Harry and Charlie.

89. A red earthenware vase, height 10½in.. (26.5cm), decorated with a hand-painted pattern 212X/XE. This demonstrates the influence of René Buthaud. Designed by Truda Carter for Carter, Stabler and Adams Ltd., from about 1924 to 1934.

90. A stylised floral pattern 900/GL. Designed by Truda Carter for Carter, Stabler and Adams Ltd., from about 1926-29. Height of vase 11⅞in. (30cm).

Shortly after Truda's birth the family moved to Cambridge so that her father could take up his position as Curator of Zoology at Cambridge University.[1] Unfortunately no information is available regarding her formal education, but presumably she studied in the Cambridge area. In 1909 her father retired to Brockenhurst, in the New Forest. A year later she travelled to London to start a three year course at the Royal College of Art, studying several subjects but in particular embroidery, which was to greatly influence her design work over the next thirty years.[2]

During her time at the Royal College of Art she met John Adams, a fellow student and later a member of the teaching staff. He was a gifted potter, originally from Stoke-on-Trent. Before taking up his teaching post he had attended evening classes at the Hanley School of Art and worked for a local tile maker for several years. He later joined the studio of Bernard Moore. In 1909 he was awarded one of ten National Scholarships to study pottery and sculpture at the Royal College of Art.[3] After completing the course he was asked to stay on and teach, which he did for two years. The couple married in 1914.[4]

At the beginning of the First World War, in 1914, they moved to South Africa where John Adams had been offered the position as Head of the School of Art at Durban Technical College, in order to set up a pottery section. While there he made a major contribution to the education system and his wife taught some of the junior art classes at the College. As well as teaching, they also produced pottery together during this period.[5] However, they became frustrated with their work at the College, finding the authorities unsupportive. In

1919 John Adams wrote to Harold Stabler, a friend from his student days at the Royal College of Art, comparing the facilities at the Durban Technical College with those of the Royal College. Stabler, an established and recognised designer in gold, and a silversmith, had met Charles Carter in 1918 and he asked John Adams to consider joining their new partnership. John Adams accepted the offer and the couple returned to England. As things turned out, the new position for her husband provided Truda with an opportunity to take on the role of designer for this fledgling company, alongside her husband.

To understand how the formation of Carter, Stabler and Adams came about, and the important role that she played as a designer, a short history of Carter and Co. is essential. The company was established at East Quay Works in Poole in 1873 (Plate 88). The site was purchased from James Walker by Jesse Carter, a successful builder's merchant and ironmonger. Jesse Carter was able to turn the business around, producing glazed architectural faience, terracotta and decorative tiling used in hotels, public houses and shops. In 1881 he took his three sons, Charles, Owen and Ernest, into the partnership. In 1895 they purchased the Architectural Pottery in order to expand. The company soon became associated with original and high quality wares, becoming one of the most successful tile businesses in the country.

When Jesse retired in November 1901 two of his sons, Charles and Owen, took over the running of the company. Owen introduced a range of lustre patterns from 1900-08. The chief designer, James Radley Young, introduced a wide range of new patterns and new shapes. In 1914 Owen Carter decided to increase production by introducing more shapes and patterns. The first pattern range featured hand-incised marks and the impressed dolphin motif. By 1914 Carter's adopted the impressed mark 'Carter and

92. The hand painted *Persian Deer* pattern 528/VU decorated on an earthenware dish, diameter 14¾in. (37.5cm). Designed by Truda Carter for Carter, Stabler and Adams Ltd., from about 1924-27.

Co/Poole'. At about this time a connection was made with Roger Fry and the Omega workshops, whose artists, including Vanessa Bell, produced a small number of innovative pots. From 1915 the majority of patterns were designed by James Radley Young and demand for the latest wares resulted in the expansion of the works.[6] Young's patterns, shown at the British Industries Fair between 1917 and 1921, demonstrated an interest in Greek, Dutch and Moorish styles. The simple Stripe pattern, and its many variations, was in production for several years. In 1920 the Monastic range was launched.

Following the death of Owen Carter in 1919, Charles took more responsibility for the works. His son, Cyril, who had joined Carter and Co. in 1905 as a representative in the London office, returned to Poole to support his father. It was largely due to his efforts that the company became so successful. He was able to secure the finances for each stage of the expansion to the works. In 1920 Carter's produced a 'Report of the Year 1920' for those who worked for them. This document outlined the state of the company following the end of the war and examined the current situation. A decision needed to be taken as to whether they should continue or close down the pottery venture, started before the war. After much deliberation it was decided to form a subsidiary company.

In 1921 Carter, Stabler and Adams was formed as a separate company, although a subsidiary of Carter and Co. Ltd. The new partners were Cyril Carter (Chairman), Harold Stabler and John Adams, each one having a specific role. John Adams was the Managing Director, although he was more involved in the development of pottery, whilst Harold Stabler was the artistic consultant. Stabler produced his own range of ornamental pieces with his wife Phoebe, who designed a group of figures for the Ashstead Pottery in about 1923 or later. The Stablers had their own kiln at their home in Hammersmith, London. As the wife of John Adams, Carter found an opportunity to design. Excellent connections in London did much to promote the company, through catalogues and in the

London stores, such as Heals and Liberty's. From the outset the directors defined their artistic policy – 'Craft techniques with a high standard of craftsmanship.'[7]

For the first few years a tremendous amount of experimentation was undertaken on the distinctive red earthenware body combined with the semi-matt glaze, introduced from 1922. Within two years this was enhanced with the use of a white slip ground with a semi-matt clear glaze. New staff were engaged, with free-hand decorators taken on directly from the local schools of art in Bournemouth. From a very early stage Carter, Stabler and Adams was known as the Poole Pottery. To assist in promotion the company produced catalogues of the latest designs in 1922, 1923 and later in 1927 and 1930. Under this new company arrangement Carter produced an extensive range of stylised floral patterns, initially building on the successful sprig and geometric style set by James Radley Young. She also created her own interpretations of his work, some of which were shown for the first time at Regent House, Kingsway in London in October 1921. The trade press reported of this exhibition: 'the results that have already been achieved by the new undertaking of Carter, Stabler and Adams are in many ways remarkable and the pottery which they have so far produced is as distinctive and fresh as any type that we might be able to cite.'[8]

From these initial patterns she developed a distinctive and original range of styles demonstrating her great interest in embroidery, particularly the styles in the Tudor and Jacobean traditions that she studied at the Royal College of Art. This interest provided her with many original and fresh design possibilities, making Poole products stand out above the many manufacturers from Stoke-on-Trent. New information has recently come to light on these and other influences. Significantly, her work has been linked to the French designer René Buthaud. Examples of his work from about 1918 show strong similarities to the patterns designed by Carter for CSA. In an unpublished paper Dr. James King compared the work of Buthaud and Carter, highlighting the similarities – 'details above

93. A selection of patterns, left to right: a hand-painted pattern on a red earthenware vase 979/SZ, from 1930-33, an earthenware bowl decorated with a stylised fish 744/OM from 1924-34, and a *Leaping Deer* earthenware vase decorated with 599/TZ, from 1934-37. Designed by Truda Carter for Carter, Stabler and Adams Ltd. Height of tallest vase 8½in. (21.5cm). Diameter of bowl 8⅝in. (22cm).

94. A hand painted vase, height 12in. (30.5cm), depicting a stylised *Blue Bird* 947/HE. Designed by Truda Carter for Carter Stabler and Adams Ltd., from about 1934-37.

95. Three earthenware vases decorated with art deco styled patterns, left to right: 333/KN and 514/UB both from 1934-37, and 856/GB from about 1934-35. Designed by Truda Carter for Carter, Stabler and Adams Ltd. Tallest vase 10¾in. (27.5 cm) high.

and below the main design share some affinity with Carter's placement of similar elements; more importantly, the exaggerated heads of the flowers and the flat rendering of the floral form look like Truda Carter's work ten years later. Since Buthaud himself was influenced by eighteenth century Bordeaux faience, he, like her, was devoted to work produced in earlier centuries.'⁹

The influence of Buthaud is evident in a number of her patterns such as (YO), (ED) and (XE) (Plate 89). Carter was also inspired by the art deco movement and the design trends from Europe that were more obvious in her work during the thirties. Outstanding designs such as (GL) and similar patterns (Plate 90) caught on straight away with the public and were featured in women's magazines such as *Homes and Gardens*. Moreover, her designs had a tremendous influence on the house style of the company. A considerable number of new wares were put together for CSA's first showing at the British Industries Fair in 1922. The stand, designed by Heals, displayed a wide selection of vases, jugs and toilet wares. Her productions certainly made an impact on the trade press, which tended to remark on the innovative patterns and the high quality of the workmanship that went into creating them. Besides showing at the British Industries Fair they exhibited at the Gieves Gallery in London, each year (Plate 91). More importantly they put together an outstanding collection of wares for the British Empire Exhibition in 1924. Of particular merit was Carter's *Persian Deer* pattern (Plate 92). This outstanding design became her signature pattern and appeared, in varying forms, on a number of occasions but notably for the pattern (TZ) from about 1930-37 (Plate 93). The CSA display also included a group of faience panels modelled by Harold and Phoebe Stabler.

96. Two interesting and lesser known patterns. The first has no known pattern number, decorated on shape 462, from about 1929-30. The pattern on the right, 966/XD, is from about 1934-37. Designed by Truda Carter for Carter, Stabler and Adams Ltd. Height of tallest item 9⅞in. (25cm).

Throughout the twenties and thirties their products were regularly illustrated in the *Decorative Art Studio Year Book*, alongside other manufacturers. The 1922 edition featured several patterns by Carter that depicted a polar bear, squirrel, owl and frog. Further designs, including fish and chicken motifs finished with simple banding, were shown a year later. In 1923 several examples of nursery wares by Carter were described by the press as being, 'amusing and delightful, and have none of that disagreeable, tasteless quaintness which many decorators seem to think a necessary quality of all art designed for the consumption of children.'[10]

The majority of the current products were marked with a backstamp reading 'Carter Stabler Adams, Poole England'. From 1925 an additional mark incorporating 'Ltd.' was introduced, and both marks continued to be used until the end of the red body period in 1934. The patterns were recorded in the company's pattern books by means of a letter code, such as (EP) or (ED). These were not used alphabetically and when some of the more popular patterns were revised some years later they either used the same code or were given a new one. Also, if a pattern featured a dominant colour, green for example, an extra letter, G, was added to the pattern code. Whilst

97. A rare pattern, 916/AW, hand-painted on a red earthenware vase, height 14¼in. (36 cm). Designed by Truda Carter for Carter Stabler and Adams Ltd., from about 1928-34.

98. One of several patterns taken from the set of *ponchoir* prints produced by French designers. This example clearly illustrates that Truda Carter used them for inspiration.

Carter's name was placed adjacent to each of her patterns in these books, her name was not put on the ware. This was in total contrast to a number of Stoke-on-Trent manufacturers who saw the sense in promoting their designers. Susie Cooper, in particular, was given a special mark for her own patterns, reading 'Designed by Susie Cooper'. The only painted mark to be found on a piece of Poole pottery was that of the decorator and not the designer. To further complicate matters the letter code was not in any order, thus making dating problematic. Patterns were hardly ever given a name.

Although Carter was responsible for the majority of the patterns, she worked as part of the design team. She adapted several patterns originally created by James Radley Young. Important contributions were made by artists and designers from London who were friends of both Harold Stabler and John Adams. A notable example was the work of Olive Bourne from the late 1920s that included the pattern Sugar for the Birds, exhibited on the company stand at the International Exhibition of Industrial Art in Leipzig in 1927.[11] At the same time, designs were often proposed by Carter's highly trained decorators, including Cissie Collette and Ernest Bantten. If she felt that a pattern had potential, then it would be used. Patterns were also created by Erna Manners, including Fuchsia (AM) and a grape pattern (NY).

The great effort and commitment by everyone at CSA was outstanding. They put together an impressive range of vases, bowls and figural items for the important Exposition des Arts Décoratifs et Industriels Modernes in Paris in 1925. Patterns by Carter included the *Blue Bird* (HE), amongst stylised floral and leaf motifs painted in purples and blues on a clear glaze over white slip (Plate 94). Many variations were produced from

99. Three hand painted patterns on red earthenware shapes from the early thirties: a red earthenware ginger jar decorated with 201/PR(G) from 1930-34, a large twin-handled vase 437/BD from 1928-34, and a red earthenware ginger jar 201/AX. Designed by Truda Carter for Carter, Stabler and Adams Ltd., from 1930-34. Height of tallest item 10½in. (26.5cm).

100. An archive photograph showing paintresses working on the current patterns. They are, from left to right: Ann Hatchard, Eileen Prangnell and Truda Rivers, from 1925.

this pattern, whilst the *Peacock* pattern, from about 1922-24, is lesser known.[12] Other notable patterns include (XE) and (OM), the latter depicting a stylised fish (see Plate 93). These were shown alongside the geometric borders, stripe patterns and figural pieces, such as The Bull, by Harold and Phoebe Stabler. The products on display must have made quite an impression with the judges as CSA were given several awards, including the prestigious Diplôme d'Honneur. Carter was awarded a Silver Medal alongside A.E. Gray and Co. Ltd., W. Adams and Sons Ltd. and Doulton and Co. Five gold medals were awarded to Bernard Moore, Gordon Forsyth and Harold Stabler, amongst others. Carter, Stabler and Adams exploited this achievement by taking out advertisements in the British trade press. Gordon Forsyth, in his official report of the exhibition, said: 'Their wares are entirely hand made, and decorated by Mrs. Adams and her assistants with freely painted designs of a modern character.'[13]

The Paris Exhibition greatly influenced subsequent designs by Carter. For some considerable time Paris had been the centre for the decorative arts. Several publishers produced portfolios of patterns suited to textiles, wallpapers and carpets. Designers were able to purchase these for inspiration and ideas. Along with other designers, Carter would have collected these sets of prints. More recently Stella Beddoe, of the Brighton Museum and Art Gallery, discovered several examples of these prints in the museum's collection that were used directly for patterns by Carter. From 'Le décor Moderne dans La Tenture et le Tissu' she used a composition by Madame Raisin for her stylised floral pattern (KN) from about 1930 (Plate 95). A more abstract design from the same publication inspired her abstract pattern (XD), painted in greens and blues (Plate 96). A lesser known pattern (AW) by Carter (Plate 97) was a direct copy of a design by the French artist E.A. Seguy (Plate 98).

A number of her designs from the early thirties also show the influence of cubism with examples such as (PRG) and (CT) produced in several colourways (Plate 99). Other patterns such as (BX) and (AP) demonstrate her interest in English surrealism.[14] Many of these patterns were so intricate and required such a high level of accuracy that a pounce was used to ensure that the work was produced to the highest standard (Plate 100).

A range of wares was exhibited at the International Exhibition of Industrial Art in Leipzig, organised by the Design and Industries Association in 1927. During that year a floral pattern (YT) was displayed at the Ideal Home Exhibition (Plate 101). One of Carter's patterns depicting a vase of flowers (JC) was reproduced as a floor mosaic for the Building Trades Exhibition in 1928. In contrast to these larger floral patterns Carter was able to devise smaller motifs suited to a practical range of items such as a biscuit barrel, cheese dish and a sweet stand, which were shown at the British Institute of Industrial Art for the Slender Purse Exhibition during November to December 1929.

Towards the late twenties Carter continued to introduce a wide range of stylized floral patterns such as (FR) in muted brown tones (Plate 106) and (ZA) depicting stylized daffodils (Plate 103). These designs maintained their position in the forefront of British design, building a reputation for quality, design and innovation. This was assisted by the continued support of stores such as Heals and Liberty's. These influential establishments promoted and sold Poole pottery. Despite the difficult times forced on British industry as a result of the economic slump in 1929, Poole was able to increase customer choice by offering new selections such as (AB), painted in browns and black (Plate 104), the (LG) pattern depicting stylized ivy (Plate 105) and (EP) a stylized floral pattern in two colour variations (Plate 102). The trade press regularly illustrated the latest products of the firm, reporting that: 'There are countless creations of beauty in pieces of noble proportions, such as large jardinières, bowls and plaques – single pieces which will sound quite a note in any furnishing scheme.'[15]

By the early thirties Poole had moved into the production of tablewares to expand its range. One of the first shapes was Studland, designed by Harold Stabler in 1930. This ware was mainly decorated with glazes but occasionally with patterns by Carter, including her (GPA) design (Plate 107), also used on decorative vases. During the thirties

101. An earthenware vase, height 10½in. (26.5cm), decorated with a hand painted stylised pattern 684/YT. Designed by Truda Carter for Carter, Stabler and Adams Ltd., from 1927. This item was shown at the Ideal Home Exhibition in 1927.

102. Two vases showing two colourways of the same pattern 966/EP and 966/GEP. Designed by Truda Carter for Carter, Stabler and Adams Ltd., about 1930-34. Height 9⅞in. (25cm).

103. Stylised floral border pattern hand painted on an earthenware vase pattern ZA (shape number unknown). Designed by Truda Carter for Carter, Stabler and Adams Ltd., from about 1926-34. Height of vase 11⅝in. (29.5cm).

104. A lesser known design, 693/AB, designed by Truda Carter for Carter, Stabler and Adams Ltd., about 1926-31. Height of vase 12¾in. (32.5cm).

several new shapes were introduced, modelled mostly by John Adams, including candelabras, lamp bases and book ends. He also modelled, with the assistance of Harry Brown, a range of flying ducks, shells, fish and racing yachts.[16] His 'two-colour glaze effects', on the Streamline shape, proved very popular and were produced in many colour combinations. This outstanding shape range was designed by John Adams. Despite critics remarking that it was ahead of its time, it became an enormous success and continued in production throughout the fifties.

Difficulties grew between Truda and John Adams, leading to their eventual divorce in 1925. However, the situation was amicable and they continued to share the same design studio. In 1929 she married Cyril Carter. After the marriage the couple spent some time planning for their new home at Yaffle Hill in Broadstone. They commissioned Edward Maufe, MA, FRIBA (later Sir Edward Maufe) to design the new marital home. The decision to build their own house gave Truda the opportunity to be creative with the interior decoration. The floor was of a cork composition in black, biscuit, green and grey-blue. She created an abstract tile design for the bathroom that was described as being a 'polished fantasy'.[17] The central hall featured a large round carpet, also to her design. This new house and interior was so significant that it was extensively featured in the magazine *The Architect and Building News*.[18] The couple would, throughout the duration of their marriage, enjoy treating guests to one of their 'at homes'.

105. A lesser known pattern, 949/LG, designed by Truda Carter for Carter, Stabler and Adams Ltd, about 1928. Height of vase 13⅜in. (34cm).

106. A red earthenware vase, 435/FR, hand painted in browns. Designed by Truda Carter for Carter, Stabler and Adams Ltd., from about 1924 to 1934. Height 11in. (28cm).

Due to increased tourism and the many guided tours given by the company, Poole Pottery constructed a Tea Rooms, designed by Howard Robertson of Stanley Hall and Easton and Robertson, Architects. Carter contributed to the interior design scheme by creating a stylised zig-zag border by means of aerography, for a modern look on the tiles around the walls (Plate 108). Her cousin, Maggie Purdie, worked in the Tea Rooms.

Throughout the thirties Poole took advantage of the important exhibitions of industrial design staged in London. In 1933 the very latest patterns were shown at both the Dorland Hall exhibition and at the Arlington Gallery, Old Bond Street, London. They also exhibited a large selection of wares at the Royal Academy Show in London in 1935, including an hors d'oeuvres set decorated with an abstract motif, a dinner service with an abstract floral motif and the *Woodpecker* pattern, both by Carter. Moreover, Carter designed an outstanding range of patterns in the art deco style, many of which were displayed in these exhibitions, including (BT) (Plate 109) and (BC) (Plate 110), a colour variation of (YE).

In the same year, at the English Pottery Old and New Exhibition, held at the Victoria and Albert Museum, she exhibited patterns for dinnerware based on a small floral motif on the Streamline shape, adding several others in 1938. However, her patterns were part of a much wider production that included new ranges such as Picotee, Everest and Sylvan, issued during the thirties, that originated from John Adams. The trade press particularly selected his range of beer mugs, with a brown mottled, semi-gloss decoration,

107. A successful pattern
produced in four colour
variations. Left to right:
334/PA from 1934-36,
697/LT from 1935-36,
203/GPA from 1934-37
and 947/LJ from 1929-34.
Designed by Truda Carter
for Carter, Stabler and
Adams Ltd. Height of tallest
item 12in. (30.5cm).

launched in 1935. John Adams informed the press that 'there can be no doubt that with better architecture, better "pubs" and a better educated public there will be room for better pots, and this is an attempt to emphasise that idea.'[19]

New tinted glazes were introduced in 1935. Carter produced a number of patterns such as (DR) to complement the body (Plates 111 and 112). By the mid-thirties many of her patterns clearly demonstrated a move towards abstraction, some resembling the art deco skyscrapers of New York, such as the Chrysler Building (Plate 110).

Whilst the first nursery ware patterns were introduced by Carter during the early twenties, others were created by both Dora Batty and Eileen McGrath. Some of these were used on decorative tiles as well. A series of birds, animals and fish was used on John Adams toilet and tea ware shapes. Carter designed *London Characters* and *Nursery Toys*, that depicted kites, a rocking horse and a rag doll. In 1935 her *Kensington Gardens* set was launched, with the trade press noting that these were essentially lines for Christmas and should sell well.[20] Carter also developed patterns for brooches with examples such as the Blue Bird motif and several stylised florals being produced. Her floral motifs also decorated an extensive range of tablewares and associated items such as biscuit barrels, posy rings, cheese dishes and candlesticks, which were added towards the latter part of the thirties to the range on offer. Carter also created some pleasing motifs for hors d'oeuvres dishes using fish and lobsters (KUA), and vegetables (KUB) for another. For a larger fish and sandwich set she used stylised fish, painted in green and grey, or alternatively pink and grey, on an alpine white glaze (Plate 113). This pattern, and a series of fruit motifs, such as pineapples, pears and grapes, for dessert ware were adapted and relaunched in about 1952. The trade press reported in 1936 that 'many useful as well as ornamental articles are now obtainable in Poole pottery, and table services in varying compositions are now being daily demanded and supplied.'[21]

108. A view of the interior of the Poole Pottery Tea Rooms, opened in 1932. Note the aerographed zigzag pattern designed by Truda Carter.

109. Three red earthenware vases decorated with abstract patterns. Left to right: 973/BT, 970/AX and 973/OL. Designed by Truda Carter for Carter, Stabler and Adams Ltd., from about 1930-34. Height of tallest vase 9½in. (24cm).

110. A white earthenware vase, height 10¼in. (26cm), decorated with an abstract pattern 429/BC. designed by Truda Carter for Carter, Stabler and Adams Ltd., 1937-41.

111. Four examples of patterns decorated on coloured bodies. Left to right: 619/DR, 598/FR,443/UI and 857/PP. Designed by Truda Carter for Carter, Stabler and Adams Ltd., from about 1935-36. Height of tallest vase 9in. (23cm).

112. Two lesser known patterns hand painted on red earthenware vases, left 995/CS and right 999/DR, the latter features a tinted glaze. Designed by Truda Carter for Carter, Stabler and Adams Ltd., from about 1928-34. Height of tallest item 8½in. (21.5cm).

113. An earthenware sandwich and fish set decorated with a hand-painted pattern, 281/UPG. This pattern was revised during the 1950s. Designed by Truda Carter for Carter, Stabler and Adams Ltd., from about 1936. Length of sandwich plate 15in. (38cm).

114. An earthenware Streamline shape tureen and cover, plate and gravy boat decorated with the *Leaf* pattern. Designed by Truda Carter for Carter, Stabler and Adams Ltd., from about 1948.

115. The *Persian Deer* pattern 684/SK hand painted on an earthenware vase, height 14⅜in. (36.5cm). An interesting reworking of the pattern from the twenties. Designed by Truda Carter for Carter, Stabler and Adams Ltd., from about 1949-50.

Production was limited at Poole during the Second World War. In 1946 the pottery started up again, although it took two years to reach any significant production. Until 1952 decorative wares were limited to export orders. The first patterns to be produced were those by Truda Carter, later under the Traditional Poole label, given to a series of gift wares and fancies. Several of her pre-war patterns, including *Spring*, based on the leaping deer motif, and *Strasbourg*, were re-introduced in about 1950 whilst her *Leaf* pattern, on the Streamline shape, was a new design from 1948 (Plate 114). A number of successful patterns such as Red Pippin and Trudiana were adapted by Ruth Pavely from original motifs by Carter. Her popular *Persian Deer* was still in production during this period (Plate 115).

In 1950 both John Adams and Truda Carter retired. Despite the proposal that she would continue to work for the company, albeit as a design consultant from home, in the end she did not make any significant contribution. Her poor health made it impossible for her to undertake any design work. The position of resident designer was taken by Claude Smale, although he did not remain in the position for long. He did however produce a limited range of items for the Festival of Britain in 1951. Carter had made an enormous contribution to design at Poole. Following her retirement, she spent her time at home in private. She died from arthritis of the spine in 1958.

For over twenty years Truda Carter was the creative force behind the patterns which placed Poole Pottery at the forefront of British design. Her contribution to the financial and artistic success of the company can be measured in many ways, not least that a group of her early popular patterns from the 1920s and 1930s are still in production as a 'commemorative' range, some seventy years or so since they were first created.[22]

CHAPTER 5

ELEGANCE WITH UTILITY

SUSIE COOPER (1902-1995)

Susie Cooper was one of the most influential and important ceramic designers of the twentieth century. Few can boast a career spanning seven decades, through the 'high days' of the art deco period to the 'swinging sixties' and beyond. Underpinning her career was a true understanding of customer taste and the latest trends in art, gently mixed with an English restraint that made her work so popular both here and abroad. She wanted to produce good designs for people with good taste but not necessarily a lot of money.

116. Portrait of Susie Cooper, about 1938.

Susan Vera Cooper was born on 29 October 1902 into a large middle class family in Station Road, Milton, just outside Stoke-on-Trent. Her parents had good standing in the local community: her father, John, was a Justice of the Peace, and her mother, Mary-Ann, had been a Sunday School teacher. Cooper, the youngest of seven children, enjoyed a happy upbringing, spending her time drawing fruit and vegetables and helping her mother with the household tasks. Sadly, her father died when she was only eleven years old. Her oldest brother took over the running of the family business, which included a bakery, butcher's and a grocery.[1] Cooper attended the local school in Milton and later a private school in Hanley.

To further her education she began attending evening classes at the Burslem School of Art from September 1918. The cost of her education was ten shillings. At the School she

117. A powder bowl and cover modelled and decorated by Susie Cooper whilst studying at the Burslem School of Art, about 1920.

118. A rare earthenware ginger jar and cover decorated with the *Cherub* pattern that was exhibited at the British Empire Exhibition in 1924. Designed by Susie Cooper for A.E. Gray and Co. Ltd. Height with lid 9¼in. (23.5cm).

119. Examples from the Gloria Lustre range. Left to right: *Cherub* bowl designed for the British Empire Exhibition in 1924; a ginger jar and cover decorated with gazelles under a fruit-laden tree (pattern 5153) and a pattern of stags decorated on a bowl, diameter 9⅞in. (25cm). Designed by Susie Cooper for A.E. Gray and Co. Ltd., about 1924-25.

undertook a range of lessons, including still life and drawing from plant form. Cooper was awarded a scholarship to attend full-time for three years in September, 1919. At the School of Art she was taught by a number of tutors, including Gordon Forsyth, the Superintendent of the Schools of Art, who was well known for placing students in employment with local pottery firms. He would later play an influential role in her career as a designer. During her time at the School she produced a number of figures, including 'Guan Yin' and a Spanish Dancer.[2] Cooper also produced a covered powder bowl with a girl's figure (Plate 117).

At that time she was interested in becoming a fashion designer and went to sit an examination at the Royal College of Art in London. As scholarships were only given to those in employment in the decorative arts, she did not qualify. To get around this problem Gordon Forsyth contacted his friend and colleague Albert Edward Gray, the owner of a small pottery based in Stoke. In order to qualify for the scholarship it was arranged that she would work at A.E. Gray & Co. Ltd., better known as Gray's, for a short time.

Edward Gray had formed this small pottery in about 1907. By the early 1920s it was well known in the trade for hand-painted domestic tablewares and toilet sets. More significantly, Edward Gray was one of the more enlightened employers, involved in the many debates on the quality of pottery and design and also working conditions. Although Gray's did not manufacture their own wares, blanks were purchased from several white ware manufacturers in the area.[3] Susie Cooper joined Gray's in June 1922, under the impression that she would be able to design.[4] Edward Gray's ideas and beliefs on good design were a major influence throughout her long career.

120. A stylised bird pattern in silver lustre decorated on a coffee set, the shape of the coffee-pot was designed by Susie Cooper for A.E. Gray and Co. Ltd. Height of pot 8¼in. (21cm).

121. Earthenware tureens and dinner plates decorated with a stylised floral pattern (8413), printed with hand-painted decoration. Designed by Susie Cooper for A.E. Gray and Co. Ltd., about 1929. Width of tureen including arms 7⅝in. (19.5cm).

During the first few months her role was as a paintress, being paid on a piece-work basis. The resident designer, John Guildford, had just left the company and subsequently a Miss Samuels was employed as his replacement. When she failed to return from a holiday, Cooper was appointed to the post of designer.[5] Although her intention was to stay with the firm for only a short time she realised that she was best suited to the potteries, explaining that: 'When I finished my art course I said to myself, what do all the students contribute to the potteries where they are born? They go to Polperro and try to paint great pictures and never again help our towns or trade.'[6]

Gray's was developing a range of lustre wares designed by Gordon Forsyth. As a student at the Burslem School of Art, Cooper had been impressed with a display of his lustre wares produced for the Pilkington Tile and Pottery Company. Forsyth produced several patterns for the new Gloria Lustre range and her first task was to copy his designs on to plaques and vases. A selection of these patterns was shown at the British Empire Exhibition in 1924, including a number of pieces designed by Cooper. She decorated a ginger jar with children underneath a fruit tree in purple and pink lustres (Plate 118).

Gray's gained considerable prestige when they showed a selection of pieces at the Exposition Des Arts Décoratifs et Industriels Modernes in Paris in 1925, winning a Gold Medal. At least two items by Susie Cooper, including a ginger jar decorated with a stylised leaf border, were shown. A number of patterns were also decorated on a series of ornately shaped coffee sets. The Gloria Lustre range was confined mainly to decorative items such as plaques, ginger jars and bowls (Plate 119). This range featured a special Gloria Lustre sun-ray backstamp. Due to the delicate nature of lustre decoration the range was limited, although Cooper introduced silver lustre patterns, particularly for plaques and coffee wares towards the end of the twenties (Plate 120). However the problems of lustre and its lack

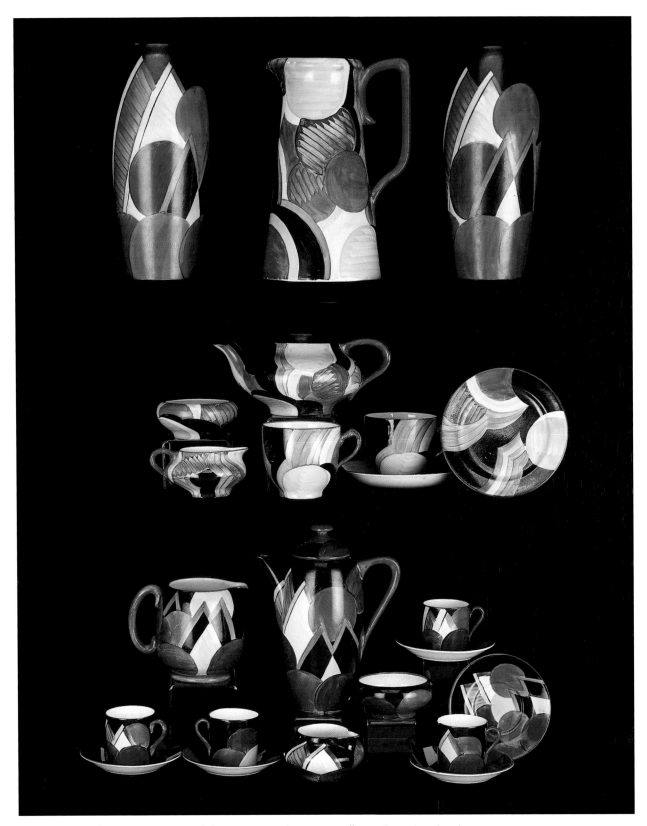

122. Collection of geometric patterns, including a *Moon and Mountains* coffee set (bottom), and similar designs, hand painted on earthenware shapes. Designed by Susie Cooper for A.E. Gray and Co. Ltd., 1928. Height of coffee-pot 4¾in. (12cm).

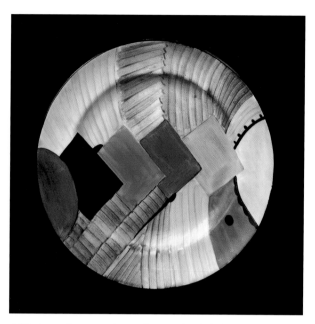

123. An earthenware plaque decorated with the hand-painted pattern *Cubist* (8071). Designed by Susie Cooper for A.E. Gray and Co. Ltd., 1928.

124. An earthenware Dutch jug, height 5½in. (14cm), decorated with a hand-painted geometric pattern (8119). Designed by Susie Cooper for A.E. Gray and Co. Ltd., 1929.

of durability necessitated a return to more durable forms of decoration.

Prior to developing her own range of lustre wares, Cooper had designed a few hand-painted floral patterns that emphasised simple brushwork effects, such as (2866), thought to be her first pattern. She found that her experience as a paintress enabled her to understand the principles of hand painted decoration and its limitations. She later commented: 'I realised that you had to design for the paintresses you had. It wasn't any good putting a lot of drawing into something which you knew they couldn't achieve. So simple brushwork came to be a feature in those early days.'[7]

To compete with the increased sales of hand-painted peasant pottery from Europe, Gray's decided to issue their own versions. Simple brush-stroke patterns were developed with Cooper's intuitive knowledge of what could be achieved in pottery decoration. She introduced a range of delicate and detailed hand-painted floral patterns for the many markets that Gray's had. Later patterns from about 1926 utilised the decorative techniques of print and enamel for patterns such as *Golden Catkin* (7671) and similar florals such as (8413) (Plate 121), both featuring the pattern name in the backstamp. Further designs included *Primula* (7813), *Iris* (7885) and *Silver Palm* (8084). More intricate patterns, perhaps targeted at the upper class section of the market, were produced on ornate bone china coffee sets. In 1926 the trade press reported that 'many of the patterns exhibited a tendency towards the futurist, if only in a mild form'.[8] Several items by Cooper were exhibited at the British Institute of Industrial Design in London in 1927.[9] Shortly afterwards, and in response to the demand for brightly coloured wares from Europe, she developed several over-glaze geometric patterns. The most notable patterns associated with this period are *Moon and Mountains* (Plate 122) and *Cubist* (Plate 123), produced on a range of tea and coffee wares, plaques and jugs. Unfortunately these thickly painted pieces

would often flake or rub.

During this period the products of the company, including those by Cooper, were marked chiefly with one of two galleon marks with the words 'A.E. Gray and Co. Ltd.' At some point during the late twenties Edward Gray decided to introduce a new modern mark, possibly to reflect the success of Cooper. The new Liner mark included the words DESIGNED BY SUSIE COOPER. Without access to the company's archives, which are now considered lost, it is impossible to accurately date the introduction of this mark, but it was probably about 1927. To further confuse the situation, some of her patterns were

125. The *Quadrupeds* nursery pattern (7742), printed in blue with hand painted decoration on a tureen and cover supplied by Johnson Brothers Ltd. Designed by Susie Cooper for A.E. Gray and Co. Ltd., 1928. Width of tureen with handles 10¼in. (26cm).

126. A view of the Chelsea Works in Burslem where Susie Cooper worked for a short period in 1930-31.

119

127. An early hand painted pattern, *Fritillary* (E/152), hand painted on the Orleans shape. Designed for the Susie Cooper Pottery, about 1930-31.

issued with other marks. Moreover, after she left the company the Liner mark was continued but with her name removed.

In 1927 Cooper introduced a wide range of banded patterns that proved commercially successful. For these banded decorations she used strident colour combinations to great effect. The popular *Harmony* range, used mainly on domestic and kitchen wares, sold for many years. Her *Layebands* (8286) pattern, named after the actress Evelyn Laye, was produced exclusively for the London store Heal's and sold well for over thirty years.[10] Lesser known banded designs include *Aquamer*, (8375) introduced in 1929 and later exhibited at the International Exhibition of Decorative Arts in Milan in 1933. The first full range of nursery wares includes *Quadrupeds* (7742/7743), a border of animals interspersed between trees, which was introduced in about 1928 (Plate 125). A rather inventive pattern featured elements from the nursery rhyme the *House that Jack Built*, whilst a lesser-known design featured Red Riding Hood on a beaker. Towards the late 1920s a limited range of patterns, many using silver lustre, was produced, some of which were illustrated in the *Decorative Art Studio Yearbook* in 1930. Notable examples include *Persian Bird* (8554).

Cooper's artistic abilities were not purely confined to pottery decoration during the late twenties. Besides developing new patterns, she contributed to the firm's display stands, chiefly for the British Industries Fairs. The trade press noted in 1926 that: 'Nobody could avoid being struck by the stand of Messrs. Gray and Co. Ltd. which was certainly designed and arranged by an artist. The lower part of the walls was of simple brown hessian cloth; and the frieze above was decorated with bright posters of a futuristic kind.'[11] A year later, for the same trade fair, she designed tall hessian panels featuring hand-painted leaping deer, complemented by geometric cushion covers featuring a red triangle. Cooper later recalled that the representatives from Bass, the brewer thought she had used their symbol.[12] The latter designs were noticed by a textiles company, Skelhorn and Edwards, which was interested in Cooper undertaking designs for them. In 1928 she was

commissioned to design the screen curtains for the Regal cinema at Marble Arch in London. The curtains remained in place until the 1960s; the design, on brown silk, featured cascading brown leaves.[13]

Cooper became increasingly unhappy with some of the hollowware shapes that she had to use. Working with differing shapes that often didn't match was very frustrating. She was able to convince Edward Gray that they needed new shapes and to this end she designed a coffee-pot and a milk jug, towards the late twenties, manufactured by Lancaster and Sons Ltd.[14] However, as she wanted to have control of both pattern and shape, she decided to set up in business as an independent designer. Cooper realised that if she stayed at Gray's she would be a decorator rather than a designer. In 1929 the decision to leave her secure job and set up on her own was taken.

At a time of economic instability the move was both audacious and adventurous. Everyone, including Edward Gray and Gordon Forsyth, who had both nurtured her talent, expressed concern at this decision. Although they were convinced that her breakthrough may have been too early, Cooper was not. Fortunately family support and financial backing to the sum of £4,000 was forthcoming. Albert 'Jack' Beeson, her brother-in-law, decided to become involved in the new venture, following the decline of his horse slaughtering business.[15] In addition, Gordon Forsyth introduced her to Albert G. Richardson, from the Crown Ducal company, who was setting up his own company at the George Street Pottery in Tunstall. He offered her space within this factory and the opportunity to design her own shapes. The fledgling company, with six free-hand paintresses, had a small studio, consisting of two rooms, a paint shop and a small office.[16]

128. A modernist design (E/297) hand painted on the Cube shape tea wares, manufactured by Wood and Sons Ltd. Designed by Susie Cooper for the Susie Cooper Pottery, 1931. Height of teapot 7in. (18cm).

129. A view of the Crown Works, Newcastle Street in Burslem, Stoke-on-Trent, 1970s.

The wares produced were rubber-stamped with a new mark, 'A Susie Cooper Production' within a triangle, and 'Tunstall' underneath. The first pieces had been decorated and were ready for firing, when the landlord foreclosed, forcing them to seek new accommodation. Sadly, little information is available on these items.

The winter of 1929 was spent searching for new premises. Eventually an ideal studio was located on the Moorland Road, not far from the Burslem School of Art. The Chelsea Works was rented from Royal Doulton, an established and profitable company. The new site was small but it suited them (Plate 126). It boasted a small showroom and a bottle kiln. An agent was established in London – Adams and Aynsley at 13 Charterhouse Street, Holborn. New patterns were developed in the same style as those produced at Gray's; simple banded and stylised floral patterns which were given a new prefix of E, to denote earthenware. In April 1930 Cooper placed her first independent advertisement declaring: 'Elegance combined with Utility. Artistry with Commerce and Practicability. Truly a strong combination'.[17] At the same time, the trade press went to great lengths to promote the young designer, describing her as 'a gifted, creative artist of the modern school of thought, one who reveals in her work a lively imagination combined with a unique capacity to achieve the maximum degree of effectiveness in pottery decoration by recourse to the simplest modes of expression'.[18]

For the time being they had to be content with buying in blank wares from various suppliers such as Grimwades, Grindleys and Wood and Sons. In particular the new firm concentrated on morning sets, coffee and tea sets, lemonade sets, cruets, cheese stands and dinnerware. Plans for the production of a group of speciality goods of 'modern expression', including figures and book-ends, were noted in the trade press.[19] In April 1930 the first order was taken from the Nottingham store Griffin and Spalding, shortly followed by another order for honey pots and morning sets from Grants Department Store in London.[20] Cooper's designs of this period consisted chiefly of free-hand florals such as *Bronze Chrysanthemums* E/96 and *Fritillary* (Plate 127), and abstract patterns including

Scarlet Runner Beans E/241. In June 1931 the trade press reported: 'Miss Cooper unquestionably reveals in her work a very sensitive appreciation of colour values, and she is, above all, a full blooded colourist. Vivid even daring, colouring is one of her strongest aids in the very direct appeal, which she makes in her distinctive creations. It will be noted by those who have come into close touch with Miss Cooper's work that she relies almost entirely upon free hand brushwork.'[21]

To expand production and meet the demands of the increasing orders, larger premises were sought. Moreover, the designer required the facilities to produce her own shapes. Fortunately Harry Wood, the Managing Director of Wood and Sons, offered her space at a small works adjacent to the Wood's site in Burslem. He was a very generous man and keen to support new initiatives. He was particularly enthusiastic having viewed a display of Susie Cooper's work at the Burslem School of Art in the summer of that year.

Charlotte Rhead had occupied the Crown Works during the 1920s but it was currently empty following extensive damage caused by a bad fire in 1926. Harry Wood offered to produce shapes based on Cooper's designs. This would provide the breakthrough she needed to be in complete control of both pattern and shape. The arrangement was that Wood's would manufacture the shapes and Cooper would purchase direct from them. She had already shown a preference for their wares, selecting them whilst she was a designer at the Gray's Pottery. The production of her shapes did not preclude her from using many of the standard Wood's shapes, such as flatware and bowls, in fact during the early thirties she utilised the Wedge, Elgreave and Cube shapes for some of her more modern designs (Plate 128).

The move to the new site took place in the summer of 1931 and once established, the

130. The *Woodpecker* pattern (E/317), printed outline with hand-painted decoration on a Kestrel shape teapot, height 4⅜in. (12cm). Designed by Susie Cooper for the Susie Cooper Pottery, 1932.

131. An earthenware Kestrel coffee pot and cover and tea cup and saucer showing two variations of the *Wide Bands* pattern. Designed by Susie Cooper for the Susie Cooper Pottery, about 1933.

Crown Works became her workplace for the next fifty years (Plate 129). The essential 'Susie Cooper' style was achieved. The designer wanted to introduce good design for those people with more taste than money, strongly believing that one should not have to pay for style as it should be part of the offer.[22] Cooper understood the current market very well and knew that she could produce moderately priced stylish wares, as the only other choices at the time were fine bone china or the shoddy goods turned out by the lesser known companies. Convinced that fine art techniques could be fitted into the industrial process, she introduced, during the thirties, a very wide range of innovative decorative techniques from crayon to aerographed decoration, the latter often successfully combined with sgrafitto decoration.

Harry Wood supported Cooper through the first few years of production until she built up her business. Initially, her wares were exhibited at various trade shows alongside the Wood's products, including Copenhagen in November 1932. Eventually Harry Wood convinced Jack Beeson that he should go to London to promote the new designs and it was arranged that Cooper would produce special boxed sets to be sent to the trade press for promotion. This enabled her to gain publicity in the national press.[23]

At the same time Cooper concentrated on producing new patterns and shapes ready for her first independent stand at the British Industries Fair in 1932. These new designs were decorated on tea sets, candlesticks and a lemonade set in the charming *Woodpecker* E/317 pattern (Plate 130). Lamp bases decorated with a Spanish Dancer and Mexican Man were displayed alongside the modern floral patterns *Briar Rose* E/328 and *Heliotrope* E/348. These items were tastefully laid out on plain natural oak tables, complemented by a painted panel by Cooper, depicting a man pulling donkeys along a road, that was placed above a selection of her wares.[24] These wares featured a new backstamp of a leaping deer, with the legend, A SUSIE COOPER PRODUCTION. To mark

her first stand an advertisement was placed in the trade press which read, 'Susie Cooper Productions, Expressing Modernity'.[25]

Of most significance was the unveiling of her first full shape range called Kestrel. It was developed with her sound knowledge of the need for a practical and functional shape that was easy to clean, poured well and could take all manner of decoration (Plate 131). Ernest Sambrook from Wood and Sons undertook the modelling. Kestrel proved very popular and remained in production for almost thirty years. The range was expanded with a notable addition, launched the following year – the tureen. The trade press and customers praised this innovative shape. The lid could be used as a separate serving dish and the set was easy to stack in a cupboard. Her consideration for the practicalities of shapes as well as decoration gave her a lead over other manufacturers. Cooper was also aware that younger people, who were buying their own pottery for the first time, wanted something reasonably priced and not too traditional. They were not interested in a full dinner service, instead opting for smaller sets, so she produced better balanced sets comprising four dinner plates, side plates, fruit saucers, gravy boat, meat plate and a divided vegetable dish. The Susie Cooper catalogue of 1932 noted that the latter item would be ideal in these days of economy of space and labour. Additional items, such as dessert ware, lamps and candlesticks were also available. Notable patterns decorated on these items include Panorama and The Homestead (Plate 132). Part of the short order range included lesser known designs such as The Seagull and Galleon (Plate 133).[26]

Cooper took the opportunity to launch her first studio wares at the British Industries Fair in 1932. The intention was that they would co-ordinate with the modern interior of a typical 1930's home (Plate 134). These incised pieces, expanded over the following years, were developed in tandem with a series of hand-painted wares of abstract patterns, stylised tulips and orchids on matt glazes (Plate 135).[27] These patterns were proudly displayed in

132. Two lesser-known patterns: Panorama (E/309) decorated on a Cube shape cup and saucer and The Homestead, decorated on an earthenware stepped jug, height 5½in. (14cm). Both shapes were supplied by Wood and Sons Ltd. and designed by Susie Cooper for the Susie Cooper Pottery, 1931-32.

133. A range of short order patterns from 1931-37. Top: *Galleon* lamp base (E/407), an earthenware biscuit barrel decorated with *The Seagull* pattern. Bottom: A *The Homestead* candlestick, Fox model, as part of a table setting from 1936-37, a small pin tray decorated with a stylised feather pattern (E/576) and a chamberstick decorated in the *Scarlet Runner Beans* (E/241) pattern. Designed by Susie Cooper for the Susie Cooper Pottery.

134. A decorated hand-thrown vase, height 5⅞in. (15cm), a rare example of a hand-painted studio piece (E/548). The item is dated on the base, 1933. Designed by Susie Cooper for the Susie Cooper Pottery.

the windows of their London showrooms during the early part of 1933 (Plate 136). The range was expanded to include several other patterns until 1938. The trade press reported that these items were 'all distinguished by original design, both in general line and in applied decoration'.[28] Both the incised and painted ranges were eventually phased out in about 1938 and were certainly not produced after the war.

New banded decorations, that had proved so popular at Gray's, were introduced with examples such as *Graduated Black Bands* (Plate 137) and *Wide Bands* (Plate 131). However, Cooper began to move away from the strident art deco colours to a much softer palette, recognising a change in public taste. She developed a subtle form of banded decoration known as wash banding, that required great skill to achieve the exact result. These sets proved popular with so many young married couples that the style soon became known as *Wedding Ring* (Plate 138). Most importantly many variations, based on the pattern, could be produced. A number were exclusive to London stores such as the John Lewis Partnership, including E/475 and E/481. These patterns proved so popular that they were heavily copied by other firms both in Britain and North America. The popular version E/479 was copied by an American company, which went as far as to call it 'Susan's Red'.[29] They were unable, however, to achieve the same subtleties of shade. Cooper recalled later that they didn't have the appropriate shaped wares to allow the paint to be applied.[30] In order to reaffirm the original production in the United States her agent placed advertisements for the pattern in the trade press declaring that Cooper's designs were: 'Conceived and potted by one of England's Oldest and Finest factories this new line with its subtle handling of colour tones has a definite place in every china department.'[31]

The British Industries Fair of 1933 showcased her latest products, including the new

135. A selection of earthenware studio wares incorporating incised, tube-lined and painted decoration. Noteworthy pieces include the *Squirrel* vase (E/345) top third from right, and a hand painted studio vase decorated with the *Orchids* (M72) pattern (bottom, second from left). Designed by Susie Cooper for the Susie Cooper Pottery, 1932-36.

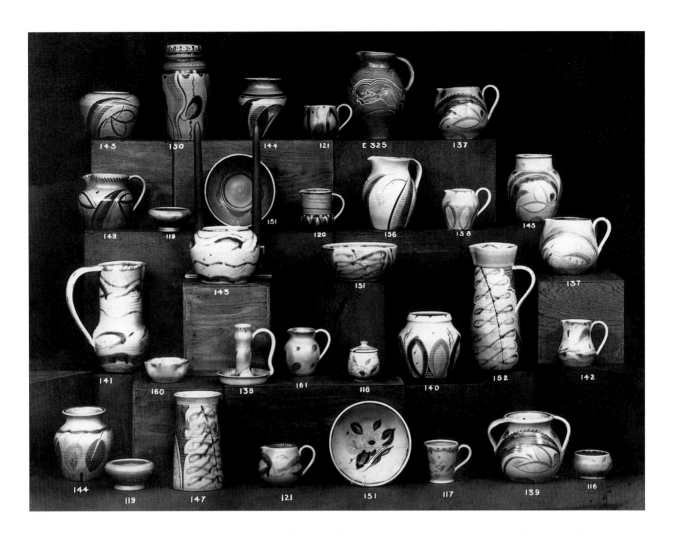

136. A period photograph showing a display of patterns and shapes available in 1932. The numbers refer to the shapes.

Curlew shape, a small bird-like form that complemented a series of crayon, tube-lined and painted designs (Plate 139). Unfortunately, Curlew did not give the designer the same flexibility as the Kestrel shape and was withdrawn after only a few years in production. For a limited period Cooper produced a range of face masks including a judge, Chinaman, an older woman and one of a young girl (Plate 140), the latter is thought to have been a self portrait. The firm also exhibited at the British Industrial Art in Relation to the Home Exhibition at Dorland Hall in London in 1933 and the Royal Academy Exhibition in 1935, where she displayed a new pattern E/912 in green enamel and crayon. This pattern proved very popular and was marketed as *Tweed* in North America. The demand for her wares inevitably led to the development of decorative treatments that could meet the increasing orders yet maintain the uniqueness and high quality of her work. She had occasionally used the traditional print and enamel method of decoration for a range of attractive floral patterns such as *A Nosegay* E/338, *Oak Apple* E/429/430 and *Freesia* E/432. In the development of her lithographs she successfully organised for her prints to be reproduced from her own art work (Plate 141). This type of ware was developed during 1934 and first tested on the North American market for feedback. With such exacting high standards the sheer quality of the reproductions taken from her original art work left many dealers refusing to believe that they were printed!

137. A selection of colourways of the *Graduated Black Bands* pattern including tango (E/496), blue (E/501) and green (E/499). Designed by Susie Cooper for the Susie Cooper Pottery, from 1933 to about 1938.

138. An earthenware Kestrel shape coffee-pot and milk jug with a Falcon shape teacup and saucer decorated with the *Wedding Ring* pattern (E/479). Designed by Susie Cooper for the Susie Cooper Pottery, about 1932. Height of coffee-pot 7in (18cm).

Her most popular pattern was *Dresden Spray*, a printed central motif with a shaded band (Plate 142). This pattern was actually created for Wood and Sons. Harry Wood had asked her to produce a range of patterns and shapes for his firm but he felt that *Dresden Spray* was too different and possibly not suitable for his market.[32] Cooper decided to do it herself by replacing the lithographic border with a hand painted shaded band. This gave her the option of producing many colour variations. *Dresden Spray* was an instant success with the buying public. Two colour variations were exclusive to Peter Jones and John Lewis. The latter stocked the pink version purchased by King Edward VIII for Mrs. Simpson. The subsequent few patterns Cooper created for Wood's were accepted by Harry Wood and also proved commercially successful. The range of functional shapes that she devised included Wren and Jay, decorated with simple patterns such as *Cavendish*, *Cromer*, *Charnwood* and *Academy*, launched at the start of 1935. Her name (and occasionally the pattern name) was incorporated into the Wood's backstamp. The *Academy* pattern was extensively advertised in the trade press and exhibited at the prestigious Royal Academy Show in London in 1935. The Wren shape was of particular interest to the trade press which reported: 'the complete creation reveals the touch of the artist's mind, in that the shape, which is primarily well-balanced, bears in the clay little incisions, or pluckings, by the tool, arranged in an orderly manner, and supported by a neat little ornament in colour appended by brushwork.'[33]

Many of the more popular designs such as *Polka Dot* E/896-898 and *Exclamation Mark* E/1188-1190 and the wide range of banded patterns were used to train the apprentices how to handle colour. Cooper felt that she had a responsibility towards the girls she employed, so several patterns were introduced to keep them in work. The

popularity of the transfer printed wares prompted her to produce further patterns, including *Swansea Spray* E/1014, *Grey Leaf* E/1161, *Long Leaf* E/1638 and *Tigerlily* E/1924 throughout the 1930s. A wide range of nursery ware patterns decorated on mugs, beakers and lamp bases was produced in about 1936 (Plate 143). Some of these patterns, including *Cowboy* E/1227 and *Horse and Jockey* E/1225, were targeted at adults, rather than at children (Plate 144).

The success of the printed wares did not limit the introduction of new hand painted patterns. At the British Industries Fair in 1937 Cooper unveiled a wide range of small composite sets and special lines that included a leaping deer table centrepiece, with matching fox and hound, intended for the sophisticated home. Also on display were the game and fish sets. The trade summarised the designer's work, stating: 'The modern range of Susie Cooper pottery is altogether wider in its scope that it was formerly: the patterns throughout are eloquent of the touch of an artist of no mean order.'[34]

In 1937 a new modern shape range called Falcon was introduced. This shape provided a form that could take all manner of decoration, and proved a successful alternative to Kestrel. Cooper employed aerography combined with sgraffito decoration of stars, swirls and crescents for a number of patterns (Plate 145). Notable printed patterns included *Tyrol* E/1496 and *Elegance* E/1701-1710. The British Industries Fair in 1938 saw the unveiling of the new Spiral shape that featured fluted edges. It was mainly produced to appeal to the export market and was decorated with floral patterns such as *Endon* E/1417, *Woodland* E/1567 and *Patricia Rose* E/1559. Cooper was not really keen on this shape for two reasons; one that it was rather difficult to apply lithographs on the curved shapes and also that dirt collected in the crevices. At about this time Cooper was

139. A rare example of the Curlew teapot, height 3⅜in. (8.5cm), aerographed in green with sgraffito decoration of diamonds (E/1186) from 1936. The Curlew teacup and saucer is decorated with a hand painted pattern on a blue glaze (E/545), from 1933-34. Designed by Susie Cooper for the Susie Cooper Pottery.

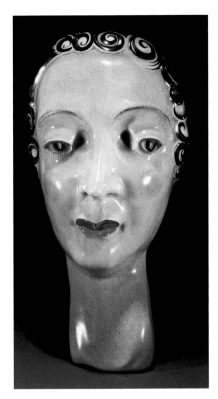

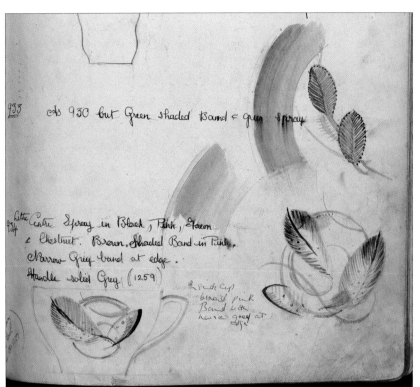

140. One of only four known face masks that Susie Cooper produced in 1933. This piece is said to be a self portrait. Designed by Susie Cooper for Susie Cooper Pottery, height of mask 12in. (30.5cm).

141. A page from the Susie Cooper pattern book illustrating *Two Leaf Spray* (E/933) and *Leaves* (E/934). Designed by Susie Cooper for the Susie Cooper Pottery, 1934-35.

commissioned to produce the tableware for the London to Paris route for the Imperial Airways and the Peckham Health Centre in London.

During the late thirties the firm established good trade with the North American provinces through her agent Fondeville & Co., at 149 Fifth Avenue, New York, who successfully marketed and displayed Cooper's work at all the major trade shows in the country. In particular Eaton's, the Canadian store, was a big customer of her wares and extensively promoted her pottery through large advertisements, emphasising the originality of this young English designer. New speciality lines were developed to meet the needs of the American table, including a modern version of the Turkey Set, used for Thanksgiving celebrations (Plate 146). She also produced smaller items, such as moustache cups and saucers, water pitchers for the boardroom and cocktail sets. Cooper later recalled: 'Just before the war was the period when we were really at the top of a wave, and we could have gone on from there to great success, I feel. But that wasn't meant to be.'[35]

In 1940 Cooper was awarded the honour of Royal Designer for Industry, the only woman from the Potteries to achieve such recognition. The other recipients of that year included Gordon Russell, Allan Walton and Anna Zinkeisen.[36] Some of her latest patterns, such as *Prairie Flower* on the Spiral shape, were used as part of the 'Britain Can Export' promotion. According to the trade press this pattern had met with an excellent reception throughout the North American market.[37] The following year similar patterns, including *Coraline*, were also featured.

142. A selection of transfer printed patterns by Susie Cooper. Top: examples of three patterns, *Tigerlily* (E/1999), *Dresden Spray* (E/1014) and *Nosegay* (E/1146) decorated on Kestrel shape coffee ware. Second row: items decorated with the *Patricia Rose* pattern (E/1894), the lesser known *Woodland* pattern (1841) on the Falcon shape from about 1939, examples of one of the many colour variations of the *Wedding Ring* pattern (E/698) decorated on a Kestrel shape teapot, milk jug and cup and saucer. Front: the *Patricia Rose* pattern (E/1657) with shaded pink border and another with a printed border (E/1890), a *Nosegay* pattern (E/995) decorated on a Kestrel shape preserve pot and cover, various tea wares decorated with the transfer printed leaf pattern (E/934), a Kestrel shape gravy boat decorated with the hand painted pattern (E/2174), a Kestrel shape soup tureen and cover decorated with the *Cactus* pattern (E/1282) and a printed *Leaping Deer* pattern on a Kestrel shape preserve pot (E/1011). 1934-49.

143. A selection of nursery ware items. Top: Divided plate printed with a cow motif (E/1436), a side plate decorated with the transfer printed *Horse and Jockey* pattern (E/1225), a divided dish decorated with a pig (E/1436). Bottom: A *Quadrupeds* (7742) sugar bowl from 1927, a *Dignity and Impudence* child's mug (E/1229), a lamp base decorated with a transfer printed motif of a duck (E/1416) and a Kestrel shape hot water jug decorated with the *Skier* pattern (E/1231). Designed by Susie Cooper for the Susie Cooper Pottery. All items about 1936-37 unless otherwise stated.

With the loss of so many skilled workers, who had left to fight in the war, very few patterns were put into production during the early years of the 1940s. After suffering a bad fire in May 1942 the decision was taken to close down the factory for the duration of the War. During this period of inactivity Cooper gave birth to her son, Timothy, in 1943, having married Cecil Barker in 1938.

Starting again with such appalling shortages of materials and skilled workers proved difficult. However her husband provided the impetus when he decided to come into the business, as did her nephew Kenneth Cooper. Setting up again seemed much harder than it had been in the early thirties. In 1946 Cooper was asked to join the selection panel to choose examples of pottery for the Britain Can Make It Exhibition, held at the Victoria and Albert Museum in London. Several of her own items were displayed, including a stylised tree design, and various seaweed motifs on Spiral shape dessert plates.[38]

For the first post-war British Industries Fair in 1947 a small display of new designs was put together featuring the *Starbursts* E/1958, *Chinese Fern* and *Tree of Life* E/2062 patterns (Plate 147), the latter being a personal favourite of the designer (Plate 148). These wares were exported chiefly to South Africa and North America, with only seconds being allowed for sale in Britain. The return to free-hand decoration was necessary as valuable stocks of lithographs had been destroyed in the fire. Several hand painted patterns featured exotic fruits painted on to large plaques (Plate 149). Cooper designed less than 250 patterns before the restrictions on the sales of ware in this country were lifted. During the reconstruction of the factory and with limited work she returned to textile design for Cavendish Textiles, a company owned by John Lewis. Whilst she reworked some of her more popular motifs such as *Patricia Rose* and *Dresden Spray* (Plate 142) she also created new ideas including a banded and scroll pattern.[39]

In early 1950 the firm decided to purchase Jason China Ltd., based in Longton. This

acquisition gave her total control over all the production process but significantly control of the manufacture of shapes. The decoration of the wares would continue to be undertaken at the Crown Works. The move to bone china production was timely, as a change in public taste soon became evident. Cooper's intention was to allow the translucency of bone china to speak for itself by designing patterns that were not overburdened by over-rich decoration.[40] Initially, a range of bone china shapes produced by Jason China Ltd. was used, including Bute, Countess and Princess, until she had the opportunity to model her own shapes. No sooner had she begun to develop the shapes than she received her first important commission. The Royal Society of Arts asked her to provide tea ware for a reception to be held in honour of Princess Elizabeth at their headquarters in London in November 1950.[41] The topical Lion and Unicorn theme was used to maximum effect, on an aerographed ground with sgraffito decoration. Due to the newness of her bone china shapes, there was a slight problem with the cups and saucers. Cooper explained: 'when we made these cups and saucers we didn't get the shrinkage quite right. The feet of the cups were a little too big for the wells of the saucer. Of course, the Queen was very observant and noted this. I had to make my explanations'.[42]

Further wares were requested by the Faculty of Royal Designers for use at the Royal Pavilion at the forthcoming Festival of Britain in 1951. For this she created the stylish *Gold Bud* C.163 pattern. To complement this set she produced biscuit plates decorated with the *Lion and Unicorn* and *Cockerel* motifs (Plate 150). A selection of her work was exhibited in the Homes and Gardens Pavilion at the event. The new *Astral* (C.11) pattern was created for the Royal Society of Arts in the spring of 1951 (Plate 151). Probably her most significant commission was to design a commemorative plaque for the Royal Society of Arts in 1954. The design, incorporating a border of words, was produced with sgraffito decoration (Plate 152). These tea and coffee wares were decorated on her exquisite Quail

144. Two rare items from the late thirties: a hand painted example of the *Horse and Jockey* pattern (E/1225), height 3⅛in. (8cm). The *Cowboy* pattern (E/1227) printed on an earthenware Paris jug, height 4in. (10cm). Designed by Susie Cooper for the Susie Cooper Pottery, from 1936-37.

145. A range of shapes demonstrating the decorative techniques of aerography and sgraffito. The two large plates depicting animals are lesser known and date from the late thirties. Bottom from right to left: An earthenware Kestrel shape teapot decorated with the *Crescents* pattern (E/1241), a Kestrel shape covered sugar decorated with the *Starbursts* pattern, a side plate in the *Swirls* pattern (E/900) from 1934, a Falcon shape cup and saucer rubber-stamped in black with sgraffito decoration from the late fifties, a Kestrel shape coffee-pot decorated with sgraffito *Stars*, about 1937-38 and an earthenware Falcon shape coffee-pot decorated with the *Ribbon* pattern (E/1406). Designed by Susie Cooper for the Susie Cooper Pottery.

shape, inspired by the quail's egg. The range included tea, coffee, dinnerware and some fancies. A new backstamp, prefix and numbering system were introduced to separate the production from earthenware. The C prefix denoted bone china with numbers starting with C.1. With such an elegant body, simple floral motifs, ferns, scrolls and spot patterns became typical during the first few years.

Several printed floral centres such as *Gardenia*, *Clematis* and *Azalea* were produced on both earthenware and bone china (Plate 153). The *Raised Spot* C.501 pattern, with its many colour variations, was a best seller and ideal for the training of new decorators. From about 1953 more complex and detailed floral motifs, including *Wild Strawberry* C.486 and *Parrot Tulip* C.621 were introduced, the latter proving popular in North America. By 1954 the production of bone china was well established to such an extent that the firm began to develop new lines, including boxed gift wares, beakers, toast racks and condiment sets. These items were exhibited at Harrods in London in 1956. Of particular interest was the range of stylised patterns for vases and the first bone china figure of Queen Eleanor of Castile, which the trade press noted, 'showed an individuality of

rhythm conveyed through line, combined with what can only be described as a sense of period, auguring that the name Susie Cooper may soon become as significantly linked with model figures as it is now with tableware'.[43] Despite being exhibited, the figurine and other special items, such as a Chinaman and bull, were not commercially produced.

Although bone china began to dominate the output of the factory, new earthenware continued to be introduced, albeit a limited amount. At the Blackpool Fancy Goods and Gifts Fair in 1957 Cooper introduced *Highland Grass* E/2311 and a new scallop tureen and a taller Kestrel tea cup and saucer.[44] Later transfer printed patterns on earthenware included *Sienna Pastel* E/2318, *Blue Orchid* E/2310, *Petronella* E/2346 and *Blue Gentian* E/2398, the latter was also available on bone china from about 1955. Some of the last earthenware patterns were hand painted, including *Ferndown* (Plate 154).

By 1960 the production of new earthenware designs was reduced. However, an Earthenware Price List dated April 1960 lists twenty-five patterns still in production, including several dating from the thirties. Although a few new patterns on earthenware were launched as late as 1963, including *Floriana* E/2417, it was phased out in about 1964. Of special interest to the press was the introduction of presentation boxed sets, produced for the more expensive patterns such as *Pomme D'Or* C.824.

The Susie Cooper Pottery suffered a disastrous blow in March 1957. A fire started in the adjacent Stanley Pottery, part of the Wood's company, and spread to the Crown Works causing an estimated £75,000 worth of damage. The trade press reported that only 'a trickle of small orders not requiring warehousing is leaving the factory'.[45]

146. An earthenware plate, diameter 10⅝in. (27cm), decorated with the *Turkey* pattern (1838), printed outline with hand-painted decoration. Designed by Susie Cooper for the Susie Cooper Pottery, about 1939-40.

SUSIE COOPER

147. A view of the Susie Cooper stand at the British Industries Fair in 1947. A number of patterns including *Tree of Life*, *Starbursts* and *Chinese Fern* are displayed.

Cooper decided to extend her product range to include bone china dinnerware, to meet increased demand but the Jason Works did not have enough spare capacity. Discussions took place with R.H. and S.L. Plant, established in about 1849, based in Longton. This company had the ovens she needed, and they were not in use. In November 1958 the two companies merged to form Tuscan Holdings Group Ltd. Shortly afterwards bone china production moved to the Plant's site, with the Jason works being sold off. The official statement regarding the merger stated: 'The new arrangements will involve the movement of staff and operatives as well as certain items of plant and machinery from the Longton factory of Susie Cooper China Ltd. to Tuscan Works, and it is hoped to complete this programme within the next few months.'[46]

Towards the end of the 1950s Cooper began to develop a taller bone china coffee cup as a response to the increasing fashion for drinking coffee. The original shape soon developed into a complete set, appropriately called the Can shape. Notable patterns of the early sixties included *Katina*, C.1160. However, one of the most outstanding patterns of the decade was *Black Fruits* C.893-898, which was developed using scraperboard techniques (Plate 155). The range, complemented by the harlequin interiors, proved very popular and was imitated by several other companies. One of her most popular patterns, *Glen Mist* C.1035, was not initially accepted on to the Design Council's Index. During the 1980s the pattern was produced exclusively for the Japanese market. The British Royal Family uses this set at Sandringham, in Norfolk.

During this period the china industry was fraught with mergers, closures and takeovers. Josiah Wedgwood and Sons Ltd. were keen to acquire Tuscan as they made low priced bone china. Tuscan had recently received several important orders from places such as the Grosvenor Hotel in London. Their volume of trade made the company a worthwhile

148. An earthenware plate decorated with the *Tree of Life* pattern, banded with sgraffito and hand painted decoration. Designed by Susie Cooper for Susie Cooper Ltd., about 1947. Diameter of plate 9in. (23cm).

149. An unusual stylised fruit pattern hand painted on an earthenware plaque. Designed by Susie Cooper for the Susie Cooper Pottery, about 1950.

investment. In March 1966 both Royal Tuscan and Susie Cooper Ltd. were taken over by Wedgwood.[47] The concern would continue production of New Chelsea, Tuscan and Susie Cooper China Ltd. Artistically there was no change in Cooper's production. In fact, Wedgwood continued to manufacture her most popular patterns produced before the takeover. At the time she told the press that her wares would reach a wider market through Wedgwood's established dealers and international links. Kenneth Cooper, her nephew, became a Director of both Susie Cooper Ltd and William Adams Ltd. The Susie Cooper showroom in London was closed and a new showroom in Wigmore Street was set up, to be shared with William Adams Ltd. Her latest patterns, including *Reverie*, C.2055, were tastefully displayed. The only obvious change was that the words 'A Member of the Wedgwood Group' were incorporated into her backstamp.

Over the next six years Cooper produced some of her most outstanding patterns, demonstrating that she was still at the forefront of contemporary design. In 1967 she went to London to seek new inspiration, visiting Carnaby Street, an attraction for young people, and returning to the Potteries with many ideas, from which she developed the outstanding *Carnaby Daisy*. Further patterns included *Columbine* C.2174, *Keystone* C.2131-2134, *Diablo* C.2150 (Plate 156) and *Pimento* (Plate 157). These contemporary patterns were popular in Scandinavia, whilst *Florida* C.2166, *Indian Summer* C.2185 and *Everglade* C.2186 were targeted towards the Canadian market Another outstanding design was *Gay Stripes* (2141-2146) produced from about 1968 (Plate 158).

However, Cooper soon realised that the new environment was very different from what she had become used to during her thirty-seven years as an independent producer. Clashes over design issues at the various selection committees frustrated Cooper, as Wedgwood were cautious about putting some of her patterns into production, fearing the financial risk.

150. Three bone china biscuit plates decorated with the *Lion*, *Unicorn* and *Cockerel* patterns, aerographed with sgraffito and gilt decoration. Designed by Susie Cooper for Susie Cooper Ltd., 1951.

151. A rare example of the *Astral* pattern (C.11) on the bone china Quail shape coffee ware. The pattern was aerographed in blue with sgraffito and gilt decoration. This set was specially commissioned for the use of the Fellows of the Royal Society of Arts in 1951. Designed by Susie Cooper.

She also felt that there was no appreciation for individuals, or their ideas.[48]

She occasionally contributed patterns to both Wedgwood and Adams. In 1968 her *Perugia* pattern, a traditional border, was decorated on the lesser known Orbit shape designed by Robert Minkin.[49] She also designed *Greensleeves* G 3182 and *Blue Mantle* G 3193, on the Wayfarer shape for Adams, in about 1969. In 1969 Cooper was asked to produce six South African floral motifs for a set of beakers for the World Wildlife Fund, sold individually boxed or as a set of six. The accompanying dinner plates depicted six different animal studies by wildlife painter David Shepherd.[50]

During the seventies Cooper produced some of her most outstanding patterns, including *Cornpoppy* C.2176, one of her bestsellers (Plate 159). Sadly the seventies were to be a period of frustration and inactivity for her, although she remained as committed to design as always. Her husband died after a long illness in 1972 and during that year she and Kenneth Cooper resigned their Directorships. She spent a great deal of time experimenting with new ideas for possible designs, creating an amazing range of trial pieces on Wedgwood blanks.[51] Outstanding designs for large bowls included *Tiger Cubs in Combat*, *Florentine Pipers* and *Chou Dynasty* (Plate 160). The latter was produced, but only in a limited run. The *Ashmun* pattern decorated a range of coffee and giftwares. In 1977 Cooper produced a range of silver lustre patterns for giftware for the Queen's Silver Jubilee which became the best selling commemorative for the Wedgwood firm, produced in a limited edition of 2,000.

In recognition of her achievements Wedgwood staged an exhibition of her work at the Sanderson's Gallery, London in 1978. Not only did this show feature examples of work throughout the decades but a wide range of incised bowls and tablewares was specially produced for the exhibition. Large and small studio vases were thrown by Elywn James and

152. This rare plaque was designed by Susie Cooper for the Royal Society of Arts to celebrate their bicentenary in 1954. The plaque is aerographed with sgraffito decoration.

153. A selection of bone china patterns decorated on the Quail shape including *Azalea* (top left), *Magnolia* (top right) and *Gardenia* (bottom left). Designed by Susie Cooper for Susie Cooper China Ltd., 1952-56.

refined by Cooper. Traditional Wedgwood shapes were used for tableware patterns such as *Pink Spiral*, originally dating from about 1950. *Blue Feather* was a reworking of a late fifties pattern with a blue banded border. All pieces were signed and dated 1978. A year later she was awarded the honour of the Order of the British Empire.

In 1980 Wedgwood launched two new patterns, *Iris* C.2212 on the Can shape and a selection of small gift wares in *Floral Lustre* and *Birds of the World*. The latter pattern originally featured a simple border but that was vetoed by the company as it was too expensive.

In a bid to rationalise the company's products Wedgwood decided to close down the Crown Works in 1980. Cooper was devastated that her company, which had successfully

154. A selection of earthenware shapes including Falcon shape ware, decorated with the *Ferndown* pattern (2374). This was one of a few hand painted patterns to be issued during the late fifties. Designed by Susie Cooper for the Susie Cooper Pottery, 1959-60. Height of coffee-pot 7½in. (19cm).

155. Examples of the popular *Black Fruits* pattern, printed on the bone china Quail shape. Designed by Susie Cooper for Susie Cooper China Ltd., from 1958. Diameter of large plate 8¼in. (21cm).

156. Notable patterns from the late sixties printed on the Can shape: *Columbine* dinner plate (C.2174), diameter 10⅝in. (27cm), the *Diablo* pattern teapot (2150) and *Keystone-Gold* (2133). Designed by Susie Cooper for Josiah Wedgwood and Sons Ltd., from 1968-69. Length of teapot from spout to handle 10in. (25.5cm).

157. A bone china Can shape coffee pot decorated with the *Pimento* pattern. Designed by Susie Cooper for Josiah Wedgwood and Sons Ltd., about 1968-69.

158. An extensive range of the *Gay Stripes* pattern (C.2141-2146), produced in many colourways, on the Can shape Designed by Susie Cooper for Josiah Wedgwood and Sons Ltd., 1968.

159. The *Cornpoppy* pattern (C.2176), printed on a bone china plate. Designed by Susie Cooper for Josiah Wedgwood and Sons Ltd., 1972.

operated for almost fifty years, was to shut down. In an attempt to appease her, she was offered a design post in any one of their subsidiary companies. After much thought she decided to relocate to William Adams Ltd, on Furlong Road in Tunstall. The move was assisted considerably by John Ryan, the manager of the earthenware division, who helped to create a familiar working environment by moving furniture from the Crown Works into her new studio.[52] Cooper developed a small range of simple and stylish patterns by means of rubber-stamping, including *Blue Daisy* on the Hexagon shape and *April* and *Meadowlands*, for Tesco and Boots respectively. Her *Florida* pattern was a reworking of a 1930's design, whilst *Blue Haze* was a new pattern from 1984. Cooper also experimented with reactive glazes, lustre and new themes such as the recumbent deer for a range of gift wares. Sadly her name was not allowed to be placed on the backstamp of the Adams ware, the Wedgwood management felt that it should not be used on earthenware. An exception was made, however, on two exclusive designs for Tiffany's in New York. For them she reworked the *Blue Polka Dot* pattern on Wedgwood's cream ware and a *Wedding Ring* pattern on the Simple shape. Despite the efforts of John Ryan to secure a good working environment she became increasingly frustrated and decided to retire. Shortly afterwards she relocated to the Isle of Man with her son Tim.

Interest in Cooper's work crystallised with a 'Pottery Ladies' television programme in

160. The *Chou Dynasty* bone china bowl (2207), printed with banded, aerographed and gilt decoration, diameter 9⅝in. (24.5cm). Designed by Susie Cooper for Josiah Wedgwood and Sons Ltd., from about 1976-77.

1985. Two years later the Victoria and Albert Museum organised a retrospective exhibition, 'Susie Cooper Productions'. To coincide with this event Wedgwood introduced three breakfast sets in *Yellow Daisy*, *Spiral Fern* and *Polka Dot*, all reworkings of patterns from the thirties. A boxed set was available for £99.00. They did not sell very well, probably due to the difficulties of takeovers and bids by other companies to purchase Wedgwood. Interest in her work saw the formation of the Susie Cooper Collectors' Group in 1990. A year later Christie's, South Kensington in London held their first specialist sale of her work, which raised over £80,000. In 1993 Cooper was honoured with an Honorary Degree from the Royal College of Art in London.

Early in the 1990s Cooper began to experiment with red clay in order to produce cockerel book-ends, intending that a small Stoke pottery would produce them for her, but nothing developed from the arrangement. In 1992 she celebrated her ninetieth birthday in great style, producing a leaping deer statue in a limited edition of ninety. She was fortunate to live to see her cost-conscious wares studied, celebrated and collected. Although she was not keen to have all her pots from different periods mixed up in a collector's cabinet, she was pleased to know that young people found her work of such interest.

Susie Cooper died in July, 1995 aged ninety-two. A special memorial service was held for her in October of the following year. In 1997 Wedgwood issued a special trio featuring the *Recumbent Deer*, an early eighties pattern that she had experimented with. She has left behind a legacy of good practical shapes, simple restrained patterns and an approach to design for everyone. Her work will continue to be studied, appreciated and collected for many years to come.

CHAPTER 6

SETTING THE NEW SHELLEY STANDARD

ERIC SLATER (1902-1984)

161. Eric Slater, photographed in the late 1920s.

The Stoke-on-Trent pottery industry was very closely knit for many years, the majority of the pottery manufacturers being family-owned. Moreover, whole families would work at a local factory in many different capacities; as decorators, packers and managers. In particular, the position of Art Director was often handed down from father to son. This was the situation when Eric Slater took over from his father, Walter, as Art Director and moved the company from traditional styles towards a modern look for the thirties by creating stylish and distinctive bone china wares. He presented the British public with an appealing blend of original patterns and shapes of such high quality that they set a new standard within the industry.

The Slater family had been involved in the pottery industry for many years. Eric Slater was born in 1902 and was raised in the Stoke-on-Trent area with his brothers and sisters. Both his father and uncle had worked as designers for Royal Doulton. In 1905 Walter Slater secured a new post as Art Director at Wileman and Co., creating a wide range of innovative wares that gave the company a reputation for high quality during the early part of the twentieth century. In 1853 Henry Wileman had formed a partnership with John King Knight, proprietor of the Foley Potteries, based in Fenton and they traded as Wileman and Knight for three years until Knight retired from the business. In 1860 Henry

162. A bone china Queen Anne shape cup, saucer and side plate decorated with the *Sunset and Tall Trees* pattern (11678). Printed in black with hand-painted decoration in orange. Designed by Eric Slater for Shelley Potteries Ltd., about 1929.

Wileman established the Foley Potteries alongside the Foley China Works. Two years later Joseph Shelley was recruited to the position of the firm's traveller. In 1864 Henry Wileman died and left the business to his two sons, James and Charles, although the latter resigned his position in 1870. In 1872 Joseph Shelley was offered a partnership with James Wileman, probably due to the sales that he had garnered for the company over the previous ten years. From this date the pottery was renamed Wileman and Co. In 1881 the son of Joseph Shelley, Percy, joined the firm and almost immediately Percy Shelley pushed for the production of the finest quality bone china. In addition, a showroom was opened in the Holborn area of London and to further promote the latest ranges agents were established in Australia and North America.[1]

When his father died in 1896, Percy was in control of the company. To maintain the high quality and originality of the wares he employed various artists and established designers, appointing Frederick Rhead to the position of Art Director in 1896. Rhead had an excellent reputation, having previously worked for both Josiah Wedgwood and Sons Ltd. and for Minton. For Wileman he produced an outstanding range of patterns including Intarsio, Urbato, Primitif and Pastello wares.[2] When Frederick Rhead left the company in 1905 the position was taken by Walter Slater. During the First World War pottery production was at a very low ebb. Walter Slater made an important contribution to the firm's production by introducing a varied range of wares. In particular he introduced a second series of the popular Intarsio range, from about 1911 to 1915. Other notable ranges include the Hunting Scenes (7684) and the Festival of Empire (7713) series that date from about 1911-12. He also produced Cloisenné (8320) in about 1920. Experiments were undertaken with lustres during this period, for a series of ornamental pieces, launched at the British Industries Fair in about 1920. A year later a substantial display of lustre ware was shown at the British

Industries Fair, and was admired by Queen Mary.[3]

Despite his father's success with Wileman and Co., Slater had no intention of following him into the pottery industry. Instead, he was interested in becoming an engineer, with an ambition to design trains.[4] After his formal education he took a position in the drawing office of the North Staffordshire Railway Company. The work was both hard and demanding and Slater soon realised that without a degree in engineering he could not continue.[5] Therefore, in 1919 he joined Wileman and Co., probably working for a number of years alongside his father learning the various skills and processes, whilst also studying. His art education was similar to that of the designers Susie Cooper and Millicent Taplin. He had a thorough training in design at the Hanley School of Art and won the prize for best student of the year in 1923, 'having evidently inherited the family trait for pottery design'.[6]

During the twenties the typical range of patterns included traditional tea wares decorated on the Dainty shape sets, designed by Rowland Morris in 1896.[7] A important part of the company's production, however, was for toilet sets decorated in traditional patterns. The late 1920s saw the introduction of charming nursery wares designed by both Mabel Lucie Attwell and Hilda Cowham, which proved enormously successful. The various patterns used many different themes and Mabel Lucie Attwell's wares in particular were in production for many years, certainly up until the outbreak of the Second World War, with some items being continued into the post-war period.[8] The company also produced jelly moulds and advertising ware. During the mid-twenties several important changes took place. In 1925 the firm changed its name to Shelley's and moved to a new showroom and agent in Holborn, London. In 1929 it became a limited company, with Percy Shelley's three sons becoming equal shareholders.[9] In that year Percy Shelley retired

163. A floral design (11839) decorated on the Queen Anne bone china shape, printed in grey with hand-painted decoration. Designed by Eric Slater for Shelley Potteries Ltd., about 1931.

164. The *Blocks* pattern
(11785), printed in black
with hand-painted
decoration. This pattern,
shown here on the Eve
shape, retaining the same
pattern number, was
originally launched on the
Vogue shape in 1931.
Designed by Eric Slater
for Shelley Potteries Ltd.,
about 1932.

to Bournemouth.

To promote the latest products and to maximise sales of the Shelley product the company took a deliberate move towards advertising more vigorously in the trade press. They appointed an advertising agency, Smedley Services, owned by Mr. W.H. Smedley, in 1925 to handle publicity targeted at the young middle class with modern tastes. To help retail outlets promote Shelley wares the company published the *Shelley Standard* from 1927 to 1931. This bi-monthly magazine gave advice on subjects such as displays, current patterns and advertising techniques. In 1931 Shelley also produced the Silver Book for the public incorporating modern stylish printing and borders with an embossed cover showing the various ranges available. Moreover, a successful marketing ploy was the Shelley Girl, depicting a stylishly dressed woman sipping tea from Shelley ware, used in trade advertisements. Further advertising was extended to national newspapers declaring that Shelley China was the latest fashion. Despite the extensive promotion undertaken the firm chose not to stand, for a number of years, at the British Industries Fairs, one of the most important trade fairs of the year. As a result there is little press coverage of the Shelley product in the trade journals of the period. It is probable that they felt their own marketing strategies were sufficient to boost sales of their latest wares.

During the mid-twenties Slater was given more opportunities by his father in the Design Studio. They worked together on a number of projects through which he gained confidence and experience. Slater's training at the Burslem School of Art, under the auspices of Gordon Forsyth, was radically different to his father's education. Under Forsyth's influence Slater recognised that he must develop a new modern approach to pottery design as the only way forward, within the context of industrial design. In 1928 he was appointed as Shelley's Art Director. Through many years in this position his modern approach to design, allied to an understanding of what the public wanted, resulted in great success. He carefully balanced the demand for the more traditional patterns and shapes whilst introducing new product ideas. Even though Slater held an important position at Shelley's he had to produce patterns to suit the company's management and to generate volume growth.[10]

As Art Director it is assumed that Slater was responsible for all the new patterns, shapes and glazes up until the end of the 1930s and during the immediate post-war period. At the same time it is also possible that other contributors may have submitted designs and the company would have used the services of open stock and suppliers of transfer printed designs from established manufacturers. Unfortunately little reference was made to Slater

165. The *Sunray* pattern (11742), printed in fawn with hand-painted decoration, on a Vogue shape bone china part coffee set. Designed by Eric Slater for Shelley Potteries Ltd., 1930.

166. The *Gladioli* pattern, printed with hand-painted decoration, on an Eve shape cup and saucer. Designed by Eric Slater for Shelley Potteries Ltd., 1930-31.

by name in the pattern books and other period material, and his name was not included on the backstamp, unlike his contemporaries such as Keith Murray, Clarice Cliff and Charlotte Rhead. Around the time of taking up his position pattern numbers had reached about 11592.

One of the first projects that Slater undertook was to modify an old tea ware shape called Antique to develop the eight-sided Queen Anne shape, launched in August 1926. The shape was traditionally styled but his new patterns gave it a modern fresh look, complementing the panels of the ware. Another pattern, *Archway of Roses* (11606), launched in September 1928, depicted an archway covered by red flowers in a garden with birds flying across the plate. This was inspired by a photograph he had seen in a London department store taken at a Buckingham Palace garden party. It must have had an impact on him as he returned to his hotel room and developed new designs depicting simple cottage scenes and gardens.[11] One of his most successful patterns was *Sunset and Tall Trees* (11678), introduced in 1929 (Plate 162). The company publicity boasted of Slater's '…new series of Garden Scenes which have met with such wonderful success both at home and overseas, where users will have a constant reminder of the beauties of the Old Country.'[12] Other notable patterns include *Sweet Pea* (11721), *Poppies* (11865) and *Cottage and Trees* (11873). The majority of these wares were decorated by means of the print and enamel technique and included stylised florals such as (11839), launched in August 1931 (Plate 163). In contrast to these wares Slater devised a series of startling patterns aerographed in black with coloured interiors, handles and covers. He later created the Princess cup shape only, as a variation of the Queen Anne shape, but this was in limited production.

Slater had been trained in the modern school of thought regarding design, with emphasis being placed on both form and function. With his experience of working with his father, his interest in engineering and his training at the local colleges, Slater was ready to move the company into a new direction by producing modern shapes and patterns that he felt would bring the firm back into the spotlight and deliver commercial success in a new market for the younger generation. In 1930 he developed the strikingly modern Vogue shape, which was unlike anything else they had produced. The range consisted of tea and coffee ware in bone china, with the dinnerware being produced in earthenware. The high standard of the bone china body and the shape made Vogue stand out above the shoddier interpretations of modern design produced by other companies. Several other manufacturers used shapes similar to Vogue, a good example being the Conical range by Clarice Cliff, but produced in earthenware.

Slater then set about creating a range of patterns that would suit the shape and also leave some plain ground. He wisely chose stylised modern abstract motifs such as *Blocks* (11785), produced in many alternate colour variations, which was used on other shape ranges such as Eve (Plate 164). Other modern designs included *Horn of Flowers* (11771). However, one of the most outstanding patterns was *Sunray* (11742), so evocative of the art deco period. This pattern was produced in several colour variations (Plate 165). A twenty-one piece *Sunray* tea set retailed at £2 8s 9d in 1930. The wide range of over fifty patterns designed for the Vogue shape caused the trade press to state that the range 'will cause people to stop and think. And if one can do that there is something to be hoped for those who, for a long time past, have been agitating for a more adventurous spirit in the manufacturing circles of the pottery trade'.[13]

Within two months the Vogue shape was followed by Mode, a modified version of Vogue. The Mode cup was slightly taller. The first pattern for this range was a simple floral design (11755) with banded decoration (Plate 167). Of the thirty-one patterns used on Mode the majority featured simple art deco motifs and abstract floral patterns combined with some banded decoration. Notable patterns included *Cornflower* (11844), *Apple* (11845), *Tulip* (11848) and *Iris* (11850). Mode retailed at a slightly cheaper price than Vogue.

Despite the good sales of both ranges, Slater was forced to respond to some of the criticisms made by both the trade and customers. The complaints focused on the solid handles of the cups that proved rather difficult to hold and the fact that hot drinks in the Vogue tea cup cooled too soon. In response, Slater developed a new shape range which answered these points yet maintained the innovative and modern feel. This new shape, Eve, was an interpretation of the Mode shape but had a firm foot at the base and an open handle. It was launched in the spring of 1932 and was in production until the end of the decade. The Eve shape was used for a number of print and enamel patterns such as *Gladioli* (Plate 166), *Crocus* (11952) and *Hollyhocks* (12019), that were available

167. A stylised floral pattern (11755), printed in black with hand-painted decoration on the Mode shape. Designed by Eric Slater for Shelley Potteries Ltd., 1930-31.

168. A page from a company catalogue illustrating the popular *Phlox* pattern (12189) on the Regent shape. Designed by Eric Slater for Shelley Potteries Ltd., from about 1933.

169. A page from a company catalogue illustrating the *Silk* pattern range (12235-12236) on the Regent shape. Designed by Eric Slater for Shelley Potteries Ltd., 1933.

with alternate colour variations, as were a number of banded patterns, such as (12133) from February 1933. Some of the later Eve patterns such as *Motif* (12293), released in May 1934, successfully combined a printed central motif with a shaded band, similar to a series by Susie Cooper, with her Dresden Spray pattern.

The introduction of the Eve shape was evidently a stop-gap before Slater could develop and introduce a new shape range that was more practical and attractive to a wider range of customers. This was the Regent shape, launched in September 1932. Its flared trumpet shape with ring handle was visually softer in form and contrasted well against the previous stark shapes that had proved limited in appeal. Over 200 patterns were decorated on Regent, and it heralded a new direction for the company. A testament to Slater's success was that Regent was still in production in the fifties. The shape was selected by Gordon Forsyth for special commendation and was also illustrated in his book *20th Century Ceramics*, published in 1936. A typical pattern was *Phlox* (12190), a naturalistic design featuring a complementary shaded band (Plate 168).

A wide variety of patterns was used on the Regent shape, including a series of banded

170. A page from a company catalogue illustrating the *Anemone Bunch* (12072) pattern on the Regent shape. Designed by Eric Slater for Shelley Potteries Ltd., 1932-33.

171. A page from a company catalogue illustrating the various colourways of the *Polka Dot* pattern (12210-12213) decorated on the Regent shape. Designed by Eric Slater for Shelley Potteries Ltd., 1933.

patterns called *Bands and Lines* from 1932, *Swirls* and *Silk* (Plate 169) from 1933. From the range of floral patterns *Anemone Bunch* (12072), a modern floral pattern, was typical (Plate 170). Slater's simple *Polka Dot* pattern, available in three or four colourways, was both stylish and restrained (Plate 171). These designs stood out above those of other manufacturers as Slater skilfully utilised the decorative method of printing. Rather than using the traditional stamp and fill method he incorporated the printed area, usually in sepia or grey, into the actual pattern to form a stylised background often giving it depth. This sophisticated use of printing is evident in patterns such as *Tulip* (12306) and *Iris* (12384). In 1934 Slater introduced the Oxford shape upon which he used a further wide range of floral, pictorial and abstract patterns.

Also in 1932, Slater developed a successful new range called Harmony Art Ware, introduced primarily on earthenware, evolved from his experiments in the design studio. The drip ware technique, as it was originally known, was discovered whilst he was applying the enamel colour to a pot on the wheel for banding. Purely by accident he stopped the wheel and the colours started to drip and merge. He then produced further

172. An earthenware teapot decorated with the *Harmony* pattern. Designed by Eric Slater for Shelley Potteries Ltd., from about 1934.

examples to show to Percy Shelley, who must have been suitably impressed. It was agreed to produce this ware on a commercial basis if the decorators could achieve the same high quality that was evident from the samples. The new range was successfully market tested in Leeds and later in London.[14] The designs were so attractive that the ware was made available for sale in both bone china and earthenware and was launched in several appealing colour variations. According to the trade press, the Queen found the Harmony Art Ware specially interesting.[15] As the range proved successful, tea and coffee wares were decorated with Harmony patterns on Vogue, Mode, Eve and Regent, alongside a range of cheese dishes, comports, ginger jars, cress dishes with stand and puff boxes, as well as earthenware tea wares and teapots (Plate 172). Existing white ware shapes were used but eventually some shapes were specially made for the range by Slater, including the volcano vase, probably seen for the first time by the trade at the British Industries Fair in 1933. This outstanding decoration echoed the Delecia pattern designed by Clarice Cliff.

With the Harmony range in production Slater started to experiment with what could be achieved with painted decoration. He created a soft pastel washband design, later called *Swirls*, decorated on the Regent shape. This range was first shown to the trade in April 1934. The opportunities for colour variation were limitless and occasionally a gold line was added to the edge of the ware.

Through the success of his new shapes and patterns Slater became a recognised designer within the industry. In 1933 he was elected to the Society of Industrial Artists

and Designers, alongside ceramic designers such as Susie Cooper, Millicent Taplin and Jack Price. In 1935 the Society held a competition for original design. Slater's submitted design gained the first prize for modern style dinnerware.

The success of the Harmony range may have prompted Slater to utilise earthenware. He modelled a number of vases, lamp bases and other assorted items that retained his strong sense of style and decoration. His handcraft range included simple spot and banded designs which proved popular. These contrasted with a series of striking vases featuring a solid black background for his patterns *Tulips* (8727) and *Jazz Circles* (8462) (Plate 173). Other notable designs include *Moresque* (8718), based on an earlier pattern by his father from about 1916-25 (Plate 174). At about the same time Shelley launched a range of 'Every Home Utility China' designed for everyday use and available in sets or individually. The range of pieces on offer was so extensive that one could purchase covered muffins, toast racks, triple trays and hot water covered bacon dishes. The publicity material emphasised that the range was efficient, economical and practical.

In 1937 the trade press reported that Shelley was producing bone china table lamps decorated to match the current range of patterns on offer.[16] The same article illustrated the Oxford shape, conservatively decorated with simple bands and gold printing, a contrast to the early Vogue patterns: 'It is definitely noticed that, both in shapes and decorations, there have been many striking changes in Shelley china quite recently. The severe angular shapes are much less in evidence, as are also many of these styles of decoration which many people are apt to describe under the sweeping term modernistic.'[17] During the latter

173. A group of lesser known patterns hand painted on earthenware by Eric Slater. Left to right: Vase decorated with *Jazz Circles* (8462), vase with the *Persian* pattern, a hand-painted bowl, vase decorated with the *Flora* pattern (8719) and vase with the *Tulips* pattern (8727).

174. Three rare earthenware vases. Left to right: Roumanian pattern (8319) decorated on shape 791, 1916-25, designed by Walter Slater, a rare blue *Moresque* vase by Eric Slater and a Volcano shaped vase decorated with the *Moresque* pattern (8718), shape and pattern by Eric Slater.

part of the decade Slater produced a range of simple 'country ware' patterns (Plate 175).

During 1938 several patterns designed by Veronica Ball were launched. There are no records or information on this designer although it is known that she started as an apprentice at Shelley's. Ironically, unlike the Art Director, her name featured on the backstamp which read 'DESIGNED BY Veronica'. This was probably added in response to the trend to give designers some recognition. Identified patterns by her include (12907) and (12908). These patterns, showing the influence of Slater, had a central motif of stylised flowers with a broad band of swirls, whilst pattern (12910) featured a ring of stylised flowers within the outer band.[18]

Like most other factories, Shelley's was greatly affected by wartime shortages of labour and skilled craftsmen. Many factories were amalgamated during the War and Shelley's was joined by neighbouring Jackson and Gosling, a company owned by Spode, and the earthenware factory was closed. The firm suffered from restrictions made by the Board of Trade but was granted a nucleus certificate allowing it to produce wares for the export market. Shelley's was licensed to export to the prominent markets in North America, Australia and New Zealand. The type of ware for these countries was essentially traditional both in shape and decoration.[19]

Due to his age, Slater was unable to join up for the Second World War. Instead he took great pride in his efforts with the Home Guard, often working through the night and then going straight to the factory in the morning.[20]

In 1945 Vincent Shelley, who had played a significant role in the success of the firm, died. As a result Slater and Ralph Tatton, the Sales Manager, were both elected to the

Board of Directors in January 1946. The task of rebuilding the business and meeting the requirements for both new machinery and a major reorganisation became the responsibility of the new management team under the chairmanship of Norman Shelley.[21]

During the immediate post-war period Slater began to experiment with new forms of decoration, moving away from some of the more overtly art deco patterns that he had introduced. He hand painted a few patterns on to large vases that were displayed in the showroom, these were probably one-off items. The patterns were preoccupied with nature using stylised leaves and feathers. Several of these were shown at the 'Britain Can Make It Exhibition' in 1946. Exhibits included a dinnerware set decorated with a stylised border of leaves, some large bowls and small ashtrays.[22] Slater was responsible for six of the patterns on show whilst the other was by Veronica Ball.

A wide selection of Shelley China was also shown at the Festival of Britain in 1951. Amongst the many Slater patterns notable examples included *Mountain Ash* (13656) and *Vine Leaf* (13659), shown in the Power and Production Pavilion. One of Slater's experimental bowls was shown in the Minerals of the Islands Pavilion.[23] His most outstanding design was *Simplicity* (13655), illustrated in the official guide to the Designs of the Festival.

For some years the management had discussed the need to adjust to new production processes when the war ended. They carefully planned to introduce new machinery to enable them to compete in an ever expanding market. Modifications to the layout of the factory were introduced by merging the two buildings into one and using the defunct earthenware factory as a warehouse. In 1946 Slater became a member of the Board of

175. A lesser known example of a printed *Country Scene* on an earthenware plate. Designed by Eric Slater for Shelley Potteries Ltd., about 1937-38.

176. A bone china mug decorated with a stylised leaf pattern that was developed from Eric Slater's experiments. Similar examples were illustrated in the *Decorative Art Studio Year Book* 1954/55.

Directors. New kilns were installed in 1946, soon followed by an electric glost oven in 1950. These improvements refined the quality of the ware and reduced losses. In 1953 the land around the factory was purchased and within a year the buildings on it were demolished to make way for new ones, built in 1960.[24]

The immediate post-war patterns and shapes were stylistically similar to those from the thirties, as they were still being produced for the export market. Of particular merit was a series of aerographed mugs with sgraffito and hand painted decoration, some of these were illustrated in the *Decorative Art Studio Year Book* in 1954/55. The foreign market demanded a combination of traditional floral styles allied to the highest quality of ware. This period also saw the introduction of new shapes, such as Henley, probably produced to appeal to a wider market, from 1938. Other shapes included Warwick, Ludlow and Stratford, the latter was designed for export. Slater's Perth shape, introduced in 1940, was decorated with a number of his patterns including the outstanding *Pine Tree and Heather* (13094). There was no change in the production of the company's wares. Apart from the more traditional patterns evident from the sales catalogues and pattern books, Slater produced a wide range of 'contemporary patterns' that were visually different from some of the more standard ones. In particular they featured simple feather motifs with banded decoration. Typical patterns included *Harmony* (13777) and *Rhythm* (13779), both on the Richmond shape. Two lesser known designs include *Forest Glade* and *Leaf*,

177. A part tea set decorated with the *Pole Star* pattern (13774) on the Richmond shape. Designed by Eric Slater for Shelley Potteries Ltd., 1954-55.

both illustrated in the *Decorative Art Studio Year Book* of 1954. One of his most distinctive patterns was the simple *Pole Star* (13774), produced from about 1955 in a number of colourways and similar to a pattern range by Susie Cooper (Plate 177). This stylistic comparison to Susie Cooper is also evident in other patterns such as *Serenity* (13783) and *Rhythm/Grey Crystals* (13803). Further patterns, used for seconds ware, included *Harmony* (2404), *Lyric* (2405) and one based on the pattern (12458) from January 1936, now called *Caprice* (2443). The latter dated from January 1960 and was jokingly called fish bones by the paintresses. The stylised leaves and ferns were also utilised successfully for a range of gift wares produced to complement the tea and dinnerwares and also to compete with the increased interest in the production of boxed gift wares, noteworthy items including a series of puff boxes.

178. A lesser known design by Eric Slater for James Broadhurst and Sons Ltd. The pattern, *Petula*, printed in black with enamelled decoration, was a popular seller for the company, about 1958-60.

Slater was a good friend of the Roper family, who owned the pottery company James Broadhurst and Sons Ltd. In about 1958 he submitted a pattern called *Petula* to the company that proved very popular and was produced in many colour variations (Plate 178).[25]

Changes in fashion and the new demands placed by customers were successfully met by Slater. His new Stirling shape, a softer organic form, included a coupe shaped plate to appeal to the North American market. The modelling was undertaken by Alan Forester, based on drawings by Slater. The shape was launched in 1956 decorated with modern stylish patterns very much in the mood of the day, including *Evergreen*, *Pastoral* (Plate 179) and *Snow Crystals* (13929). Another popular pattern was *Fantasy* (14190). In contrast to the new contemporary styles the traditional Queen Anne shape was in production for a limited period. The Stirling shape was followed by Avon, introduced in 1964 and used for a range of contemporary patterns such as *Fiord* (14280), a border pattern in pinks (Plate 180), *Hathaway* (14307), a large sunflower motif quite unlike anything previously produced, and *Naples* (14281).

From the late thirties Shelley's had attempted to make a significant impact on the Canadian market. From 1938 they produced a special line of wares stamped 'Ideal China' on each piece. Patterns ran from 051 to 0721. This line included a wide range of patterns, both abstract and floral, and was withdrawn in 1966.

In 1956 John Evans, a former apprentice who went on to study and graduate from the Royal College of Art, rejoined the company as a designer, but only stayed for a year or so.[26] In May 1965 Shelley Potteries Ltd. changed its name to Shelley China Ltd. Within a year, following the death of Norman Shelley, the company was taken over by Allied English Potteries, owned by the parent company S. Pearson & Sons Ltd. This group had more recently acquired Thos. C. Wild & Sons and Royal Crown Derby Porcelain Co. Ltd. At this point the Shelley family connection with the company ended and the Shelley site

179. A bone china cup and saucer and plate decorated with the *Pastoral* pattern (13893), printed on the Stirling shape. Designed by Eric Slater for Shelley Potteries Ltd., 1957.

was used for the production of Royal Albert bone china. The production of Shelley bone china ceased.[27] Slater was kept on by the organisation but working more in the management area, rather than on shape and pattern design. In 1971 AEP merged with the Doulton Group. Slater retired from work in 1972 at the age of seventy and enjoyed an active retirement, pursuing his interest in sports and golf and his passion for vintage cars, especially the MG.[28]

In 1984 Slater died, leaving a legacy of good design, simple shapes and an understanding of quality, originality and practicality. His shapes and patterns have come to epitomise the art deco period, attracting an increasing number of collectors. Over the last fifteen years Shelley China has become tremendously collectable, with special annual sales in leading auction rooms. The Shelley Group, a collectors' club established in 1986, now boasts members from all over the world.

180. A bone china part tea set printed with the *Fiord* pattern (14280). Note that the tea pot is lesser known. Designed by Eric Slater for Shelley Potteries Ltd., 1964.

CHAPTER 7

THE HANDCRAFT DESIGNER

MILLICENT TAPLIN (1902-1980)

Millicent Taplin made an important contribution to the productions of Josiah Wedgwood and Sons Ltd., an incredible achievement for any designer, not least one from a traditional working-class background. Due to her commitment and understanding of hand-painted decoration she became one of Wedgwood's most important designers, working successfully alongside Keith Murray and Victor Skellern who also rose to prominence during the 1930s. Taplin was prominent in the introduction of new contemporary designs, many for the lithographic process, during the fifties and early sixties. At the same time her work as teacher and trainer of Wedgwood's paintresses guaranteed the high quality of workmanship that the firm was renowned for.

Millicent Jane Taplin was born on 29 July 1902 into a working class family. They lived in a terraced house in Vine Street, Hanley. Her father, John, worked as a sanitary presser at the Whieldon Sanitary Pottery. Her mother, Lucy, besides looking after Millicent and her two brothers, Eric and Joshua, worked as a lithographer at a local pottery firm to supplement the family's income. Taplin's formal education was undertaken at the local Church of England school until the age of thirteen. After leaving school she took a job working as an assistant in a millinery shop. However, after only a month she was awarded a three-year scholarship from her old school to attend evening classes at the Stoke School

181. Portrait of Millicent Taplin, working on Rhodian Ware, 1928.

of Art. During her education she undertook a regular art and design training which included drawing, painting and throwing. Her tutors encouraged her to develop her artistic skills. Combining a full time job with evening classes must have been a challenge, and she later recalled that her experience as a student was rather sombre. The evening classes were not as lively as the daytime sessions and her only regret was that she did not have any time to indulge in student whims![1]

When Taplin showed an interest in ceramic decoration, her tutor told her that if she really wanted to paint he could secure her a job with Green's of Fenton, a small manufacturer. This informal introduction was the start of an illustrious career in the pottery industry lasting over forty-four years. Her role as a liner at this small firm was sadly not very interesting and she became rather frustrated with painting gold lines on to cups and saucers. Although this was her introduction to employment in the industry, she realised that the job lacked prospects. It was also poorly paid, her wages were only a half-a-crown a week. As she became increasingly impatient she began to look for an alternative position to make use of her skills and provide her with opportunities in design.

A position was secured at the prestigious firm of Minton's (established 1793) as a trainee paintress. The company was based in Stoke and renowned for the high quality of their wares. The majority of their productions, in both earthenware and bone china, were based on eighteenth century styles. During the early part of the twentieth century they made a conscious effort to develop modern wares. One of the outcomes was the Secessionist range, directly inspired by Viennese design, developed by Leon V. Solon and John Wadsworth from about 1902. The latter designer became Art Director in 1909. However, by the time Taplin joined the firm they had both left.[2] At Minton's, she learned how to paint the well known Pansy, Forget-me-Knot and Rose patterns that the company was justly famous for. This work enabled her to develop her hand-painting, standing her in good stead for future opportunities. This job was also poorly paid, and offered little opportunity for promotion within the company.

In 1917 she was able to secure a position with the prestigious firm of Josiah Wedgwood and Sons Ltd., established in 1759 and based in Etruria, Stoke-on-Trent. The company had a tradition of employing artists and designers in order to ensure the continuation of good design. The founder pioneered new production techniques, shapes and bodies such as Jasper. Underpinning his work was a belief in uniting art and industry. Taplin was appointed as a free-hand paintress working on tea wares, for which she was paid two shillings a week for the first six months. Shortly afterwards she was transferred to piecework in the hand-painting department, under the supervision of Ethel Tatton. They worked for forty-seven hours a week, starting each morning at eight o'clock. During her first few years of employment she continued to undertake evening classes for three or four nights a week at the Stoke School of Art. In particular she studied free-hand decoration and pottery painting. Further classes were taken at the Burslem School of Art on two afternoons a week, as part of her apprenticeship. Taplin commented: 'When I joined the firm there were about twenty hand paintresses working on piece work. After a while I was producing handcraft tea sets, dinner sets and fancies decorated with brushstrokes. They sold like hot cakes.'[3]

Before Taplin joined the company Wedgwood had established the production of hand-painted wares designed by Alfred and Louise Powell. Alfred Powell first submitted designs to Wedgwood in about 1903, convincing the management that a return to free-hand decoration for fancies, tea and coffee wares, could be commercially popular. An arrangement was set up whereby they would decorate blank wares at their London studio, to be transported to the factory for firing. In 1907 Wedgwood established a new studio for the

182. Pattern book entry for the Rhodian range, designed by Alfred and Louise Powell for Josiah Wedgwood and Sons Ltd.

Powells at 20 Red Lion Square in Bloomsbury. Wedgwood provided them with their own thrower and attendants expressly to produce one-off pots. The first exhibition of their work was held in the studio in May of that year. The success of these hand-painted wares came at a time when Wedgwood had made a conscious decision to change its traditional market and products. Although they gave the Powells a free hand in decoration, with a studio at Etruria at their disposal, the firm could not afford to employ them to produce pottery for a limited market. Therefore more commercial designs were introduced that could be produced in much larger quantities. At the same time, on a suggestion from Louise Powell, the firm revived some of the hand-painted designs from the original pattern books dating back to the eighteenth century. Not only did the Powells influence the firm's design output for the following twenty years, including the training of the free-hand paintresses, but they also inspired the young Taplin.

Together with a few other free-hand paintresses, she was selected to work in the Powell studio at Etruria. The thorough training they were given by Alfred Powell commenced with copying butterflies and birds on to paper, eventually progressing to free-hand painting on to blank wares. Although the training was slow, they were soon painting border patterns based on original Wedgwood designs from the eighteenth century. In about 1919, the Powells developed Rhodian, a style inspired by Rhodes, encompassing many variations on both earthenware and bone china wares. These patterns were often so complex that they had to be adapted so that the free-hand paintresses could complete the work and it could be produced commercially. In recognition of the additional time needed to complete the work, they were given extra pay. The Rhodian range (Plate 182), decorated on plaques, vases and dinnerware, was launched at the British Industries Fair in 1920.[4] Wedgwood promoted these new designs by producing several large trade advertisements. With the range proving so popular both at home and abroad further patterns were introduced, such as Persian from about 1926. These ornamental designs required a high level of skilled workmanship. As demand grew for hand-painted pottery more free-hand paintresses were recruited from the local schools of art.

The Powells were based in London for most of the working year, thus having limited contact with Wedgwood. They respected Taplin and worked with her on the development of new patterns. They also entrusted her to supervise the production of their patterns. On a number of occasions their designs were too intricate to be produced commercially, which was frustrating for both parties as they were always original and attractive. The Powells also recognised Taplin's free-hand skills and her experience in decoration, therefore giving her the important responsibility of adapting such patterns, where possible, by simplifying or reducing the amount of free-hand decoration required so that they could be applied to the range of shapes currently in production. This was a major responsibility and a positive step for such a young designer. The fact that the Powells, who had done so much to revive the fortunes of the Wedgwood firm, had entrusted Taplin with their designs, must have been noted by the management. They may not have had such success with their more commercial line without Taplin's skills.[5]

During the mid-twenties the Powells' work was regularly shown as part of the Wedgwood display at the major exhibitions and trade shows. These included the British Institute of Industrial Art Exhibition held at the Victoria and Albert Museum in London in 1923 and the British Empire Exhibition in 1924. They exhibited alongside other leading producers of pottery including W. Moorcroft, Carter, Stabler and Adams Ltd., Royal Doulton Ltd. and William Adams Ltd. For the influential Exposition des Arts Décoratifs et Industriels Modernes, held in Paris in 1925, Wedgwood presented an impressive display of their most outstanding products produced over many years, complemented by a selection of their latest designs. The display included a silver lustre coffee set designed by the Powells. Not surprisingly, Wedgwood received good press coverage for their display. Gordon Forsyth wrote, in the official review of the event: 'Wedgwood is not hide bound by tradition, and has devoted much care and thought to experimental work.'[6]

At about this time Taplin went to Paris, possibly to attend the Exhibition. Her visit generated a great deal of excitement in her family. It is not known how she funded the trip but the family was now slightly better off, with the wages of Taplin and her brothers coming into the household. With this income they were able to purchase a house on Oak Hill, just off London Road, Stoke, in about 1930. However, once Millicent and her brother Josh had married and moved away there was less money coming in and therefore fewer opportunities for their younger brother, Eric.[7]

During the late twenties the hand-painted patterns were proving so commercial that Wedgwood decided to set up a handcraft studio in 1926 to develop new ranges and maximise on future sales. Taplin was put in charge of the handcraft studio with the assistance of Margery Hall and Mary Simpson, who came from the Burslem School of Art, recommended by Gordon Forsyth. A year later the hand-painting department merged into the handcraft department, significantly increasing the number of free-hand painters. This department produced ranges by other designers, such as Victor Skellern, in addition to those by the Powells.

Taplin's experience of adapting and modifying patterns by the Powells over several years enhanced her practical skills and sound understanding of the limitations and possibilities of free-hand decoration. As demand grew, more girls were brought into the studio and were trained by Taplin. Eventually she began to produce her own designs, which were stylistically very similar to the Powells' work. Some of her earliest designs include *Buds and Bells*. Taplin also experimented with a range of stylised patterns on a number of wares (Plate 183). Taplin's painted monogram, a T above M, was often added to the hand painted earthenwares. Her handcraft patterns were given an 'S' prefix.[8]

One of the free-hand paintresses was Star Wedgwood (the daughter of Major Frank Wedgwood), who was also taught by Alfred Powell. Star Wedgwood designed several important and popular patterns such as Turkey Oak in 1932, Stars and Lady Jane Grey. In 1937 Star Wedgwood designed the Coronation pattern for the Coronation of George VI. Despite the harsh business climate and the difficulties that all manufactures faced following the Wall Street Crash in 1929, Wedgwood was able to stage a celebration, in 1930, to commemorate the birth of Josiah Wedgwood I in 1730. Louise Powell designed the special Bicentenary vase, decorated with stylised silver lustre vines and limited to an edition of fifty vases only. A pageant was organised by a committee of civic dignitaries to celebrate the man's work, with exhibitions held throughout the country.

In 1930 the company's trading surplus was a mere £44 which was a great drop from over £7,500 the previous year. This situation continued to worsen to such an extent that by the first quarter of 1932 losses were in the region of £6,829. Cuts in staff and wages were inevitable if the company was to continue production, although great efforts were undertaken to minimise redundancies. Sharon Gater noted that 'to some extent Wedgwood had been living on the reputation of its past achievements, but in the early thirties it began to take steps to recapture its position as a pioneer in high quality ceramics'.[9]

The responsibility of improving the contemporary situation of the the company can be attributed to the efforts of the new management team. To begin the restructuring of the works a new manager Hensleigh Wedgwood was appointed alongside Norman Wilson, as works manager. Improvements included starting a programme of modernisation and the imposition of a new management structure. In 1934 Victor Skellern, who had worked for the company since 1923, was appointed to the position of Art Director, succeeding John Goodwin. Victor Skellern had studied part time at the Burslem and Hanley Schools of Art and was taught by Edward Bawden at the Royal College of Art. Victor Skellern returned

183. A handcraft vase, hand painted in various colours. Designed by Millicent Taplin for Josiah Wedgwood and Sons Ltd., about 1928.

to Wedgwood as the only specially trained and educated art director. He was responsible for the company's successes during the following decades.[10]

Following restructuring, a brief was introduced for producing new patterns, under a very strict design policy. In order to increase profits the management were keen to promote a restrained modern style of decoration utilising simple painted motifs, thus allowing them to compete in the mass market by producing medium priced wares for the discerning buyer with sophisticated tastes. A letter from the management to the travellers noted: 'Starting in 1934, the number of new patterns put out per year will be strictly limited.'[11] At the same time, many of the expensive ornamental wares, such as the Fairyland Lustres, were cancelled. Victor Skellern co-ordinated design matters and introduced of a group of free-lance designers such as Keith Murray and Eric Ravilious. The popular shapes and patterns that Keith Murray designed for vases, coffee wares and other items made an outstanding contribution, restoring Wedgwood's reputation as a leading design company. His work was featured in major exhibitions and trade journals throughout the thirties. John Skeaping's animal figures enjoyed similar coverage. In the same way that Taplin had been influenced by the Powells throughout the twenties she was influenced again by Victor Skellern, with whom she worked closely for over twenty years.

Throughout the thirties Taplin produced an attractive range of stylish and topical patterns for tea, coffee and fancies, utilising various decorative techniques and glazes. Whilst many of these were styled with a hint of the art deco period she also produced patterns on more traditional shapes, on bone china and earthenware. It was during this period that she firmly established herself as a designer, which was quite an achievement given the considerable changes and upheavals within the firm. In about 1930 she used the Cane ware body for a series of stylised floral and leaf patterns for tea, coffee, early morning sets, dinnerware, fruit sets and cruets. A notable pattern, *Sunlit*, a stylised trellis border with floral motifs, was also produced on decorative vases, jugs and toilet sets (Plate 184). Another example of this period was *Papyrus* (W.H.3095), featuring a hand painted centre motif and stylised border. This design proved so popular that further variations were produced during the fifties – pink (W.4079) and blue (W.4080). As early as 1931 her work was featured in the *Decorative Art Studio Yearbook* which illustrated a tea for two in a stylised floral design (A.M.H. 8357) painted in silver lustre and red with a black band to the edge. At the same time, Taplin produced a range of stylised floral borders that appealed to the traditional Wedgwood market (Plate 185).

In 1932 Taplin married Joe Winfield and soon afterwards they moved to a newly-built house on Bank House Road in Hanford, Stoke-on-Trent. Some years later her parents moved house to be closer to their daughter.[12]

All new designs produced by the free-lance designers and the design team, including Taplin, were subject to a selection process. Twice a year the designs were laid out on a large table for the directors to remove any items that they deemed to be unsuitable. A second selection was made by the directors' wives, who selected items that they

184. The *Sunlit* pattern, hand painted on a Cane body. Designed by Millicent Taplin for Josiah Wedgwood and Sons Ltd., about 1930.

particularly liked. After this a meeting was arranged with the firm's travellers to ask for their reaction to the selected pieces they considered, with their experience, would sell. At one particular meeting in 1933 the examples shown by Taplin, including patterns on both the Paris and Colonial shapes (G.H. 7835), were commented on. A request was made for further samples of one particular pattern to be 'produced in various graded colour schemes' for the next meeting.[13]

As Wedgwood began to recover from the slump, exhibitions of the latest wares were organised to promote their artistic achievements. The British Industries Fairs in London provided an opportunity for the trade buyers and trade press to examine the latest products. From these events recognition of Taplin's contribution was forthcoming, both in the trade press and as part of the marketing strategy of the company, throughout the thirties. Wedgwood promoted its latest productions vigorously by taking out full page advertisements featuring illustrations of the ware. A typical example from the period illustrated a group of John Skeaping animals, vases and tea ware by Keith Murray and coffee ware by Taplin, all under the legend 'Wedgwood A Living Tradition'.[14]

Taplin's most popular and successful designs included *Moonlight* (S.196), an outstanding simple design of broken and wavy lines in silver on a silver grey groundlay (Plate 186) and *Green Lattice* (S.235), featuring a diaper pattern hand painted in green with a silver line to edge. *Falling Leaves* (S.243) featured small leaf motifs painted in green and grey (Plate 187), on the Globe shape designed by Norman Wilson in 1935. Both *Falling Leaves* and *Moonlight* were available in tea sets, early morning sets, coffee and a twenty-nine piece breakfast set. The success of the *Falling Leaves* pattern prompted several variations to the design, including a version called *Autumn Falling Leaves* (S.329) and a border version (W.H.3960) was produced a few years later. Her *Silver Buttercup* (A.M.H. 9612) pattern depicted stylised floral motifs painted in matt platinum, on a Moonstone glaze, on the Bow shape range. Taplin also produced a limited range of patterns, some in silver lustre, for the Annular shape, designed by Art Director John Goodwin and Tom Wedgwood in about 1932.

Following the Gorell Report of 1932 a number of exhibitions took place in London to show the public examples of good design. Companies such as Wedgwood and Moorcroft had always put good design at the forefront of production but smaller factories could not afford to invest in design and tended to copy and adopt the latest styles superficially. One of these exhibitions was 'British Industrial Art in Relation to the Home' organised by the Design and Industries Association and staged at Dorland Hall, Regent Street, London in 1933. Exhibitors included Susie Cooper, A.J. Wilkinson Ltd., Carter, Stabler and Adams Ltd. and A.E.Gray and Co. Ltd. The trade press noted that Wedgwood 'provided very clear proof of their determination to maintain their leading position in the industry. More than that however, it seemed to emphasise the fact that they are very definitely in touch with modern artistic leanings and capable of responding to this and even of giving a marked lead in special directions. Restrained modern styles of decoration

predominated as, for example, the application of simple, hand painted motifs, with colour lines at the edge, on a deep cream glaze. A case in point was pattern A.M.H. 9038 shown as having been designed by Millicent J. Taplin.'[15]

By the mid-thirties Taplin was at the height of her career. In 1934 she became a member of the Society of Industrial Artists, increasing her reputation as a leading designer. She became a member of the National Council of the Society during the Second World War. In 1935 her work was shown, as part of the Wedgwood range, at the prestigious Royal Academy exhibition. Good reviews were forthcoming for the Wedgwood products and in particular herself. The reviewer described her as 'a talented young lady who actually operates at the factory, and of whom it has been said that she is concerned not with art on industry, but art in industry'.[16]

For the Silver Jubilee Celebrations Taplin designed a tea ware pattern (S.254) on the Globe shape using silver lustre and painted decoration, each piece marked '1910-1935' on the base. From about 1935 she developed new patterns to decorate a range of embossed and traditional shapes such as Catherine, Wellesley, Corinthian, Patrician and Edme. In particular she used an attractive eighteenth century shape featuring a shell edge. Taplin also designed several patterns on shapes designed by Keith Murray, these include a stylised floral border (Plate 188) and *Springtime*.

To display its very latest achievements in design Wedgwood organised an exhibition at the Grafton Galleries in London between April and May 1936. Victor Skellern designed and organised the setting for this prestigious exhibition. The aim of the show was three-fold – to show the results of experiments in new design at Etruria, to illustrate the marriage between art and industry and to re-affirm the company's strong links with tradition. The catalogue stated: 'There is no conflict between the best of the new and the best of the old.'[17] Louise Powell, Victor Skellern, Keith Murray, Star Wedgwood and John Skeaping exhibited new ranges. Taplin exhibited the most – a total of eleven designs, including three stylised floral designs on the new Alpine Pink body, developed by Norman Wilson. These

185. A typical floral pattern, hand painted on a bone china cup and saucer. Designed by Millicent Taplin for Josiah Wedgwood and Sons Ltd., about 1930-34.

186. The *Moonlight* pattern (S.196) hand painted on a bone china coffee cup and saucer. Designed by Millicent Taplin for Josiah Wedgwood and Sons Ltd., about 1932-34.

patterns, (W.K. 3327, 3238 and 3239) were decorated on the Globe shape for tea, coffee and early morning sets. Her other designs included *Moonlight* (S.196) and *Wintermorn* (S.221), the latter on tea wares (Plate 189). A twenty-one piece tea set in the *Wintermorn* pattern was priced at £3.15.0. The majority of these patterns retailed at prestigious stores including Heal's, Saville and Co. and Spokes and Smith.

The exhibition also provided the management with an ideal opportunity to outline the latest moves by Wedgwood regarding relocation of the factory. For several years the directors had been deliberating on the future of the Etruria site, which was unsuitable for the current methods of production. There was also a growing problem of subsidence which could not be solved, nor could it be ignored; some parts of the factory were ten to fifteen feet below the level of the canal. In 1935 the directors decided that production would cease at Etruria and the firm purchased 382 acres near the village of Barlaston, south of Stoke-on-Trent, for the sum of £30,000. This site was allocated for a new factory, to be designed by Keith Murray and Charles S. White, with internal layouts to be developed by Tom Wedgwood and Norman Wilson. A press release of 1936 noted: 'The Wedgwood tradition prescribes a duty to the future as well as to the past generations; and the new venture is being launched with confidence on a rising tide.'[18] The foundation stone was laid in September 1938 and although it was hoped that the building work would be finished by the following year, construction continued, despite the War, until 1940.

In 1937, without having to submit any examples of her work, Taplin was placed on the National Register of Designers alongside prominent artists such as Susie Cooper, Eric Slater and Sam Talbot, the designer at Gray's Pottery. During the thirties her former tutor, the well-respected designer and artist Gordon Forsyth, asked her to start teaching at the Burslem School of Art in the evenings, but despite this recognition she felt that her poor education

187. Several bone china tea wares decorated with the hand-painted *Falling Leaves* pattern (S.243). Designed by Millicent Taplin for Josiah Wedgwood and Sons Ltd., about 1934.

and lack of design qualifications hindered her progress. Some years earlier, after completing her apprenticeship, Taplin had decided to develop herself further by undertaking a course at the Royal College of Art in London. Sadly she was unable to take up a scholarship to study as her family was unable to support her financially. She believed that had she undertaken the course she could have become the Wedgwood Art Director.

In 1938 a special exhibition was organised at Wedgwood's Hatton Garden showrooms in London. The trade press, praising the company's work, selected a design by Taplin, observing: 'A tea service, pink panelled and gold spotted, taking the number S.408, impresses us as being both up to date in spirit and very smartly rendered.'[19] A year later Wedgwood staged another special display featuring new patterns by Taplin such as *Chinese Aster*, painted on the distinctive Moonstone glaze and decorating a wide range of vases and bowls. Her work was prominently displayed alongside that of John Skeaping and Keith Murray. Four of her new patterns were promoted with individual full page advertisements, including *Briar* (S.420) on both bone china and earthenware, *Summer* (S.417), *Spring* (S.418) and *Autumn* (S.419). Further designs, including *Daisy Diaper* (S.403) *Fern Leaf* (S.421) and *Thistle* (S.422) date from about 1939 whilst others, such as *Dahlia* (W.H.3632) date from about January 1940.

Taplin's work was well represented on the Wedgwood stand at the New York World's Fair, 1939, by a *Moonlight* coffee set and a stylised leaf design on a Moonstone vase. (A.M.H.9516).[20]

With the outbreak of the Second World War further production of new wares was inevitably limited. To maximise profits, patterns were rationalised, with the decorative Jasper and other ornamental wares being withdrawn. From 1942 Government contracts predominated with utility ware being produced by Wedgwood. At the same time the

number of staff dwindled from 11,000 to 600 at Barlaston and seventy-five at Etruria. Sales of Wedgwood ware in America were higher than those of the previous year. Needless to say, the development of new designs, under such appalling wartime restrictions and conditions, was practically non-existent and as a result the London showroom was closed.

Gordon Forsyth approached Taplin again to ask her to teach full time at the Stoke School of Art, and she accepted. The designer maintained her links with Wedgwood, not least by spending one day a week at the Burslem School of Art, with Victor Skellern and Frank Dearden, learning about lithography. The firm was intending to introduce this process into their production during the post-war years, so it was important that staff designers were fully aware of the new medium. However, following the end of the hostilities, she returned to the company to develop a wide range of hand-painted patterns, as lithographic decoration had not been fully integrated into the firm's repertoire at this point. Her free-hand designs, from 1942, included the notable *Cynthia* (W.3976) which featured a solid yellow band with a central floral motif, decorated on the Globe shape. Other patterns of the period include *Westover* (W.3981), *Windmoth*, *Windrush* (W.3973), *Vanity Fair*, *Chestnuts*, *Acorn* (G.H.5600) and *Greensleeves*.

Victor Skellern was keen to see the introduction of lithographic designs for bone china and earthenware production. Wedgwood had never used lithographic decoration on its wares, apart from one occasion in the late 1870s. The company was reluctant to introduce this form of decoration as it believed that it would diminish the company's reputation for high quality and would force the closure of the hand painting department. However, the introduction of lithography seemed more favourable to the firm following the success of patterns, by Eric Ravilious. During the same year the hand painting department moved to Barlaston. The first lithographic pattern to go into full production was Charnwood, introduced in 1944, a floral design based on a pattern from the early nineteenth century,

which became a bestseller for over twenty years. At the same time Wedgwood reissued several nineteenth century patterns including Bullfinch, Napoleon Ivy and Willow, to appeal to the North American market. Taplin successfully utilised the lithographic medium for a range of popular patterns during the late forties and early fifties. One of the first was *Kingcup* (W.4050), a border design of yellow flowers introduced around 1948. The pattern was inspired by an actual specimen in her garden and was illustrated in the *Decorative Art Studio Year Book 1952/1953*. The designer recalled: 'One morning I was leaving the house, Joe plucked a Kingcup from our garden pool and commenting on its loveliness, asked if I'd ever really looked at one. I was rushing off to spend a few hours at the factory and took it along with me. I put it on my desk and eventually began to draw it.'[21] Another range of patterns, decorated with stylised floral motifs, was illustrated in the same year. This was a series of resist lustre patterns in either gold or silver on beer mugs designed by Keith Murray (Plate 190).

In 1955 Taplin became Head of the Wedgwood School of freehand painters. With the responsibility of running the studio and developing new patterns she set about creating a more artistic environment for her paintresses. To make the decorating shop more attractive she produced some decorative screens. Hand painted murals depicting dancers and stylised floral borders were placed around the walls of the workshop alongside boldly painted abstract and stylised floral decorations (Plate 191).[22] Sadly, throughout the fifties there was a gradual decline in the production of hand-painted decoration, albeit for the more expensive ornamental wares. A few years earlier however she had designed a selection of sensitive hand-painted patterns, many in silver lustre, for Norman Wilson's 'Unique Ware', a range of unusual contemporary free form shapes (Plate 192). This range often featured contrasting glazes such as a crackled transparent glaze inside the ware with a stone coloured exterior glaze. These special pieces were marked with 'NW' alongside the standard Wedgwood marks. She must have appreciated these short-run designs as it

190. A set of three resist lustre patterns. Designed by Millicent Taplin for Josiah Wedgwood and Sons Ltd., about 1951-52. (Shape designed by Keith Murray.)

saddened her that hand-painted decoration was on the decline.

The change in production coincided with the reorganisation and development of the firm's approach to marketing and promotion. During the Second World War new London showrooms had been purchased, though they were not opened until 1949. They were divided into three individual rooms for bone china, earthenware and new designs, the latter room designed by Keith Murray in 1951.[23]

The new premises incorporated sales, display and public relations offices. Alan Eden-Green was appointed as the first Director with responsibility to oversee the first of many national advertising campaigns by Wedgwood. The *Wedgwood Review* magazine, which provided up-to-date information on new products, was distributed to retailers across the world. In 1961 the Design Research Unit examined the company's logo, packaging and colours with the intention of standardising its image. This was extremely important in an increasingly competitive market. Simultaneously, further changes were taking place within the Wedgwood management team. There was a clear move away from family

191. The Handcraft Studio photographed during the fifties.

involvement which was confirmed when Josiah V resigned from his post as Managing Director to be succeeded jointly by Norman Wilson and Frank Maitland Wright.

Increased trade with the North American market after the War prompted the Wedgwood management to strengthen and develop these links. They employed Alan Price, an English designer, who had trained at the Royal College of Art. He was based in the New York office with the intention that he would maintain regular contact between New York and the Barlaston factory. The *Pottery Gazette and Glass Trade Review* in 1955 highlighted this new strategy and explained how the firm believed new designs should be developed for the large North American market. The article also outlined the successful teamwork approach to design. Victor Skellern was joined by Peter Wall, as assistant art director with two full time designers – Ulla Goodman and Millicent Taplin. The article illustrated several patterns, including two by Taplin, *Sunset* and *Sunrise*, featuring the same lithographic central motif with alternate shaded banded decoration, on Queensware shapes.[24] Another of her patterns, *Pinehurst*, an on-glaze print design, was highlighted in the *Pottery and Glass* trade magazine in 1954.[25]

In 1956 Victor Skellern and Millicent Taplin worked together on a new lithographic pattern called *Strawberry Hill*. This simple border design was submitted for the Design Council Awards for Design of the Year in 1957 (Plate 193). Out of 35,000 entries, twelve products were chosen by the judges. *Strawberry Hill* received an award for Wedgwood, alongside Midwinter Pottery, which had submitted plastic tableware. This prestigious and

192. A stylised floral pattern decorated on an earthenware lamp base. Designed by Millicent Taplin for Josiah Wedgwood and Sons Ltd., about 1936-38. (Shape designed by Norman Wilson.)

193. A bone china soup bowl and plate printed with the *Strawberry Hill* pattern. Designed by Millicent Taplin and Victor Skellern for Josiah Wedgwood and Sons Ltd., 1956-57.

gratifying award guaranteed phenomenal sales and critical praise for a design extensively advertised in bridal magazines. One of the judges, Milner Gray, commented: 'This exceptionally fine example of lithographed on-glaze pattern of strawberry foliage and fruit accords admirably with the classic shapes of the Wedgwood fine bone china which it decorates. The restrained colour and delicate execution emphasise the quality of the china.'[26]

In 1959 Taplin took responsibility as Foremistress of the china enamelling department following the retirement of Nellie Edwards, who had worked for Wedgwood for over fifty years.[27]

After more than thirty years of working for Wedgwood, Taplin decided to retire in August 1962. Following her retirement the studio was closed down. As there were no skilled free-hand painters at the works she had to paint her own retirement bowl. She decided to return to something that she clearly enjoyed – teaching pottery decoration at the Stoke College of Art. She took things a little easier and enjoyed, with her husband, a more relaxed life in their new bungalow on Meaford Road in Barlaston, near to the Wedgwood factory. Besides working in the garden, taking her dog for long walks and dressmaking. Taplin remarked that she was 'still finding enough time to do a little painting now and again'.[28]

She became involved with village life at Barlaston, taking on the role of treasurer for the good companions' group, which organised informal events.[29] This hard working and practical designer died in 1980 at the age of seventy-eight. Her work, once a bench-mark for quality and originality, has yet to be fully appreciated by design historians, collectors and those interested in twentieth century design.

CHAPTER 8

THE SKILL OF THE ART DIRECTOR

Victor Skellern ARCA, FSIA, NRD (1909-1966)

Throughout the twentieth century, ceramic designers worked in different capacities as owners, art directors or sometimes free-lance. For over thirty years Victor Skellern held an unrivalled position with Josiah Wedgwood and Sons Ltd. Not only did he design an impressive range of patterns and shapes but he also successfully co-ordinated design matters at Wedgwood. He is credited with bringing several artists and designers into the company. Throughout his career he remained a private person, unwilling to court the press and promote himself. He was described by Josiah Wedgwood as having 'artistic ability, co-operative personality, the capacity to study appreciatively different materials, techniques and tastes'.[1]

Victor George Skellern was born in 1909 in Fenton, Stoke-on-Trent. His parents were both schoolteachers; his father Harry taught for many years at the Cauldon Road Council School in Hanley, retiring at the age of sixty-one. He was a prominent organiser of school sports and was selected to play for the Fenton Cricket Club. Skellern's grandmother worked in the decorating shop at E. Brain and Co. Ltd.[2] Following his formal education, Skellern joined Josiah Wedgwood and Sons Ltd. in 1923, at the age of fourteen. He served his apprenticeship in the decorating shops and design studios. At the same time he studied part time at the Burslem and Hanley Schools of Art. Like other students, he

194. Portrait of Victor Skellern in the Wedgwood Design Studio, 1950s.

195. A plate, diameter
8¼in. (21cm), printed with
the *Forest Folk* pattern.
Designed by Victor Skellern
for Josiah Wedgwood and
Sons Ltd., introduced in
about 1934-35.

studied under Gordon Forsyth. He was awarded several prizes including the certificate of The Royal Society of Arts for pottery design.[3]

Shortly after joining Wedgwood, Skellern became assistant to John Goodwin, who had been the Art Director since 1909. They enjoyed a good working relationship. Skellern is credited in the factory records with painting several designs, mainly floral, in 1930.[4] John Goodwin, seeing Skellern's potential, encouraged him to enter for a scholarship to study at the Royal College of Art and Wedgwood released him so that he could attend a three year full-time course there, funded by a scholarship from the City of Stoke-on-Trent. While there he studied under Edward Bawden, a well established artist known for his wood engravings. Skellern specialised in stained glass window design. Most importantly, the three years at the College put him into contact with several important designers and artists who were later commissioned to design for Wedgwood.

Skellern completed his course in 1934. On his return to Wedgwood he was appointed Art Director, following the retirement of John Goodwin during that year. By taking up this position Skellern became the first professionally trained designer at Wedgwood, making him rather unique. Sharon Gater of the Wedgwood Museum commented, 'he brought to his new job an unusual combination of qualities – of management ability, perception, humour and lack of pretension'.[5] Skellern was also a very practical person who

understood how a designer should develop his latest patterns. He explained: 'Good design grows out of a sure understanding of good techniques. Therefore, a designer must have a sound understanding of technical limitations, and be able to appreciate the technical advice of his colleagues. On the other hand, he should be sympathetically understood when he ventures into the field of technical speculation. No designer can remain churning out new and interesting ideas if technical development is moribund.'[6]

During the thirties his new designs carefully balanced decoration and shape to create a completely unified object. His patterns were topical and reflected the current interest in the modern style, later known as art deco, with notable examples including *Sylphides* (W.K.3230) and *Snow Crystals* (W.K.3244). These were soon followed by a range of handcraft patterns such as *Anahita* (S.303), *Green Leaves* and *Persian Ponies* (Plate 196). Like other Wedgwood designers, his work was featured in the major exhibitions of the period including the British Art in Industry Exhibition at the Royal Academy in London in 1935. Examples of his work included his *Forest Folk* pattern (Plate 195), illustrating the influence of Edward Bawden's wood engravings. Another of his notable patterns, *Seasons*, featured four individual motifs reproduced in a graphic style, complemented by a stylised border (Plate 197). The designs, representing the labours of the four seasons, were printed in sepia. One of the motifs was used by Wedgwood for the company

196. A bone china box and cover decorated with the *Persian Ponies* pattern. Designed by Victor Skellern for Josiah Wedgwood and Sons Ltd., about 1934-35.

197. A plate decorated with the printed *Spring* pattern from the *Seasons* range. Designed by Victor Skellern for Josiah Wedgwood and Sons Ltd., from about 1934-35.

Christmas card in 1935.[7]

Significantly Skellern was involved in the introduction of new shapes such as Corinthian, which he produced in conjunction with Kennard Wedgwood in 1935. This shape, adapted from old moulds, featured a moulded border of leaves and was used for a number of new patterns including *Hampton Court* in 1937. At the same time he re-designed the Florentine pattern, originally introduced in the 1880s. This became one of his most successful patterns and was produced in a number of colour variations. Skellern's aims with regard to pottery design and decoration were outlined in an article by Maurice Rena in 1936, who said: 'Modern forms should be utilitarian and harmonious. There was all the difference in the world between good modern design which interprets fundamentals in human manner and "Modernistic" experiments in crazy geometry. Mr. Skellern wishes to emphasise the beauty of the material itself and is aware that applied decoration should indeed be decorative, conscious of its background and capable of enhancing the unity of the whole.'[8]

As Art Director, Skellern also co-ordinated the promotional activities of the company and most importantly the trade exhibitions. In particular, he designed the layout for the Grafton Galleries Exhibition in 1936. This exhibition featured the work of Keith Murray, Millicent Taplin, Star Wedgwood, Louise Powell, John Skeaping and Skellern himself. Alongside his tableware patterns, such as *Snow Crystals*, he also exhibited a black sgraffito bowl in olive green and a bowl in egg yellow in a separate display entitled 'Stoneware and Earthenwares in Special Glazes'.

In 1937 Skellern became an Associate of The Royal College of Art. The following year a further exhibition to promote the latest Wedgwood products was held at the London

BARLASTON

store Heal's, entitled 'Modern Developments in the Wedgwood Tradition'.[9] During the latter part of the decade several patterns such as *Greyfriars*, *Morning Glory*, *St. James* and *Woodstock* were launched, soon followed by *Fairford* and *Wildflower* during the forties.

Skellern made an important contribution to Wedgwood during the latter part of the thirties when he invited a number of artists and free-lance designers to submit patterns. These included Rex Whistler, Edward Bawden, Laurence Whistler and Clare Leighton. Skellern designed a new coupe plate for Clare Leighton's series of plates entitled New England Industries Series.[10] Skellern co-ordinated their individual contributions throughout development and production. Sharon Gater noted: 'It is important to recognise that one of the strongest qualities brought to the job of Art Director by Skellern was the ability to give one hundred per cent attention to the work of other designers without fearing his own status. Thus he was able to nurture the talents of those who came to ceramics from other disciplines with only a rudimentary knowledge of the technical demands of ceramic design.'[11]

Skellern worked very closely with Eric Ravilious during the latter part of the decade. They corresponded regularly to discuss the design issues and ideas for both new shapes and patterns. On a number of occasions, Skellern advised Ravilious how to go about the various methods of pottery decoration. During this period Ravilious developed new designs including Garden, Travel, Persephone and Garden Implements. In October 1938 Skellern sent Ravilious a letter explaining how lithographic sheets were produced and how the design could achieve maximum use from them.

Following the decision to move the company from the Etruria site to Barlaston a number

198. A commemorative mug produced on the occasion of the move from Etruria to Barlaston in 1940. Designed by Victor Skellern for Josiah Wedgwood and Sons Ltd., 1940. Height of mug 4⅞in. (12.25 cm). (Shape designed by Keith Murray.)

199. The *Green Leaf* pattern, printed on the Queen's shape. Designed by Victor Skellern for Josiah Wedgwood and Sons Ltd., from 1949.

of important events took place. In September 1938 the foundation stone at Barlaston was laid following a speech by Josiah Wedgwood V. In September 1940 a set of black basalt vases, designed by Skellern to demonstrate the crafts of throwing, turning and ornamenting, were laid under the foundation stone.[12] A duplicate set was also produced. To commemorate the move, Skellern produced an engraved design that was reproduced on the Keith Murray beer mug (Plate 198). The central motif depicted the new factory whilst on the reverse a view of Barlaston Hall accompanied small vignettes symbolising engineering, architecture and building. Apart from the standard mark on the base the following words were added: 'Presented by Josiah Wedgwood and Sons Ltd.' The alternate version, with pattern reversed, included the words: 'Wedgwood Barlaston Summer 1940 from first firing biscuit and Glost through Wedgwood Brown Boveri Electrically Fired Tunnel Oven 1200c.'

With the advent of the Second World War production of pottery at Wedgwood slowed down considerably. For some time Skellern acted as an auxiliary fireman. He was of an age to sign up for the war effort but the Wedgwood management wanted to keep him at the factory. Wedgwood protested to the Ministry of Labour in 1943 asserting that Skellern held an important position at the factory, and with his knowledge of the decorative techniques and production processes it would be incomprehensible that he would not be able to continue his work at Wedgwood. The management wrote to the Board of Trade explaining that, with the loss of other important staff, they could not continue to run the design department.[13] Wedgwood succeeded and Skellern remained at the factory and developed a practical range of eighteen functional and practical shapes called the Utility range. This set included three plates, designed to stack on top of each other, and a coupe soup to be used as a bowl for fruit or for serving soup. The cup, without handles, could be used as a sugar bowl.

At the same time Skellern worked closely with Frank Dearden at the Burslem School of Art exploring the issue of lithography. Skellern's foresight and experience convinced him that lithographic transfer prints could be produced to the highest standards for Wedgwood. However, the Wedgwood management was not initially keen on this method of decoration, feeling that lithography would detract from the high quality of current production and tarnish the company's reputation. Fortunately, as he was held in such high esteem Skellern was able to convince the management to produce a number of trials. He later recalled: 'Tablewares are very intimate objects, and their decoration is usefully seen at very close range – literally, at the end of one's nose. Reproducing fine line

work by these printing processes can give extraordinarily good results. Here it is possible to reproduce the artist's own calligraphy.'[14]

The extensive display of Wedgwood products at the 'Britain Can Make It Exhibition' in London 1946, included sixteen patterns by Skellern. One of these was (S.406), a hand-painted pattern on bone china. With his thorough understanding of the market both in this country and North America, Skellern carefully developed a series of new patterns. A notable example that demonstrated his appreciation of the market included the traditionally styled pattern *Green Leaf*, from 1949 (Plate 199). An earlier version of this pattern was printed in outline and then filled in by hand but Skellern's updated version was entirely printed. This successful pattern, a best-seller in the North American market, was decorated on the Queen's shape, originally designed for Queen Charlotte in 1765. The pattern was later shown at the Festival of Britain in 1951.[15] During the late forties and early fifties Skellern's patterns, such as *Astral*, *Evenlode*, *Pimpernel* and *Winchester*, were regularly illustrated in the *Decorative Art Studio Year Book*. *Sandringham* was illustrated in 1951/1952 and *Wild Oats* in 1955/1956. The latter pattern was very popular and was used by the Duke and Duchess of Windsor on the *SS America* as they sailed from South Hampton to New York in November 1954.[16]

During November to December 1949 Skellern, accompanied by John Wedgwood, went on an official sales trip to the United States of America. The intention was to visit the many stockists of Wedgwood ware and to examine public tastes and fashions so that they could capitalise on this important market. Skellern recorded the visit in a large format diary, illustrated with many snapshots and other ephemera. They visited several important department stores in New York, Chicago and Dallas. During his visit to New York, Skellern was taken around the Bronx and then to Coney Island. He recorded his experiences noting that, 'There is a field for contemporary ceramics designs from Wedgwood and one which we must pursue, not with the hope of immediate bulk reward

200. An example of the studio wares introduced during the late fifties. Designed by Victor Skellern for Josiah Wedgwood and Sons Ltd., from about 1956-58. Height 10⅜in. (26.3cm).

but to maintain the reputation and prestige of Wedgwood, which is undoubtedly higher here than in England.'[17]

Throughout his career, Skellern also turned his artistic abilities to other aspects of the Wedgwood company. In conjunction with other designers, he redesigned the London showrooms in September 1953, introducing new fittings and lighted egg boxes to display individual pattern ranges. He also designed the layout and production of company catalogues and often designed the front covers. One notable example was the cover for the booklet, 'The Making of Wedgwood at Barlaston', in grey, blue and green. He also undertook special production pieces such as the special Cranwell Memorial Vase made for the chapel at RAF Cranwell in 1953. This large piece featured a coat-of-arms and supports modelled by Eric Owen and finished with a speckled glaze, created to imitate the stone of Hopton Wood.[18]

Around the mid-fifties, following a request from the London showrooms, Skellern produced a range modelled by Eric Owen. This collection included vases, oval bowls and cactus pots featuring ribbed banding decorated with a Moonstone glaze (Plate 200). Each piece was produced in a series of four sizes and retailed from about 7s to 57s.[19] This range, that proved very popular for over ten years, bore a striking similarity to the work of Keith Murray. However, unlike his contemporary, Skellern's name was not included on the ware, which was stamped with the standard mark – 'WEDGWOOD of ETRURIA & BARLASTON, MADE IN ENGLAND'.

Skellern had the ability to assimilate the many aspects of what constituted a good design by identifying the various aspects for consideration. At a talk to the British Pottery Managers' and Officials' Association at the North Staffordshire Technical College he declared: 'Decoration is not simply a question of quantity. The use of a great number of processes, firings and hours of work is not the measure of the excellence of a good design. Decoration should add a sustained interest to the pot. It should enhance the shape-making play by texture and colour in the same way as a composer builds up a symphony from a single melody – or maybe the melody itself is sufficient. It is a question of values.'[20] A strong element that Skellern excelled in was teamwork. In 1956 he worked closely with Millicent Taplin to create the Strawberry Hill pattern. This simple border design was awarded a Design of the Year Award in 1957.[21] During the same year Skellern designed the new Savoy shape. Although modern in style, it fitted the Wedgwood look of the period and was decorated with a number of pleasing patterns such as Partridge in a Pear Tree by Norman Mackinson.[22]

In 1959 Skellern undertook a number of important tasks that included the development of commemorative wares. He designed the London jug and mug that was first used for the 250th anniversary of the birth of Samuel Johnson. Each piece bore the quotation 'When a man is tired of London he is tired of Life'. In 1966 this pattern was an award winner at the Souvenir competition staged by the British Travel Association and the Council for Industrial Design.[23] To celebrate the 200th anniversary of the founding of

201. The *Shakespeare* earthenware mug, printed and hand coloured in blue and yellow. Designed by Victor Skellern for Josiah Wedgwood and Sons Ltd., 1964. Height 4⅝in. (11.8cm).

Wedgwood, Skellern designed a black Basalt mug, depicting the Churchyard works, Etruria and Barlaston. The individual vignettes featured an ivy leaf border, printed in gold.

During the late fifties Skellern also designed several successful patterns, including *Asia* and *Avocado*, both from 1959. The *Asia* pattern won the Gold Medal at the State Fair, Sacramento in 1959. *Avocado* was decorated on the Catherine shape, based on the important service that Wedgwood supplied to Catherine the Great of Russia in 1774. In 1963 Peter Wall and Robert Minkin worked together on the 'Design 63' experimental project that gave them freedom to develop highly individual works. Skellern no doubt played an important role overseeing this project. For the 400th anniversary of the birth of William Shakespeare in 1964 Skellern designed six historical mugs that were awarded a Design Council Award. One of these depicted various characters from his plays, such as Hamlet and Henry IV. Inside the mug the dates 1564 and 1964 were hand coloured in blue and yellow, respectively (Plate 201). The design was sponsored by the 1963 Shakespeare Anniversary Council, Stratford upon Avon.

As Skellern began to suffer from ill health he took the decision to resign from his position in 1965. A year later he died. Wedgwood had lost its most innovative and honourable all-round designer. He could not be replaced. Instead, two managers were recruited. His significant contribution to Wedgwood during what was probably the most difficult period of the company's history during the twentieth century deserves both recognition and reassessment.

CHAPTER 9

SIMPLICITY AND SCULPTURE

KEITH MURRAY ARIBA, RSA (1892-1981)

202. Portrait of Keith Murray holding a black basalt vase (shape 3877), about 1936-37.

Keith Murray was one of the most innovative designers of the twentieth century. Originally trained as an architect, he moved into the fields of ceramics, glass and silver during the economic slump of the early thirties. Through his work he promoted a new approach to both shape and decoration that concurred with the principles of modernism. Murray encouraged a better understanding of modern design noting that Simplicity and Sculpture were the keys to good design.[1]

Keith Day Pearce Murray was born on 5 July 1892, in New Zealand, into an affluent family. His father, Charles Henry Murray, a stationer by trade, was born in Peterhead, near Aberdeen in Scotland. His mother Lilian Day Murray (née George) was born in Nelson, New Zealand.[2] The Murray family was based in Stokes Road, Mount Eden, close to Auckland. He had a brother, Charles. During his teenage years Murray studied at the Kings College in Remuera, Auckland. In 1906 the family decided to emigrate to Britain to live, the reason for this is unknown. When they had settled into their new home Murray attended the Mill Hill School in London, from the summer term 1906 until the following year. He then undertook a college education, at a slightly older age than was usual, between 1913 and 1915. After his father's death his mother returned to New Zealand, where she remarried.[3]

With the onset of the First Word War Murray joined the Royal Flying Corps in June 1915 and then the Royal Air Force in France from April 1918, until the end of the hostilities. He was awarded the Military Cross in 1917 and the Croix de Guerre Belge. He returned to London in 1919, where he trained as an architect at the Architectural Association School in Bedford Square, graduating in July 1921. He won the Stanhope Forbes Prize for best colour work. He was elected an Associate of the Royal Institute of British Architects, after completing the Special Examination for those students whose training had been interrupted by the War.[4]

For some years he was employed by the architect Maxwell Ayrton FRIBA, at the architectural practice Simpson and Ayrton, which was responsible for the British Empire Exhibition at the Wembley Stadium in 1924.[5] Murray also taught at the Architectural Academy between 1923 and 1925 but little is known of his other activities. He produced a number of paintings during this period, a notable example being a pen and wash drawing entitled 'Rue Montmartre' from 1925, possibly done during his visit to the Exposition des Arts Décoratifs et Industriels Modernes in Paris. Three years later an exhibition entitled 'Drawings from Spain', was held at the Lefevre Galleries in London in October 1928. The exhibition consisted of over thirty paintings,[6] studies of buildings, such as cathedrals, in Avila

203. The *Cactus* pattern (946a), engraved on a tall glass vase, height 15⅛in. (38.4cm). Designed by Keith Murray for Stevens & Williams Ltd., about 1935.

204. An unusual jet black glass floor lamp, 43¼in. (110cm) high. Designed by Keith Murray for Stevens & Williams Ltd., about 1935-36.

205. An engraved liqueur decanter and stopper, a glass beaker designed for the Royal Institute of British Architects and an engraved decanter and stopper (521a) dated 1934. Designed by Keith Murray for Stevens & Williams Ltd.

206. A group of vases and bowls designed by Jean Luce and illustrated in the *Decorative Art Studio Year Book* of 1932.

and Salamanca. Prices ranged from five to fifteen guineas and it is evident from the designer's copy of the catalogue that several works were sold, including 'Saint Miguel, Segovia' purchased by Maxwell Ayrton. Despite this initial success Murray seems to have exhibited no further examples of his work.

During the twenties Murray became interested in glass, inspired by one of his friends who had a large collection. He purchased some Victorian pieces, paying between ten shillings and two pounds for them. He gradually analysed what he felt was wrong with these examples and decided that their shapes were poor.[7] He was particularly interested in the range of Swedish glass exhibited at the Exposition des Arts Décoratifs et Industriels Modernes, where he would have seen examples by Orrefors, the leading Swedish manufacturer. Murray noted some years later: 'It was only at the Paris exhibition of 1925, where I first saw modern continental glass, that I realised for the first time that there was no reason whatsoever why English glass should not be beautiful too. It was, in fact, only a matter of design and good taste.'[8]

British design commentators during this period gave great praise to the current

207. Three bowls, shape (3753) decorated with a matt green, matt straw and blue glaze. Designed by Keith Murray for Josiah Wedgwood and Sons Ltd. Introduced in 1933. Height of tallest bowl 6½in. (16.5cm).

208. Four examples of the (3801) shape vase decorated in moonstone, matt green, blue and grey. Designed by Keith Murray for Josiah Wedgwood and Sons Ltd. Introduced in 1933. Height 5⅞in. (15cm).

209. A tall hand-thrown shoulder vase, shape (3805), height 11in (28cm), decorated with a matt straw glaze. Designed by Keith Murray for Josiah Wedgwood and Sons Ltd. Introduced in 1933 and in production for several years.

210. A hand-thrown vase, shape (3802), height 8½in. (21.5cm), decorated with a matt straw glaze. Designed by Keith Murray for Josiah Wedgwood and Sons Ltd. Introduced in 1933.

Scandinavian designs following an important exhibition in Stockholm in 1930. The following year an exhibition of Swedish Industrial Art was staged at the Dorland Hall, London between March and April. Murray was attracted to Swedish design, which was simple, plain and modern. He was drawn to Simon Gate's work for Orrefors, who would later influence Murray's approach to form and decoration. Furthermore some of his later work for Wedgwood bore a distinct resemblance to the glass designs exhibited at the Swedish exhibition.[9] The designs for glass that he saw, produced in Finland, Austria and Sweden, convinced him that English glass should be given a modern expression to compete with the European manufacturers. Several British manufacturers were very positive about this exhibition, leading them to review their current product ranges and possibly emulate some of the styles and designs.

During the late twenties and early thirties the economic problems endured by British industry directly affected architectural practices throughout the country and as a result Murray was unable to establish himself as an architect. He lived in a studio flat at 3a Gloucester Road, South Kensington, and due to his difficulty in gaining work he would spend long hours sitting in the local park trying to decide what he should do.[10] In about December 1931, Murray started to develop glassware designs, on paper, which he felt met the requirements

for contemporary glass. During this formative period of design his good friend Major Longden introduced him to Harry Trethowan, Sales Director of Heal's, and Arthur Marriot Powell, the owner of the glass manufactory Whitefriars. He agreed to produce six experimental pieces but it soon became apparent that his designs were not suited to their production process. Murray was forced to look for other possible manufacturers. After several unsuccessful contacts he was put in touch with Hubert Williams-Thomas, the Managing Director of Stevens & Williams Ltd., who was prepared to work on a selection of trial shapes designed by Murray and had already discussed Murray's designs with two influential men, the designer Gordon Russell and Sir Ambrose Heal, the influential furniture designer and owner of the fashionable store, Heal's,

The history of Stevens & Williams Ltd. goes back to 1776, when Robert Honeyborne established the factory. The Williams-Thomas family was connected with the glass works from about 1824. In 1845 William Stevens and Samuel Cox Williams took over the company and in 1870 a new factory was built on Brierley Hill in the West Midlands. Stevens & Williams Ltd., under the artistic director John Northwood I, soon gained a reputation for high quality lead crystal glass, with agents in Australia, New Zealand and South Africa. The company exhibited at the Exposition des Arts Décoratifs et Industriels Modernes, but their highly decorated designs were not in the modern style, harking back to an earlier period. During the early thirties the name was changed to Royal Brierley Crystal following its appointment as the Royal British Glass makers.[11]

During 1932 Murray took his prototypes to the company and the Director chose three designs that he considered most suitable for its production. Murray commented: 'Now began a period of alterations and editing in which I had to adapt myself to the materials and the processes, and in which the factory had to adapt itself to my conception of form.'[12] The resultant glasswares must have appealed to the management as a formal agreement

211. An unusual shoulder vase, shape (3820), height 7in. (17.8cm), decorated with a matt blue glaze. Designed by Keith Murray for Josiah Wedgwood and Sons Ltd. Introduced in about 1933-34.

212. Four beer jugs, left to right, (3845), (3844), (3974) and (3822). Although these items were featured in company advertising material it seems that all but (3822) were discontinued after a few years. Designed by Keith Murray for Josiah Wedgwood and Sons Ltd. About 1933-34. Height of tallest jug 9¼in. (23.6cm).

was made for Murray to design for Stevens & Williams Ltd. Murray was contracted to work for them for three months a year, being paid in the region of £225 annually, plus expenses. The only stipulation was that he was to design glass solely for them for the duration of the contract. Murray concluded that if he could secure three other freelance positions he could earn £1,000 a year, quite a considerable sum in those days.[13] The first examples of his glass were shown at an exhibition at the London showrooms in October 1932. These included cocktail sets, vases, sherry sets and decanters. In contrast to Murray's work there was also a display of the company's standard products that were stylistically very different. In December of that year Murray showed a Mr. Stephen Tallents, Secretary to the Empire Marketing Board, around the London showrooms. Following this productive meeting with the designer he wrote to Stevens & Williams Ltd. to inform them that at the annual dinner of the Design and Industries Association he had paid a brief tribute to this new enterprise and promised that he would do what he could to enlist further interest.[14]

Murray produced over 150 designs each year. Whilst the majority of his patterns were plain, banded or tinted he also designed many intricate floral, geometric and abstract patterns. One recurring motif was the *Cactus* design (946a), produced in many different versions (Plate 203). Lesser known patterns include one depicting a helicopter (350a), a leaping deer (705a) and seagulls flying above the sea (801a). All his work was entered into the Keith Murray Description Book and given a number, ranging from 100a to 1198a, although this last number had no shape alongside it in the book. However, establishing dates for his designs has proved rather problematic. A stylised green glass vase (591a) was exhibited at the Paris Exhibition in 1937.[15] Not all of his designs were actually put into production and it is noteworthy that he was not the only company designer. Each piece he made was marked with his initials and 'Royal Brierley'. The company extensively advertised his work through special brochures and trade advertisements. The first advertisement declared: 'Something fresh at last to satisfy a growing demand. Specimens of this achievement in Modern Glassware can be inspected in our London showrooms.'[16]

Within a few years new lines such as bathroom sets, in various colours, and sherry and

213. Examples of three beer mugs designed by Keith Murray, each decorated with a champagne glaze. Left to right: (3810) (3970) and (3971). About 1933-34.

liqueur sets were selling alongside more unusual items including a glass candlestick and an audacious glass floor lamp, probably designed to appeal to the bachelor flat owner (Plate 204). Murray undertook a number of important commissions in glass, furthering his own reputation as an innovative designer and enhancing that of the company. In November 1934 he designed a set of wine glasses and tumblers decorated with star motifs, for the Banqueting Suite of the Royal Institute of British Architects on the opening of their new building (Plate 205). A year later he designed glassware for the new Orient cruise liner *SS Orion*.

Royal patronage was forthcoming at the British Industries Fairs throughout the thirties. In 1934 the trade press reported that the Duchess of York had purchased some pieces in black and flint crystal. The same reporter noted the remarks made by the Queen at the Royal Brierley stand, 'I suppose those are rather expensive? the Queen remarked when examining some of these new pieces, but an assurance was promptly forthcoming that this was not the case. We are out to beat the foreigner was the reply of Mr. Williams-Thomas, jnr.'[17]

Murray's strongly held beliefs on good design for glass, and later for ceramics, were enthusiastically asserted in a number of articles for journals and in lectures to designers and manufacturers. Some of these articles were printed in influential magazines such as *Design for Today*, which gave him the opportunity to outline his own thoughts on design for glass, explaining that form was more important than pattern, and if used it should work to express the form. He also believed that designers should work within the capabilities of the facilities available. He was very critical of the type of British glass decoration that tended to cut heavily into the shape. However, it seems that on occasion he may have been asked to produce the same type of ware. This was echoed in a review of his glass in 1933, which noted: 'He does not abuse cutting and has created some glass that is both romantic and functionally agreeable. It is when he tries to compromise and employ our excellent cutters to do only a certain amount of labour that he fails to come off, and the moulded examples also seem not quite good.'[18]

Firmly established as a contemporary designer, Murray was approached by Josiah

214. Archive photograph
used to promote the beer jug
and mugs in about 1935.

Wedgwood and Sons Ltd. in 1932. For a number of years Wedgwood had been feeling the effects of the economic slump, following the Wall Street Crash of 1929, and was making a concerted effort to improve its position. The new Chairman, Josiah V, was an economist who had recently gained a degree at the London School of Economics. Despite being slightly inexperienced in design matters, he was determined to introduce innovative new designs that would maintain their high reputation, but more importantly restore the company's profits. He was assisted by Tom Wedgwood, his cousin, and the production manager Norman Wilson. Josiah V took the decision to rationalise production and concentrate on simple modern tablewares. In 1934 Victor Skellern was appointed as Art Director, having recently qualified from the Royal College of Art. Wedgwood's reputation for commissioning artists skilled in areas other than ceramics had rather lapsed since the eighteenth century. The need to introduce talented designers, such as Murray, was both economically and artistically based.[19]

Murray's introduction to the company was organised by Felton Wreford, the manager of the London showrooms. Murray's visit to Wedgwood was fruitful and he was shown the important aspects of design, production and decoration. Before a formal arrangement was made he was asked to assist in the development of the Annular shape, designed by Tom Wedgwood and John Goodwin. Murray was asked to design the two vegetable dishes, that were modelled from his drawings in about October 1932. This distinctive range, developed for Rouard of Paris, was launched in 1933. Following this exercise a formal arrangement was made between Murray and Wedgwood whereby he would work for them for forty-eight working days a year and be paid a fee of £125 per annum, with a monthly retainer plus royalties.[20] His appointment was to design new shapes for the

company rather than patterns, unlike the other free-lance designers. Murray studied the various production processes at the factory, enabling him to gain a thorough appreciation of the skills of throwing and turning, assisted by Norman Wilson, who played a significant part in Murray's success. His pieces were traditionally thrown and finished on the lathe to give them sharpness, successfully achieved by skilled craftsmen. The decision to make his wares by hand was partly economic. Firstly, with the financial difficulties faced by the company, the development of costly moulds was ruled out and secondly, this form of manufacture would secure the jobs of the skilled men. Murray often watched the head turner, Tom Simpson, at work, sometimes directing him in a particular way. These first productions, made in Queen's ware, do bear a striking resemblance to a series of earthenware flower vases and bowls with a matt finish by Jean Luce of Paris (Plate 206).[21]

Murray must have started work immediately as a full range of pieces was ready in the spring of 1933. These featured horizontal banding or incised bands that made them look as though they had been machine made. They were entered into the standard Wedgwood shape book and it is assumed that his first shape was (3753), which was the first entry (Plate 207). An important aspect of Murray's shapes was the distinctive glazes that were used on them. These were developed by Norman Wilson. The choice of matt glazes included grey, straw, deep ivory, green, turquoise and a cream coloured glaze called champagne. Norman Wilson recalled that there were a few problems during the development of this range, as the design team found that some of the matt glazes were easily marked by silverware. These were subsequently withdrawn. Unusually for the company, Murray's facsimile signature was incorporated into the company backstamp which read: 'Keith Murray, WEDGWOOD, MADE IN ENGLAND.'

Murray's work was launched during a period of heated debates about mass production, employment and other important issues that were threatening the survival of the pottery

215. Two examples of black basalt showing a beaker (3884) and vase (3870). Designed by Keith Murray for Josiah Wedgwood and Sons Ltd., from about 1934-36. Height of vase 5⅛in. (13cm).

216. A drawing of a black basalt vase in the Wedgwood Shape Book, about 1934.

217. Two examples of the ribbed coffee set in black basalt or with a moonstone glaze. Designed by Keith Murray for Josiah Wedgwood and Sons Ltd. in about 1934. Height of coffee-pot 7¼in. (18.4 cm).

industry. Interestingly, his wares did not sell well initially and it was only when the design commentators of the period and the trade press started to praise this new and innovative approach to pottery design that they became popular.[22] His work was first displayed at the British Industrial Art in Relation to the Home Exhibition, at Dorland Hall, in the summer of 1933. The display included the (3753) bowl, produced in four sizes, and the vase (3765), that bore a similarity to the Annular range. Also on show was a smaller vase (3801), featuring incised banding (Plate 208) alongside a large shoulder vase (Plate 209) and a footed bowl (3806) (see page 16). These were also illustrated in a company advertisement in the magazine *Design for Today*, in July of that year. The trade press reported: 'the special object of demonstrating qualities of form and colour, and the development of a classic tradition on modern lines, rather than the technical skill of elaborate ornament.'[23]

In order to reach a wider market advertisements were placed in the leading design magazines with the emphasis being placed on the fact that they were stylish but affordable wares, suitable for the modern home. Wedgwood's publicity boasted: 'Keith Murray has seen how to build on the Wedgwood tradition an entirely new style of design, making full use of Wedgwood craftsmanship and fineness of material. His designs are characterised by virile shapes and clear cut lines.'[24] Murray's work was also displayed at the fifth Triennale in Venice in 1933, where he won a gold medal. He was informed of this by letter from E.R. Eddison, of the Department of Overseas Trade.[25]

In November 1933 over 124 different items were shown at the London department store, John Lewis, on Oxford Street. At about this time Wedgwood produced a special sales catalogue to illustrate Murray's range of items, divided into sections such as 'Vases and

Bowls', 'Mugs and Jugs' and items 'For Desk, Table and Mantelpiece'. The selected patterns ranged from 3753 to 3881, and included the (3802) vase (Plate 210) and the (3820) vase (Plate 211). The beer jugs, produced in grey, straw or deep ivory glazes (Plate 212), were illustrated alongside the beer mugs (Plate 213). Two lesser known shapes, a jug (3843) and mug (3810), were available in white, green and deep ivory glaze. Further shapes and glazes were added. The most popular of these, (3810), was extensively advertised in the trade press and found favour with many design commentators including Herbert Read, who declared that these were better than anything else in modern English ceramics (Plate 214).

Over the next few years Murray continued to add several new shapes with a number in Black Basalt bodies, perfected by Josiah Wedgwood I in the late 1760s, for a series of bowls, vases and beakers (Plate 215). These were entered alongside his other shapes into the standard Shape Book (Plate 216). The shapes used ranged from about 3813 to 4062, and were also used for matt glazes. For a limited period Murray's wares were produced in new experimental bodies such as Bronze and Copper Basalt for a range of items, including a vase (3818), a beaker (3884) and a tobacco jar (3862). These retailed from 11/9, 6/3 and 16/3, respectively. Murray also developed a shape for a coffee set, but it was rejected by the Wedgwood selection committee in favour of an older shape that was modified so that the spout wouldn't drip.[26] The ware, featuring ribbed decoration, was produced with a moonstone glaze and also on Black Basalt, although only the coffee pot, milk and sugar were produced on the latter body (Plate 217).

A range of cheaper shapes was introduced by Wedgwood based on Murray's designs.

218. These two slip-cast items were first introduced in about 1936. Both the bath salt jar (4125) and the powder bowl (4113) are decorated with a matt green glaze. Designed by Keith Murray for Josiah Wedgwood and Sons Ltd. Width of bowl 5¾in. (14.6cm).

219. Six cocktail cups (3999) decorated with a matt green glaze. Designed by Keith Murray for Josiah Wedgwood and Sons Ltd. about 1933-34. Height 3in (7.5cm).

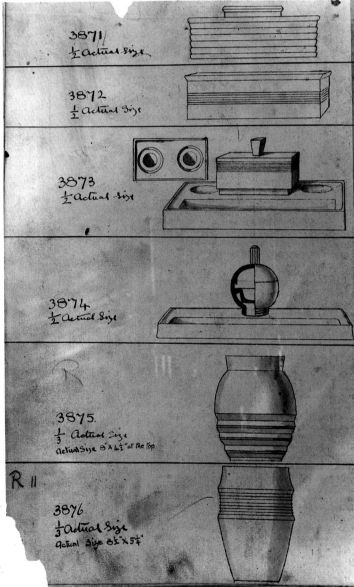

220. An entry in the Wedgwood Shape Book showing the various small gift ranges designed by Keith Murray in about 1934-36.

These were slip cast, a method used by Josiah Wedgwood many years earlier. This process, updated by Norman Wilson, allowed for faster and cheaper production. The range included simple fluted vases, table lamps and smaller pieces such as an ink stand (3873), ashtray (3881), cigarette box (3871/72), powder box (3866), bath-salt jars (Plate 218) and cocktail cups (Plate 219). These items were all entered into the company's Shape Book (Plate 220). The slip-cast beer mugs, decorated with either an ivory or champagne glaze, retailed at half the price of the tankards shown at the Royal Academy of Arts in 1935. These mugs had ribbed sides, skilfully disguising the seam marks left by the mould.

Observing Murray's skilled work with these more practical items may have prompted the written request from Josiah Wedgwood V in October 1933, for Murray to design patterns that could be more economically produced: 'What I should like is for you to turn your attention to the design of new cheap shapes, attractive to modern eyes, for the essential pieces of dinner and tea sets. Along with alternative suggestions for patterns of a simple character for hand painting, engraving or litho.'[27] Murray created a wide range of patterns for both table and dinner wares. The first thirteen of these were in development by April 1934.[28] One of the first was *Iris* (AMH 9613), a hand painted pattern in green and platinum on a moonstone glaze on the Trent shape, advertised in November 1934. Further patterns included *Green and Silver Willow* (S.22), *Red Pimpernel* (AMH 9548) and *Radio*. A notable design was *Lotus*, a stylised sprig, produced in two colourways – russet red and bronze (S.70) and green and silver (S.203). This distinctive pattern was decorated on tea sets priced at £2.3s.6d and early morning sets for £1.0s.6d (Plate 221). Further patterns included *Tulip*, *Wheat Border* and *Weeping Willow*, also known as *Green Tree* (AL 9679) (Plate 222). Murray also designed the decoration for the Savoy Hotel's new china, featuring banded decoration in platinum and green, with the monogram.

Around 1934 Murray was approached by the prestigious Mappin and Webb Ltd. to produce a number of silverware items for them. The company was keen to be represented in the forthcoming British Art in Industry exhibition at the Royal Academy in 1935. As the criteria for selection stated that items had to demonstrate an understanding of modern design, it was decided to commission Murray. He designed several items, including a tea

221. An example of one of the few patterns for tableware designed by Keith Murray. This example is *Lotus* (S.70) on a bone china teapot and jug, about 1935-36.

222. An earthenware plate decorated with the *Green Tree* pattern. Designed by Keith Murray for Josiah Wedgwood and Sons Ltd., about 1933-34.

service, silver tankard, a silver bowl with ivory feet and three presentation cups (Plate 223). The silver tea set retailed at £30 in 1935. He also designed some cheaper electroplated items such as a cocktail set (Plate 224) and a casserole dish and part tea service (Plate 225). Many of these items were exhibited at the Royal Academy. Although the company published a special catalogue, the range, according to the designer, was not produced in great numbers.[29] At the same exhibition Murray also exhibited over twenty-five different items in glass, including a rose bowl, various vases and a lemonade jug. In the accompanying exhibition catalogue he was credited with designing a hair brush coromandel and iron for G. Betjemann and Sons Ltd.

The display of Wedgwood ware at the Royal Academy included vases, bowls and Murray's coffee ware. His (3805) vase was described in the catalogue: 'This tall vase has personality. It can dominate its setting, or become an unobtrusive essential to a well-planned room. It is also an admirable lamp holder.'[30] However, the trade criticised Murray, stating: 'His incurved tankards have not, to me, such a good flow, and the cream half pint with its ungainly and inappropriate handle and its high foot rim (as if reducing one's half) suggests that Mr. Murray has still some distance to travel on the ceramic path. I liked his zoned coffee set, but it seemed a trifle lacking in plasticity and flow, as is natural enough in an architect.'[31]

In 1935 an exhibition of Murray's design work, including glass, ceramics and silver, was staged at the Medici Gallery in London. This solo exhibition, the first of its kind, was opened by Sir William Llewellyn, President of the Royal Academy of Arts. It presented a tremendous

range of individual items produced over a mere three years and included over one hundred Wedgwood pieces. Also included was a small range of Unique Ware, produced with Norman Wilson. The most expensive item for sale was a dinner service decorated in the *Irish* pattern, priced at £15.10.0. Over one hundred glass items were shown, ranging from a cut crystal decanter, a cut amethyst vase and a cut bottle vase, the latter priced at £3. In his introductory speech Sir William Llewellyn said that Murray '…is the first designer from the dominions to achieve prominence in Britain and the first industrial designer to host a one man show. He has displayed great courage and has made a very significant contribution to industrial design in this country. His work is marked with great simplicity'.[32] Murray's work

223. Three silver presentation cups designed by Keith Murray for Mappin and Webb Ltd, 1935.

224. An electroplated cocktail set and bowl designed by Keith Murray for Mappin and Webb Ltd, about 1935.

225. A part silver tea set designed by Keith Murray for Mappin and Webb Ltd., 1935.

proved very popular in both Australia and New Zealand. At about this time the large David Jones department store in Sydney showed an extensive range of his current shapes under the banner 'Modern Classics'.

Alongside his range of ceramics for Wedgwood, Murray continued to develop outstanding and critically acclaimed designs for Stevens and Williams Ltd. He designed a bathroom set which was presented to the Duke and Duchess of Gloucester for their wedding in 1936.[33] A year later he produced a stylised design for a glass plaque for the Architectural Association as a presentation piece to Geoffrey Shakespeare. Murray also designed a number of special commemorative wares for the forthcoming Coronation of King Edward VIII. Whilst many were decorated with the Royal Coat of Arms there were a few more innovative items such as the Empire Bottle, with a coin in the stopper, that featured an engraving of the globe with waves and 'Rule Britannia' in the middle of the item.[34]

A selection of Murray's ceramics and glass was exhibited at the Paris Exhibition in 1937. Of particular interest was a green glass vase, thought to be made specially for this show, decorated with deep cuts in the glass and also unmarked.[35] Towards the late thirties the impact that Murray had made for the company began to wane as other manufacturers adopted his modern style and approach. By 1938 his designs were marketed alongside the standard products made by the company. His *Whitville* range, incorporating a wide range of items, was illustrated in the 1939 catalogue (Plate 226). Murray's contract was probably not continued after the Second World War although some of his patterns, including those decorated with both fish and cacti, were illustrated in the 1955 catalogue.

In 1936 Murray was among the first ten designers to be appointed to the Faculty of Royal Designers for Industry by the Royal Society of Arts. Others included Eric Gill, Harold Stabler and Tom Purvis. This faculty was limited to forty members. In the same year Wedgwood held a prestigious and important exhibition at the Grafton Galleries in

London, displaying examples of the latest pieces by all the Wedgwood designers. Murray showed a wide range, including a jug (3845), a vase (3765) and a bone china teapot and cream jug decorated with his *Lotus* (S.70) pattern. He also displayed four styles of lamp base, although fixtures and plain shades had to be purchased separately (Plate 227). At about this time he also produced some book-ends, available in different glazes (Plate 228) and a series of fluted ware such as shape (4116) (Plate 229).

The new slip wares that Murray developed for a range of vases, bowls and practical items are particularly interesting (Plate 230). These pieces combined the cream coloured earthenware body with blue, green, yellow or brown glaze. Some were turned on the lathe to reveal the cream coloured body underneath, thus revealing the beauty of the forms which have an almost classic dignity (Plate 231). Over twenty-eight different shapes – vases, ashtrays, cigarette boxes and other items – were produced with shape numbers between 4192 and 4253. Some of these two-colour glazes enjoyed a revival when relaunched after austerity measures were lifted in 1952.[36]

By the late thirties Murray was moving away from pottery design into his architectural practice. A selection of his shapes was shown at a special exhibition at Wedgwood's Hatton Garden showrooms in London in 1939, alongside the work of Victor Skellern, Millicent Taplin and Eric Ravilious. Some of Murray's last designs for Wedgwood included two dramatic items – a tall plain vase (Plate 232) and a round vase (4326) (Plate 233). His (4319) shape was dated October 1939 in the shape book.

Murray's outstanding shapes were so popular that they were used by other Wedgwood designers for patterns that were markedly different from Murray's own work. His series of beer jugs and mugs was used by Victor Skellern and Millicent Taplin for both handcraft patterns and commemorative wares. For the Coronation of King Edward VIII a number of

227. Two hand-thrown lamp bases, both decorated with a moonstone glaze, (3955) and (3956). Designed by Keith Murray for Josiah Wedgwood and Sons Ltd., about 1933-34. Tallest lamp base 11in. (27.9cm) high.

Murray's shapes were used, including a tankard and cigarette box featuring relief decoration by Arnold Machin.[37] A lesser known pattern, although probably not by Murray, was inspired by a visit from George Robey, the music hall comic who was performing at the Theatre Royal in Hanley.[38] His famous crescent-shaped eyebrows formed a border pattern, painted in platinum (C.6107) or brown (C.6110). Murray also undertook some freelance work, including the styling of tyres for the Dunlop company.[39] Although no further information is available, this does demonstrate his versatility as an industrial designer.

With his primary interest in architecture Murray went into partnership with Charles White. Their first commission was to design the new Barlaston factory. Tom Wedgwood, Norman Wilson and Murray visited America, Switzerland and Italy to look at new factory designs and organisation.[40] A number of proposals were worked on (Plate 234). A good working relationship was formed as the development of the new site continued. Norman Wilson recalled that 'he was a calming guide, philosopher and friend and architectural tutor. Apart from being an architect Keith was a very methodical and hard headed administrator. We were bursting with ideas and excited by the prospect of putting theory into practice'.[41]

In 1939 Murray was elected a Fellow of the Royal Institute of British Architects, having been proposed by Maxwell Ayrton, Robert Atkinson and C.H. James. In 1940 the new Wedgwood factory was opened. As a commemoration, one of Murray's beer mugs was produced featuring a Victor Skellern design. A new mark was introduced for Murray's work, that of a simple 'KM Wedgwood' motif. Production of his work continued

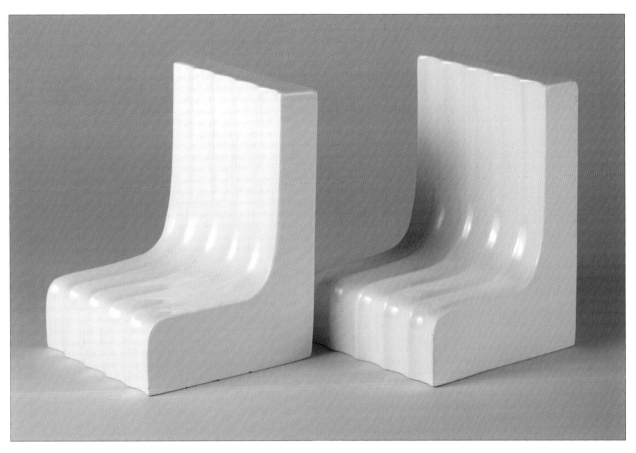

228. A pair of bookends decorated with a white gloss glaze. Designed by Keith Murray for Josiah Wedgwood and Sons Ltd., about 1936-37. Height 5½in. (13.8cm).

229 A lesser known hand-thrown fluted bowl (4116), height 5½in. (13.8cm), decorated with a moonstone glaze. Designed by Keith Murray for Josiah Wedgwood and Sons Ltd.

230. Three pieces from the slip ware range decorated with a celadon glaze. Vase (4198), bowl (4254) and urn (4225). Designed by Keith Murray for Josiah Wedgwood and Sons Ltd., about 1936-52. Height of tallest piece 8¼in. (20.9cm).

throughout the Second World War. Without any hesitation, he returned to the Royal Air Force between 1939 and 1941 as Squadron Leader in the RAF Volunteer Service. From about 1940 a new backstamp was introduced that featured his initials 'KM'. Murray became rather tired of seeing his name on each piece.[42]

Alongside other pottery companies, Wedgwood displayed a wide range of exhibits at the 'Britain Can Make It' exhibition in London in 1946. A total of 140 Wedgwood items were selected by the Council of Industrial Design, making Wedgwood the largest exhibitor. Whilst Murray showed eleven pieces, including a vase (4248) and a mug (3810), no glass designs were evident. The illustrated catalogue, 'Design 46' does not feature any Murray pieces for Stevens & Williams Ltd., but seven pieces designed by Tom Jones, who had designed for that company for several years.

In 1946, the Wedgwood management decided to introduce a new tableware range suitable for large scale production in earthenware that could take all forms of decoration, including plain for the home market and decorated for export. They commissioned Murray, in conjunction with the company's own technical staff, to design a new range that would conform to the post-war requirements and be pleasing in form and function, packaging and storage. Initially Murray submitted drawings that were then made up by the modeller. Three different teapots were made with the selected shape undergoing testing in a number of homes before receiving the final seal of approval. Murray also developed the Commonwealth service with the Wedgwood design staff (Plate 235). The final shape had several important features – there was no drip or backflow from the spout. Murray credited this to the modeller.[43] The Commonwealth service formed part of a special display of Murray's work organised by the Royal Society of Arts entitled 'Designers

231. Slip wares decorated with a celadon glaze. Vase (4217), height 8¼in. (20.9cm), and plant pot (shape number unknown). Designed by Keith Murray for Josiah Wedgwood and Sons Ltd., from about 1936.

at Work', alongside Susie Cooper and R.Y. Gooden. Between 1945 and 1947 Murray was the Master of the Faculty. A few years later a number of his vases were displayed at the Festival of Britain in 1951.

Murray produced a staggering range of shapes throughout his Wedgwood period. Those that were popular and remained in production were featured in the Wedgwood Catalogue of Bodies and Shapes 1940-1950. Such was his contribution that his work was given a separate section, with seven pages of shape illustrations and references. In 1951 the London Wedgwood showrooms were re-designed by Murray, R.Y. Gooden and R.D. Russell. Murray was given the task of re-designing the room for the company's latest products, and the bone china room. The new showrooms featured several inset glass cases, large tables for the display of pottery and special display shelves. When the showrooms were expanded in 1957, the accompanying press article illustrated Wedgwood's current range of products, including wares by Norman Wilson and the Strawberry Hill pattern by Victor Skellern and Millicent Taplin.[44] Interestingly, no items by Keith Murray are visible from the selected illustrations. For some years it was assumed that production of his work had ceased during the fifties. However, new information indicates that a limited number of his items were still being produced until the late sixties, as the designer continued to receive royalties. One of his powder bowls, in a bone china body, was still in production in 1982. Eventually Murray signed away his rights and retired.[45]

During the latter part of the forties Murray met Mary Beatrice de Cartaret Hayes, the daughter of Lt-Colonel R. Malet, during a holiday in Somerset. In January 1948, when her divorce came through, they married. Josiah Wedgwood was his best man. Their daughter, Constance, was born towards the end of the year. Murray then decided to retire from

232. A tall footed vase (4325), 11⅞in. (30.3cm) high, decorated with a moonstone glaze. Designed by Keith Murray for Josiah Wedgwood and Sons Ltd., 1939.

233. A hand-thrown vase (4326), height 7¼in. (18.4cm), decorated with a moonstone glaze. Designed by Keith Murray for Josiah Wedgwood and Sons Ltd., 1939.

freelance design to concentrate on his architectural business.[46] The Ramsey, Murray and White architectural practice was responsible for a number of important commissions. The practice, situated above the Wedgwood Showrooms in Wigmore Street, London, had over thirty employees during the early fifties. In 1952 they designed the concrete hangars for London Airport.[47] Shortly afterwards Basil Ward joined the practice, resulting in the change of name to Ramsey, Murray, White and Ward. They later designed a number of industrial buildings, including the Air Terminal in Hong Kong, a housing estate at Edenbridge on the Thames and laboratories in Oxford.[48]

In 1967 Murray retired completely from his architectural practice, although he acted as a consultant for a period of time and certainly up until 1969.[49] On his retirement Josiah Wedgwood and Sons Ltd. presented him with a large black basalt bowl decorated with words in gold inside the piece, with facsimile signatures on the base, also in gold. During his retirement Murray spent time enjoying trout fishing near his home in Blandford, Dorset.

He must have been proud of what he had achieved in painting, glass, pottery and architecture, as he kept several examples of his work and also retained all his records, including leaflets, cuttings and photographs, which are now enjoyed and cherished by his family. Murray died on 16 May 1981. His friend and colleague Norman Wilson wrote a touching obituary in which he said: 'Keith taught us to keep our feet on the

ground whilst allowing occasional floating in the clouds. He had impeccable taste and judgement borne out by the lovely elevation of the original Barlaston factory and by his elegant pottery shapes.'[50]

Recent interest in his work began to develop following an exhibition organised by the Victoria and Albert Museum in 1977. Two years later a selection of his work was shown in the influential Thirties Exhibition in London. Typically, prices for his work have steadily risen in recent years as more people begin to seek new collecting areas. However, his modernist and undecorated ceramics seem to appeal to only a small range of collectors. In many respects Norman Wilson summed up the contribution made by Murray – 'He was a man of many parts who has left behind much evidence of his excellent work.'[51]

234. Drawing by Keith Murray of the proposed new Wedgwood factory at Barlaston.

235. An archive photograph illustrating various items for the Commonwealth service. The teapot was designed by Keith Murray for Josiah Wedgwood and Sons Ltd., about 1947-48.

CHAPTER 10

DESIGNER FOR WEDGWOOD

ERIC RAVILIOUS (1903-1942)

236. A portrait of Eric
Ravilious, 1940.

Eric Ravilious was one of the most important British artists to emerge during the inter-war period. He undertook many prestigious commissions in the early part of his career, establishing himself as a prominent wood engraver and illustrator. His introduction to ceramics came after working with furniture and glassware. Producing some of the most innovative designs for Josiah Wedgwood and Sons Ltd. in the four years preceding the Second World War, he demonstrated that art and industry could combine with excellent results. Sadly, his life was cut short by the War. Ravilious also made an influential contribution to British art and illustration, bringing to his work a sense of humour, freshness and humility. In this area his achievements have been celebrated and documented through exhibitions and books. This chapter concentrates mainly on his work as a designer for Josiah Wedgwood and Sons Ltd.

Eric William Ravilious was born on 22 July 1903 in Acton, South London; he was seven years younger than his brother, Frank, and had a sister, Evelyn. Catherine, the first-born child of Frank and Emma Ravilious, died when only two years old. When his father's drapery business failed, the family moved to Eastbourne, setting up an antiques shop. Following his early education Ravilious studied at the Eastbourne Grammar School from

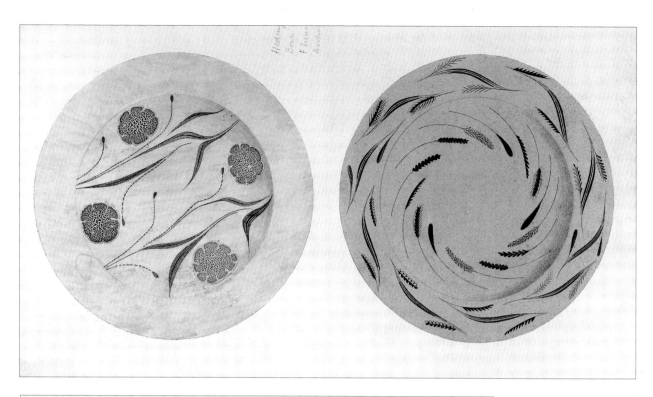

237. Early examples of proposed designs submitted by Eric Ravilious to Josiah Wedgwood and Sons Ltd., 1936.

238. The King Edward VIII Coronation Mug (CL 6203), printed in sepia with hand-painted decoration in yellow with a pale blue band on an earthenware body. Designed by Eric Ravilious for Josiah Wedgwood and Sons Ltd., 1936.

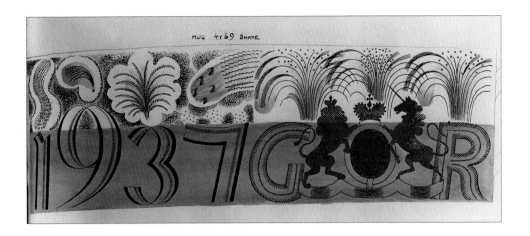

MUG 4169 SHAPE

1937 G R

1914.[1] In December 1919 he took the Cambridge Senior Local Examination Award, after which he was awarded a scholarship to attend the Eastbourne College of Art. The strict regime there expected students to attend daily, including Saturday mornings, with evening sessions on Tuesdays and Thursdays.

In 1922 Ravilious won a scholarship to the diploma course at the Design School of the Royal College of Art, where he studied lettering, design, life drawing and composition. However, as his grant was insufficient he had to cram the three year course into two. Amongst the other students there were Henry Moore, Edward Bawden and Douglas Percy Bliss. According to Edward Bawden, Ravilious was often to be seen in the students' common room, playing ping-pong or sitting with girls in the old broken-down armchairs.[2] Paul Nash helped him to develop his skills in watercolour painting and encouraged him to take a more experimental approach to wood engraving. Ravilious spent a lot of time in the School of Engraving which, Edward Bawden recalled, '…was a privilege granted to few, admission being by application to the Professor, Sir Frank Short, who did not give it readily to students of the Design School as they could not be expected to reach even a moderate standard of good drawing.'[3]

Ravilious chose mural decoration for his examination subject. Students were expected to prepare the gesso panels, using egg tempera and grinding earth colour, following Cennino Cennini's ancient recipes. However, Ravilious chose not to follow the established procedures and used bought-in gesso powder and ordinary colours for his mural. He passed with distinction and was awarded the Design School Travelling Scholarship to Italy, where he spent time in Florence, Sienna and Volterra. Following his return he became increasingly interested in wood engraving. A fine example is an illustration used for the cover of the *Gallimaufry*, the RCA student magazine, in June 1925.[4] Having finished his education at the Royal College of Art, he set up a studio in 1925 with Douglas Percy Bliss. Throughout the rest of the twenties he exhibited his work with Edward Bawden and Bliss. Paul Nash recommended Ravilious to a number of important people in the arts and also proposed him for membership of the Society of Wood Engravers.[5]

To make ends meet he taught for two days a week at the Eastbourne School of Art, from September 1925, but continued to live in London. Whilst teaching he met and fell in love with one of his students, Tirzah Garwood. Already nearly engaged to the son of a close friend, the arrival of Ravilious on the scene caused a good deal of parental

240. An earthenware teapot, height 6¼in. (16cm), decorated with the *Persephone* pattern (AL 9984), printed in sepia with hand-painted decoration in blue. Designed by Eric Ravilious for Josiah Wedgwood and Sons Ltd., 1936.

241. A selection of earthenware dinnerwares including a tureen and gravy boat decorated with the *Persephone* pattern.

242. A later version of the *Persephone* pattern printed in gold on the Leigh shape. Designed by Eric Ravilious for Josiah Wedgwood and Sons Ltd. for Queen Elizabeth II's Coronation banquet in 1952.

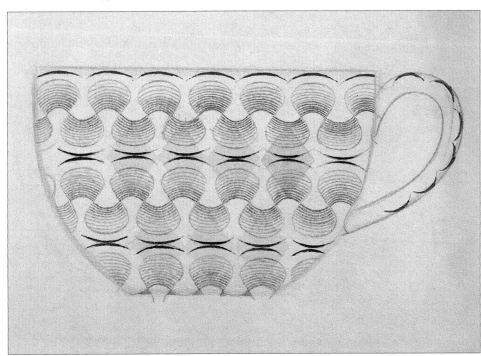

243. An example of a submitted design by Eric Ravilious, 1936, that was not put into production.

opposition, which caused Tirzah to look beyond the confines of Eastbourne and move to London to pursue her artistic career. The couple became engaged, and married in July 1930, Edward Bawden being the best man. After a honeymoon in Cornwall they moved into a top floor flat in Stratford Road, Kensington. To boost his income Ravilious took up a part-time teaching post at the Royal College of Art.

In 1928 Sir William Rothenstein asked Ravilious and Bawden to produce sketches for a mural, based on London, for the refectory at Morley College.[6] The first drawings were rejected by Sir William, who then suggested a fantasy theme. He was delighted with the result when each artist produced his own murals decorated with a variety of scenes from Shakespeare's plays, contemporary life and old English dramas.

In 1932 Ravilious and Bawden rented Brick House, in Great Badfield, Essex as a base for landscape painting. When Edward Bawden's father bought the house as a wedding present for his son on his marriage to Charlotte Epton in 1934, Ravilious and his wife moved to nearby Bank House in Castle Hedingham. During this period, Ravilious undertook several important commissions, including designs for a publication of *Twelfth Night* for the Golden Cockerel Press, published in 1932. In 1933 a notable commission came from the new Midland Railway Hotel in Morecambe, Lancashire. The hotel, designed by the architect Oliver Hill, required a mural for the circular tea room and bar. Ravilious chose the theme of Day and Night for the two circular panels.[7]

In 1933 he held his first one man show at the Zwemmer Gallery in London, showing thirty-seven watercolours. Three years later a second one-man exhibition was held at the

244. Artwork illustrating the *Alphabet* pattern. Designed by Eric Ravilious for Josiah Wedgwood and Sons Ltd., 1937.

245. An earthenware jug and mug decorated with the *Alphabet* pattern (CL 6261), printed in black with hand decoration in blue. Designed by Eric Ravilious for Josiah Wedgwood and Sons Ltd., 1937.

same gallery. This show included watercolours of Essex and Sussex landscapes, and also a drawing for a decoration for glass. In 1937 the Council for Art and Industry asked Ravilious to create an exhibit on the theme of Tennis, for the Sports Section of the British Pavilion and to design the cover of the British programme for the Paris Exposition of 1937.

His introduction to the decorative arts came about when Cecilia Dunbar-Kilburn, a fellow student from his days at the Royal College of Art, set up a shop in partnership with Athole Hay, the Registrar of the RCA, selling objects of applied art. The shop, called Dunbar Hay, at 15 Albemarle Street, London, was to sell furniture, textiles, pottery and glass of the highest quality. Ravilious was commissioned to design the trade card and was paid a retainer for several years. He designed a suite of dining room furniture comprising a mahogany table and a set of chairs with a star pattern inlay. The shop also sold his designs for glass made by Stuart and Sons, and his successfully his designs for Josiah Wedgwood and Sons Ltd.

In 1933 Ravilious was asked to submit designs for glassware to Stuart and Sons Ltd. of Stourbridge, responding to the Gorell Report recommending better design in industry. An exhibition entitled 'Modern Art for the Table' was planned to take place at Harrods in London in 1934. Ravilious made his contribution alongside some of the leading artists and designers of the period, including Gordon Forsyth, Dame Laura Knight, Dod Proctor, Paul Nash and Graham Sutherland. He designed at least four different patterns, including one of stylised leaves decorated on a tall vase and another featuring horizontal and slanting engraved bands on a sherry glass. His decorative designs were marked 'DESIGNED BY ERIC RAVILIOUS' and 'Stuart England'. This exhibition also displayed a range of earthenware tablewares based on submissions by some of the leading artists of the period, including Duncan Grant, Dame Laura Knight, Graham Sutherland and Ben Nicholson. These wares were produced by Clarice Cliff at A.J. Wilkinson Ltd. and E.

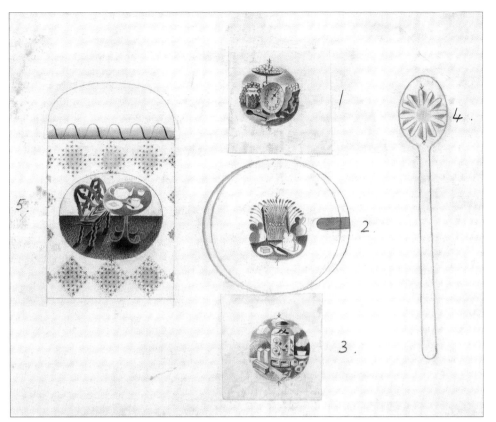

246. Artwork for the *Afternoon Tea* pattern, showing the various motifs and decoration for the proposed spoon. Designed by Eric Ravilious for Josiah Wedgwood and Sons Ltd., 1937.

247. A Queen's ware preserve jar decorated with the *Tea Set* pattern. Designed by Eric Ravilious for Josiah Wedgwood and Sons Ltd., 1937.

Brain and Co. As some of the designers' wares were not ready in time for this important exhibition, they were shown a year later at the British Art in Industry Exhibition at the Royal Academy.[8]

Ravilious' first contact with Josiah Wedgwood V, the Chairman of Josiah Wedgwood and Sons Ltd., came in November 1935 with a telegram urgently requesting a meeting. The company was keen for him to produce a range of patterns. He travelled up to Stoke-on-Trent with Cecilia Dunbar-Kilburn to meet Tom Wedgwood and Victor Skellern, the Art Director. Ravilious toured the factory, observing the various production processes. Following discussions he agreed to develop some trial designs suited to pottery decoration. Sharon Gater, at the Wedgwood Museum, points out that 'the decision to employ Ravilious on a free lance basis reflected the desire of Josiah Wedgwood V to revitalise the surface pattern. By recruiting the services of an artist whose expertise lay outside the field of ceramics, he hoped to make a departure from stale decorative motifs, which had usually relied on floral or foliate subject matter.'[9] Hence his rejection of the initial designs proposed by Ravilious in May 1936, featuring stylised ferns and grasses (Plate 237). Ravilious collected nineteenth century porcelain, especially transfer printed vignettes, and his new designs were based on updated versions of these. Ravilious mentioned other, lesser known, trial patterns in

248. A bone china cup, saucer and milk jug decorated with the *Afternoon Tea* pattern (W 3514) printed in black and groundlaid in green on the Leigh shape. Designed by Eric Ravilious for Josiah Wedgwood and Sons Ltd., 1938.

249. The *Boat Race Day* pattern (CL 6263), printed in sepia with hand-painted decoration on the Harvard Bowl and Burslem Vase. Designed by Eric Ravilious for Josiah Wedgwood and Sons Ltd., 1938. Height of vase 9⅞in. (25cm).

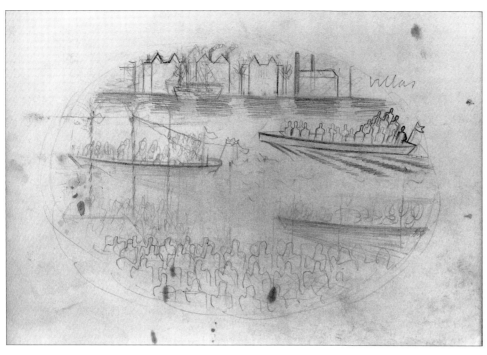
250. An original sketch for the *Boat Race Day* design by Eric Ravilious, 1938.

251. An untitled watercolour known as 'Garden Flowers on Cottage Table', an interior of Ironbridge, from 1941. 22in. (56cm) x 20⅜in. (51.75cm).

252. An earthenware plate decorated with the *Travel* pattern (TK 472), printed in black with hand painted decoration in turquoise on a grey body. Designed by Eric Ravilious for Josiah Wedgwood and Sons Ltd., designed in 1938 but not put into production until 1952.

correspondence with his friend Helen Binyon. In July 1936 he wrote, 'today I've been trying out ideas for a potting design with a sort of picture all over, a sea piece founded on an old engraving of mine of last year with what Hennell called the palimpsest island. There is a whale spouting somewhere. The thing has a look of the coast of Greenland which was the intention, but so far the border has beaten me. I must have another try at it.'[10]

In July 1936 Ravilious returned to Wedgwood with his proposed designs. A second visit was made the following month, staying with the Wedgwood family. His range of trial patterns was cautiously welcomed by Wedgwood because they felt they were a little too advanced for their customers. In August 1936 Ravilious wrote to Helen Binyon: 'You will be sorry that the family think my beautiful designs above the heads of their public and that to begin with something should be done safer and more understandable. I argued about this most of the afternoon. The argument is whether to alter the present way of doing things in a hurry or attempt it by degrees. I was for a clean sweep and they want a method of slow percolation: it all means that I'd better think of some new designs – something if possible that suits all the markets at once so I must go back and see if I am clever enough to do this.'[11]

Despite this minor setback, Wedgwood was exceedingly pleased with Ravilious' Coronation mug design and wanted to begin production as soon as possible to be ready for the forthcoming Coronation of Edward VIII in 1937 (Plate 238). The pattern, decorated on a new Queen's ware mug, featured a stylised version of the Royal coat of arms and exploding fireworks, rather different from the usual Wedgwood approach. This probably explains why Josiah Wedgwood V initially questioned whether he had made the right decision in commissioning Ravilious.[12] The Coronation mug (CL6203) was printed in sepia with an enamelled band in turquoise and decoration in egg yellow, ready for the Christmas market of 1936. The only shop in London to stock the mug was Dunbar Hay and the first customer was Mrs. Simpson.[13] However, as historical events unfolded the British public were informed in December 1936 that the forthcoming monarch had decided to abdicate. The Coronation mug was immediately withdrawn. Within a year an announcement was made that Edward's brother would be crowned.

253. A range of earthenware tablewares decorated with the *Travel* pattern, including a coffee pot and a gravy boat and stand

254. Two wood engravings by Eric Ravilious. Left: Snowstorm from the *Kynoch Press Note Book*, 1933 and right, from *Fifty-Four Conceits* by Martin Armstrong, 1933. This was used for the *Travel* pattern.

255. A pencil drawing of a greenhouse by Eric Ravilious that may have been an idea for the proposed *Greenhouse* pattern.

256. An example of a proposed design by Eric Ravilious submitted to Wedgwood in about 1936. Note the rubbed-out drawing of a greenhouse in the background.

With the assistance of Ravilious, Wedgwood adapted the pattern for the Coronation of George VI (Plate 239). Two versions were produced: the first (CL6203) and the other in an alternative colourway with a green band and pale red decoration (CL6225). The design was revised in 1952 for the Coronation of Queen Elizabeth II in 1953. This version was printed in sepia with a pink lustre band and lemon yellow decoration (CL6484).

Following the success of the Coronation mug, Wedgwood asked Ravilious to design for them for six weeks each year, with royalties paid on sales. This business arrangement was conducted amicably with both parties enjoying the development of new patterns for the next few years. Initially Ravilious had expressed to Wedgwood that he wasn't happy that he was unable to inspect the finished pieces before they were given to the travellers. Ravilious also wanted to train up one of Wedgwood's engravers so that his work would be reproduced to the highest standard. Victor Skellern recalled later: 'I persuaded Ravilious to let us cut the first pattern and get his comments. I sent prints to him, and the reply was full of unbounding joy and enthusiasm – this was the engraver he wanted. I had found the right man who knew exactly what he wanted. When he next came to the factory I had to admit that every one of the engravers – and there were ten of them – had each done a separate part of the engraving; he took this very well, and remarked, "I will never again argue about the Wedgwood engraving any more, these chaps are without doubt the finest engravers I have ever met".'[14]

His association with Wedgwood did not curtail Ravilious' other creative interests. His new commitments did, however, require him to resign from his teaching post in 1937. Amongst many commissions he produced chapter headings depicting motifs such as fish and lobsters for the *Country Life Cookery Book*, written by Ambrose Heath. During the latter part of 1936 Ravilious started work on an important commission for the production of

twenty-four lithographs, each depicting a different shop front, for a book entitled *High Street* written by J.M. Richards, published in 1938. During that year Ravilious went on a painting expedition to Bristol with John Nash.

Ravilious' first tableware pattern to be produced was based on a pencil and wash sketch called 'Harvest Festival and Loaves', a drawing he had made at the Castle Hedingham Harvest Festival. This still life subject included cornucopia, loaves and fish modelled in bread by his wife.[15] The pattern was developed and launched in December 1936 as *Harvest Festival*. Within two years it was being advertised as *Persephone* (Plates 240 and 241). The pattern was available in four colourways on a number of

257. An earthenware meat plate, 14¾in (37.5cm) wide decorated with the *Garden* pattern (TL 259), printed in sepia with hand-painted decoration. Designed by Eric Ravilious for Josiah Wedgwood and Sons Ltd., 1938.

258. Examples of the various studies used for the *Garden* pattern.

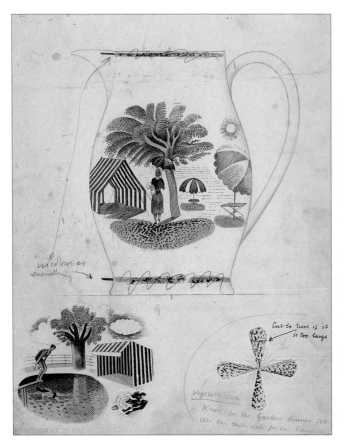

259. A lesser known proposed design that was developed from the *Garden* pattern. Designed by Eric Ravilious for Josiah Wedgwood and Sons Ltd., 1938.

shapes, printed in sepia with a band in either yellow (AL 9983), blue (AL 9984), pink (TL 154) or vine green (TL 155). The yellow and blue versions were produced in great quantity. The complete dinner service for six was priced at £3.14.0. During the war years the pattern was produced without hand colouring.

In 1952 the Coronation *Golden Persephone* on Lincoln bone china in four different versions of the pattern was put forward as Wedgwood's bid to produce a service for the Coronation Banquet of Queen Elizabeth II, to be hosted by Sir Anthony Eden, Secretary of State for Foreign Affairs. Against fierce competition from other leading manufacturers, Wedgwood won the contract. A total of 1,200 pieces were made, each bearing the Royal coat of arms as the central motif (Plate 242).

A lesser known pattern, *Troy*, was introduced for a limited period and shown at the British Industries Fair in the early part of 1937, initially decorated on the Grecian shape but few samples were made. In 1952 samples were produced on Lincoln bone china as an alternative to the Coronation *Persephone*.

Ravilious started to develop a pattern based on the alphabet during 1937. The *Alphabet* pattern consisted of two bands of motifs placed under the individual letters (Plate 244). The range consisted of a jug, plate, porringer, double egg cup, two sizes of mug and a lamp base. *Alphabet* was produced in several colourways and was launched in 1938, although the designer presumed that the set would be available for the Christmas market of 1937 (Plate 245). This, he was advised, wasn't possible due to other production commitments. Wedgwood wanted to feature all Ravilious' latest designs at a special exhibition in London in February 1938. The range was later revised with some discussion on using coloured bodies for the series but concern was expressed that the coloured bands might not show up. In 1939 Wedgwood promoted Ravilious' *Persephone*, *Boat Race* bowl and *Alphabet* under the banner 'The Three Ravilious Patterns'. This advertisement explained how the alphabet letters on the bowl were not placed above the corresponding image, 'so that this causes a lot of fun puzzling out which pictures and letters go together'.[16]

Some of Ravilious' designs were inspired directly from his artwork. In 1936 London Transport commissioned him to produce four illustrations for a poster for the Green Line Bus routes. One of the motifs, depicting tea ware on a garden table, inspired a new pattern for a preserve jar. Ravilious submitted drawings for the preserve jar with matching spoon (Plate 246). In response to these Victor Skellern wrote to him commenting: 'I have put in hand for making the jam pot as per your drawing, with a fitting as approved when you were here. A sample in biscuit should be ready in about three to four weeks.'[17] However, it was decided that the spoon was not an essential addition. Josiah V wrote to Ravilious explaining: 'although your design for a spoon looks most attractive, pottery spoons with jam pots are, in fact, precious little use and we propose to delete this.'[18] The preserve jar, firstly called *Tea Set*, was launched in 1937 (Plate 247) in three colourways. The design must have proved successful, as it was soon suggested that it should be extended into a tea set (Plate 248). Wedgwood sent Ravilious various examples of shapes so he could select the most suitable. In February 1938 the set was relaunched as *Afternoon Tea*, on the Leigh shape, offered in

260. The *Garden Implements* pattern, printed in sepia on a Liverpool jug. Designed by Eric Ravilious for Josiah Wedgwood and Sons Ltd., 1939.

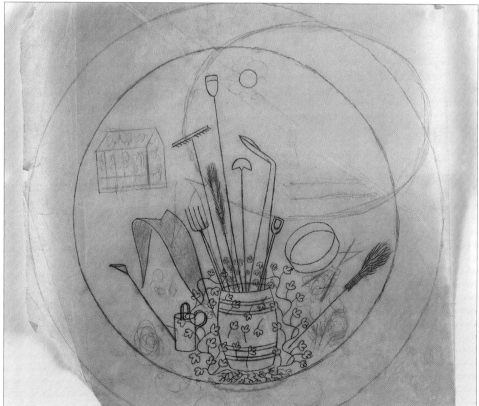

261. A sketch design on tracing paper by Eric Ravilious for the *Garden Implements* pattern for a 10in. (25.4cm) plate. Interestingly this pattern was not used for flatware.

262. A pencil study of sunflowers by Eric Ravilious, about 1938. 17in. (43cm) x 21in. (53.4cm).

263. A pencil sketch of rhubarb and a rhubarb enforcer by Eric Ravilious, from 1938. 8⅞in. (22.7cm) x 7in. (17.7cm).

four colour variations, including printed in black and painted in yellow and green (W3494) and printed in sepia and ground laid in green (W3495). In 1939 the pattern was advertised as also being available in breakfast and coffee sets.

One of the most outstanding designs by Ravilious was the *Boat Race Day*, produced in

264. A watercolour study of acanthus leaves in a white jug by Eric Ravilious, probably before 1939. 20⅝in. (52.5cm) x 17⅞in. (45.5 cm).

1938 (Plate 249). This special set, one of the designer's favourites, featured individual scenes from the Boat Race, for which Ravilious produced several sketch ideas (Plate 250). Wedgwood sent the giant egg cup-shaped Burslem Vase in biscuit and a life size sketch of the vase with no handles for Ravilious to work out the scale needed for such large pieces. During this experimental period the vase featured in several of his paintings (Plate 251). Wedgwood asked Ravilious to bear in mind that the engravings should be interchangeable both for the Harvard Bowl and for the Burslem Vase.[19] The design was formalised by April 1937 and the samples returned to the factory. As the engravings were expensive Wedgwood wanted to pursue the possibility of using them further, on other forms of pottery, to maximise on the initial outlay. Wedgwood suggested that items such as cocktail sets could be decorated with one of the oval patterns, asking Ravilious to submit sketches for the suggested shapes but these did not go beyond the ideas stage.[20]

Early in 1938 Wedgwood requested Ravilious to submit a range of proposed patterns for the production of new dinnerware ranges. The letter asked: 'We should like you, if possible to give us a fair number of alternatives to choose from, say half a dozen, though you will understand that we should only be able to adapt one of these for engraving this autumn. Would you think in terms of a plain printed pattern and a printed and hand enamelled pattern.'[21]

Responding to this, Ravilious spent some time developing two new patterns – *Travel and*

265. The reverse side of the *Garden Implements* pattern, showing the various vignettes. This version with the gold decoration is uncatalogued and therefore is probably a trial. Designed by Eric Ravilious for Josiah Wedgwood and Sons Ltd., 1939.

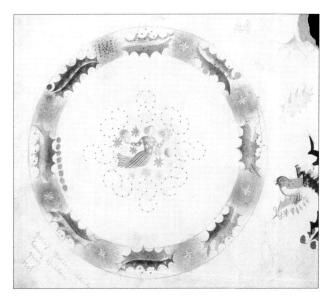

266. Artwork for the *Noel* pattern from 1939.

Escape and *Garden*. The *Travel* pattern (TK 472), as it soon became known, consisted of over ten different motifs including an aeroplane, steam train and a cruise liner, printed in black on a Windsor grey body, with some hand painted decoration (Plate 252). *Travel* was decorated on a number of shapes and combinations of sets (Plate 253). Some of these motifs derived from his previous illustration work such as the aeroplane from his illustrations to *Fifty-Four Conceits* by Martin Armstrong, 1933 (Plate 254), whilst the train motifs were originally illustrated in *The Hansom Cab and the Pigeons* by L.A. Strong, 1935.[22] The yacht motif was taken from a newspaper cutting in one of his scrap books, which he compiled with cuttings, postcards, his own drawings and designs and useful reference material. Due to wartime austerity measures, *Travel* was not put into production, despite some trials being made, until September 1952.

In the course of correspondence during June 1937 between Ravilious and Wedgwood,

267. An earthenware dinner plate, diameter 11¾in. (29.8cm), decorated with the *Noel* pattern, printed in sepia with hand-painted decoration. Designed by Eric Ravilious for Josiah Wedgwood and Sons Ltd., 1939.

268. Artwork for the London Underground Plate by Eric Ravilious, 1939.

269. A pencil sketch of a proposed design by Eric Ravilious for Josiah Wedgwood and Sons Ltd., probably 1938-39.

reference was made to a proposed pattern called 'Greenhouse', to be decorated on the Burslem Vase. This did not materialise, not because the design wasn't appealing but because to use a single pattern only on a vase would have proved too expensive.[23] A detailed design of a greenhouse exists which may have been the intended pattern (Plate 255), though one may have expected a more stylish shape. An early proposed trial pattern of ferns and leaves, from 1936, indicates a rubbed out drawing of a greenhouse underneath the central motif (Plate 256). This greenhouse may have been intended as the primary subject idea for the forthcoming *Garden Implements* pattern.

Within a year of the 'Greenhouse' design rejection, Ravilious submitted the new *Garden* pattern (Plate 257). This outstanding range featured over ten different scenes, including a man on a diving board, a lady on a swing, a woman with an umbrella and a lady feeding birds (Plate 258). The finalised patterns were forwarded to Wedgwood so that the engravings could be started. In June 1938, as soon as Tom Wedgwood had seen them, he wrote to Ravilious saying: 'I am delighted with them, particularly the *Garden* pattern; you must have put in a tremendous lot of work on these patterns since you were down here, and I do think you are to be congratulated on the result.'[24]

Garden was launched in 1939 on various earthenware shapes in six initial colourways, including golden orange (TL 259), blue (TL 270) and green (TL 275). Bone china samples of the pattern were produced in September 1952 for the Coronation bid. Ravilious developed the trial design for a Liverpool jug. The main motif was taken from the *Garden* pattern, but in a pink colourway. This idea seems not to have gone beyond the ideas stage and was not produced (Plate 259). It is possible that the problems in sorting out the various existing motifs on the Liverpool jug may have prompted Ravilious to create a completely new pattern. His *Garden Implements* lemonade set, launched in 1939, was based on the small barrel motif in the *Garden* pattern, contrasting with nine small circular motifs on the reverse. Ravilious produced a number of sketches to develop the main design (Plate 261). These drawings formed the motif (Plate 260). For the reverse pattern, Ravilious examined

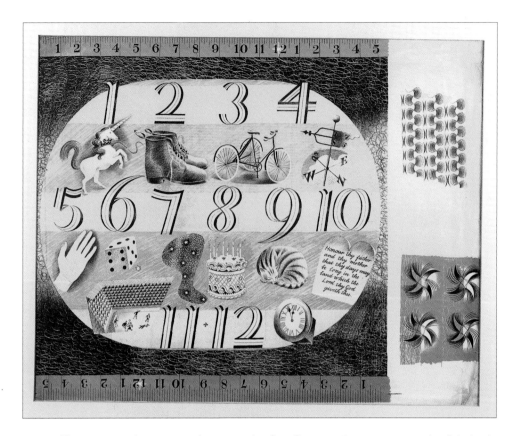

270. A lithograph design for a cotton handkerchief. Designed by Eric Ravilious for the Cotton Board, 1941. 17½in. (45cm) x 17¼in. (44cm).

271. A pencil sketch of the proposed design for the *Barlaston* mug. Note the bottle kilns and barge that were not included in the final version. Designed by Eric Ravilious for Josiah Wedgwood and Sons Ltd., 1940

some of his previous drawings such as a study of sunflowers (Plate 262), a study of rhubarb and enforcer (Plate 263) and a painting of acanthus leaves in a white jug (Plate 264). These were used, alongside other designs, for a collage of motifs (Plate 265).

Whilst Ravilious was developing new ideas, Wedgwood was in the process of considering the introduction of lithographic decoration. In 1938 Victor Skellern wrote to Ravilious explaining how lithographic sheets were manufactured, carefully outlining that as many parts of the printed design as possible had to be fitted on to one sheet to make it cost-effective. Skellern noted that centre only patterns were the most effective as printed borders were not required.[25] Ravilious experimented with the lithographic form of

272. The *Barlaston* mug, printed on earthenware. Designed by Eric Ravilious for Josiah Wedgwood and Sons Ltd., 1940.

decoration for his *Noel* pattern (Plate 266), intended for the Christmas 1939 celebrations but not ready until the following year. Each piece featured an individual seasonal motif such as a Christmas pudding, holly leaves, a robin and a design of a mythical lady with stars. The plates were finished with a decorative holly border with the individual letters of 'NOEL' included (Plate 267). Sadly, this pattern did not go into production and only a few pieces of *Noel* were ever made. Samples of this pattern, exhibited at a trade show in North America, were then given to the Victoria and Albert Museum in London.

In 1939 Ravilious was commissioned by The Department of Overseas Trade to design a stylised map of the British Commonwealth for the British Pavilion at the New York World's Fair. His design consisted of several motifs made from metal. Three of his paintings, including 'Channel Steamer Leaving Harbour' were also shown in the British Pavilion. The original drawings for the New York World's Fair were later used as designs to decorate a large bowl submitted by Ravilious to Wedgwood during that year. It depicted people and animals from the continents against a stippled pink background but was never produced. The pattern name, *Four Continents Bowl*, was given some years later.[26] During the same year Ravilious also designed the London Underground Plate, a commemorative item for the London Passenger Transport Board (Plate 268). Felton Wreford, manager of the London showrooms, wrote to Ravilious in March to inform him that the pattern would decorate a low shaped bowl to be designed by Keith Murray, but due to the impending wartime restrictions, only a sample was produced. Ravilious also submitted a design of circles to Wedgwood but this was not produced either (Plate 269).

When war was declared in September 1939, Ravilious volunteered to work at Hedingham Observation Post and in February 1940 he was offered a position as an official war artist and given an initial six month contract. After Chatham, Sheerness, Whitstable and Grimsby he went to Norway and the Arctic Circle and later in the war was based at Newhaven, with the task of drawing the coastal defences. He produced a large number of watercolours, including 'Barrage Balloons'. Between commissions

233

273. The artwork for a proposed floral pattern developed by Eric Ravilious for Josiah Wedgwood and Sons Ltd. in 1941.

Ravilious created a series of ten lithographs entitled 'Submarine Series' that were sold at the Leicester Galleries in London. He also designed for the Cotton Board but only one design, for a child's cotton patterned handkerchief, reached a trial stage and none were put into production (Plate 270). A lesser known stylised design for the Cotton Board featured yellow tea pots and cups.

Despite the busy schedule and his creative demands Ravilious was able to develop a new proposal for Wedgwood – a design to commemorate the relocation of the works from Barlaston to Etruria in 1940 (Plate 271). The *Barlaston* mug skilfully depicted examples of Wedgwood ware in the kiln surrounded by stylised flames and a portrait of Josiah Wedgwood (Plate 272). War conditions were curbing the pottery industry and Ravilious wrote to the company: 'I suppose the lithographed Wedgwood mug, the new one, is held up for a bit, or will you produce it at all now there is a war, hope so – it would be nice to see a homage to Josiah Wedgwood someday!'[27]

In 1941 the Ravilious family, with their three children, moved from Castle Hedingham to Ironbridge Farm in Essex. Ravilious submitted a floral pattern to Wedgwood, but it was not produced (Plate 272). On 28 August 1942 he received his third commission, taking him to Iceland. He then joined an Air Sea Rescue mission on 2 September, from which he failed to return and was presumed dead.

Four years after his untimely death a total of thirty-three pieces of his work for Wedgwood were exhibited at the Britain Can Make It exhibition in London in 1946. When restrictions were lifted on the sale of goods in Britain his patterns proved very popular and his work continued in production for a number of years. Always ahead of its time, the quality and originality of his work has not diminished. Examples are still highly sought-after, a testament to his originality and style.

CHAPTER 11

THE SPIRIT OF THE FIFTIES

Alfred Burgess Read ARCA, RDI, FSIA (1898-1973)

274. Portrait of Alfred Read, 1954.

The devastation inflicted on British industry and the subsequent clearing up after the Second World War had a marked effect on pottery manufacturers. The mid-century period saw Poole Pottery trying to bridge the gap between austerity measures and full production. To start up again they realised they needed a designer with vision and a creative outlook to move the company forward. The position was offered to Alfred Burgess Read. At the time he was established as an industrial designer in lighting rather than a designer of ceramics. However, during the fifties he successfully worked with a number of people, including skilled craftsmen, to produce an outstanding range of contemporary pottery. Despite his important contribution to the history of the Poole Pottery and to British design, little is known about this artistic and enigmatic man.

Alfred Burgess Read was born on 29 May 1898, in Willingdon, Sussex. He was educated at Eastbourne Grammar School and later at the local School of Art. During the First World War, between 1918-19, he served as Second Lieutenant in the Welsh Guards. He then studied metalwork at the Royal College of Art between 1919 and 1923. Upon graduation he successfully won the Rural Industries Bureau Travelling Scholarship to Italy in 1923. As he had just married Phyllis Barbara Walker, from

275. The *Kitchen* pattern,
decorated on tiles. Designed
by Alfred B. Read for Carter
and Co. Ltd., from about
1923.

Harrogate in Yorkshire, the scholarship turned into a sort of honeymoon.

On his return Read and his associates set up the Clement Dane Advertising Studio in the Strand, London.[1] He was an educated and cultured man, interested in the work and philosophies of the designer Walter Gropius. Read took the opportunity during the early twenties to travel to Germany and visit the Bauhaus. He examined their individual and innovative response to the need for good industrial design. No doubt he was influenced by their ideas.

In 1924 Read left the country for one year to work for a French lighting company, Bagues. Little information is available about his role there, and in 1925 he was offered a Directorship by Troughton and Young Ltd. in London. This forward-thinking industrial lighting company moved to 143 Knightsbridge during the early thirties. Read re-designed the company's offices, incorporating an orderly system for storing technical drawings and other such material. The main office was decorated with pale grey walls and chrome furniture.[2] During this period Read, with several other designers, pioneered the new international modern style. He developed designs for free-standing and wall lamps, which established him as a leading designer of lighting during the thirties. In 1933 he was awarded the Ayrton Premium of the Institute of Electrical Engineers.[3] His work was often illustrated in the important journals of the period such as *The Decorative* Art *Studio Year*

276. An external view of the Poole Pottery Ltd. factory during the fifties.

Book. Read also contributed articles on industrial design and wrote a book entitled *Lighting the Home*, published in 1938. His significant contribution to industry was acknowledged in 1940 when he was made a Royal Designer for Industry by the Royal Society of Arts. One of his most important industrial designs was the Versatile Reflector, first shown at the Design at Work Exhibition in 1948 and in production for some considerable time.[4]

Despite his national recognition as an industrial lighting designer, Read is probably better known today for his contribution to the work of Carter and Co., the tile manufacturer, and its subsidiary pottery company Carter Stabler and Adams, formed in 1921. Although his main involvement was during the fifties, his association with the tile side of the business goes back to the early twenties. A friendship was formed with Cyril Carter, probably through Read's involvement in the work of the Design and Industries Association. Throughout the twenties both companies invited a number of artists and designers, mainly from the Royal College of Art, to submit patterns. In 1923 Read designed a charming pattern for tiles called *Kitchen*, that featured various motifs such as a fish on a plate, and some vegetables (Plate 275). Although not immediately included in the range, *Kitchen* was followed some years later by *Playbox*, and both patterns remained in production until the 1960s.[5]

In about 1930 Troughton and Young Ltd. were commissioned to design the lighting for Yaffle Hill, the new home that had been designed for Cyril and Truda Carter by the architect Edward Maufe. This outstanding modernist house included electric light fittings designed by Read and was featured in several important architectural and design magazines.[6] Read and his wife would often stay at Yaffle Hill during the thirties. His firm friendship with the Carters resulted in Read's appointment in 1952 as Head of the Design

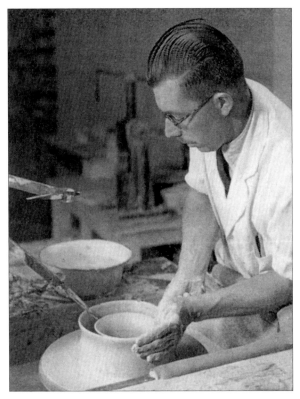

277. Guy Sydenham throwing a pot, about 1954.

278. Ruth Pavely applying a pattern by Alfred B. Read to a hand-thrown vase, about 1954.

279. A selection of earthenware plates, bowls and beakers decorated with the *Coronation* pattern. Designed by Alfred B. Read for Poole Pottery Ltd., 1953.

Unit, set up to serve both the pottery and the tile works.

Having enjoyed tremendous successes during the thirties, Poole Pottery had experienced a number of problems when re-starting after the War. As soon as was possible, major reconstruction began with over seventy-five per cent of the factory being demolished to make way for a new building.[7] (Plate 276) In 1947 Roy Holland was appointed Works Director and in 1950 Lucien Myers succeeded John Adams as Managing Director. Also in 1950, Claude Smale, a recent graduate from the Royal College of Art, was appointed to the design post vacated by John Adams on his retirement. He worked closely with Ruth Pavely, who had joined Poole in 1922 and had worked with Truda Carter to produce a collection of commemorative wares for the forthcoming Festival of Britain in 1951. Claude Smale, together with Guy Sydenham, designed a selection of hand-thrown vases that were in production for most of the fifties.[8] Smale's appointment was brief, however, lasting a mere six months, thus leaving the company without a designer until Read's appointment in 1952. Read therefore took up the position as Head of the Design Unit. His principal role at Poole was as a replacement for Reg Till, designer at the tile works, who had left in 1951. Carter's were first in the field with silk screen printed patterned tiles and these were being widely specified by architects in the early 1950s, thus creating a great deal of design work for prestigious

280. A large hand-painted *Coronation* dish produced in a limited run of twenty-five. Designed by Alfred B. Read for Poole Pottery Ltd., 1953. Diameter 15½in. (39.5cm).

281. A selection of tablewares including *Constellation* (OK), *Adraine* (OS), *Feather Drift* (NN) and *Ripple* (OV). The floral pattern (right) is Trudiana, based on a pattern by Truda Carter. Designed by Alfred B. Read for Poole Pottery Ltd., 1954.

282. A selection of Streamline shapes decorated with the hand-painted *Ripple* pattern (OV). Designed by Alfred B. Read for Poole Pottery Ltd., 1954.

contracts. The status of Read as a Royal Designer for Industry must have given prestige to the Poole Pottery. Leslie Hayward commented in his book on Poole Pottery: 'Under Read's direction Poole embarked on a period of close co-operation between artists and technicians that resulted in a range of stylish and elegant wares whose unity of shape and decoration expressed totally the spirit of the fifties.'[9]

Read worked closely with two people – Guy Sydenham and Ruth Pavely – both members of the Design Unit. Sydenham, who had joined the company in 1932, was the company's senior thrower and worked closely with Read to develop a number of shapes

for hand-throwing or casting (Plate 277). Read clearly benefited from Guy Sydenham's considerable skills and experience. The same system would have probably been followed for the range of surface patterns that he developed. Ruth Pavely would have adapted Read's patterns to the various shapes, and then trained the paintresses in suitable methods of marking out the pots before painting. Unlike the 'traditional' patterns, no pounces were used. Although the influences on Read's designs are unclear, it is probable that he looked to Swedish design. Some of his first patterns were similar to the work of Ingrid Atterberg,

283. A selection of wares. Left to right: 686/YF.T, 691/YF.I; 185/YF.P. Designed by Alfred B. Read for Poole Pottery Ltd., about 1953-55. Height of tallest vase 11⅝in. (29.5cm).

284. A selection of hand-thrown shapes decorated with the PK.T pattern. Left to right: Shape vase 704, vase 711, vase 700, vase 715. Designed by Alfred B. Read for Poole Pottery Ltd. Shapes 704 and 715 date from 1953-55, 711 and 700 are both from 1955-59. Height of tallest vase 10⅝in. (27cm).

241

285. A range of
Contemporary patterns. Left
to right: a carafe
698/PK.C, from 1959-62,
a vase 694/PJ.B from
1955-59, a carafe
698/PL.T from 1959-62, a
vase 694/PK.T from 1955-
59, and a carafe 698/PJ.L
from 1955-59. Designed
by Alfred B. Read for Poole
Pottery Ltd. Height of tallest
item 15⅜in. (39cm).

the designer who worked for the Uppsala-Ekeby AB in Sweden. Her range of pottery, called Graphica, was illustrated in *Design* magazine in 1951. The same edition featured an article by Read entitled 'Versatility in Lighting'.[10]

For the most part, Read worked on his designs from his studio at the Carter & Co. Ltd. offices at 44 Bloomsbury Street, London. He would travel down to the factory from time to time to see how his designs were being developed. Read turned his attention to the production of a number of commemorative wares for the forthcoming Coronation celebrations of 1953. These patterns mostly featured the Royal Coat of Arms. One range of vases and beakers was complemented with banded decoration (Plate 279). In contrast to those wares, Read also produced an outstanding dish with a calligraphic border that read: 'Her Majesty Queen Elizabeth, Coronation June 2nd 1953' (Plate 280). This item was displayed at the Tea Centre, in Regent Street, London, alongside Read's experimental work, in 1953. He then developed a range of patterns that included *Ariadne* (OS), *Ripple* (OV), *Feather Drift* (NN) and *Constellation* (OK), decorated on the Streamline shape that he updated in 1954 (Plate 281). His patterns were also used for a wide range of shapes including mugs and jam-pots as well as dinnerware (Plate 282). During that year the distinctive black panther glaze was introduced and Read created several complementary patterns such as (QW), a stylised Greek key border and a stylised leaf motif (TQ).[11] Some years later the designer David Queensberry poignantly noted that it was '…a great shame that Read did not produce a tableware shape in the contemporary style as it would certainly have rivalled Midwinter's Stylecraft and Fashion ranges.'[12]

Read's most important contribution to Poole Pottery was his series of 'Contemporary' shapes and patterns for vases. These first shapes consisted of eight items, each given a code number ranging from 692 to 715. The various sizes of each item were allocated different numbers. Read also used a variety of established shapes, including the four

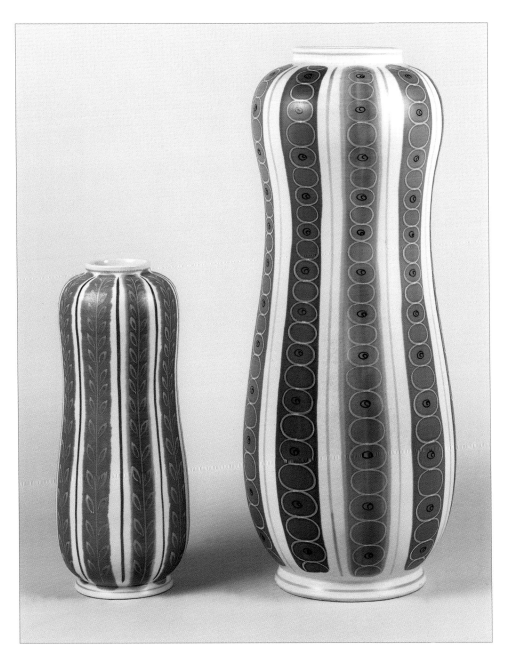

carafes (688-691) and four vases (684-687) designed by Claude Smale and Guy Sydenham. These experimental pieces, the combined efforts of the Design Unit, were shown for the first time at the Tea Centre in London in 1953. By 1954 a range of patterns had been designed by Read that were both simple and fresh, using banded decoration effectively combined with stylised motifs such as ferns (YF), produced in four colour variations (Plate 283). Another notable design from this outstanding range of patterns was (PK.T) that consisted of vertical coloured bands (Plate 284). Read developed several other patterns, including (PK.C), (PL.T) and (PJ.L), that were more complex, using vertical bands with overpainted decoration of squares and circles (Plate 285). The (PG.T) pattern incorporated a more formal vertical band of leaf motifs (Plate 286). Most of this range was stamped with the stylised Dolphin motif, with the words 'POOLE ENGLAND, HAND

286. Two contrasting items. Left: Earthenware vase 700/PG.T, from 1953-55. The taller earthenware vase, 702/PL.T., 17⅝in. (45cm) high, dates from 1959-62. Designed by Alfred B. Read for Poole Pottery Ltd.

287. A collection of shapes by Alfred B. Read and Guy Sydenham, glazed in solid colours. About 1954-57.

MADE, HAND DECORATED'.

The new 'Contemporary' range was featured in the important journals and magazines of the period, again placing Poole Pottery at the forefront of British Design. In 1954 a range of white earthenwares decorated with one colour glazes were introduced. The colours included lime yellow, ice green and magnolia (Plate 287). During that year a large collection of Poole Pottery was donated to the Pitt-Rivers Museum in Farnham following a suggestion by the current curator that the museum should have examples of notable local craftsmanship. The collection included pieces from the early part of the century, several patterns by Truda Carter and a number of items by Read. The local press noted that 'his striking new hand painted patterns on vases and carafes represent an entirely new departure in design at Poole, while yet retaining a link with the earlier style.'[13]

In 1955 Ivor Kamlish, a recent graduate from the Central School of Art, was appointed as Read's assistant. He worked closely with Read, solely at the tile works. Read submitted a number of linear patterns for tile designs to Carter and Co. These appeared in the company's catalogue of 1958 under the banner 'Dolphin Screen Printed Ceramic Tiles' alongside contributions from Robert Nicholson.[14]

In 1956, whilst undergoing treatment in a local sanatorium after suffering from tuberculosis, Read developed sketch ideas for a range of free-form shapes for floral arrangements. From these sketches eight slip-cast shapes were produced. These were decorated with a number of patterns by Ruth Pavely and Ann Read, such as Loops (PW), Stars (FS), Tadpoles (PX), Ravioli (GG) and Basket (GB) (Plate 288). Read's daughter, Ann, had joined the Tileworks in 1952 after studying at the Chelsea School of Art in London. She later transferred to the Pottery and developed several patterns for plaques and other items.[15] Following his recovery, Read also designed a wide selection of shapes that included a club ashtray (shape 357), egg cup on stand (shape 104), butter dish (shape

354) and cheese dish (shape 355). These were illustrated in the New Giftwares supplementary leaflet in 1958.

Probably due to his poor health, Read resigned his position in 1957. In 1959 Poole Pottery issued a new trade catalogue that illustrated the latest range of free form pieces, including the current tablewares, beer mugs, nut bowl and a gentlemen's set. Read's patterns were illustrated in this catalogue and in subsequent publications from 1960 to 1962.

When Read was in better health he returned to Troughton and Young Ltd. Towards the end of his life he lived at Blandford Forum in Dorset. He died on 10 October 1973. His obituary noted that Read was a craftsman in metal who designed and made silverware and jewellery. The same article also observed that he drew buildings with a Ruskinian manner and was an accomplished painter.[16]

As examples of Poole Pottery from the twenties and thirties, particularly the work of Truda Carter, are becoming both harder to find and rather expensive, collectors have begun to look into new periods of collecting. The innovative and original designs of Read are proving to be in demand. His works, due for reassessment, can safely be considered as modern design classics. During a presentation to the Poole Collectors' Club in September 1996, David Queensberry noted that 'The free-form shapes and decorations designed by Alfred Read in the mid-fifties stand up today as being amongst the most interesting ceramics in the "contemporary style".'[17]

288. A selection of patterns designed by Ruth Paveley decorated on shapes designed by Alfred B. Read. These are Horizontal Rope 719/HY, Ravioli 717/HOU and Loops 724/PW, all from 1956. Height of tallest vase 14in (35.5cm).

CHAPTER 12

MIDWINTER MODERN

JESSIE TAIT (b.1928)

289. Portrait of Jessie Tait in the Design Studio, 1952.

Jessie Tait was one of the new breed of contemporary designers to emerge from a country at war and deprived of innovative and exciting pottery. She created colourful patterns for a new generation of young people who wanted taste at affordable prices. From a very early age she was determined to contribute her own style to ceramic design and was inspired by the work of Susie Cooper. Her designs for the Midwinter Pottery during the 1950s and 1960s caused a sensation and were very successful. From the late seventies onwards she produced designs for both J. & G. Meakin and Johnson Brothers, which have yet to be evaluated and appreciated.

Dorothy Jessie Tait, born in Tunstall, Stoke-on-Trent on 6 March 1928, is the youngest of three children, with two brothers. Her parents met during the First World War. Her mother, born in Kent, was quite artistic, according to Tait. Like so many of her generation she had been unable to pursue her creative skills as her immediate responsibility was to raise a family. However, she wanted her children to have the opportunity to do something different.

Following her formal education at a school in Tunstall, Tait enrolled at the Burslem School of Art in 1940, after passing the entrance exam at the age of thirteen. She spent two years in the Junior Department, run by Mr. Johnson, being taught a wide range of subjects such as

still life by Miss Brough, throwing by Harold Thomas and Celtic design by Miss McBride. Tait also attended a whole range of classes including life drawing, plant drawing, anatomy and architecture. In particular, Leonard Brammer taught the students etching and engraving. One half of the course, however, was set aside for general subjects such as English, some of these being taught by a Miss Farrington. Tait also attended the night sessions at the School of Art which she described as 'stimulating and informative'.[1]

She was fortunate to be able to move to the Senior Department with financial help from her elder brother. There she was taught throwing by William Ruscoe, whilst Mr. Deardon taught lithography, in the school's cellar. During her three years in the Senior Department she was sent to the firm of A.E. Gray and Co. Ltd., on a work placement for two weeks, where she was encouraged to explore and experiment in pottery decoration.

Sadly, whilst Tait was in the Senior Department, Gordon Forsyth, the Superintendent of the Art Schools, became ill and had to be replaced. The acting principal was the well-respected writer, designer and painter Reginald Haggar. Eventually Professor Baker was appointed to the position. As her enthusiasm for painting in oils increased, Tait became interested in pursuing a career as a fine artist, with an ambition to study at the Royal

290. A large earthenware meat plate, diameter 13¾in. (35cm), decorated with the hand-painted pattern *Primavera*, from the Stylecraft range. Designed by Jessie Tait for W.R. Midwinter Ltd., 1954.

291. An earthenware side plate painted with the *Fiesta* pattern, from the Stylecraft range. Designed by Jessie Tait for W.R. Midwinter Ltd., 1954. Diameter of plate 6¼in. (16cm).

College of Art in London. Despite taking part one of the entrance exam in 1945, and securing a grant, it soon became apparent that she needed to work in local industry to help support her family. Her father had just retired from the Gas Board. In seeking a job she was assisted by Professor Baker, who was very aware of her determination to design and make her own statement.

In 1945 Professor Baker was able to secure Tait a post with H.J. Wood, at the Alexandra Pottery, Burslem, as an assistant to Charlotte Rhead. This famous designer, well known for her outstanding range of tube-lined designs, had joined the firm in 1942 after leaving Crown Ducal. It was a good start for Tait, who had an advantage of already having been taught slip trailing whilst at college. Further training in tube-lined decoration was given by the woman in charge of the decorating shop. Tait must have believed that she would be able to realise her dream of becoming a designer within the firm. However, it was soon clear that this was impossible, as the firm was operating under post-war austerity measures, with limited supplies of materials and staff. It was restricted to producing ornamental wares for orders placed on the export market. Tait's role was chiefly involved in the production of Charlotte Rhead's designs. Not surprisingly, she became dissatisfied with the work, feeling that she had little opportunity to develop. In spite of reassurances from Charlotte Rhead that

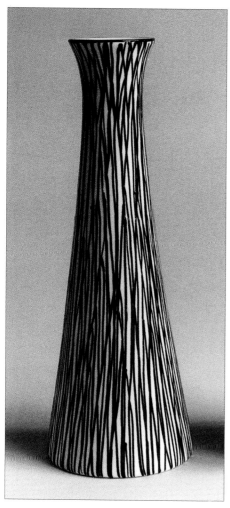

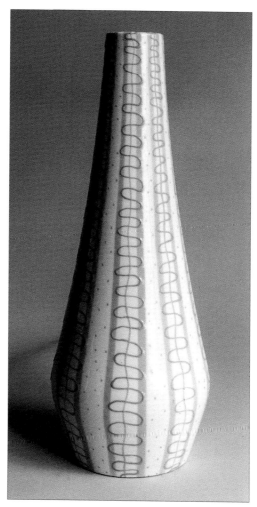

292. A candlestick decorated with the *Tonga*
pattern, tube-lined in black slip. Designed by
Jessie Tait for W.R. Midwinter Ltd., 1954.

293. A lesser known decorative vase, tube-lined with
hand-painted decoration, probably a trial pattern by
Jessie Tait, about 1955.

she would eventually be able to design, Tait was disillusioned. After working with the firm
for only six months, she saw Professor Baker at night school and told him of her
disappointment with her job. He asked if she would like to be interviewed for a vacancy
at the firm of W.R. Midwinter.

The Midwinter firm was a small family concern, initially established at the Bournes Bank
site in 1910. It later moved to the Albion and Hadderidge Potteries on Navigation Road
in Burslem, following expansion in 1914.[2] Typical patterns of the 1920s included Blue
Willow and a series of amusing nursery wares such as Jack Sprat and Old Nat King Cole.[3]
Their range of traditional shapes included Belle and Avon. During the Second World War
most of the factory was closed, in part used by both the Ministry of Defence and the
Ministry of Aircraft Production.[4] Tait took a portfolio of her design work to the interview,
and was offered the job by Mr. Midwinter, Senior. After working a week's notice at the
Alexandra Pottery, she started her new job in August 1947. At about that time the
Midwinter company was about to embark on modernisation, including the formation of a

new decorating department, packing office and the installation of new equipment.

Tait had settled into her post when Roy Midwinter, the son of the owner, returned after five years as a pilot in the Royal Air Force. Although he started at the bottom, working in the various departments to gain experience, he was to play a major role in the success of the firm and importantly in Tait's career for over thirty years. In order to understand production and manufacturing processes, he also studied at the local technical college to gain a manager's certificate.

Typical patterns of the late 1940s included traditional printed designs such as Rural England, and stylised florals. With the burden of restrictions on the sales of ware in Britain still in place, the factory made what it could sell to the export market. At that time, modern design was not seen as important.

To fight off the post-war gloom, a range of Handcraft patterns was produced in underglaze crayons, ranging from stylised leaves to pictorial patterns. These were produced by a team, including Tait. Although they were given a free run on the designs they were always aware that they had to be speedy enough to earn wages.[5] In 1950 Roy Midwinter became Sales and Design Director, helping to re-establish the company's good fortunes by encouraging the development of new modern design and updating the current range. Roy Midwinter encouraged Tait to create new designs using her own ideas, albeit on a range of traditional wares, including the Hudson shape. These designs provided an opportunity to train the decorators to undertake more detailed and intricate hand-painted decoration. The first steps into the modern style of design are evident in patterns such as *Moonfleur*, introduced in 1950, which featured incised forms with clay stains in grey, beige and blue. A painted version, in green and blue, was also produced. Typical patterns such as *Parkleigh*, *Regal* and *Wynwood*, featured hand-painted leaf borders with gilt decoration whilst *Maytime*, a floral border, was a transfer printed design from her original artwork. As early as 1952 Roy Midwinter was keen to promote the role of Tait as the firm's designer, by featuring her name in various trade advertisements and on the backstamp. Several other designs were produced during this period but these have yet to be attributed to her.

As Sales Director, Roy Midwinter went on a tour of the North American market in August 1952, taking with him a range of patterns not really designed for export, which not surprisingly received a cool response.[6] Colonel Keene, the influential buyer for Eaton's Stores in Canada, bluntly told him: 'I will shoot the next man who comes all the way over from Stoke to show me some more English Roses.'[7] Despite his criticism, he did give Midwinter some advice, telling him to visit the West Coast of America to examine the latest shapes and patterns by American designers such as Eva Zeisel, Raymond Loewy and Russell Wright, who were leading the way with softer, more organic shapes. Roy Midwinter examined these new ranges and found that the American public favoured coupe shape plates that were rimless. Several examples were despatched to the Midwinter factory for them to examine, followed by many cables between Roy Midwinter and the factory. As soon as he returned to the factory the project was discussed further. His

experiences told him that North American customers wanted something new and different. It was decided that Midwinter would produce a full-scale version of its own shape range for the export trade and the British market once restrictions were lifted. He realised that this was a big financial risk but he believed in the project. The Stylecraft range was developed from a number of sources, not least the skilled work of William Lunt. Inspiration for the coupe plate came from a nut bowl. Stylecraft consisted of forty practical and functional shapes which were to be ready for the Blackpool Fair in February 1953. This gave them less than six months to complete the whole production.

The development of new patterns was given to Tait, who was inspired by these new shapes. Working from her own studio, she began to develop designs, having access to all the relevant departments and choosing always to work on biscuit ware rather than on paper. Firstly she looked at contemporary interior design and furnishings for inspiration. Her aim was to put her own personality into the ware and attain something in design, understanding that she needed to capture the mood of the day and to design pottery that complemented the modern interior. Several floral designs were created to appeal to the housewife, who usually bought the household pottery. Tait co-ordinated the development and production of thirty-six new patterns for the Stylecraft range. The range was put together using bought-in lithographs, Tait's designs and those from outside designers. One

294. The striking *Zambesi* pattern, hand-painted in red and black on an earthenware Fashion shape tureen and cover. Designed by Jessie Tait for W.R. Midwinter Ltd., 1956. Width of tureen 9⅞in. (25cm).

of the first and most outstanding successes was Encore, a combination of a bought-in lithographic centre motif with a hand-painted shaded band. It was so popular that the factory could not cope with the increased orders.[8] Other successful bought-in lithographs included Pussy Willow.

The production of new hand-painted designs was quite an undertaking, as the paintresses were unfamiliar with such complex designs. In order to achieve the desired effect many patterns required a pounce. To enable them to gain the skills and confidence Tait would sit with them and demonstrate how to achieve the desired effect in hand painting. When she was busy her assistant would inspect the work to make sure the standard of decoration remained high and that there wasn't too much variation in the patterns.[9] Tait's notable designs for Stylecraft included *Primavera* (Plate 290), an outstanding hand-painted design that used several colourful abstract motifs, reminiscent of the Festival of Britain, from 1951, and later modified for the Fashion shape. *Homeweave* was a very simple plaid decoration produced in a whole range of colour variations and was later copied by many pottery companies. The detailed *Ming Tree* was decorated by means of print and enamel, whilst the colourful *Fiesta* pattern was hand painted (Plate 291).

Tait supervised the patterns produced by the free-lance designers brought in by Roy Midwinter, who were well known for their contemporary designs. She modified these

295. A period photograph taken in the newly designed showroom, 1956. Note W.R. Midwinter, senior (front, centre).

designs, where required, so that they would fit on the shapes. The Riviera pattern, by Hugh Casson, became an outstanding success and sold for many years. The artist Peter Scott developed Wild Geese in about 1955, proving popular throughout the fifties and also the sixties. The production of all the patterns had to be complete in time for the important trade fair in February 1953. Fortunately, simultaneously, restrictions on the sale of goods in Britain were lifted. The launch of Stylecraft was accompanied by an extensive publicity campaign, and the trade press noted: 'The new Stylecraft tableware cannot strictly be described as a copy of American coupe ware, but rather an improved version embodying all the advantages of its American counterpart, but possessing also other characteristics likely to make it more acceptable here.'[10]

Roy Midwinter targeted the younger generation in particular by producing starter sets for newly-wed couples. Each pack contained four cups, saucers, plates, dinner plates and oatmeal plates. Associated items such as tureens and condiments could be purchased separately. When Stylecraft was launched there was little competition within the industry and Midwinter was viewed by many of the more traditional companies as something of an oddity. However, as sales continued to rise beyond the trade's expectations several companies began to copy the range.[11] The trade press highlighted the firm's achievements and recognised the important role that Tait had played in the realisation from first idea to the launch of the range – 'a quiet, unassuming artist, Miss Tait has not hitherto achieved prominence as a pottery designer. Her work for Midwinter's, however, shows that she is one of the industry's most promising young artists, of whom more will be heard in the future.'[12]

With Stylecraft selling well, Tait became involved with the Clayburn Pottery, established

296. Three examples of patterns on the Fine shape. Left to right: *Mexicana* from 1966, *Sienna* from 1962 and *Spanish Garden* from 1968. Designed by Jessie Tait for W.R. Midwinter Ltd. Height of tallest coffee-pot 8¼in. (21cm).

297. An example of one of the many *Spanish Garden* kitchen accessories produced from about 1970. Height of pot 7⅞in. (19.5cm).

by William Lunt and Mr. Edgerton in 1953. Initially the intention was to produce a few pieces to present to family and friends but production began to increase, mainly undertaken by William Lunt. The appropriate equipment was installed at a works located in Milner Street in Hanley and it soon became a commercial venture, with the aim of producing a range of individual studio items. Lunt employed his sister-in-law, Mary Lunt, to be responsible for the decorating, and Mrs. H. Oldacre to cast and sponge, both working on a part-time basis.[13] Roy Midwinter became a partner in the venture, taking on special responsibilities for sales. The Midwinter firm had exclusive rights to the products of the studio. The intention was that designs should conform to contemporary trends in interior furnishing and decoration. To enable Tait to complete the patterns, a box of blank wares, such as vases and lamp bases, would be dropped off at her home for her to decorate. Her stylish patterns used various floral motifs and animal forms.[14]

Popular motifs created by Jessie Tait at Midwinter were often interpreted by the Clayburn paintresses and therefore cannot be attributed to her. Tait didn't sign the wares that she designed as she was working for Midwinter at the same time. Instead, these pieces were marked with the words 'Individual pottery by Clayburn, Staffordshire'. When William Lunt decided to leave the area, the firm had to shut down.

For a limited period in 1956 Tait produced a range of patterns for vases and flasks for Midwinter. Her decorative wares for Clayburn should not be confused with these items,

which were decorated with tubelined or banded decoration such as *Tonga* (Plate 292). She designed ten shapes, including a water flask (201), beaker (202), vase shapes (203-206 and 209) and two candlestick holders (207-208). Each piece was clearly marked with the words 'designed by Jessie Tait' and constituted the only shapes that she designed for Midwinter. Tait also produced a range of individual patterns at the Burslem School of Art and occasionally at home (Plate 293).

To remain market leaders, Roy Midwinter developed a new shape range called Fashion. This range, which he created with William Lunt, went a step further in the direction of modernism. Despite some production problems, Fashion was launched at the British Industries Fair in 1955. Four of the first six patterns: *Festival*, *Falling Leaves*, *Pierrot* and *Capri*, were designed by Tait. The *Festival* pattern was inspired by her trip to the Festival of Britain a few years earlier. This complex design, using several different colours, required the use of a pounce to recreate the abstract symbols. Contemporary marketing promoted the design as portraying 'the gaiety and fun associated with a festival, depicting streamers, balloons and confetti'. The trade press observed: 'the handles, spouts, lips and knobs, have assumed graceful free flowing, curved shapes, which harmonise perfectly with the main bodies of the pots themselves to give an ensemble of unique beauty'.[15]

Tait went on to design over forty further patterns including *Chopsticks*, *Driftdown*, *Magic Moments* and *Cuban Fantasy*. New decorative techniques were exploited to create

298. The *Country Garden* pattern printed on a Fine shape earthenware coffee-pot, height 7½in. (19cm). Designed by Jessie Tait for W.R. Midwinter Ltd., about 1968.

299. A large Fine shape earthenware plate, diameter 10⅜in. (26.5cm), decorated with the printed *Valencia* pattern. Designed by Jessie Tait for W.R. Midwinter Ltd., about 1968-70.

patterns such as *Savanna*, using sponged motifs. Tait also experimented with the moulds by cutting into the clay to create a grid-like effect, which was then complemented by sponging areas with colour, on the *Mosaic* pattern, from about 1960. Her *Toadstool* pattern was developed to match a fabric design of toadstools produced by the firm Rosebanks. The Midwinter family used the Cassandra pattern, a bought-in transfer printed design, at their home.[16] The *Flowermist* pattern, featuring stylised flowers, reflected the styles of contemporary textile designs. Tait's outstanding *Zambesi* pattern (Plate 294), featuring an overall zebra print design with solid red decoration, was launched in 1956. This pattern proved so popular that it was widely copied by other manufacturers. This design, alongside Cassandra, *Cherokee* and *Monaco*, featured in a Midwinter advertisement giving the firm an opportunity to boast: 'Here is a selection of Jessie Tait designs on Midwinter Modern Fashion shape Tableware. They are modern in conception and provide harmony of colour and design to match modern furnishings and home decor while giving a fresh look to table layouts.'[17]

Tait designed the majority of patterns, with others commissioned by Roy Midwinter from young designers, mainly from London. He encouraged them not to be limited by the confines of pottery production. Terence Conran produced Salad Ware, Nature Study, Plant Life, Chequers and Melody between 1955 and 1957, all proving commercially successful. He also produced black and white designs for a series of fancies featuring vintage cars, flying machines and paddle-steamers. He redesigned the firm's showrooms,

300. The *April Showers* pattern printed on the MQ2 shape. Designed by Jessie Tait for W.R. Midwinter Ltd., from 1967. Width of plate 6⅞in. (17.5cm).

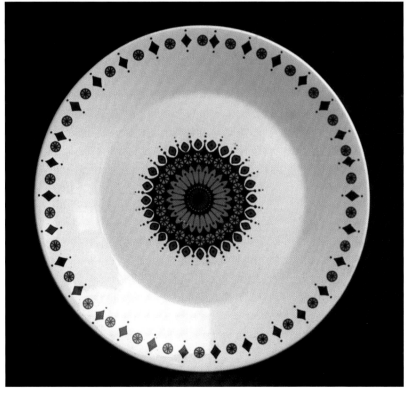

301. An example of the lesser known *Inca* pattern, originally designed by Jessie Tait for Midwinter but used by J. & G. Meakin Ltd., in about 1972.

302. The *Impact* pattern, printed on the Studio shape coffee-pot, height 9¼in. (23.5cm). Designed by Jessie Tait for J. & G. Meakin Ltd., about 1972.

providing a sympathetic setting for the Midwinter product (Plate 295).[18] John Russell contributed Magnolia, Carmen and Countryside, whilst Colin Melbourne modelled animals, such as giraffes, bison and jaguar, for a series of 'contemporary figures' advertised by the firm in the trade press in 1957. A few Stylecraft patterns, such as Riviera, were adapted for the Fashion shape. To meet demand from the North American market Roy Midwinter requested a modern version of the Thanksgiving turkey plate. Tait created an audacious pattern called the *Gay Gobbler*. She also designed several nurseryware patterns, including a beaker depicting a pink elephant and tea ware with aeroplane, cricket bat and spinning top motifs.[19]

As early as 1960 Midwinter discussed the introduction of a new shape to lead the industry towards new standards in pottery design. The decision to develop this shape coincided with the trend for a whiter body. In 1961 Clive Rogers, the Works Director, undertook the research necessary to produce a body with improved colour, strength and durability.[20] Through its development it was apparent to the team that the shape should be modern and English, not to be confused with German, Swedish or American styles. Roy Midwinter commented that when designing for tableware one should always start with the

coffee-pot.[21] The shape was designed by Professor David Queensberry, Head of the School of Ceramics at the Royal College of Art. He worked very closely with Sid Machin, head modeller at Midwinter. Before a satisfactory shape could be achieved thirty-one modifications were made to the prototype for the Fine shape.

This new shape was designed to take all forms of decoration, despite the move away from expensive painted designs. The range consisted of tea, coffee and dinnerware with some smaller items being produced as well. A new backstamp incorporating the words 'Fine Tableware' was introduced. In October 1961 fifty-three surface patterns were shown to the trade in North America. The twelve patterns selected comprised eight modern and four classical and were later shown, with six others, at a South African trade fair for further selection.[22] The final selection, previewed at the Blackpool Fancy Goods and Gifts Fair in March 1962, was Queensberry Stripe, Evesham, Meadow, Golden Leaves, Olympus, Kingcup, and *Whitehill* and *Sienna* by Tait. The latter pattern was one of the most outstanding and popular patterns produced by the company and was extensively advertised in the trade press both at home and abroad (Plate 296). Most importantly, the influential Canadian store Eaton's recognised the pattern's potential, securing its exclusivity in the Canadian provinces. It was also accepted by the Design Council for their Design Index. In 1972 the trade press reported that 20,000 dozen pieces a week of *Sienna* were being produced.[23]

In 1964 Roy Midwinter spoke at a lunch-time meeting of the Design and Industries Association and outlined how the company had converted, with the introduction of the Fine

303. Examples of patterns for the Stonehenge range. A *Caprice* coffee-pot and jug decorated with the *Blue Dahlia* pattern. Designed by Jessie Tait for W.R. Midwinter Ltd., 1972. Height of coffee-pot 6⅞in. (17.5cm).

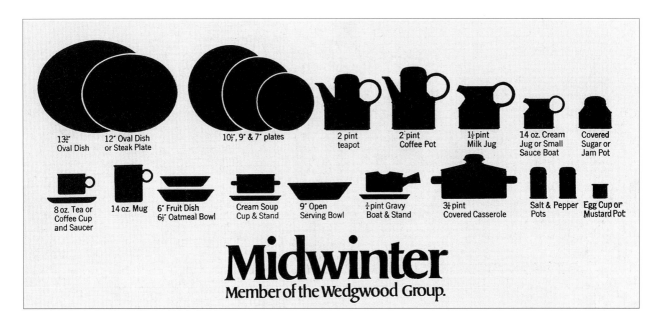

Within the leaflet image the following labels appear:

13¾" Oval Dish | 12" Oval Dish or Steak Plate | 10½", 9" & 7" plates | 2 pint teapot | 2 pint Coffee Pot | 1½ pint Milk Jug | 14 oz. Cream Jug or Small Sauce Boat | Covered Sugar or Jam Pot

8 oz. Tea or Coffee Cup and Saucer | 14 oz. Mug | 6" Fruit Dish 6½" Oatmeal Bowl | Cream Soup Cup & Stand | 9" Open Serving Bowl | ½ pint Gravy Boat & Stand | 3¼ pint Covered Casserole | Salt & Pepper Pots | Egg Cup or Mustard Pot

304. A publicity leaflet showing the many shapes produced for the Stonehenge range.

shape, into a pottery fashion house: style first, price second, a method of working that suited the size of factory.[24] A year later he formed a local branch of the Association.

To maintain the introduction of new stylish designs, several young designers, including Barbara Brown and Nigel Wilde, were commissioned to produce patterns. These were first shown on the company's stand at the Blackpool Fair in 1964. Four black panels displayed photographs of the individual designers and examples of their work. Simultaneously, a selection of more traditional items was introduced to increase sales in the more conservative market. At the same time, hotel ware and at least 360 figures and shapes were phased out.

Tait produced over twenty-five individual designs for the Fine shape with notable examples including *Mexicana* and *Spanish Garden* (Plate 296). The former was a hand-painted border design in orange and greens that was later reproduced, due to demand, by lithography. In 1964 a coffee set was priced at £3 7s 6d. The most successful pattern on the Fine shape was *Spanish Garden*, introduced in 1968 and in production for almost twenty years. Tait was given an open-ended brief to interpret the original inspiration, which came from a Liberty tie worn by both David Queensberry and Roy Midwinter at the same party. They were so amused that they thought it worth discussing whether it would make a good ceramic design.

The popularity of this pattern and new demands from the buying public prompted Midwinter to develop co-ordinated matching kitchenware. The pattern was licensed to two companies to be reproduced on kitchen items such as chopping boards, frying pans, cake tins and bread bins, but did not prove popular (Plate 297). The trade press noted in 1972 that the best selling patterns, *Country Garden* (Plate 298), and *Spanish Garden*, 'stood out in the High Street shops like gazelles in the snow, different and improbable in their combination of elegance, liveliness and low price.'[25]

Tait went on to design several more important patterns on the Fine shape, including *Jasmine* and *Berkeley*, dating from the late sixties. Further patterns included *Michaelmas*, *Sunglow* and *Valencia* (Plate 299). Whilst *Sienna* and Queensberry were available until

305. The *Nasturtium* pattern
decorated on an
earthenware side plate from
the Stonehenge range.
Designed by Jessie Tait for
W.R. Midwinter Ltd., from
1974. Diameter 7in.
(18cm).

1978 the Fine range was entirely withdrawn by 1982.

The sixties was a period of great success and change for Midwinter. Growing demand prompted Roy Midwinter, in 1963, to consider expansion in order to increase production. In 1964 Midwinter acquired the long established A.J. Wilkinson Ltd., and the Newport Pottery based in Burslem. Both Roy Midwinter and H.C. Rogers became joint Managing Directors of the two firms, with Mr. A.B. Walton appointed as Sales Director and Mr. Thistle as Works Manager.[26] About 300 members of Wilkinson's staff were kept on, which helped to speed up delivery of orders. Within two years all production was moved to this site and the company began a radical reorganisation of the works and the installation of the latest machinery. The old Midwinter site at Hadderidge was sold to the firm of Bolton's, an engineering company.

In 1966 some modifications were made to the Fine shape that included the removal of the knob on the tea and coffee-pots. Not only was this an economical move but it also made it possible to place a motif on the top. During this period the first proper oven-to-tableware range was produced by Midwinter. The new range, comprising twenty-nine items, was called Trend. This fluted ware utilised coloured glazes such as black, olive, white and blue which proved problematic, as matching the ware after firing was difficult. Despite the reliance on a coloured body, Tait did design one pattern for this range called

306. A photograph of Jessie Tait working on patterns for the Chelsea Collection, 1972.

Sherwood, carefully combining the green glaze with simple stylised motifs on the lids and covers of the wares. Her name featured on the backstamp. Trend was first shown at the Blackpool Fair of 1965, alongside similar versions by Poole and Johnson Brothers.

The Portobello shape was produced by the Canadian potter David Long in 1966. Glazes used on this shape included Conifer, Maple and Spruce, suggesting a marketing move towards the Canadian market. Despite poor initial sales, the range was given a second push a few years later. Tait designed one pattern, not named, featuring a stylised floral medallion in brown on the flat ware and lids with hollowwares glazed in brown. Despite publicity photographs being taken of her pattern, it was not produced until a few years later, on the Stonehenge shape, as *Medallion* and *Blue Dahlia*.

During the late sixties a new shape range was developed that was to be called the MQ2 shape, designed by Roy Midwinter and David Queensberry. Based on a cylinder and sphere, it evolved from a desire to introduce something a little more elegant for the period. Its development proved difficult, with no fewer than forty cup shapes being produced before a satisfactory solution was achieved. Tait developed a wide range of patterns for the MQ2 shape and from these three contemporary florals were selected. Her *April Showers* and *September Song* patterns, with overtones of the art nouveau style, were identical but produced in two different colourways (Plate 300). The two other patterns used on this shape were Tait's *Columbine* and Pierrot by Nigel Wilde. However, the application of transfer prints proved difficult due to the shapes of the wares.[27] The MQ2 shape was launched at the Blackpool Fair in 1968 and consisted of a teapot, sugar, coffee cream, covered vegetable bowl and teacup and saucer. Sadly MQ2 received such a cool reception from both buyers and the trade press that it was phased out after a couple of years. *April Showers* was later used on the Fine shape, but renamed *Springtime*. Tait developed a similar range

for the Pedestal giftware, also for the 1968 Blackpool Fair. These items included a bowl, lidded preserve pot, beaker and condiment set. Despite being illustrated on the cover of the *Gift Buyer International* magazine in February 1968, they did not go into production. Midwinter was over-stretched and unable to meet the increasing orders, compounded by the relative failures of the MQ2 and the Portobello ranges.

In 1968 Midwinter was taken over by the long established firm of J. & G. Meakin, based at the Eagle Pottery in Hanley. Meakin was formed by two brothers, James and George Meakin, in 1851. They designed and produced pottery chiefly for the North American market. Meakin tableware was standard equipment on the wagon trains that carried settlers westward across America to open up California.[28] After the Second World War the works were modernised and extended. Family involvement in the business had dwindled to such an extent that by 1958 a new team of Executive Directors led by Mr. Joe Grundy, as Chairman, and Mr. D. Jones, as Vice Chairman, was formed.[29] This successful company had produced a wide range of designs both in the traditional print genre and more recently contemporary patterns such as Allegro and Garden Party for the Studio shape, introduced in 1964. Over sixty per cent of all production was exported to North America. Many patterns were developed by Mr. Trigger, who later retired. Phil Forster, employed to take over his role, was responsible for developing semi-contemporary patterns such as floral borders and stylised designs. At the time of the takeover the

307. A selection of coffee and dinner wares decorated with the *Monticello* pattern, printed on the Heirloom shape. Designed by Jessie Tait for Johnson Brothers Ltd., about 1981-82

Managing Director of Meakin's informed the trade press that the move enabled Midwinter to cope more swiftly with the demand for its distinctive modern designs and that the aim was for the group to seek quotation on the stock exchange. The combined assets of the group were £1 million. This merger provided an opportunity to exchange experiences and to pool resources to create an even larger share of the tableware market.

Shortly after the takeover, several patterns by Tait, already proofed for the Midwinter product, were taken on by Meakin. These included *Inca* (Plate 301), *Baroque*, *Galaxy*, *Mandalay* and *Impact*, for the Studio range (Plate 302). Meakin's also produced a new shape range based on Midwinter's MQ2 called Apollo, launched at the Blackpool Fair in 1970.[30] *Minuet*, one of the stylised patterns used on Apollo, was based on Tait's *Reverie* pattern for Midwinter. Sadly the aesthetics of this new interpretation of the shape were not successful and it appears not to have been in production for long. Both *Inca* and *Impact* were, according to the company, 'best sellers' and featured in a major promotional campaign organised in conjunction with *Woman's Own* magazine. A full colour centre spread was included in the magazine in April 1972. Meakin's Joint Managing Director was quoted: 'We are looking for national coverage and dominance plus the facilities to show in full colour as many patterns as possible.'[31]

Within two years of Midwinter relocating to the Meakin site both companies were taken over by Josiah Wedgwood and Sons Ltd. This company had recently made several acquisitions including Susie Cooper Ltd., Coalport, Johnson Brothers Ltd. and William Adams Ltd. Assurances were given to Meakin staff that their terms of employment would be respected.[32] Roy Midwinter, without doubt, viewed the takeover and the support that Wedgwood could offer him as an opportunity to finally break into the North American market. He said: 'For the first time all the ends are tied up, finance, design, distribution and promotion.'[33]

The Wedgwood Group requested a new shape range from Midwinter, prompted by a request from the US Wedgwood division. The new oven-to-tableware shape that they developed was designed by Roy Midwinter and Sid Machin. The original inspiration for the shape was based on the billy-can used on canal boats. The concept was to base the patterns on the style of bargeware, using the same colours, but that proved problematic.[34] The Stonehenge range consisted of twenty-six practical shapes including a one size cup for both tea and coffee and an open casserole which doubled as a fruit or salad bowl (Plate 303). Each piece was dishwasher safe and completely resistant to acids and alkalis. The surface patterns were developed to reflect rustic themes, using attractively bold floral patterns. They even went as far as to state that the Stonehenge range was inspired by the shapes and textures of nature. A special feature was made of the integral glaze colour available in either a sage, dark brown or pale cream finish. The first patterns, launched at the Blackpool Fair in 1972, included *Blue Dahlia* and *Caprice*. One of Tait's last designs for Midwinter was *Nasturtium* (Plate 305), which was withdrawn in 1976 due to the high levels of cadmium in the glaze.

Following further rationalisation by Wedgwood in about 1974, Jessie Tait was transferred to work for both J. & G. Meakin Ltd. and Johnson Brothers Ltd. Although the working environment was different from that enjoyed at Midwinter she was still in close contact with Roy Midwinter. In 1975 David Johnson took over as Managing Director of Midwinter, staying in this position until 1980.[35] In his new role, Roy Midwinter was responsible for co-ordinating design over the entire Wedgwood Group. At the same time Eve Midwinter developed new designs for Stonehenge. Meakin's speciality, by the early seventies, was the mass production of fashionable wares on a range of shapes but chiefly the Studio range, which comprised over thirty separate items. Under the banner 'A Bull in a China Shop', the firm extended its tableware range with the introduction of traditional designs with modern interpretations. A simple border pattern, *Wicker*, was produced in various colourways on the Liberty shape.

Some of Tait's designs were also taken on by Johnson Brothers Ltd., formed in 1833 by three brothers, Harry, Fred and Alfred. Over the years they had established a good business and export trade. The firm was famous for its range of traditional designs, such

308. An earthenware plate, coffee pot and cup and saucer decorated with the *Fleur L'Orange* pattern. Designed by Jessie Tait for Johnson Brothers Ltd., 1981-82.

309. The *Bonjour* pattern, printed on an Heirloom shape dinner plate, diameter 8⅞in. (22.5cm). 1981-82.

as Indies, Old Britain's Castles and the Dawns, the latter being self-coloured wares. During the early 1970s it decided to break away from tradition and produce modern ranges of tableware, uncertain of success.[36] Fortunately, with Tait, the company had an experienced and innovative designer to produce the contemporary patterns that it required. Despite the rather conservative North American market, the new initiative did prove successful. One of the first ranges was the Chelsea Collection developed by Tait (Plate 306). The four patterns, *Pimlico*, *Cheyne Walk*, *King's Road* and *Sloane Square* were launched in 1974. This collection's success convinced the company that it could capitalise in a new market, whilst still producing traditional patterns. The A La Carte range, featuring three floral patterns by Tait, *Fancy Free*, *Straw Hat* and *Honey Bunch*, was launched in 1975. The floral motifs were restricted to the plates and fruit bowls. Several patterns were decorated on a number of lesser-known shapes such as *Alpine* on Tivoli, and *Brookside* on the Cresta shape. The success of these ranges prompted Brian Greatbatch, Sales Director, to inform the press: "Now we intend to devote a good deal of our design activity to developing casual elegance in our products. With the new patterns, we can now offer a very wide variety, something for almost every taste."[37]

The Country Range, introduced in about 1979 on the Studio shape, was extensively publicised and marketed with full colour brochures featuring four patterns; Windswept, Poppy, Hedgerow, and a Tait design, *Wayside*. Following improved printing techniques developed by John Cope, some new patterns by Tait originally intended for the Meakin product were used instead by Johnson Brothers, as they found them so outstanding.[38] These patterns were showcased in a major promotion for the North American market entitled

'Pleasure of the Provinces.' Patterns included *Provincial*, *Monticello* (Plate 307) and *Fleur L'Orange* (Plate 308). One of the most outstanding designs of the period, also marking a change in artistic direction, was *Bonjour* (Plate 309), designed by Tait for the Heirloom shape. The promotion included two patterns for the Laura Ashley store: Petite Fleur Burgundy and Petite Fleur Blue on the softer Cottage shape. Unfortunately the Pleasure of the Provinces became a victim of the changes and rationalisations within the earthenware division of the Wedgwood group. Although some patterns continued in production, others were withdrawn. Eventually the Meakin backstamp was phased out and all subsequent designs by Tait were produced for Johnson Brothers. Lesser known patterns include *Deauville* and *Tulip Time*.

In 1980 Josiah Wedgwood and Sons Ltd. purchased the firm of Enoch Wedgwood, based in Tunstall, re-naming the firm Unicorn Pottery shortly afterwards. Johnson Brothers utilised the modern Marquess shape, designed by Lord Queensberry, for several patterns, including *Jessica* by Tait. The 'Bull-in-a-China-shop' logo, introduced by J. & G. Meakin during the early sixties, was later used by Wedgwood as the brand name for the Creative Tableware Division encompassing Johnson Brothers, Midwinter, Unicorn and J. & G. Meakin.[39] In 1983 Johnson Brothers noted that, 'today the accent is on increased development in body, shape and pattern: the great importance of good design has constant attention, as have technical improvements and techniques'.[40]

The Johnson Brothers design team worked either to specific briefs, on site feedback or self-inspired initiative but the commercial angle was always present. In an increasingly competitive market the company operated a very strict selection panel for all proposed

310. An earthenware cup and plate decorated with the *Starbursts* pattern, printed in red. Designed by Jessie Tait for Johnson Brothers Ltd., about 1981-82. Diameter of plate 6¹¹/₁₆in. (17cm).

311. Coffee wares and dinnerware items decorated with the *Sweetbriar* pattern, printed on the Regency shape. Designed by Jessie Tait for Johnson Brothers Ltd., about 1984-86.

patterns. From more than a thousand different designs developed each year about twelve or so were selected for production, taking into account the opinions of the overseas agents and world-wide distributors. These important contributors were supplied with up-to-date colour photographs of the prototypes. Tait produced many trials and experiments, chiefly on plates, towards this selection date.

Leading department stores and supermarkets started to request exclusive patterns for their customers and the team of designers created patterns to satisfy these demands. One of Tait's first exclusives was *Camelot* for Boots on the Trend shape, launched during the late seventies. Her *Scandinavia* pattern was exclusive to Sainsbury's, whilst *Winchester*, on the Heritage shape, was an exclusive to British Home Stores and *Starbursts* (Plate 310), exclusive to Marks and Spencer. Her stylised floral patterns such as *Rose Garden*, *Floral Dance* (Plate 312) and *Sweetbriar* (Plate 311) were all produced on the elegant Regency shape. The popular *Thistle* pattern, from 1984, was derived from a wallpaper pattern produced for Laura Ashley.[41]

By the late eighties Tait had developed several progressive modern florals and fruits alongside some more traditional patterns applied to ornate shapes, a notable example being *Vintage*, a pattern of ivy motifs. Fresh and colourful patterns were *Lucerne*, *Springfield*, *Lynton* and *Lugano* (Plate 313). The latter was produced on textiles, place mats and tablecloths. The teapot retailed at £24.95 and a cup and saucer at £4.65 in March

312. The *Floral Dance* pattern, printed on the Regency shape. Designed by Jessie Tait for Johnson Brothers Ltd., about 1984-86.

313. Tea wares decorated with the *Lugano* pattern. Designed by Jessie Tait for Johnson Brothers Ltd., about 1992.

1992.[42] The London shape was used for a range of patterns such as *Bloomsbury*, *Park Lane*, Mayfair and *Kensington*. Despite this success, by the late eighties Tait began to consider that it was probably the right time to retire, rather than reaching the stage where she no longer enjoyed the work. The company, without doubt, did not want to lose such an important and experienced designer and asked her to stay on. Tait continued, albeit on a part-time, three days a week basis, for a further six years.

In 1991 the company dropped the established Bull-in-China-Shop logo. In 1993 the Wedgwood Company decided that the design team should relocate to the Barlaston based design department. Not wishing to move into the open plan studio, Tait decided to retire in December of that year.

Following her retirement, she has been working on a free-lance basis for Far Eastern and British companies. In recent years her work, particularly from the fifties, has become highly collectable and sought-after, which she must find very satisfying.

CHAPTER 13

BEAUTY ON A BUDGET

Kathie Winkle (b.1932)

314. Kathie Winkle, 1960s.

During the sixties and seventies very few designers created such a wide range of stylised and abstract patterns as Kathie Winkle. This was a considerable achievement given the limitations of the printing and decorating process imposed by the management at James Broadhurst and Sons Ltd. Her designs, almost 120 of them, were produced for the mass market and reached the homes of many ordinary people who could not afford expensive pottery. Her work was popular in both Britain and North America, promoted under the 'Beauty on a Budget' banner.

Probably the person most surprised at her success would be Kathie Winkle herself. This unassuming and very friendly lady was born on 10 September 1932 to Emily and Horace Winkle. She was born in a house once lived in by the famous potter William Adams. During her formal education at the local Penkhull County Modern School, art lessons were regarded as unimportant and therefore they took place only occasionally. More emphasis was placed on housecraft and needlework.. Winkle left school at the age of fourteen. In her early twenties she attended an evening class for one term with a friend to learn how to apply on-glaze colours to glazed ware. At that time she had no ambitions to become a designer. Her younger sister went to art school and later worked in an art studio for a local factory for a few years.

315. *Pedro* was the first pattern by Kathie Winkle, printed with painted decoration, introduced in 1958. Diameter of plate 6½in. (16.4cm).

316. This *Harvest* pattern is one of two designs, printed with painted decoration. Designed by Kathie Winkle for James Broadhurst and Sons Ltd., from about 1964. Diameter of plate 6⅝in. (16.7cm).

A family connection enabled Winkle to gain employment with Shorter and Co., at the age of fifteen. Her uncle, Percy Hull, was the head fireman at the firm, as his father had been. He was able to secure her a job there as a free-hand paintress. Winkle's eldest sister and her cousin also worked there as paintresses. The company was established in about 1878 when Arthur Shorter, who had previously worked as an apprentice at Minton's, purchased a small pottery works in Copeland Street, Stoke-on-Trent with his partner James Boulton. In 1894 Arthur Shorter bought, and managed, the firm of A.J. Wilkinson Ltd., based in Burslem, whilst his partner remained at the original works.[1] His son, Arthur Colley Shorter, joined the company after leaving school in 1900 and his other son, John Guy Shorter, took charge of the Shorter factory in 1905. From about 1906 the firm became known as Shorter and Sons. In 1918 Arthur Shorter retired, leaving his two sons to run both potteries.

Kathie Winkle joined Shorter's in 1947, being paid 22/6 per week at the age of fifteen, which increased to about £3 a week when she was seventeen. The factory had fully recovered from the war restrictions and new ideas were being explored for hand painted domestic wares and fancies. During the thirties Mabel Leigh had produced a range of innovative Period Pottery, despite only staying with the firm for a short time. Winkle was required to work on the various ranges, including Majolica, character jugs and the many fancies and sgraffito ware. She gained a great deal of experience in free hand decoration, noting later that working at Shorter's was a marvellous grounding for her. She learned all kinds of decorating skills including sponging, free-hand painting, shading, etching, mottling and she also worked on the clay, undertaking incised decoration on the 'green state' before the pieces were fired. Another of her many tasks was painting in the eyes of the popular fish ranges established in the thirties. Winkle recalled that Colley Shorter was known to visit the factory and each year would send out a Christmas card to

317. An earthenware side plate, diameter 6⅝in. (16.7cm), decorated with the *Orchard* pattern, printed with painted decoration. Designed by Kathie Winkle for James Broadhurst and Sons Ltd., from about 1963.

318. A large bowl, diameter 7⅝in. (19.4cm) decorated with the *Viscount* pattern, printed with painted decoration. Designed by Kathie Winkle for James Broadhurst and Sons Ltd., from about 1963.

each of the employees from himself and Clarice Cliff-Shorter.[2]

The market for novelties was strong during the late forties. In particular small giftware items such as posy rings, table lamps and character jugs were popular. Winkle decorated some of the Toby jug ranges, revived from the late thirties. She recalls the grumpy-looking 'Scottie' character, produced in different sizes, whose tartan kilt required careful painting. In about 1949 the company launched a series of Toby jugs based on the Gilbert and Sullivan operas, originally modelled by Clarice Cliff with the assistance of Betty Silvester, ten years earlier. This extensive range again demanded skilled free-hand work. Some of the older paintresses were not very keen to work on these pieces, being concerned that they would get headaches! Winkle and a friend both offered to do the work, asking for an extra pound a week. Not expecting to be taken up on the offer, they were summoned to see Mr. Harry Steele, the Managing Director, who agreed to the wage increase. This was an interesting position, but the wages were rather poor, as they were paid from a bonus system and not on piecework, so after two and a half years she decided to look for other employment.

In April 1950 Winkle joined the firm of James Broadhurst and Sons Ltd., as a paintress. This firm was established in 1847 and later settled at the Crown Works in Longton from 1854. It was chiefly involved in the manufacture of earthenware tea ware, dinnerware and general tableware at the lower end of the scale. By 1870 it had moved to the Portland Pottery in Fenton. The Managing Director of the firm, Peter Roper, joined in 1928, gaining experience by working in all the departments at the works. Before undertaking war service Roper had ordered a gas-fired glost tunnel oven, which was installed in 1947. This new machinery was part of the plan to modernise and re-organise the site from 1946. The demolition of three bottle kilns created space for the erection of new buildings to provide a larger underglaze decorating department.[3]

319. An earthenware milk jug decorated with the *Mikado* pattern, printed with painted decoration. Designed by Kathie Winkle for James Broadhurst and Sons Ltd., from about 1963. Height 3½in. (9cm).

320. An earthenware cup, saucer and plate decorated with the *Safari* pattern, a printed and painted border design. Designed by Kathie Winkle for James Broadhurst and Sons Ltd., about 1963.

During the immediate post-war period the company was chiefly concerned with the production of tea ware for the export market. The weekly output had risen from 6,500 dozen a week in 1948 following the installation of the gas-fired glost tunnel. By 1956 16,000 dozen pieces were coming off the production line and over 200 staff were employed at the works.[4] The existing bottle and glost ovens were demolished and replaced by continuous kilns. The reorganisation of the biscuit warehouse was undertaken alongside the enlargement of the glost warehouse. In 1957 a new showroom was opened on the first floor of the works, adjacent to the office of the Managing Director.[5] Overseas agents were established in Australia, New Zealand, South Africa and Canada. By the end of the decade agents in Norway, Finland, Sweden and Denmark were added. The company was always busy, even at times when other firms were short of orders. It was able to provide what the customer wanted, 'Cheap and Cheerful' was its motto and it prided itself on a speedy delivery service.[6]

The main decorating process was underglaze painting, lining and rubber-stamping by hand, as transfer-printing was not in use. The hand-stamping was completed by about six people with twenty to thirty paintresses. A new emphasis was placed on simple underglaze decoration with some on-glaze decorations also being produced. Typical examples of the late fifties included Tyne, Maytime, Saxon, Crocus and Clyde. Margaret Turner was the designer responsible for many of the patterns during this period. The Petula pattern, produced in several colourways, such as yellow or blue, was designed by Eric Slater, Art Director at the Shelley Potteries and a friend of the Roper family.[7] The firm occasionally bought in rubber stamps from the open stock range of W. Bennett & Co. who produced all the rubber stamps for Broadhurst's own in-house designs. Reg Chilton, joining the company as under-decorating manager in about 1952, produced several patterns from these open stock rubber stamps. Contemporary designs for the mid-fifties included the popular Wheat Rose, Alton, Bouquet and Hawaii. The Revel pattern was extensively publicised in the trade press and sold well for many years.[8] The majority of these designs featured a simple mark with the words 'Broadhurst, Staffordshire England'.

Very little free-hand decoration was undertaken at Broadhurst's. Winkle's work was involved with the stamp and fill method, by which the outline of the pattern was stamped on to the ware and then the colour was applied to the spaces in the pattern. She was paid on a piecework basis. The occasional samples and special pieces that she did increased to such a point that the management offered her the opportunity to design on a full-time basis, which she accepted. Her commitment to the company was to play a major part in the success of the firm during the sixties and seventies. The fact that she had already worked with the firm for eight years before her promotion gave her terrific insight and understanding of the limitations and possibilities in design. Her experience as a paintress put her on very good terms with the team of paintresses. All her design work had to be produced within the limitations of the printing and decorating process. The firm would request her to produce half a dozen designs suitable for printing on the Malkin rubber stamp machines, that printed the pattern on to the ware. Her selected patterns, submitted on paper, were then used to produce the engraving plates, to create the moulds for the rubber stamps. The print was then applied at the biscuit stage, after the first firing, with the colours painted by hand before the second firing. This process sealed them under the glaze, making them detergent and dishwasher proof. All applications of colours had to be costed by Reg Chilton who would time every stroke for each pattern to price the cost of the piece. The lowest price scale would probably have one application of colour, with very few painted strokes. Winkle would sometimes have the opportunity to produce designs that required more colours.

As early as 1960 the firm initiated direct selling in presentation packs through Littlewoods, Great Universal and Grattan, which lasted for several years. A large export

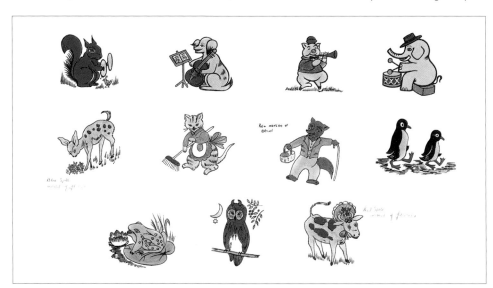

321. Artwork showing the various motifs created by Kathie Winkle for egg sets for a London store during the sixties.

322. The lesser known *Bamboo* pattern, printed with painted decoration. Designed by Kathie Winkle for James Broadhurst and Sons Ltd., from about 1962. Diameter of plate 6⅜in. (16.2cm).

323. An earthenware plate, diameter 6⅝in. (16.7cm), decorated with the *Calypso* pattern, printed with painted decoration. Designed by Kathie Winkle for James Broadhurst and Sons Ltd., introduced in about 1964.

market was developed through overseas agents and the many trips that the Koper family and their representatives made to countries such as Australia and Canada. Although Winkle started to design in about 1958, the most recent patterns by Reg Chilton and Margaret Turner were going into production, marketed through trade exhibitions and press advertisements. In 1961 the Calypso pattern by Reg Chilton and the on-glaze Matador and Shanghai patterns by Margaret Turner were noted in the buyers' notes of the trade press. These patterns, alongside Margaret Turner's, Tahiti, were illustrated in one of the firm's advertisements in February 1963.[9]

Some of Winkle's first designs were stylistically similar to those previously issued by the company. One such example was *Pedro* (Plate 315), depicting a Mexican fisherman. Her *Carmen* pattern of stylised roses was similar to Wheat Rose by Margaret Turner. Several designs, including *Albany*, dating from about 1959, were promoted in 1964.[10] Whilst some patterns, such as *Newlyn*, were produced on the Coupe shape, the majority were decorated on the Rim and Riviera shapes. The Tudor shape consisted of a cup, sugar and cream shape that the factory used alongside condiment sets bought in from another company. *Newlyn* was exported to the major department store Eaton's in Toronto, who sold a 100 piece service for almost thirty dollars. The *Harvest* design (Plate 316), another simple centre motif of wheat and leaves in autumnal shades, was an exclusive for the Timothy White's chain of shops. Its popularity prompted a similar version some years later.[11] These early wares utilised the current backstamp, with the word 'Broadhurst's' in italics.

Influences came from a range of sources, including contemporary textiles and interior decoration. Successful patterns produced by their competitors prompted Broadhurst's to develop new patterns. The Harlem pattern, for instance, created from open stock rubber

324. An earthenware dinner plate, diameter 9½in. (24cm), decorated with the *Barbecue* pattern, printed with painted decoration. Designed by Kathie Winkle for James Broadhurst and Sons Ltd., 1967.

stamps, was introduced following the success of patterns such as Midwinter's Zambesi design, introduced in 1956. Harlem proved successful but was not designed by Winkle. In many respects the most important influences on her were requests from the management. She was asked to develop four geometrical patterns for an important sales and promotional trip to Australia undertaken by Stephen Roper, the Sales Director, in February 1964.[12] During that year Michael Roper, the Director and Technical Manager, went on a six month sales trip to Canada visiting Toronto, Vancouver and Montreal, joining Edward Willis of Staff Sales Ltd., the Canadian agent, from about 1959.[13] Patterns such as *Palma Nova*, *Autumn* and *Orchard* (Plate 317) were typical of the period. The latter was developed after a suggestion from Peter Roper, who wanted a fruit pattern added to the current range. Winkle created a suitable motif combined with a bright colour scheme. However the Canadian agent thought it would not sell decorated in the selected colours and suggested that a colour scheme of yellows and browns would be more suitable, to which Winkle responded: 'You don't have brown oranges and apples.'[14] The pattern, with its new autumn colours, was a best seller for the company.

At the Blackpool Fancy Goods and Gifts Fair of 1964 several new designs, including *Viscount* (Plate 318), *Mikado* (Plate 319) and *Safari* (Plate 320), were displayed. *Viscount* was one of her most popular and became a best seller for the firm throughout the sixties and seventies, clearly following a fashion trend for stripes in wallpaper and interior decoration. These simple striped patterns such as *Kontiki* and *Radiance* fitted perfectly into the limitations of the printing process and were cost-effective, with only two colour brushstrokes required. A lesser known pattern was *Bamboo* (Plate 322). The range of

325. The earthenware 'Kofti Pot' designed by Kathie Winkle. The pattern on this piece is Rushstone, not a Kathie Winkle design. Introduced in about 1967-68. Height 6⅛in. (15.5cm).

shapes that Winkle used was very plain and simple and included the Coupe and Rim, the latter combined with Delta cups, sugars and creams. Most of these patterns were issued with the general company backstamp that read 'STAFFORDSHIRE ENGLAND Est. *Broadhurst* SINCE 1847'. Around this time the Canadian agent suggested that Broadhurst's should incorporate the Kathie Winkle name and the words 'dishwasher safe' into the backstamp. He felt that the designer's name would give the ware more identity. Therefore 'A Kathie Winkle Design' was incorporated into the mark in about 1964. Patterns such as *Mandalay* and *Lagoon* were issued with the new mark from the start.

Winkle's other responsibilities within the company included despatching the trials and samples that she produced for specific clients. When required she would give guided tours to school parties, important visitors and foreign buyers. Although her role was significant to the success of the firm she did not attend many of the trade fairs and had no proper involvement in the creation of the firm's stands. She did produce display boards for in-store promotions. A promotional advertisement noted that: 'Our organisation is completely up to date and planned on modern streamlined enabling us to give quality and excellent value and to guarantee delivery on time.'[15]

In order to develop new designs, Winkle and Stephen Roper would look through open stock catalogues selecting those that they felt fitted in with their house style. Winkle would then work up the pattern by adding hand-painted decoration. One such example was a border design of circles within squares, named Concord. The popularity of this design prompted Reg Chilton to quickly sketch a similar pattern that she then drew up for the printing process. This new

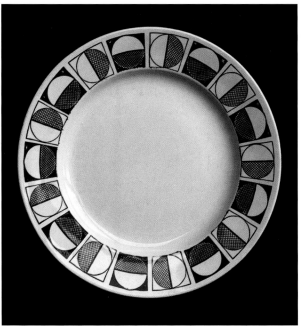

326. An earthenware plate, diameter 9½in. (24cm), decorated with the *Barbados* pattern, printed with painted decoration. Designed by Kathie Winkle for James Broadhurst and Sons Ltd., from about 1967.

327. The lesser known *Eclipse* pattern, printed and painted on an earthenware plate, diameter 9½in. (24cm). Designed by Kathie Winkle for James Broadhurst and Sons Ltd., from about 1971.

interpretation was called Rushstone, introduced in about 1965. The pattern turned out to be one of the best sellers for the company. As it was developed from Reg Chilton's sketch, the design cannot be attributed to Winkle, although her name is on the backstamp with the pattern name.

In 1965 Broadhurst purchased Sampson Bridgwood and Sons Ltd., based at the Anchor Works in Longton. The management, according to the press, intended to continue and expand the production of hotelware alongside the introduction of table lines in general earthenware.[16] The site was much larger than the Portland site and included some recent modernisation. Several of Broadhurst's patterns were produced at the Sampson Bridgwood and Sons Ltd. works. Winkle had a very limited involvement with the company, designing only a few patterns, including badged ware for the hotel market. At about this time Broadhurst's had a regular contract with Ford's of Croydon to produce large quantities of egg cups each year for the Easter celebrations. Several sets were produced annually, featuring four motifs. The designs, grouped into sets of motifs, included animals playing musical instruments, such as a pig with a flute and an elephant playing the drums (Plate 321). More stylised designs had motifs such as a deer, cow, frog, owl, duck and a cat sweeping with a broom.[17] These wares were sold unmarked, due to their size, so the identification of Winkle's patterns has to be based on stylistic grounds.

Towards the late sixties new designs became visually more complex. Broadhurst's wanted to produce a new shape, suitable for rubber stamping, to keep up with the current trends. Winkle drew up a sketch for the coffee pot for the modeller. The shape was introduced during the mid-sixties, when leading firms such as Midwinter, Portmeirion and Wedgwood were also launching new shapes. The Riviera shape, featuring ribbed edges on plates and on the pots, was limited to coffee and tea ware, covered and open sugar, cream jugs,

328. An earthenware cup and saucer decorated with the *Barbados* pattern, printed in 22 carat gold. Designed by Kathie Winkle for James Broadhurst and Sons Ltd., 1967. Height of cup 2¾in. (7cm).

plates, oatmeal fruit, soup, open scallop and other smaller items. The standard mark was changed slightly to incorporate the shape name. The Coupe shape was used less from the late sixties onwards and was eventually phased out.

New patterns for 1967 included *Moselle, Palermo, Acapulco* and *Corinth*. However, the most outstanding pattern of this period was *Calypso*, a stylised floral centre spray with an intricate border decorated on the Rim shape (Plate 323). This pattern should not, however, be confused with an earlier one designed by Reg Chilton in about 1961.

In February 1969 the trade press reported that Broadhurst's had appointed Mel Robbins as export assistant, noting that he was to travel to Scandinavia to call on current agents and customers. Sales in this region had increased significantly over the last twelve months. During the same year Stephen Roper went on a successful trip to Canada to promote the new Riviera shape.[18] Winkle was requested to produce several drawings, using autumn colours, for him to take as examples. The trade press mentioned a new coffee pot that without doubt was the 'Kofti pot' she designed, modelled by Stan Edge, the head mould maker. The Kofti pot, a combination of tea and coffee pot, was ideal for the wide range of starter and combination sets that Broadhurst's were currently promoting in the North American market (Plate 325). The continued demand for the Rushstone pattern prompted the management to expand the co-ordinated boxed sets by offering matching linen and cutlery, supplied by another company. The Connoisseur set pack contained thirty pieces of pottery, twenty-four pieces of stainless steel cutlery and twelve pieces of Irish linen.[19] Eventually these popular sets, for other patterns such as *San Tropez*, included glassware but did not feature the individual pattern motifs on the cutlery. Specific wares were produced for the North American market including sets of mugs, fruit nappies and small round dishes that were often mistaken for ashtrays! Best selling patterns such as *Michelle* and *Kimberley* were sold with glasswares which reproduced the pattern printed in gold on each piece. Broadhurst's then produced kitchenware, including a chopping board, cutlery, pans and matching utensils decorated with the popular *Calypso* pattern.[20] The success of the kitchenware prompted the company to issue another kitchenware pattern called Marrakech. This pattern, produced as a lithographic transfer, was stylistically very different from the current output. The repeating floral border in red and turquoise with lids in solid orange is not a true design by Winkle. It didn't prove as popular as *Calypso*.

329. An earthenware cup, saucer and plate decorated with the *Compass* pattern, printed with painted decoration. Designed by Kathie Winkle for James Broadhurst and Sons Ltd., from about 1968. Diameter of plate 9½in. (24 cm).

At about this time the company began to advertise its wares more vigorously by taking out full colour trade advertisements to promote the latest patterns. These included *Tarragona*, *Mardi Gras*, *Barbecue* (Plate 324) and *Mexico*, the latter was created to link in with the Olympic Games of 1970 being held in Mexico City. Her popular *Barbados* (Plate 326) was also produced in all over 22 carat gold, without any hand-painted decoration, in a separate department (Plate 328).

During the same year the sales arrangements of both Sampson Bridgwood and Sons Ltd. and Broadhurst's were finalised when British Pottery Limited became their manufacturing agents. The organisation had a large showroom on King Street in Longton. This association was to last until 1976.[21] At about this time, Broadhurst's described themselves as being, 'Earthenware manufacturers of low priced tea and dinner ware in a wide range of contemporary patterns.'[22]

The sales potential of the export market prompted the firm to produce an export catalogue in 1968. This important document lists the many designs by Winkle, including the popular *South Seas* and *Tenerife*. However some of these overseas companies demanded exclusive rights to certain patterns. Stephen Roper was not prepared to limit one design to one firm, which would mean losing out on worldwide sales. Therefore he suggested that they could have the desired pattern but in different colours with a new pattern name. For example, *Seattle* was a colour variation of *Michelle*, whilst *Bridgewood* was reworked and called *Capri* in about 1971. Several late sixties patterns were given names that evoke faraway exotic places such as *San Marino* and *Monaco*. The intricate *Monte Carlo* pattern, a trailing floral design set against a trellis frame, was painted in greens and browns. North American stores such as Eaton's, Sear's and Freeman's emphasised both the quality of the ware and the competitive prices in their marketing. They declared that in purchasing their latest products

the customer was buying 'Beauty on a Budget', whilst Eaton's advised 'Let forty-five pieces of English Ironstone brighten up your summer table!'[23]

During the early seventies Broadhurst's maintained a strong hold on the business by producing a range of artistic and traditional designs. Notable examples of the more artistic styles include *Harrow 4*, a pop art asymmetrical pattern, an exclusive for a major London department store. Sadly it was unsuccessful. Winkle's distinctive *Eclipse* pattern (Plate 327), was produced in two colour variations and dates from 1971. A similar audacious pattern was *Compass* (Plate 329), which according to the designer encapsulated her distinctive style of circles and squares within each other. The original concept came about from an idea by Stephen Roper, who wanted an overall design incorporating a squares and circles motif, that had previously only been used for border patterns. Another design, *Roulette* (Plate 330), was based on one of the many samples that she had developed for the home market and mail order. She noted that 'It caught on straight away and lasted for quite a while. The pattern was named by the glost warehouse manager Denis George, he looked at the drawing I had done and said it reminded him of a roulette wheel.'[24]

Broadhurst's, in line with market trends, developed a new range of studio tableware called Sandstone. This distinctive soft oatmeal base was their attempt to produce a higher grade of tableware. Winkle created six stylish designs including *Snowdon, Moorland, Hillside, Morning Glory* and *Country Lane* (Plate 331).[25] The other patterns are less typical of her work, being printed in one colour. The lesser known *Snowdon* design utilised the *Roulette* print, decorated with fashionable bands of purple and green. At about this time a new palette-shaped backstamp was introduced to emphasise the art side of the range. In contrast, production of the more traditional patterns was continued. Winkle was asked to make a new rubber stamp version of the longstanding *Indian Tree* pattern (Plate 332), which had been

330. An earthenware plate, diameter 9½in. (24cm), decorated with the *Roulette* pattern, printed with painted decoration. Designed by Kathie Winkle for James Broadhurst and Sons Ltd., from about 1971.

331. An earthenware plate, diameter 9½in. (24cm), decorated with the *Country Lane* pattern, printed on a matt glaze. Designed by Kathie Winkle for James Broadhurst and Sons Ltd., 1972.

332. An earthenware dinner plate, diameter 6⅝in. (16.7cm), decorated with the *Indian Tree* pattern, printed with hand painted decoration. Designed by Kathie Winkle for James Broadhurst and Sons Ltd., 1971.

produced successfully at Sampson Bridgwood and Sons Ltd. for many years. The pattern was launched in about 1972, proving popular with the overseas market and was given its own special mark. Trade leaflets and publicity of the period indicate that both *Indian Tree* and *Calypso* could be purchased with single colour cups instead of the repeated pattern, possibly to increase customer choice. By 1973 the two factories were extremely busy, with a workforce of 630 and a turnover of almost £1.5 million. A year later the derelict Crown Clarence works in Longton were purchased, later to be named Churchill China.[26]

During the early 1970s typical patterns included *Zodiac*, *Kimberley*, *Cordoba*, *Muscouri* and *Sombrero* (Plate 333). Her *Seychelles* pattern was suggested as a follow-up to *Calypso*. The *Wild Flowers* range was stylistically far removed from Winkle's other work, featuring more than eight different motifs, which she drew for the set. Each motif included the Latin flower names, such as *Borago Officinalis*, *Anagelli Arversus* and *Dryas Octopetala*. The pattern, printed in brown on the Rim shape and hand-painted in a range of colours, was given a special backstamp. Winkle later described the printing of this pattern as a production nightmare because the Rim borders on plates and saucers caused difficulties. After a few years the pattern was issued without hand-painted decoration (Plate 334).

In 1975 the company celebrated the success of the Rushstone pattern after the fifty millionth piece had been fired. During the same year, Broadhurst's invested in the construction of a new extension to enable them to break into the print market for the first time. In about 1976 the English Scenes range of printed patterns was launched, produced by the Dekram printing method. These were followed by Constable Prints based on the work of John Constable, from engravings produced at the Transgrave Studios. Winkle had no involvement at any stage with this range. Many of her earlier patterns were still popular

333. An earthenware bowl, diameter 7⅝in. (19.2cm), decorated with the *Sombrero* pattern, printed with painted decoration. Designed by Kathie Winkle for James Broadhurst and Sons Ltd., 1972.

334. An earthenware dinner plate, diameter 9½in. (24 cm), decorated with the *Wild Flowers* pattern, printed in brown. Designed by Kathie Winkle for James Broadhurst and Sons Ltd., 1975.

with mail order companies both at home and abroad as late as 1976. These included *Viscount, Calypso, Sombrero* and *Indian Tree*. Lesser known patterns included *Fleur, Verdi Green* and *Verdi Brown*. Further agents were established in Austria, Belgium, Gibraltar, Holland, Italy and Portugal. The Silver Jubilee 1977 mugs in maroon were produced at Broadhurst's, where a facility for once firing was available, at that time.[27]

After twenty years of designing for the firm, Winkle decided that she would like a change, and became involved with quality control. As a result, the management contracted the John Russell Studio to develop a range of patterns based on the Kathie Winkle style. They came up with, amongst others, Agincourt, Tashkent and Alicante. However these new designs continued to use the backstamp incorporating the Winkle name, as it was registered and good for marketing. She managed to have her name removed from the designs which were not her own but this use of the 'Kathie Winkle design' backstamp now makes it difficult to attribute designs to her.

In 1982 Broadhurst's set up an in-house design department to co-ordinate all the group's design work and in 1992 Winkle retired from the company. In recent years her work has become quite collectable following articles in collectors' magazines and coverage on television programmes. Moreover, collectors are always looking out for 'the next big thing' now that the work of Susie Cooper, Clarice Cliff and in some respects Jessie Tait is beyond the reach of ordinary collectors. The fact that all her work was hand-painted and featured her name on the backstamp will contribute to the increasing demand. Winkle finds all the interest amusing and complementary, to such an extent that she has started to collect her own work from car boot sales, charity shops and antique fairs. With the keen interest in her work prices have started to rise gradually, much to the designer's surprise!

CHAPTER 14

A DESIGNER FOR THE MASS MARKET

JOHN CLAPPISON (b.1937)

335. John Clappison in the Design Studio, about 1965. Note the range of trial and experimental items on the shelves.

It is somewhat difficult to imagine that a small pottery situated on the East Coast of Yorkshire could have risen to international status during the sixties and seventies. Several contributory factors led the Hornsea Pottery to success, not least the hard work and determination of the founder members of this family-run business. Innovative and good quality design has always been the surest way of attracting new markets and increasing sales. This is how the Hornsea Pottery set about expanding its share of the market and at the same time becoming known as one of the leading pottery companies. The driving force behind Hornsea's success was the young and innovative John Clappison. He played such a vital role, yet still remains a relatively unknown designer.

The Hornsea Pottery was located in East Yorkshire, below the fishing port of Bridlington. The pottery was established in 1949 by Desmond Rawson, Colin Bentley Rawson and Caesar Philip Clappison. Prior to this the two Rawson brothers had only made plaster of Paris ware. Pottery production did not commence until Caesar Philip Clappison had financed them and they were able to buy a second hand kiln. Philip Clappison had been suffering from ill health for several years and decided to sell his butcher's business. His doctor suggested that to keep himself busy in retirement he should visit the Rawson brothers.

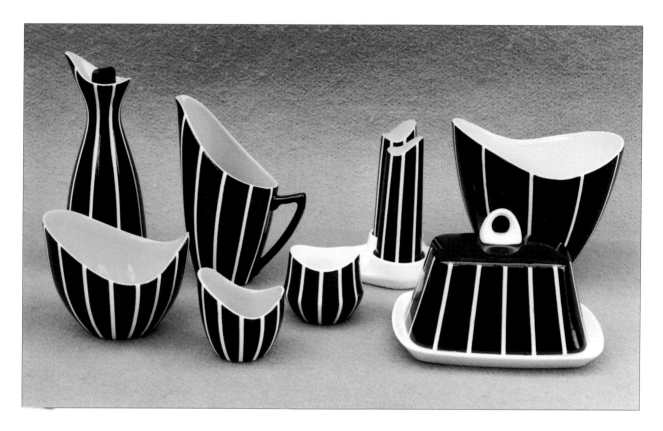

338. A selection of earthenware vases, gift wares and dishes decorated with the *Elegance* pattern. Designed by John Clappison for Hornsea Pottery Ltd., about 1955-59.

After meeting them he decided to become involved in the pottery and invested the money from the sale of his business in the Hornsea company on 1 April 1950. Philip Clappison put £875 into the business, Desmond Rawson £675 and Colin Rawson £150.[1] The Clappisons then became involved in all aspects of operation. The initial business proved successful and larger premises were sought after only a year. They moved from a small property in the town to a rented property known locally as 'The Old Hall', one of the largest houses in the area. In March 1954 the Hornsea Pottery officially became the town's biggest employer. However, this success demanded further relocation.

During July, 1954, the pottery moved to a twenty-eight acre site on Edenfield Estate, Marlborough Avenue, Hornsea, formerly a brick and tileworks, established in 1864. The site had been used as a piggery before the sale, so work had to be done to make it operational. About sixty-five staff were employed during this period.[2] Production at the time was predominantly small items such as character jugs, vases, boots and clogs, impressed with the word 'Hornsea' or a simple 'H'. Further items included an outstanding range of modelled animals such as giraffes, panthers and dogs, skilfully created by Marion Campbell. Further stylised figures and African figures, decorated in black, were introduced in 1956.[3] Once production was running smoothly tourists holidaying in the area started to visit the pottery for factory tours.

William John Clappison, the son of Philip and Enith, was born in Hull in 1937. He was brought up in a family that appreciated the arts; his father played the violin and also enjoyed painting. Clappison attended the local schools in the area before gaining a place at the High School for Arts and Crafts in Hull from 1950 to 1953. This informative and creative education led him to enrol at the Hull Regional College of Arts and Crafts, for a

four year period, where he gained a National Diploma in Design, Special level in
Ceramics. His exam piece was a lamp base decorated with motifs of wild flowers he had
collected as a child. Clappison produced a self-watering plant pot modelled in the shape
of a head in 1956, small fish dishes decorated with a feather-combing pattern and small
pig models. He also produced a range of bon-bon dishes that were thrown on the wheel
and experimented with transfer printed designs for a set of cruets.[4]

As his parents were heavily involved with the Hornsea Pottery, Clappison would spend
time there during the holidays, modelling in clay. Eventually he started to design for
Hornsea. His first pieces heralded the firm's new direction into the production of tableware
design with his heart-shaped *Honeymoon* range, launched in 1955, targeted at newly-

338. Several practical items
from the lesser known
Ulrome range. The shapes
were designed and
modelled by John Clappison
for Hornsea Pottery Ltd.,
about 1958.

weds. During the same year he introduced the distinctive *Elegance* range of small vases, bowls and jugs, decorated with a vertical in the contemporary style (Plate 336). This decorative technique was achieved by a labour-intensive method of applying masking tape strips to the ware before each item was aerographed with a colour. The effects were dazzling and the range proved very popular. The trade press reported: 'an excellent sale for the range of striped pottery, tables inlaid with hand painted creative tiles – ideal for tea pots and so on.'[5] Three years later the pottery company Burt and Edwards (Hull) Ltd., produced a similar range called Mooncloud.[6]

The Rawson brothers saw great potential in Clappison. In 1957 Desmond Rawson took him to the Royal College of Art in London to arrange a special one year course, for which the company paid his fees. During the course Clappison specialised in industrial design and ceramics. He stayed in lodgings in Fulham. His tutors were Peter O'Malley and Arnold Machin. Clappison recalled that the advice given to him by Arnold Machin was, 'Why don't you make the cup like a saucer and the saucer more like a leaf?' In some respects Clappison had an advantage, as he had already gained considerable experience in the development of industrial ceramics, which probably explains why he felt that he learned little. As a result he spent a lot of his time at the Victoria and Albert Museum and the Natural History Museum in South Kensington. He also regularly examined the products in leading London stores, such as Heal's.[7] Clappison gained the Faculty of Industrial Design, Certificate in Ceramics at the Royal College of Art, where he must have made a good impression, as the Principal, Professor Baker, suggested that he would greatly benefit from a further two years of study. However, Clappison decided to return directly to Hornsea. During his studies he had continued to submit his ideas to the company, including his

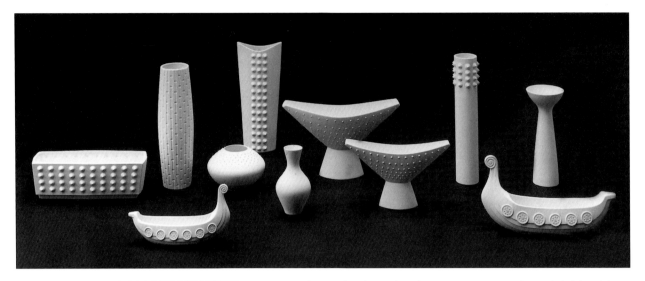

340. Several examples of items from the Home Decor range that included the *White Thorn*, *White Frost* and *White Bud* patterns. Designed by John Clappison for Hornsea Pottery Ltd., introduced in 1960-62. Tallest item 11in. (28cm).

341. A *White Thorn* tall vase and flower trough. Designed by John Clappison for Hornsea Pottery Ltd., introduced in 1960-62. Height of vase 11in. (28cm).

Tricorn range, illustrated in the *Decorative Art Studio Year Book* for 1958/59 and advertised in the trade press.[8] This was followed by the table set called *Ulrome* that featured impressed marks in the speckled glazed surface (Plate 338). This was the first Hornsea ware to be entered on the Design Council's Design Index list.

In 1958 he was appointed as Chief Designer for the Hornsea Pottery Co. Ltd. As a design studio did not exist at the pottery, a small brick outbuilding was given to Clappison to use. This was situated at the rear of the sales office in the marketplace. Once established in this studio, Clappison developed a whole range of patterns for tablewares, fancies and gift wares that would take the company to the forefront of British design. Eventually all design development took place in a specially built studio, designed by Clappison, away from the main factory. The studio, directly overlooking a pond, had space for Clappison, Michael Walker, Alan Luckham and Gordon Helliwell; the latter was in charge of graphics, photography and publicity material. This building housed a kiln for the team to use for trial patterns. Alan Luckham, the chief modeller, came from Stoke-on-Trent to join Hornsea in 1959. He was experienced and worked closely with Clappison for several years.

Clappison was decisive and clear as to what he wanted to achieve. With his experience at Hornsea he was fully aware of the possibilities, and more importantly the limitations, of the company and its workforce. The opportunity to develop hand painted decoration was not possible as it was very costly and the workforce had little knowledge of the process on a commercial scale. Furthermore, the use of bought-in transfer printed sheets was ruled out, probably as they were far too costly for a small company such as Hornsea. Clappison wanted to develop an individual style, through

342. Examples of John Clappison's work for the Hornsea Pottery. A jardinière decorated with the *White Bud* pattern, part of the Home Decor range. Hornsea Pottery Ltd., 1960-62.

343. A rare earthenware *Fish Light*, decorated with sponged decoration. Designed by John Clappison for Hornsea Pottery Ltd., 1961-63.

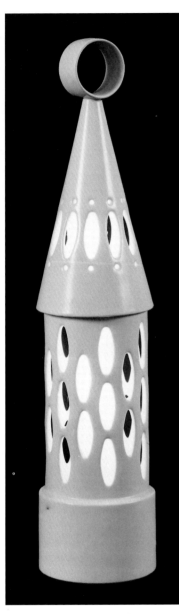

344. A rare earthenware *Abbey Light*. Designed by John Clappison for Hornsea Pottery Ltd., 1961-63.

experimentation and new techniques, that eventually became known as the 'Hornsea Look'. He understood the need to create something very different from other manufacturers. New shapes were developed by experimenting with paper sculpture from the large quantity of white cartridge paper that he had ordered, which didn't please the management.[9] He had done this with his earlier shapes, such as *Tricorn*, whilst undertaking his studies.

One of the first results of these experiments was a series of tall cylindrical shapes forming the basis for his *Summit* range, which featured vertical indentations on the body (Plate 339). The decoration was formulated by Michael Walker during an experiment in which he sprayed the colour on to the ware and then wiped off the surface, thus leaving the colour inlay, creating a distinctive utilitarian look.[10] This decorative process was both economical and easy to undertake. *Summit* was launched in 1960 on an extensive range of practical wares such as condiment sets, preserve pots, jugs, sugar sifters and cheese dishes. *Summit* was so successful that it was in production for many years. Several other shapes and patterns evolved from this range over the next few years, including Conifer, Spruce and the range of Studio Craft.

In 1959 Clappison travelled to Denmark to visit the Royal Copenhagen Porcelain factory, meeting Nils Thorsson, the Design Director. Clappison also went to Kahler Keramic, a studio pottery at Naestved, Denmark, where he was very impressed with the work of Nils Kahler and bought several examples. These were sgraffito decorated and covered with a Persian blue glaze. This type of transparent glaze would ultimately be used on the *Heirloom* range, introduced by Clappison a few years later. The Kahler pottery also produced slipware pieces which were decorated using cow horns as slip trailers! Clappison was so impressed with the slipwares that his interest in this form of decoration for Hornsea was renewed. This important trip was followed up three years later when the Sales Director, Bob Hindle, and Clappison spent a whole day at the Gustavberg Pottery, the influential Swedish company, meeting the designer, Stig Lindberg and also Gunnar Nylund, who had just left Rorstrand to work at Gustavsberg's. They also visited several small studio potters in Stockholm. A pot purchased from a potter named Gerd Heymann was to influence Clappison's *Saffron* design, particularly the colourway. In 1960 Clappison visited Milan with Colin Rawson for the Triennale. He was impressed with the work of Rut Bryk and the large ceramic and wire birds made by Birger Kaipiainen for Arabia. They also visited the workshop of the Italian designer Bruno Munari whilst in Milan. These trips had a great and lasting influence on Clappison.[11]

During the same year Clappison introduced a stylish and distinctive range of matt glaze shapes called Home Decor (Plates 340 and 341). These wares were originally glazed in various colours, unsuccessfully, so the decision was taken to use plain glazes. The pieces were decorated with a subtle matt glaze in three decorations – *White Frost*, *White Thorn* and *White Bud* (Plate 342). A wide range of shapes, such as Viking Boat planters, was modelled for this range. Home Decor gave Hornsea a leading edge in the industry.

In complete contrast to the modern contemporary wares such as the Home Decor range, in 1960 Clappison also introduced a series of comical giftwares that he called *Keyhole* bon-bon dishes. The printed centre motif depicted a topless woman, which caused quite a controversy. A similar pattern, although more traditional, was called *Tasty Dish*. A wide range of cruets on wooden stands was also manufactured during the late fifties and sixties.

In 1961 Clappison produced a range of lights including the *Fish Light*, decorated with sponged motifs (Plate 343). His *Abbey Light*, an outstanding piece of pottery, was entered on to the Design Index in 1962.[12] It retailed at £6.15.6d (Plate 344). These pieces, intended as background lighting, were displayed on the company stand at the Blackpool Gifts and Fancy Goods Fair in 1962 (Plate 345). During the same year, following a request from Desmond Rawson, Clappison produced a stylised elongated bust of a young girl, modelled by Alan Luckham. These figures were used for lamps and plant pots, although very few were made (Plate 346). Clappison's *Aphrodite* vase from January 1961 featured a relief decoration produced with a matt white glaze (Plate 347). In 1977 two other sizes of the vase were produced. All three sizes were sold in the unglazed cream vitramic finish.

By the early sixties the Hornsea Pottery was expanding and gaining a great deal of local and national press interest. Despite his significant design contribution to both patterns and shapes, over many years, Clappison's name was not incorporated into the backstamp. This contradicted the policy of featuring the designer's name on each piece as a strong marketing ploy, practised by companies such as W.R. Midwinter Ltd. and James Broadhurst and Sons Ltd. His new *Studio Craft* range, from 1960, was formed from a combination of some of the shapes used for *Home Decor* and the decorative process exploited by *Summit*. The range included large vases, jardinières, plant pot holders, bulb bowls and bulb troughs. A similar variation was *Lattice*, also from 1960.

345. A period photograph of the Hornsea Pottery Ltd. stand at the Blackpool Fair in 1962. The stand was designed by John Clappison with the graphics by Gordon Helliwell. Note the lesser known studio items on the shelf, top left, by John Clappison. These were never sold to the public.

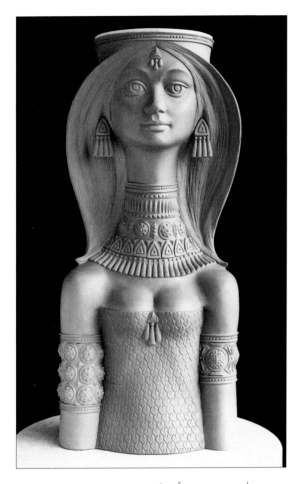

346. A lesser known 'Woman Figure' designed by John Clappison and modelled by Alan Luckham, for Hornsea Pottery Ltd., 1962-63.

Clappison also tried his hand at marketing, by designing the current shell-shaped company logo. In 1961 he gave the factory buildings a new Mediterranean look by painting them in yellows, blues and pinks, but the Rawsons felt that this was far too garish and they were changed back. In 1963 he designed the firm's exhibition stand for the Blackpool Gifts and Fancy Goods Fair. The theme was 'The Seaside Potters' and featured solid teak shelves contrasting with large photographic panels of pebbles (Plate 348). On display were some of the brand new ranges, including *Summertime*, probably one of the most extensive collections of items, that incorporated spice jars, egg cups and oil and vinegar bottles. The lids of the storage jars were cork-lined and supplied with separate slide-off transfers that could be applied by the customer to label contents, such as 'Spice' or 'Coffee' (Plate 350).[13] Also on display was *White Wedding*, a collection of classical vases, jardinières and plant pots glazed in matt white and matt black. Publicity photographs were taken of Judy Harland, Blackpool Girl of the Year, holding examples of the range on the company stand. The display also included the new innovative range of *Leaf* patterns, such as maple, chestnut and bramble, devised by Clappison in 1962. These individual motifs were created by taking casts of each leaf, which were then incorporated into the moulds (Plate 349). The decoration of the leaf, in coloured slip, was applied to the mould and then the item was cast. This technique, devised by Michael Walker, achieved outstanding results.[14] These items featured a special leaf backstamp.

Hornsea was among the pioneers of direct printing. Clappison had an idea for a machine that would print directly on to cylindrical pots when he was a student at the Royal College of Art in 1957, and produced some rough working drawings of such a device. This idea was shown to Desmond Rawson who visited him at his lodgings in Fulham in December of that year. Several years later, Desmond Rawson saw a machine printing milk bottles which used a similar method to the one that Clappison had devised. One of these machines was ordered in about 1964. The technique took some considerable time to perfect. The first design to be used for this process was a black scroll pattern on a range of storage jars, designed by Gordon Helliwell. However, it was not until 1964 that the first silk screen printer was purchased by the company. As it was a small model, only beakers could be decorated.[15] Clappison therefore produced a range of *Zodiac* patterns (Plate 351), which proved popular and generated several others over many years.

In October 1966 the company made a great effort to promote its new ranges and the latest products by staging an exhibition at the Ceylon Tea Centre in the Haymarket, London. Clappison made wall hangings using glazed and unglazed stoneware (Plate

352) which were exhibited alongside the forerunners of the *Muramic* range of wall plaques. These innovative items were not marketed. Notable examples include Indian Woman (Plate 353) and a similar design (Plate 354). Clappison also experimented with small 'jewelled' stones, made in red clay. These were not made commercially (Plate 356).

The most important product on display was the new Heirloom range designed by Clappison. This extensive range of wares was initially decorated with the *Heirloom* pattern (Plate 355). Before the range was launched the Rawsons asked Clappison to extend the height of the coffee pot (Plate 357), following on from the staggering success of Portmeirion's Totem range on the tall Cylinder shape. The *Heirloom* pattern developed from Clappison's experimentation with calligraphic pens. From numerous sketches and drawings he developed the distinctive motif that later formed a repeating pattern. The choice of the glazes used was influenced by his earlier student work.

The *Heirloom* range proved a massive success and was soon followed by *Saffron* (Plate 358) in 1970 and *Bronte* in 1972. To achieve the distinctive pattern the biscuit wares were screen printed with a resist medium prior to glazing, so the glaze covered the unprinted parts of the design, creating contrasting semi-matt areas. The thicker glaze

347. The *Aphrodite* vase, featuring relief decoration with a gloss white glaze. Designed by John Clappison for Hornsea Pottery Ltd., 1962-63. Height 5¾in. (14.5cm).

348. A period photograph of the Hornsea Pottery Ltd. stand at the Blackpool Fair in 1963.

349. Several examples of the *Leaf* range. Designed by John Clappison and Michael Walker for Hornsea Pottery Ltd., 1962-63.

produced a relief effect that enhanced the design. This distinctive style was much admired by the trade press and other manufacturers and proved so successful that the Fauna range of plant pots and vases was withdrawn. Only the Fauna mugs and cruets were retained to sell alongside the Heirloom range.

In complete contrast to the functional ranges like *Summit*, Clappison turned his hand to a number of innovative ceramic pictures that he called *Muramic* wall plaques, with varied and unusual subjects, ranging from an owl on a tree to Queen Elizabeth I. A special area

350. Three storage jars from the *Summertime* range. Designed by John Clappison for Hornsea Pottery Ltd., 1962-64.

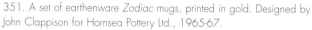

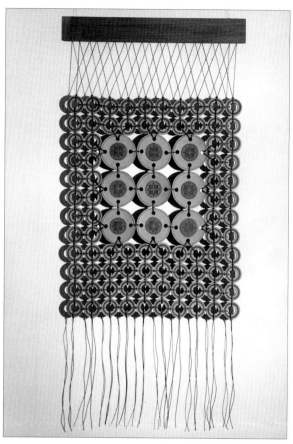

351. A set of earthenware *Zodiac* mugs, printed in gold. Designed by John Clappison for Hornsea Pottery Ltd., 1965-67.

352. One of the very few wall hangings that John Clappison produced in 1966.

was set aside for the development of these very labour-intensive pieces. They were, however, deleted within six months of starting production. Clappison also produced a limited series of textile ceramic screens during the latter part of the sixties.

In 1968 Hornsea purchased automatic spraying equipment to apply to coloured earthenwares. The trade press reported that productivity had increased by 300 per cent. Moreover, savings were made through less wastage.[16] Clappison's imaginative designs had made Hornsea so successful that new facilities were required for the manufacture of wares. In 1970 the company purchased a thirty-six acre factory site in Lancaster to run on the same lines.

During the sixties the Hornsea Pottery became a great tourist attraction, building on the efforts of Clappison's mother during the first years of production. In 1969 over 300,000 people visited the site and considerable efforts were made to provide a range of high quality facilities. Amenities included a picnic area, children's playground, a collection of exotic birds and a garden centre.[17] The seconds shop was one of the most popular attractions. Apart from the opportunity to see how a Hornsea pattern was made, visitors were also allowed to enjoy the extensive grounds.

An important reason for the success of the Hornsea Pottery was the continuous release of mugs and beakers decorated with a whole range of images, slogans and messages

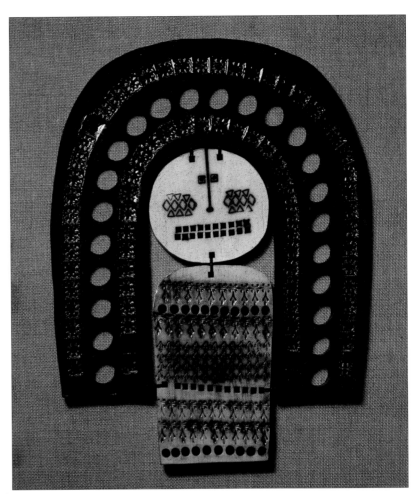

353. A forerunner of John
Clappison's *Muramic* murals.
It depicts an *Indian Woman*.
Produced in about 1966.

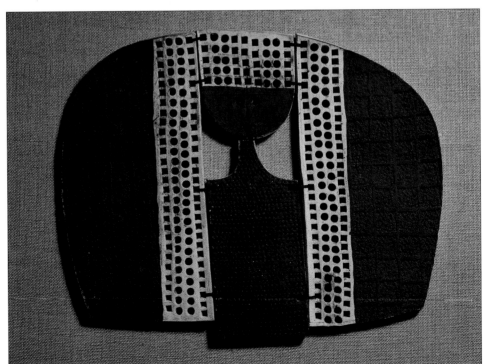

354. A rare mural depicting
a woman, from about
1966.

designed by Clappison, from the late sixties. Notable examples include half pint mugs decorated with patterns such as *Nessie, Mermaid, Bird* and *Dragon* (Plate 359). The latter was designed to coincide with the Investiture of Prince Charles in 1969. As the management wanted to gain maximum sales from the design, the idea of using commemorative words on the piece was ruled out. Instead, Clappison carefully incorporated the Prince's insignia on to the Dragon. He always injected a touch of humour into his designs, very evident in his 1970 *Train* pattern, depicting the 'toff' in the first class compartment, the worker in second class and the burglar in the goods van! Further sets were produced throughout the seventies, including the amusing 'The World's Best' series, and others featuring 'Fish' and 'Piggy' motifs.

Despite his outstanding success at Hornsea, Clappison faced difficulties and clashes with the Rawson brothers which developed into an untenable situation. He resigned as Design Director on 7 July 1972. When he left Hornsea, almost all the products currently in production were his designs.[18]

355. An earthenware coffee-pot, cup, saucer and milk jug decorated in the *Heirloom* pattern. Designed by John Clappison for Hornsea Pottery Ltd., 1967-87.

On the 1 October 1972 Clappison began work as Chief Designer for Ravenhead Glass at St. Helens, Lancashire, manufacturer of mass-produced glass for the retail and licensed victuallers' trades, taking over from the retiring designer, Hardie Williamson. Throughout the period of his contract, Clappison worked from home, visiting either the factory in St. Helens or the Head Office in Sunbury-on-Thames, about once every two weeks. He created many commercially successful designs such as *Topaz*, *Olympiad* and *Solar*. He also contributed to the development of the successful *Siesta* range (Plate 360) and produced designs for other items such as wine glasses (Plate 362). Some of his glass patterns were accepted by the Victoria and Albert Museum in London. However, his most outstanding design was the 'Bar Masters' range of glasses for licensed victuallers in 1973.

357. Michael Walker working on the *Heirloom* coffee pot.

358. A coffee set decorated with the *Saffron* pattern. Designed by John Clappison for Hornsea Pottery Ltd., 1970-92.

Sales totalled hundreds of millions of items. Whilst working for Ravenhead, Clappison devised a way of presenting glass designs in three-dimensional form without the need for a standard model. His three-dimensional simulating machine was essentially a black box with a high speed motor that revolved, thus creating a visual image of the design. This was an advantage as the designer could post these designs to the company. Clappison recalled: 'It has always been difficult to assess the exact three-dimensional appearance of

359. A collection of earthenware mugs. Top: *Train* (1970); centre: *Mermaid* (1969-70), bottom: *Bird* (1969-75), *Nessie* (1969-71) and *Dragon* (1969-75). Designed by John Clappison for Hornsea Pottery Ltd.

360. A boxed set of *Siesta* glassware that John Clappison contributed to. Ravenhead Glass Ltd., about 1973. Height of glass 2¾in. (7cm).

361. A promotional photograph inllustrating the *Midas* pattern, printed in gold on a black glaze. Designed by John Clappison for Hornsea Pottery Ltd., about 1976.

362. A detailed drawing of a wine glass design by John Clappison for Ravenhead Glass Ltd.

a glass in drawings, the main difficulty being that a drawing always makes glass look proportionately fatter than it will actually appear when made.'[19]

After Clappison's departure it soon became apparent to the Hornsea Pottery that it had lost a very good and original designer who had been responsible for its success. Several pleas were made for him to return, which he did in January 1976, as 'House Designer', creating the *Sequel, En Suite* and *Midas* designs (Plate 361). His *Impact* range from 1977, was accepted on to the Design Council Index. A range of trinket boxes called *Strata* was designed and initially manufactured by Clappison in 1980. The distinctive decoration was made from coloured clays. Slabs of multicoloured stratified clay were made and from these thin sections were taken and placed in the moulds prior to casting. After firing the box lids were polished flat on a lapidary wheel. Each box had a different configuration of stratified clays.[20] These boxes won a gift award at the National Exhibition Centre, Birmingham in 1983 (Plate 363).

During Clappison's absence from Hornsea, the management had contracted the Queensberry/Hunt Design Group, which had introduced the very successful Contrast range of shapes. On his return it had not been made clear to Clappison that this group had exclusivity on shape design, which he must have found rather limiting. Despite continued growth during the late seventies, Hornsea Pottery suffered from the recession in 1981. Attempts to recover by changes in management and design policy failed to save the company, so in 1984 it was put into the hands of the receivers and the entire design team, including Clappison, was made redundant in order to cut costs.[21]

After such an outstanding career, Clappison was soon re-employed as Head Shape designer at Royal Doulton. He moved to Nantwich, Cheshire with his wife and youngest

son in July 1988. His position as group shape designer meant that he worked for Minton, Royal Albert, Crown Derby, and Doulton Hotel and Airlines Division. He designed the Gallery (Plate 30) and Warwick shapes in 1992, followed by a range of cookware and everyday ware, from 1997 and 1998 respectively. Clappison also designed several individual items for Crown Derby.

After more than forty years in the pottery business, ill health forced his retirement in 1998 at the age of sixty-one. During the course of his career he has been interested to see his work increase in value and become collectable. In 1986 he donated over forty examples of his work to the Victoria and Albert Museum's permanent collection.

363. A selection of giftwares decorated with the *Strata* pattern. Designed by John Clappison for Hornsea Pottery Ltd., 1983.

364. A selection of wares from the Gallery range, designed by John Clappison for Royal Doulton Ltd., 1993.

CHAPTER 15

REFRESHINGLY DIFFERENT

EVE MIDWINTER (b.1926)

365. Eve Midwinter working on the Stoneware range, 1979.

The success of contemporary wares produced by the Midwinter company during the fifties and sixties was without doubt due to the firm's commitment to original and high quality patterns and shapes. Whilst Jessie Tait's patterns of that period had established Midwinter's reputation, it was the contribution of Eve Midwinter which carried this success through until the eighties. She was pioneering in the development and introduction of new glaze decorations, innovative patterns and shapes. However, she was not just a designer but also an accomplished stylist who projected the image of the Midwinter product throughout the style-conscious eighties, later on working as a free-lance designer for several other companies.

Eve Midwinter has always maintained that her contribution to pottery design was down to good luck and good timing. Her sense of style and appreciation of good design was clearly influenced by her family and their various interests. Her Russian father, John Wyse, with his two brothers, moved to India, leaving their home country just before the Russian Revolution. At the age of fourteen he became a wine merchant and then a surveyor for the North Western Railway in Lahore. Some years later he became a Colonel in the Indian Army. Her mother was Enid Little. Eve was born in 1926; her sister Jacqueline was born

two years earlier and her brother David in 1930. Her father was interested in the
decorative arts and in particular the Georgian period, especially furniture. His appreciation
of the fine arts must have encouraged Eve's understanding of good classic design.[1]

Having spent most of her early life in India, she came to England, aged seven, to attend
a co-educational school in Huntingdon. Her parents were good friends of the Midwinter
family, owners of a small pottery manufactory in the Potteries. The Midwinter's son, Roy,
attended the same school, but he was four years older. In about 1941, after her formal
education was finished, she returned to India until the end of the War. During this period
she joined the Women's Auxiliary Corps. (India) as a subaltern. By 1946 she had come
back to Britain to live with the Midwinter family at Rockwoods, Longton Road in Stone,
becoming very good friends with Roy's sister, Joy.[2] In 1946, after five years of service in
the RAF, Roy Midwinter was employed in the family firm. His father wanted him to learn all
the important aspects of running a successful business by working in each department. He
also suggested that he should attend technical college to add to his knowledge.[3]

Having developed an interest in the fine arts and portrait painting, especially the
Impressionist and the Pre-Raphaelite periods, Midwinter considered attending college. Her

367. A Fine shape coffee-pot decorated with the *Roselle* pattern, introduced in about 1963 and a *Tango* gravy boat and stand, 1969. Designed by Eve Midwinter for W.R. Midwinter Ltd. Height of coffee-pot 7½in. (19cm).

368. The lesser-known *Poppy* pattern, transfer printed on an earthenware bowl, diameter 6¼in. (16cm), from the Studio range. Designed by Eve Midwinter for J. & G. Meakin Ltd., in about 1972.

mother wanted her to attend the Slade School of Art in London. Ultimately it was decided that she would take a place at the Burslem School of Art, closer to the Midwinter's family home, in about 1948. However, nine months into the course Roy proposed to her and she left the School of Art. To make her wedding dress, her parents brought white silk with silver hand-embroidered detail with them from India.[4]

For most of the fifties Midwinter was responsible for looking after her children; Richard, born in 1949, and a daughter, Julie, born in 1954. At the same time Roy had embarked on revitalising the company, introducing modern patterns and stylish shapes that would put the Midwinter company at the forefront of British design.

For some years Eve Midwinter worked for the Pottery in an unofficial capacity. She visited London each month in order to buy examples of contemporary design, such as textiles, to be used at the firm for ideas and inspiration. By the early sixties her involvement had developed to such an extent that she was responsible for the styling of the firm's trade stands, a notable example being the Blackpool Fancy Goods and Gifts Fair of 1962, that launched the new Fine shape. She creatively devised four individual and contrasting room themes such as 'Victorian' and 'Contemporary' for each of the new designs, Sienna, Whitehill, Queensberry Stripe and Evesham. One particular room featured Regency style wallpaper and period light fittings. Eventually she began to create her own tableware patterns,

369. A coffee set decorated with the *Maidstone* pattern, aerographed in orange with printed decoration, from the Studio range. Designed by Eve Midwinter for J. & G. Meakin Ltd., about 1972-74. Height of coffee-pot 9¼in. (23.5cm).

in a limited form, for which she was unpaid.

In 1960 her first pattern, *Bella Vista*, was launched (Plate 366). It was developed from a suggestion by her father-in-law who was aware of a popular floral design produced by a competitor. He asked her to create a similar version, that once completed was handed to Jessie Tait for adaptation to fit the Fashion shape range of giftware. Examples were illustrated in the trade press as late as September 1961. *Bella Vista* was also produced on the new Classic shape, introduced during the same year, to appeal to the more conservative market. Midwinter also created *Vegetables*, a hand-painted pattern of stylised vegetable motifs, with trailing leaves in green.[5]

Her second pattern, *Roselle* (Plate 367), was a simple repeating stylised pattern in blue and green, produced by on-glaze lithograph, with lids and saucers in a matt blue glaze, introduced on the Fine shape in 1963. The pattern proved popular for many years, after which it was re-styled with the saucers and lids being changed to a green and blue band.[6] This pattern, and Oakley by Jessie Tait, was exclusive to the Boots chain of stores and to Timothy White's, marketed and backstamped as part of the 'Stylist Tableware' range. With two successful patterns in production, Midwinter spent more time in the studio, becoming conscious of the practicalities of designing on a commercial scale. Her next design, *Tango*

370. An earthenware Stonehenge shape tureen decorated with the *Creation* glaze. Designed by Eve Midwinter for W.R. Midwinter Ltd., 1972.

(Plate 367), featuring bold stylised flowerheads in orange and yellow, was introduced in 1969. For the first time, her name was incorporated into the backstamp, which read 'Designed by E. Midwinter'. During the development of *Tango*, Roy Midwinter had explained to her that one could never cover more than a third of the ware in lithographed pattern. Being experienced in design, she carefully introduced white breaks in the form of leaves, so that they would register in the same way that textile designs are developed, enabling the pattern to cover a much wider space.[7] This stunning design remained in production for over six years. She also submitted a few patterns for the forthcoming MQ2 shape, designed by Roy Midwinter and David Queensberry in 1966. These were banded patterns, inspired by the psychedelic fashions of the period, in clashing colour combinations such as red and purple, and lime green and blue, in both thick and thin bands. Unfortunately the public did not take to the new shape range and as a result the patterns were not used.

The Midwinters were very good friends with Susan Williams-Ellis and Euan Cooper-Willis, who ran the small but innovative Portmeirion Pottery, established in the early sixties. On a number of occasions they visited them in North Wales, occasionally scuba-diving together. Indeed, Susan Williams-Ellis painted Roy's portrait underwater.

Sadly, the Midwinter marriage deteriorated and they divorced in the mid-sixties. Given the difficult time, Midwinter needed a new impetus and decided to take up an open invitation from Susan Williams-Ellis to work with her. She joined Portmeirion in 1967 at probably one of the most exciting periods in the company's history. Her role was as an assistant designer to Susan Williams-Ellis' assistant designer! Her short time there was diverse and interesting, working in each department, recalling later that it was quite a chaotic factory. As part of her work she was asked to produce a set of drawings based on an old newspaper article, depicting Victorian ladies and gentlemen riding unusual bicycles, for a range called Velocipedes. This design was used on storage jars, plates, coffee sets and giftware.

371. Two Stonehenge plates decorated with the *Sun* and *Earth* patterns. Designed by Eve Midwinter for W.R. Midwinter Ltd., 1973.

372. An earthenware Stonehenge shape coffee-pot decorated with the *Earth* pattern. Designed by Eve Midwinter for W.R. Midwinter Ltd., 1973.

373. An earthenware dinner plate decorated with the *Wild Oats* pattern. Designed by Eve Midwinter for W.R. Midwinter Ltd., about 1974.

Portmeirion was currently producing the popular Totem range that had been in production for at least four years. Midwinter attributes much of her knowledge and skill with glazes to working there, noting in particular the problems with the flow glazes on the Totem range. The tall coffee pots had to be fired separately from the rest of the range, making matching the smaller wares with the coffee pots a production nightmare. Susan Williams-Ellis became increasingly dissatisfied with her chemists, therefore she put Midwinter in charge of glazes. This new position gave her first-hand experience of working with glazes and patterns which she would later exploit for her own distinctive patterns for the Midwinter Pottery. Whilst working at Portmeirion, Midwinter had the opportunity to develop a limited range of patterns, including a small box and cover decorated with a stylised pink floral border and some tea ware featuring a zebra print pattern, but these were not put into production.

Despite their recent divorce, Roy Midwinter asked her to consider returning to work for him, at a time when the firm had undergone enormous changes. It was taken over by J. & G. Meakin in 1968, although production remained at the Albion and Hadderidge works. The Meakin/Midwinter company then began refurbishing the A.J. Wilkinson site that Midwinter had purchased in 1964. Following the subsequent acquisition of both companies by Josiah Wedgwood and Sons Ltd. in 1970, the Midwinter firm transferred to the Wilkinson site, whilst the design team and sales moved to J. & G. Meakin Ltd., at the Eagle Pottery based in Hanley. The Wedgwood Group sold the Albion and Hadderidge Works to the engineering company William Bolton, which in turn sold the site to John Maddocks whose own building had been recently demolished to build a new 'Kwik Save' supermarket. The site then became the home of Royal Stafford China but due

374 Three earthenware plates, diameter 10¼in. (26cm), decorated with the patterns *Greenleaves, Autumn* and *Rangoon*. Designed by Eve Midwinter for W.R. Midwinter Ltd., 1974-76.

to structural problems, the premises were closed and will soon be demolished.[8]

Following the takeover by Josiah Wedgwood and Sons Ltd., Roy Midwinter became the Group Design Co-ordinator. Working on a part-time basis for J. & G. Meakin, Midwinter played a more important creative role, with two of her most recent designs, originally intended for Midwinter's Fine shape, used by Meakin's on their distinctive Studio shape. Her *Poppy* design (Plate 368) was influenced by Susie Cooper's best-selling Cornpoppy pattern for Wedgwood in 1971; Midwinter's pattern also became a big seller for the firm for several years. Two of her patterns, *Bianca*, a large abstract flower motif, and *Maidstone* (Plate 369), were developed as a result of the many experiments that she undertook to create original design. Both patterns featured self-coloured hollowwares complemented by a textured design decorated on plates, lids and saucers in assorted colours, as part of the *Maidstone* range. Her name was not incorporated into the backstamp. Little information is available on any other designs that she may have produced for J. & G. Meakin.[9]

In 1972 the Midwinter Pottery introduced Stonehenge, an innovative range that successfully created a studio-style appearance in shape, colour and decoration. It was launched at the Blackpool Fair in that year. She was not involved in the development of the initial patterns but, drawing on her recent

375. The *Spring Blue* pattern decorated on an earthenware Stonehenge shape milk jug, height 5in. (12.5cm. Designed by Eve Midwinter for W.R. Midwinter Ltd., 1974.).

376. Two patterns for the Stonehenge range. Plate decorated with *Strawberry* and covered sugar with *Riverside*. Designed by Eve Midwinter for W.R. Midwinter Ltd., about 1974-78. Diameter of plate 7in. (18cm).

experience at Portmeirion, she began to experiment with reactive glazes. The many trials that she produced led to the production of the distinctive *Creation* glaze (Plate 370). This was a real breakthrough for the company. However, she credits three men, Ron Carter, Harry Webster and Gordon Stanley, with helping her to achieve the successful glaze and subsequent designs for commercial use. Ron Carter, employed at Cookson, glaze manufacturers, developed a system that enabled reactive specks to be suspended in the glaze by coating them with plastic so when fired in the kiln they would remain in the glaze finish. To give the glaze a burnished feel he made up a small amount of iron oxide manganese that was painted around the edges of the ware.[10] Wedgwood Canada was very impressed with the Creation glaze, placing a large order for the ware.

The production of Creation did have its problems. Eve Midwinter was forced to fight against the sceptical workers who disapproved of her ideas. Historically, contamination in the glaze was a pottery's worst enemy. This probably explains why on a number of occasions members of staff kept throwing away the specially mixed glazes, thinking that they were not pure. In the industry any piece of pottery with blemishes to the glaze was considered to be a second. However, she skilfully reversed this by turning seconds into firsts. As sales increased, more of the factory was taken over with the production of the Creation glaze for the Stonehenge range and as a result many Fine shape patterns were discontinued.[11] Creation was featured in several important magazines and trade journals, including the influential *Design* magazine. A twenty-one piece tea set was priced at £9.43 and a twenty-four piece dinner service at £20.17.[12] Marketing focused on its sophistication, durability and the fact that it was dishwasher safe. The company boasted: 'In these days of mass production it's refreshing to find slight variations in decorations normally associated with the expensive hand-thrown studio pottery. Close examination proves that each piece is unique.'[13]

377. An example of the *Denim* pattern decorated on a Stoneware cup, height 2⅜in. (6cm), and saucer. Designed by Eve Midwinter for W.R. Midwinter Ltd., about 1979.

Subsequent designs that she produced over the next ten years featured the Creation glaze. One of the first was *Sun* (Plate 371), that was developed following a request made by Wedgwood Canada. This outstanding pattern was inspired by a collection of Italian design magazines, one of which included a colour spectrum shading from deep orange to pale yellow. Gordon Stanley, a founder director of Precision Studios, helped develop the in-glaze lithographs for her, that could be placed on to the ware. The actual design was created, in some respects, by accident as she was so keen to see the finished pattern that she decided to cut circles out of the coloured sheets, placing them in an arrangement and running the joins with oxide glaze edging. The experiment was successful, although the piece was left on the shelf in the factory for some time. It was not until Mike Eccles, President of the Canadian Division of Wedgwood, happened to come across this sample that he decided it had great potential and therefore should be produced. Colour variations were appropriately called *Moon* and *Earth* (Plate 372). Publicity material for these three innovative patterns was original, with life-size replicas of the plates being printed in the form of leaflets for prospective customers to request. The advertisements encouraged them to send a stamp and receive a plate to try it out on the dining room table!

Midwinter wanted to put oxide into the printing medium to create depth and after little success she turned to Harry Webster, the founder director of Transgrave Studios. She explained what she was trying to achieve and asked how this new decorative colour could be successfully produced to a commercial standard. He helped produce the very deep engravings to print the patterns, using a ferric-oxide based colour. To create the reactive glaze an opaque glaze was used so that the ferric-oxide would push through, forming the reactive texture. This technique was used for the best-selling *Wild Oats* pattern that featured soft brown wheatsheaves on a pale oatmeal glossy glaze (Plate 373).

Moreover the pattern name proved rather controversial as it had another meaning. The journalists loved the insinuations that indirectly helped to sell it. *Wild Oats* sold well in North America, Germany and Britain. Further patterns, using the Creation glaze, were simpler and more stylised, using a minimal colour range in order to blend with the distinctive body. Notable examples include *Greenleaves*, *Autumn* and *Rangoon*, the latter incorporating hand-painted bamboo canes (Plate 374).

In about 1974 the Seasons Collection was launched, including *Winter*, *Summer* and *Spring Blue* (Plate 375), all designed by Midwinter.[14] New patterns continued to be introduced throughout the early part of the eighties, among them *Riverside* (Plate 376). The Midwinter Pottery confidently boasted: 'We've come a long way since Creation.'[15]

At some time during the late seventies Wedgwood moved the Midwinter Pottery design team back to the A.J. Wilkinson site. Wedgwood invested a considerable amount of money installing new equipment in the factory. The new design team, headed by the Midwinters, operated from the old Malkin Tile building, as the Newport Pottery was closed down during the War. Carol Lovatt, who had previously worked as a paintress at Coalport, joined the team in 1980. Her skills in free-hand painting were needed to produce the samples and trials to send out and to show the management. When the design team wasn't very busy she was encouraged to develop some of her own ideas for the Stonehenge range and one of her first patterns was Seascape, produced in the *Wild Oats* colours. New patterns and shapes were developed through a team effort rather than individually. During the subsequent years several young designers were appointed to work with Midwinter. These included Laura Kemp, Pat Speak, Janet Crisp, Janet Dunham, Lynn Boyd and Angela Atkinson. Contributions to design matters also came from outside

379. A collection of Style shapes including an undecorated beverage dispenser pot, a Style shape tureen decorated with the *Confetti* pattern designed by Eve Midwinter and right, items decorated with Rainbow, designed by Carol Lovatt, both from 1983-85.

consultants, such as Derek Healey. The central room at the site was equipped with a large table in the centre, a big sink and several display shelves, with offices along the corridor from the central room. Reiner Muller, the Art Director for Wedgwood (USA) would look through all the samples and select those that he thought would be commercially successful. The Spanish Garden, *Roselle* and *Riverside* patterns, the latter designed for the Fine shape by John Russell, were still the best selling lines for the Midwinter Pottery in 1980.

Responding to market trends, Midwinter developed a new range towards the end of the seventies, called Stoneware. It was the intention that decoration should be avoided, thus allowing the body of the ware to speak for itself. Roy Midwinter admired the work of Robin Welch, an East Anglian based potter, and commissioned him to create the shape range. As it was his first experience of working in an industrial situation he worked closely with Sid Machin, the firm's modeller.[16] Given that the North American market was very important to the company, Roy Midwinter took prototypes to New York City to carry out market research. It was imperative that they should be successful and appeal to this market. He consulted department stores such as Macey's and Bloomingdale's to receive feedback on the prototypes. Their comments were then sent back to the company with any instructions for further modifications if required. The design team was very conscious of developing practical shapes that were multi-purpose, such as stackable bowls and plates that could double up for pizza and tarts. The range included tea, coffee and dinnerware. Roy Midwinter commented: 'A pattern that fails is a disappointment – but a shape that fails is a disaster because all patterns are designed for that shape. With studio pottery you are selling the shape; you can't cover it with elaborate patterns.'[17]

A range of samples concentrating on glazes and textures to complement these shapes

380. An earthenware Style shape tureen decorated with the *Carnival* pattern. Designed by Eve Midwinter for W.R. Midwinter Ltd., about 1983. Width of tureen 10¼in. (26cm).

was sent out to the United States as part of the market research. The results of this valuable research informed the company that plain ware would not be popular. Robin Welch felt that the shapes should remain undecorated.[18] The need for some form of decoration necessitated further trials. At the same time she worked on the glazes, making sure that they were resistant to scratching and thermal shock – important factors demanded by customers. The initial samples received a very good reception at the international trade fairs in Birmingham, Frankfurt and Atlantic City. The four introductory patterns were Natural, Blueprint, *Hopsack* and *Denim*, the latter two were designed by Midwinter (Plate 377). Whilst Natural relied on the plain body Blueprint, designed by Janet Dunham, featured a fringed blue band. Sadly it took over two years for the Wedgwood company, which initially wanted to put the range out under their name, to decide what to do with it. Without these delays the range may have been more successful. Even though it proved very popular with the North American market, British taste was moving away from the seventies' stoneware look. The public wanted something a little more modern and therefore this range was not popular. Further patterns including Rossetta, Provence, Shetland, Terrene and Brownstone were introduced. In 1981 Midwinter and Lynn Boyd designed the lesser-known pattern *Petal*, on an oatmeal glaze, on the Stoneware range. This pattern was commissioned by Marks and Spencer's. Unfortunately nothing came of it as the store did not allow enough time for the production of publicity and in-store displays to promote the range.[19] One of the last patterns on Stoneware was Braid by Laura Kemp, introduced in about 1985.

By the start of the new decade the Midwinter Pottery had built up a healthy export market, with over seventy-five per cent of goods being exported, in particular to North America and Germany. *Wild Oats* remained the best-selling pattern both at home and abroad. In 1981 Roy Midwinter decided to retire from the Wedgwood organisation to set

381. The promotional leaflet for the Bizarre Collection of Clarice Cliff reproductions, 1985.

up his own design consultancy. He produced designs for the Federation Potteries that were reminiscent of the fifties retro look, popular in the early eighties. He also gave other firms the benefit of his experience. At about this time Midwinter became a Senior Designer within the Wedgwood group. During the same year Roger Marsden, the Managing Director of Midwinter, informed the trade press: 'as far as the future for stoneware products goes, I feel that there is still mileage in the rustic look which has been popular for so many years. Having said that, our new patterns are moving towards a more sophisticated and feminine look and this is the way the market is going.'[20]

This new look took the form of a white version of Stonehenge chiefly targeted at the Australian market. New patterns included *Invitation* (Plate 378) and *Wild Cherry* by Midwinter and Aztec by Angela Atkinson. In line with market trends the Cookware range was introduced, consisting of items such as avocado and soufflé dishes, ramekins and flan dishes. The first three patterns, introduced in 1982, were *Invitation*, Ratatouille and Still Life, Carol Lovatt designed the latter. Also around 1982, the Stoneware shape was used to create the Tempo range, an earthenware version of Stoneware. Four patterns, Duet, Nocturne, Orbit and Blue Crosses, not designed by Midwinter, were decorated on this range. The Tempo range was completely phased out after about three years.

Midwinter realised that the market was moving towards a more sophisticated and feminine look for the 1980s. With her ability to anticipate the style of the period she began to develop, with her team of designers, a new shape and pattern range for the new decade. The designers made inspiration-seeking trips to New York and San Francisco to examine the latest trends and tastes. In some respects the new shape range came about because she was less than keen to use existing shapes for her own patterns. This dissatisfaction prompted her to develop her own shapes, based on stylish ovals. Mike Pawluk, the company's Design Administrator, an experienced ceramics technician, advised at an early stage on the feasibility of her new concept. He was a great help to Midwinter for several years. She was able to persuade a friend to produce the three-dimensional prototypes to show the sales team. According to the designer: 'I was aiming at a feminine shape, something more elegant and lighter than we have made in the past. I like ovals, and if you look there are ovals within ovals at the handle and lid of the beverage dispenser.'[21]

The Style range was both innovative and revolutionary, yet it took three years to get into full production. The initial range was launched in 1983 with an extensive publicity campaign in major magazines such as *Cosmopolitan*, *Homes and Gardens* and *Ideal Home*. The marketing strategy focused on the individuality of the range with the slogan 'Style, Refreshingly Different'. A four page colour leaflet for publicity and advice on in-store displays was distributed to retailers.[22] The range featured a stylish beverage dispenser that acted as both the tea and coffee-pot. Alongside the standard shapes, a selection of fancies and gift wares, such as napkin rings and small vases, were produced (Plate 379). A unique oval-shaped tea warmer that had a space inside for a small candle was designed by Midwinter. The range consisted of six patterns. She created both *Confetti* and *Carnival* (Plate 380). Carol Lovatt designed Crystal, and Pat Speak created Carousel, Calypso and Cameo. The undecorated version was called White. The most attractive pattern was *Confetti*, with its distinctive glaze treatment. The speckled glaze of pretty pastel dots, bursting on to the surface in a random manner, captured the mood of the day. However, it was subject to production problems as the various speckle sizes were hard to reproduce to a satisfactory standard, although this was eventually resolved. Carol Lovatt also designed Celebration, Chromatics, Coral Mist and Rainbow (Plate 379); the latter pattern was targeted at the German market but proved unsuccessful. The Calypso pattern was later developed for the Cookware range. The Confetti glaze was exclusive to Midwinter for the first twelve months, after which competitors were able to purchase it for use in their own manufacture.

Despite its visual elegance the tea pot, or beverage dispenser as it was marketed, was not very practical. The handle was fragile and tended to break during firing. Moreover the purchaser was required to retain the grey plastic support, which functioned as a protective stand for use in the dishwasher. Midwinter recently referred to it as the handbag![23] Although orders for the Style range were accepted up until December 1986, Carousel, *Carnival*, Celebration, Chromatics and Crystal were phased out during 1985. The whole range was cancelled three years later. Interestingly, one of the most popular Midwinter patterns, Spanish Garden, designed by Jessie Tait in 1968, was briefly decorated on the Style shape, truly a rarity! However this and other unusual items, transfer-printed with old-fashioned village scenes and birds were probably trials which managed to get into the public domain.

At a time when the major chain stores wanted their own exclusive patterns, Midwinter designed a new oven-to-tableware shape called Orient in 1985. The range consisted of tea, coffee and dinnerware, with a sugar bowl and cover that was often mistaken for a

small ginger jar. Her *Forget me Knot* pattern featured a series of thin black lines cascading over the plain white body and knotting in the centre. Orient was the plain undecorated version. They were chiefly targeted at the Canadian market but didn't sell well. Lynn Boyd created a simple trailing floral motif that did not go into production. The Orient range had a rather limited run of just over a year.

In 1985 the growing interest in the art deco period inspired Midwinter to produce a range of giftware based on the work of Clarice Cliff. Several patterns and shapes were recreated, called The Bizarre Collection, the name of the original designer's first range from 1927 (Plate 381). The patterns included Honolulu, Melon, and Umbrellas and Rain. The reproductions consisted of a Summerhouse charger, Umbrellas and Rain conical bowl and Honolulu on a mei-ping vase. The six sugar sifters were decorated in Crocus, Rudyard, House and Bridge, Pastel Melon, Pastel Autumn and Red Roof Cottage. Each individual item was stamped 'Royal Staffordshire Pottery by Clarice Cliff, Made in England.' The larger pieces informed the purchaser that the edition was limited to 500. A date mark '85' was impressed on the back. However, achieving the same distinctive 'art deco' look with

382. A selection of earthenware coffee and dinnerwares from the *Lincoln* range, developed by Eve Midwinter for Barratts of Staffs. Ltd., about 1987.

383. Examples of coffee and dinnerwares decorated with the *Trellis* pattern, printed in either pink or blue on the Regal shape. Designed by Eve Midwinter for Barratts of Staffs Ltd., about 1988.

its vibrant colours proved difficult as some of the colours had been banned several years earlier. These patterns were produced as a limited edition. The publicity leaflet claimed that the new range: 'Is destined to create the same surprise and admiration as when it was first unveiled.'[24] When they proved rather difficult to sell, Harrod's purchased the remaining items. The Bizarre Collection was complemented by three further patterns, Oranges and Lemons and Melon by Lynn Boyd and Crocus by Angela Atkinson, these were based on original examples. However the patterns were simplified for the lithographic process.[25] Crocus decorated the Stonehenge and Cookware ranges, but unlike the original it was transfer-printed. Further patterns, developed by Midwinter, included a novel breakfast set, comprising a mug, standard cereal bowl, eggcup and three sizes of plate, called *Good Morning*. A three-piece boxed set of plate, bowl and mug retailed at £9.40.

Possibly due to what Wedgwood saw as failures with the Style and Orient ranges, the final shape by Midwinter had to be both utilitarian and not too daring. Reflex was based on the Simple shape, designed by Peter Wall for William Adams in the late sixties. Susie Cooper used this functional range, which had a vitrified white ceramic body, for her Blue Haze and Florida patterns in about 1983.[26] The shape was modified to include a slightly different knob on the lids and rounded handles for the hollowwares. The range included tea, coffee and dinnerware and a few smaller items including ramekin dishes. Reflex was launched in 1986 with eight new banded and floral decorations. *Montmartre*, designed by Eve Midwinter and Lynn Boyd, was inspired by Claude Monet's kitchen at his house in Giverny, France.[27] The strong solid band in yellow contrasted with the thin bands either side in blue. Originally the team wanted the bright yellow band to be hand-applied but this was not possible due to financial costs. To promote this pattern at the forthcoming trade fair the design team set up a French café table to showcase the design. Further patterns included Rhapsody by Lynn Boyd and Enchantment by Carol Lovatt. The latter designer also created Nouveau whilst Angela Atkinson was responsible for both Blaze and Symphony. In 1986 new patterns, including Pimlico, Quarto, Domino and White Reflex were introduced. Wedgwood issued both Versailles and Avignon, variations of *Montmartre*, after Eve Midwinter had left the company.

In July 1986 Midwinter resigned from the company to pursue other work. As a leaving present she was given a tall vase, hand-painted with stylised birds and flowers decorated by her team of designers at Wedgwood. Lynn Boyd, recruited from her degree show by Midwinter, developed artwork for a special range of 'Roland Rat' giftware. The items included tea ware, an oval money-box, cereal bowl, tankard, toothbrush beaker and a mealtime set. Consultations also took place with Tony Hart, the popular BBC television art presenter, regarding the production of giftware such as ceramic jigsaws depicting the popular animated character, 'Morph'.[28]

Following the takeover by Waterford in 1987 a rationalisation of the firm's products resulted in the cancellation of several designs. The Midwinter factory closed in April 1987 and shortly afterwards the site was demolished and turned into a housing estate. The most successful patterns, such as *Wild Oats*, *Creation* and *Invitation*, on the Stonehenge shape, and some Reflex patterns, were continued after that date. These were dealt with by Creative Tableware, based in Hanley. Despite the closure, Wedgwood continued to use the Midwinter name for some years.

After such a prestigious career and with a reputation for quality designs, Midwinter undertook various free-lance jobs. One of her first contracts was with Maw and Co., a firm established in 1850 in Worcestershire which later moved to the Benthall Works in Shropshire. It produced lustre and enamel painted tiles for hall and fireplace decoration. In 1960 it was purchased by Campbell Tile Co. Ltd. and four years later a merger took place with Richard Tiles, which merged in 1968 with H. & R. Johnson Ltd. Two years later the original site closed down and production moved to Staffordshire.[29] The company was based in Tunstall. The opportunity for Midwinter to design for Maw and Co. was made possible by a new Government initiative that aimed to encourage smaller companies to invest in design. The Government, in part, funded her wages. She developed a range of designs for floor and wall tiles. The wall tiles featured a subtle raised edge whilst the floor tiles looked more to tradition.

Shortly afterwards, another post presented itself which was to be more challenging and successful for Midwinter. In 1987 Barratts of Staffordshire Ltd. contracted her to act as a design consultant. During the same year Norman Tempest, previously Sales Director

384. A modern fruit pattern called *Sorbet*, hand painted on a range of earthenware shapes. Designed by Eve Midwinter for Royal Stafford Tableware Ltd., about 1998.

Manager at the Midwinter Pottery, joined the firm. During the fifties Barratts was a family-owned business that produced cheap earthenwares for boxed sets. Eventually the company was sold to Great Universal Stores. When this firm decided to sell off its outside interests the pottery section was sold. Between 1986-87 the firm was run by the management but soon went into receivership. A new owner, Stanley Cohen, purchased the company, which was later renamed Barratts of Staffs. Ltd. Prior to this takeover, good modern design had not been a feature. The firm's products had been very run-of-the-mill, with no quality control or, as Midwinter explained, 'straight out of the kiln and on to the shelves'.[30]

Seeing potential for the company, the owner wanted to take the firm's wares more up-market by producing fine earthenware like Mason's. The most immediate requirement was the production of new shapes and patterns. With all her years of experience, Midwinter could see that there was a gap in the market and set about looking through the firm's archives and moulds. During her investigations she came across a small plate and coffee can which had not been produced since the twenties, featuring a border of embossed fruit. This was the starting point of the firm's success. New moulds were made with additional shapes such as the cover dish designed by Midwinter and Fred Hackney. The classic *Lincoln* pattern (Plate 382), as it came to be marketed, featured a warm glaze and proved popular. The backstamp depicted the firm's distinctive front gates as the trademark. In 1988 a hand-painted version of the pattern, called *Vine*, featuring green leaves and purple grapes painted in water-based colours, was initially not viable as the firm's decorators were unable to be swift enough to make the range commercial. To solve the situation the company brought in some young people on the Government's Youth Training Scheme who proved very capable and were more productive that the firm's decorators. To the surprise of the firm, the hand-painted *Lincoln* designs proved very popular with the Japanese market for at least three years. *Lincoln*, which eventually became an exclusive to British Home Stores, sold individually or in a boxed set for new householders, was very successful and has remained in production for over ten years, becoming in some respects the firm's bread and butter.[31] Midwinter continued to develop similar patterns, most notably a simple painted border design of embossed fruit called *Country Fayre*, produced especially for the Guild of Fine China Retailers. Another version called *Ashford* was produced for Debenhams. Her *Songbirds* and *Trellis* patterns (Plate 383), both on the Regal shape, were printed in either pastel blue, pink or green. A more traditional pattern was *Samarkand*, produced in black edged with a gold line.

In about March, 1992 Barratts purchased Royal Stafford, established by Thomas Poole in Longton around 1840. The firm later moved to the Maddocks site, previously the home of the Midwinter factory. It relocated to Navigation Road in Burslem some years later. In the difficult business climate of the period the firm had sadly gone into receivership. Until their amalgamation in 1993 the two companies operated separately, becoming known as Royal Stafford Tableware from 1994. Following these changes all new patterns were released under the Royal Stafford name. Many other designers produced patterns for the company, including Julie Pople whose designs included Geo Floral and Naturelle.[32] These patterns, as well as Midwinter's *Bordeaux*, were decorated on the new Classique shape developed by Fred Hackney, Julie Pople and Midwinter. She also reworked the longstanding and popular pattern *Asiatic Pheasant* for the firm, giving it a contemporary feel.

Whilst working as a designer for Barratts, Midwinter undertook work for other companies, in particular for Maw and Co. Although they had a resident designer, they commissioned her to produce a range of patterns for vases in the Moorcroft style. She worked closely in the decorating shop with Margaret Brindley, the firm's supervisor, who once worked for Susie Cooper as a free-hand paintress. The attempt to recreate the Moorcroft look, both in terms of colour and style, was fraught with difficulties because the firm had always been involved in the production of tiles rather than decorative pieces. More importantly, Maw and Co. were not able to reproduce the distinctive style of Moorcroft despite several attempts with different treatments.

Tube-lined decoration was also ruled out in favour of moulded ware, probably due to financial costs and perhaps the lack of skills available.[33] Instead, Midwinter drew the pattern on to the selected vase, and then the modeller created a relief decoration. At this point she was unsure about the colours that should be used and Roy Midwinter produced the artwork for her to demonstrate the desired effect. For one of the first trials the ware was aerographed with a dark blue glaze. The pattern was hand painted on to the ware using glaze colours that unfortunately tended to blend with the base colour. This and associated problems were finally resolved. When the first pattern, *Wisteria*, was finally produced Margaret Brindley proudly took the item around the showroom to show everyone who had played a part in getting the pattern right. Midwinter designed only a few patterns for the company, including *Basket Fruit* and another in a Japanese style. These were not very successful, as the marketing material was not put in place by the company. After only twelve months she decided to move on to more artistically challenging projects that could be realised to a higher standard.

With her inherent understanding of good design and contemporary tastes Midwinter produced a wide range of stylish tablewares for Royal Stafford Tableware during the mid-nineties. Her *Newport* and *Fairfax* patterns were typical. One of her most recent patterns is *Sorbet* (Plate 384) featuring a single fruit motif, such as an apple or orange, combined with a printed textured border, exclusive to the Boots stores in 1998.

Following the end of her contract with Royal Stafford Tableware she has successfully carried on working as a free-lance designer, often collaborating with other designers on new concepts and ideas. More recently she has worked for Carter and Edwards in Stoke-on-Trent. She has been able to enjoy recognition for the outstanding and influential work that she has produced over many years. Largely due to her inspiration, the Midwinter company will always be acknowledged for its pioneering approach to design, especially during the fifties.

CHAPTER 16

FROM DELPHIS TO ROYAL DOULTON

ROBERT JEFFERSON (1929-1998)

385. Robert Jefferson outside the Poole Pottery, admiring the new ceramic wall mural, 1963.

During the 1920s and '30s the Poole Pottery established a reputation for innovation and high quality. In the immediate post-war period the company introduced a range of contemporary patterns on free form shapes, again establishing itself as a leading manufacturer. Towards the latter part of the fifties Robert Jefferson moved the company into a new period of artistic, critical and financial success, placing Poole at the forefront of British design. He went on to design an outstanding range of tablewares for the Purbeck Pottery, then moved forward to produce a range of successful modelled figures and animals for Royal Doulton, Royal Crown Derby and Minton in an outstanding career spanning over forty years.

Jefferson was born in Southport on 24 January 1929 to Harold, a local solicitor, and his wife, Margaret. He was educated at Lancaster Royal Grammar School. In 1945 he studied at the Liverpool College of Art for a year, followed by two years of National Service with the King's Royal Regiment, Lancashire. When his regiment travelled to Trieste, Jefferson visited a number of galleries and museums in Northern Italy, Germany and Austria.[1]

In 1949 he went to the Burslem School of Art. While studying at the college he also worked under Agnete Hoy, the Danish potter, at the Bullers Art Studio in Milton. For one year Jefferson learned a great deal about pottery, glazes and decoration. Unfortunately, the Bullers Art Studio,

set up in 1932, was closed in 1952. At the Burslem School of Art he was awarded a travel scholarship by the British Pottery Manufacturers' Federation to visit France, Germany and Scandinavia, where he met the influential designer Stig Lindberg. Jefferson was influenced by Swedish design and meeting this international designer must have consolidated his interest.

On returning to Britain, Jefferson gained a scholarship to attend the School of Ceramics at the Royal College of Art (RCA) in 1951. As students of the RCA were allowed unlimited access to the Victoria and Albert Museum, he spent a great deal of time in the ceramics department there, studying the exhibits. One project required students to select a particular item and then recreate the piece, in detail. Jefferson chose a Leedsware tea pot. His remarkable gifts were recognised when examples of his work were shown in the influential *Design* magazine, after only one year of study. The magazine illustrated a pickle jar with stand, modelled and decorated with a black band and gold lustre.[2] A year later *Design* illustrated a condiment set decorated with a green glaze and a tall vase with a strong Swedish influence, decorated with an abstract pattern.[3] On completion of the course in 1954 Jefferson gained a Des.RCA. When he left he listed his occupation as 'teacher and freelance'.[4]

One of Jefferson's first jobs was as a decorator for a wealthy lady based in Knightsbridge, who had her own kiln and made mugs to give to friends as presents. This unusual employment ended when he forgot to switch the kiln off![5] He then secured a post teaching at a school in Gravesend for a short period. In 1954 he designed the pattern for the Royal Doulton tableware on the new Orient Line ship, *Oronsay*.[6] Before the official launch Jefferson and his wife were shown around the ship.

386. A casserole dish, height 6⅛in. (15.5cm) decorated with the *Lucullus* pattern, aerographed in blue, the lid decorated with a black print and hand-painted decoration. Designed by Robert Jefferson for Poole Pottery Ltd., about 1962.

387. A selection of earthenware shapes decorated with the *Lucullus* pattern and two storage jars decorated with the *Green Diamond* pattern. Designed by Robert Jefferson for Poole Pottery Ltd.

388. A selection of lesser known earthenware studio pieces decorated with in-glaze techniques that were first shown at the Tea Centre exhibition in 1961. Designed by Robert Jefferson for Poole Pottery Ltd.

389. A large earthenware plaque, length 16in. (40.5cm), decorated with a stylised owl. Designed by Robert Jefferson for Poole Pottery Ltd., 1962-63.

Subsequently, he worked at the Odney Pottery in Cookham, Berkshire. Odney Pottery was one of several small craft workshops established by the John Lewis Partnership, employing people with problems, some following wartime experiences. While there, Jefferson produced a wide range of small items such as cruet sets, bone china vases and trays decorated with various hand painted motifs. Following the introduction of new management, these craft workshops were closed down in about 1956.[7] Jefferson then undertook a wide range of freelance work for various companies, including the Langley Mill Pottery, based in Nottingham, and silk screen printing designs for Johnson Matthey and the Meyercord Company of Chicago.[8] He also designed tableware patterns for Minton's, and a range of Barbecue oven shapes and patterns for Lovatt's.

In 1956 Jefferson returned to Staffordshire to take up the full time position as Lecturer in Ceramics at the Burslem School of Art, where his students would have benefited from his industrial experience. However, as any gifted designer will always be dissatisfied solely

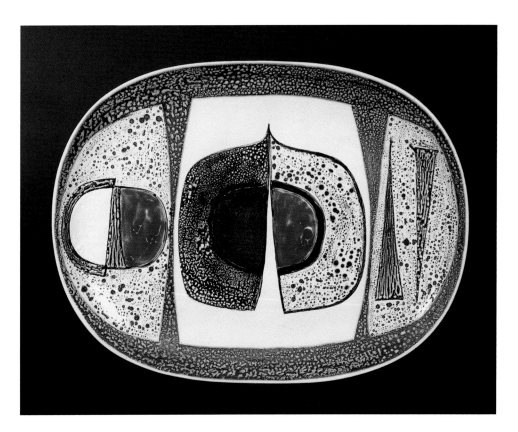

390. A large earthenware plaque, length 16in. (40.5cm), decorated with a stylised apple motif, from 1962-63. Designed by Robert Jefferson for Poole Pottery Ltd., 1962-63.

with teaching, Jefferson started to seek employment as a designer at a pottery company. He had firm beliefs about the many issues of design and noted in 1958: 'Every designer, if he is a little honest, knows that he can produce both good and bad work. What we need then is a yardstick by which we can produce work which is consistently of a high standard and if we can reach the sublime sometimes, so much the better.'[9]

At this time the Poole Pottery required a new designer to develop fresh, innovative designs. Lucien Myers, the Managing Director, persuaded the management to invite Jefferson to spend two weeks of his summer holiday at Poole, to familiarise himself with factory processes and as a result he was offered a permanent position at the Pottery.[10] Ironically, his connection there went back to the previous summer when he had taken a number of his work colleagues from the Odney Pottery to look at modern production techniques at Poole. Moreover, an example of one of his college pieces, a bowl decorated with stylised fish, had been illustrated in a series of articles by John Adams (see Directory of Designers) in *Pottery and Glass* in 1951.[11]

In 1958 Jefferson was appointed Resident Designer, having worked a term's notice at the Burslem School of Art. The Jefferson family moved to Dorset, to a house in Parkstone that had been built for an artist. The living room was a studio with an enormous north-facing window. The late fifties was a transitional period for Poole Pottery. The free-form shapes originated by Alfred Read and designs by his daughter Ann and Ruth Pavely were still in demand but new ideas and designs were needed for tableware, which by the mid-fifties had begun to dominate the company's output. The management also wanted to introduce new products reflecting the public's interest in modern interiors and fashions, and at the same time to replace the extensive range of hand-painted ware that was known as

Traditional Poole. Jefferson's initial task was to install the Murray Curvex decorating machine and to design patterns for copperplate printing. He developed a technique of printing on the raw glaze before firing, that created in-glaze colour. His first pattern, *Pebble*, launched in 1960, was available in two versions, black and white or grey and white, both on the Streamline shape. Printing by this process however was limited to flatware, which meant that the hollowware pieces were finished in solid colours. To overcome this limitation Jefferson next developed a silk screen technique of printing and painting on the raw glaze to create 'in-glaze' colour in the traditional Poole manner.[12] He also spent some time sorting out the current products of the firm. In 1963 he remarked that, 'Being outside the swim of Stoke-on-Trent all my thoughts concentrate on the necessity of being different. An out potter would be foolish to try to produce the same type of ware which the potteries can produce better with their vast technical and labour resources. I try to get a sense of the clay into my designs and to use clay in its most natural forms.'[13]

Jefferson's next major contribution was an oven-to-tableware range consisting of fifteen pieces with a contemporary feel. This was to be the first major venture since the company's expansion, a pre-requisite of this being an extension of the company's manufacturing and firing capacity which was completed in 1960. In developing the range Jefferson considered all the problems such as sharp corners and the individual function of each piece in order to make it practical and visually pleasing. 'Nothing is worse than a pot with handles which are so designed that one burns one's fingers when taking it from the oven, or lids which fly off as soon as the pot is tipped. Easily-held handles, tight fitting lids and well designed dishes which bear a relation to the purpose for which they are meant, should be the goal of all designers.'[14] Once the prototypes were produced, rigorous testing was

391. A large earthenware plaque, length 16in. (40.5cm), decorated with an abstract pattern. Designed by Robert Jefferson for Poole Pottery Ltd., 1962-63.

392. An abstract pattern hand painted on an earthenware studio dish, diameter 13½in. (34.5cm). Probably designed by Robert Jefferson for Poole Pottery Ltd., 1962-63.

393. An earthenware studio dish, diameter 16½in. (42cm), decorated with a stylised fish. Probably designed by Robert Jefferson for Poole Pottery Ltd., 1962-63.

undertaken to make sure they were of the highest quality. The company informed the trade press that in well over a year the number of oven-to-tableware items returned under the guarantee covering breakages has been less than half of one per cent.[15]

The oven-to-tableware range, decorated with a Cameo finish in either Blue Moon, Celadon Green or Heather Rose, was launched in 1961, and although it proved popular, there was a general criticism that the solid colour with white contrast looked rather plain. Jefferson preferred plain ware, feeling that to add decoration would be to gild the lily.[16] Despite this, the very successful *Lucullus* (Plate 386) and *Herb Garden*, silk screen printed patterns designed by Jefferson, were introduced in 1962-63 and these in time supplanted the plain Cameo finishes.

The oven-to-tableware range was followed in 1963-64 by the introduction of Contour tableware, designed by Jefferson along traditional Poole lines and used with both Twintone and Cameo colours and printed patterns introduced to appeal to the modern housewife. The hand printed and painted patterns were well received by the trade press which felt that they were quite striking and in harmony with the idea of cookware. A heater stand could be purchased for both the oval and round casserole dishes. Jefferson also designed the new packaging materials, made by Albert E. Read Ltd.[17]

In 1965 Jefferson's Compact range was introduced. It consisted of fifteen items including a casserole, sauce boat and egg cup. The range was designed to be space-saving, ovenproof and multi-purpose, initially decorated with bright glazes in either Chestnut, Charcoal or Choisya and sold alongside the twin-tone ranges on the Contour shape. These wares were marked with a number of standard backstamps, with the words 'Detergent and Dishwasher Proof Colours' added later. Poole continued to produce some of the hand

painted floral patterns originally created by Truda Carter. The two main pattern groups in the Traditional range were simplified Sprig and Elaborate, but special designs such as Ship plates, the Persian Deer and other full elaborate patterns dating from the twenties and thirties continued to be painted.

When it became apparent that demand for the traditional painted wares was in decline the new Managing Director, Roy Holland, decided to change the approach to design. He sent Jefferson to London to investigate which types of ware would yield between £50,000 to £100,000 of sales per year.[18] A decision was taken to set up a studio producing new artistic lines which would bring Poole to the forefront of British design once again. Poole would be one of the first British potteries to set up such a studio, which was a relatively new concept in Britain but a regular feature of many leading potteries in Scandinavia. The idea was first suggested in 1950 by John Adams to Cyril Carter, who agreed that a separate studio should be set up outside of the normal routine of the factory production.[19] In one of his regular articles for the trade press John Adams asserted that there was 'an urgent need for design research as well as for science – the two are indivisible – and we are considering the idea of a studio on the factory with a picked team to find new avenues for bulk production and to add prestige to the factory'.[20]

To this end Jefferson started to develop innovative studio shapes and patterns with a modern look (Plate 388). The first results included a range of tall vases and pebble vases decorated

394. An earthenware vase (shape no. 9) decorated with coloured glaze. Pattern and shape designed by Robert Jefferson for Poole Pottery Ltd., 1963. Height 5⅛in. (13cm).

329

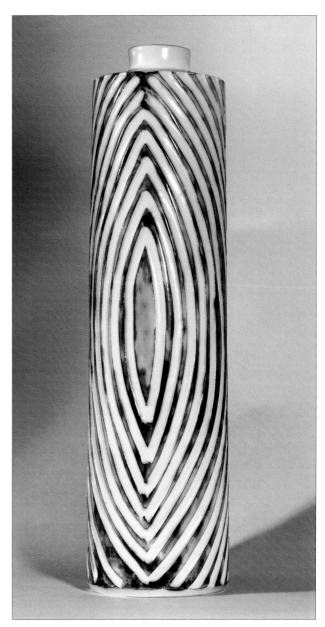

395. An earthenware vase (shape no. 16) decorated with coloured glaze. Pattern and shape designed by Robert Jefferson for Poole Pottery Ltd., 1963. Height 10⅛in. (25.7cm).

396. An earthenware vase (shape no. 50) decorated with an abstract pattern. Pattern and shape designed by Robert Jefferson for Poole Pottery Ltd., 1963. Height 15½in. (39.4cm).

with stylised patterns using in-glaze techniques. These were exhibited for the first time at the Tea Centre Exhibition in London's Regent Street in January 1961. A wide selection of large plaques and studio dishes decorated with contemporary patterns, such as a stylised owl (Plate 389) an apple motif (Plate 390) and an abstract pattern (Plate 391) were to follow. These were produced alongside a range of plaques and vases. These were all marked with the POOLE STUDIO backstamp and the Dolphin motif, used between 1962-64. Following the success of these studio wares a decision was taken by the management to develop the range from 1963. Further productions included a studio dish depicting stylised people (Plate 392) and another depicting a fish (Plate 393), probably designed by Jefferson.

397. The ceramic mural designed by Robert Jefferson situated at the front of the Poole Pottery factory, 1963.

Jefferson designed several new shapes, including vases, dishes, trays and bowls for the Delphis studio range. Many of these were decorated in contrasting colours and stylised patterns (Plates 394 and 395). The range also included a selection of tall vases, a typical example decorated with an abstract motif (Plate 396). These items were marked 'POOLE STUDIO england' with the Dolphin motif, issued from 1964 to 1966, giving some indication of date. The majority of Jefferson's were not signed by him, although some are marked with his initials, in monogram.

These pieces were launched as 'The Delphis Collection', delphis being the Greek word for dolphin. The range was limited to ornamental wares such as dishes, bowls and vases in various sizes. The trade press described the various decorative techniques: 'some being very simple examples of direct glazing or painting. Some are the result of two or three firings in the kiln. Others are created by using wax resist with different applications of colour and glaze. There are partially glazed pieces with a sgraffito or carved surface inlaid with vitrified slip. Colours and glazes range from dark browns, lambent blues and greens to brilliant oranges and reds. Particularly interesting is an aventurine-type glaze with a burnt amber colour in which crystalline gold flecks scintillate under a bright light.'[21]

Delphis set a new standard of artistic and technical achievement under Jefferson's co-ordination. During the latter part of 1962 and early 1963 he also developed a ceramic mural made up of tiles that represented the products of the Poole Pottery (Plate 397). The design, completed on various sizes of tiles in coloured glazes, was erected on the end elevation of the factory.[22] During the development he was assisted by Vic Thomas.

Tony Morris, a gifted painter, had joined the company in 1962 to work firstly for the tile works and from January 1963 with Jefferson. He was born in 1942 and later educated in the fine arts at Newport School of Art. In 1963 Morris assisted Jefferson in glazing the mottled rectangular tiles on the north-eastern corner of the Pottery, a feature of the new factory tour entrance. Morris also designed individual pieces, a notable example being the

398. Two examples of the *Bokhara* range. Left: hand painted on an earthenware jam pot 375/OH.B (note the shape pre-dates the introduction of this range); and right, an earthenware preserve jar 657/OG.B. Designed by Robert Jefferson for Poole Pottery Ltd., 1964. Height of preserve jar 4in. (10.2cm).

'Sun Face' tile panel from 1964-68. The company press release announced that the designers were given complete freedom to develop their own ideas, unhampered by commercial considerations.[23] Moreover, they declared that a decision to market a given piece would be based upon design merit rather than potential sales or ease of production. From the start the collection was meant to incorporate an ever-changing range of patterns, evolving on an individual basis. The company went so far as to boast that some pieces were unique and that 'the prices cannot bear any strictly commercial relationship to production costs in view of the fact that the studio has, of set purpose, not been organised on any rigidly economic basis.'[24]

The Delphis Collection was launched at Heal's in London in October 1963, officially opened by the designer Sir Gordon Russell, a former Director of the Council of Industrial Design. The range was imaginatively displayed with enlarged photographs of pottery-making and some examples of the pots in sand. The initial range of forty pieces included vases, plates and bowls. Simultaneous displays of the Delphis Collection were exhibited in Leeds, Ipswich, Bristol, Nottingham, Manchester, Glasgow, Cambridge, Guildford and Birmingham. The company declared that the range was introduced 'to give the public an opportunity to see some of the endless possibilities which modern ceramic techniques can provide and, at the same time, to use the studio for the development of new techniques and ideas which will be useful in the production of the firm's standard ranges'.[25]

By early 1964 there was a shortage of work for the hand paintresses. Although some were made redundant, others were kept on by Poole. Jefferson was asked by the management to design a series of hand-painted wares to keep the decorators in work and he developed a range of hand-thrown jars and vases called *Bokhara*. Nine basic shapes were produced, some of which were hand painted with broad brushwork patterns decorated by means of the in-glaze technique which has been a feature at Poole since the 1920s. The patterns featured repeating stylised borders (OHA) in mustard colours (Plate 398). These detailed patterns of the *Bokhara* range contrasted with those wares such as (JB) that were decorated with a distinctive Sapphire Blue Glaze (Plate 399). They were

individually priced between 10/6d and 26/3d for the larger items. Jefferson effectively used contrasting glazes for a set of plaques and trays in the shape of birds, fish and daggers, a new departure for the company (Plate 400). According to Poole, these individual items could be: 'Hung in the kitchen, living room, dining room, nursery or bathroom, they will brighten and add charm to any surroundings'.[26]

To complement these new products Jefferson designed the Helios table lamp range for the home or business, 'free from the frills of bygone styles'. These were produced in different sizes with a choice of six lamps, all but one featuring relief moulding with either a midnight blue, charcoal matt or olive green glaze. The sixth example featured a black leaf print on a snow white glaze or a white leaf on a black panther glaze. The shade was made from opal perspex. These innovative items were launched in 1964 under the heading 'New Lamps for Old'. The tallest lamp retailed at £4 18s 6d whilst the cheapest was £2 2s 0d.[27] The Helios range was publicised alongside a series of nursery wares that Jefferson produced for a mug, plate and bowl depicting a polar bear, zebra, panda and other zoo animals. These were printed in black with a colour wash band in either a sunshine yellow or blue moon finish.

Jefferson also introduced the *Green Diamond* storage jars with cork stoppers in 1963 (Plate 387). These pieces were sold at Heal's in London. A wide range of patterns and shapes by Jefferson was shown in the Poole sales catalogue for 1964, including new items such as a butter box, toast rack, beaker and a mug in three sizes. One page was devoted to the many shapes for cruet and oil and vinegar sets available in current patterns. By 1971 the standard range of hand-painted simplified patterns, featured in the 1964 sales catalogue, were decorated on Delphis shapes rather than the earlier ones. Some of the Elaborate patterns were marketed as the 'Connoisseurs Corner' in 1973, but phased out by 1980.

399. Further shapes from the *Bokhara* range. An earthenware vase decorated in blue and black 674/2 JB and an earthenware kitchen jar decorated with the same colours 659/JB. Designed by Robert Jefferson for Poole Pottery Ltd., 1964. Height of vase 6¼in. (16cm).

400. A selection of earthenware wall plaques and trays featuring raised line decoration finished with coloured glazes. Top left: Bird (shape 393), 6½in. x 8⅜in (15.9cm x 21.3cm; top right: Fish (395); bottom left: Bird (394) and right, Dagger (396), length 12¼in. (31cm). Designed by Robert Jefferson for Poole Pottery Ltd., 1964.

From 1965 the Delphis Collection was marketed increasingly as a hand-painted range with individual designs on a series of individual shapes. The pieces were for the most part unique, using a wide range of topics and themes. Christine Tate, a member of the design team, together with Tony Morris, would sometimes spend up to a week on subjects such as fish, animals, sunflowers, sun faces, clowns and circus themes.[28] Many Delphis patterns, due to the nature of pattern development, were not formally recorded, making attribution of patterns to individual designers problematic. Clearly, a team effort was the general approach. Jefferson noted at the time that introducing new patterns was: 'no problem, there are so many patterns. I produce a drawing of the decoration, and the design team produce the end product. One week we may be working on decorative owls, in the next week landscapes in the district, for example the Harbour and its boats. All our decorations became somewhat stylised with the passing of time.'[29]

After making such a prolific artistic contribution to Poole over an eight year period Jefferson effectively worked himself out of a job. Moreover, he felt that he had explored all the design possibilities for the company. At the same time Poole was not ready to introduce a stoneware range, in line with other companies, as this would have required a new body, possibly fired at a much higher temperature. To take on a new challenge Jefferson left in 1966 to take up the position of designer at the newly formed Purbeck Pottery. He was not replaced with a full time designer. In May 1966 Poole opened the new Craft Section. At the same time a new Delphis Range was introduced, stylistically different from, and not to be confused with the earlier Delphis Studio Collection. This new range, which by 1971 used predominantly red, yellow, orange and green glazes and featured a new backstamp, did not include any reference to 'studio' as the previous mark had done. By 1971 over 4,000 pieces of Delphis were being produced each week but this steadily declined until it was phased out in about 1980, when it had lost much of its impact. New ranges were introduced during the seventies, including Aegean, developed by Leslie Elsden, formerly a line manager in the glaze spraying department, launched in 1970. He was assisted from the start by Carole Holden but by 1972

401. A selection of
earthenwares from the
Country Fayre range,
decorated with the hand
painted *Pheasant* pattern.
Designed by Robert
Jefferson for the Purbeck
Pottery Ltd., about 1966-
67.

others were to join him. This range was phased out in 1980. From 1972 Guy Sydenham,
with a small team including Beatrice Bolton and Susan Dipple, introduced and developed the
Atlantis range which was discontinued in 1977. The Ionian range was more elaborate and
was developed by Julia Wills but was in production only during 1974-75. In 1971 the Poole
Pottery, a subsidiary of Pilkington's Tiles Ltd. since 1964, became an autonomous unit within
the Thomas Tilling Group. In 1983 Tilling was taken over by BTR, another finance group, but
since 1992 Poole Pottery has been operating as an independent company.[30]

402. A selection of
earthenwares from the
Country Fayre range,
decorated with the hand
painted *Oatmeal* pattern.
Designed by Robert Jefferson
for the Purbeck Pottery Ltd.,
about 1966-67.

403. A lesser known shape range and pattern. Designed by Robert Jefferson for the Purbeck Pottery Ltd., about 1966-67.

The Purbeck Pottery was formed in 1966, based at the Branksome China Works in Westbourne, Bournemouth. Before setting up the pottery, Peter Barnes (formerly employed by Poole) and Jefferson had discussed the possibility of starting a pottery at Corfe Castle. However, when they were joined by Stanley Laws (an accountant) and Gordon Ede (a chemist), both previously employed by Poole Pottery, the plan changed. Financial backing was forthcoming from Jack Turner to establish the Purbeck Pottery.[31] Almost immediately Jefferson started to develop trial runs for new shapes and patterns that were formalised by September 1966. His shapes, made from a highly vitrified body, included the distinctive Country Fayre range that was used for a wide range of patterns such as *Pheasant*, banded in greens and browns (Plate 401). The distinctive look was so difficult to achieve that there was a high loss factor. Another pattern, *Oatmeal*, featured a large stylised floral motif in celadon green (Plate 402). Of particular note was an audaciously styled new coffee pot that resembled a Greek design, decorated with a old gold spot border on a black matt glaze (Plate 403). During his period of work at Purbeck Jefferson also designed a wide range of studio vases, trays and small items, assisted by George Janes, a modeller, who had also joined them from Poole Pottery. The small trays were inlaid with crushed glass that was colour stained to create a dramatic effect.[32]

One of his most successful tableware ranges was *Toast*, a simple handcraft styled range, first produced on the Plymouth shape in about 1968 (Plate 404). This shape range was also used for a number of studio glazes. His Portland shape was decorated with, amongst others, the *Brown Diamond* pattern that is still in production, albeit decorated on modern shapes. A range of smaller items was produced, such as cube or cylindrical money boxes, depicting pop art

405. Roseate Terns, a model designed by Robert Jefferson for Royal Doulton Ltd., 1975.

404. A selection of earthenwares from the *Toast* range. Designed by Robert Jefferson for the Purbeck Pottery Ltd., about 1966-68.

styled figures of Long John Silver and stylised men and women printed in black on a white ground or gold on a matt black ground. Some of these patterns featured mottoes such as 'Do not open yet'. Jefferson also produced a game pie casserole dish with a moulded lid of a pheasant, sold complete with two real feathers. Further new ranges included tankards that were hand painted in lustres. At the same time a series of mugs was produced decorated with medieval pursuits on a matt glaze outside and finished with a bright glaze inside.[33] Jefferson produced a range of modelled figures based on Greek mythology which were successful in Switzerland and also a range of modelled animal and bird studies that included owls, squirrels, badgers and foxes. These animals proved popular and were in production for ten years. Early examples were individually signed by Jefferson. The general productions were marked with a stylised backstamp depicting two mugs in reverse so that the handles represented the initials of the company and a hand holding a paint brush and the words 'Purbeck England'. By 1969 Jefferson had produced so many tableware patterns and shapes and various fancies that his services were no longer required.[34] He decided to leave Purbeck and return to Lancashire and resumed his former role as a freelance designer, eventually being retained by Royal Doulton.

In 1972 Jefferson joined Royal Doulton as a freelance sculptor, working closely with the Design Director, Joseph Ledger, who had previously carried out a number of commissions for Carter and Co. Ltd. during the fifties. They teamed up on a range of projects for Royal Crown Derby, Royal Doulton and Minton. One of Jefferson's first tasks was to model a series of birds and animals set in their natural habitats for Royal Doulton. This successful series included

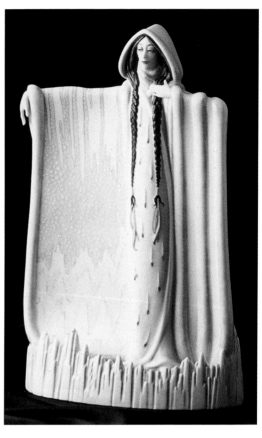

406. Four modelled figures for Royal Doulton Ltd. by Robert Jefferson. Printemps, Hiver, Eté and Automne.

Roseate Terns, from about 1975, aimed at the collectors' market and produced in a limited edition (Plate 405). In 1978 Jefferson modelled his first figure for Royal Doulton, called Harmony. This outstanding piece, inspired by the art nouveau style, was so successful that it confirmed Jefferson's modelling skills. Several further models were produced over the next few years. Other ranges such as the outstanding Myths and Maidens collection included Europa and the Bull, Diana the Huntress, Lady and the Unicorn and Leda and the Swan.

In 1981 Jefferson produced several animal and bird paperweights, decorated in traditional patterns, for Royal Crown Derby. They were an outstanding success and further additions were added to the range. Some of these items have, throughout the years, been reproduced in limited form for specialist stores and for the company's collectors' club. These pieces are highly sought after by paperweight collectors. The Classic Collection for Royal Crown Derby was designed by Joseph Ledger and modelled by Jefferson in 1986. This series represented the four goddesses, Persephone, Dione, Penelope and Athena. This was followed by a series of modelled items for Royal Doulton Ltd. based on the work of Alphonse Mucha called Les Saisons (The Seasons), featuring Printemps, Automne, Eté and Hiver (Plate 406). These outstanding figures were produced annually until 1999 in a limited edition of 300. Jefferson also modelled a series of Royal Cats, again designed by Joseph Ledger. These were soon followed by a series of national dogs such as a Scottie, Welsh greyhound and Afghan hound. Another outstanding range was inspired by the world's great lovers through history, from Antony and Cleopatra to Robin Hood and Maid Marion. These finely modelled pieces were a major contribution to the range produced by the firm. Two years later he introduced a commemorative range of twelve goblets, The Twelve Days of Christmas.[35]

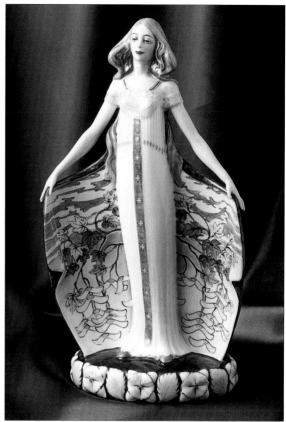

During the late seventies the Poole Pottery invited designers not employed by the company to submit designs for a new shape range. Technical developments made it possible for them to produce hotel ware for the first time. Jefferson's elegant Style shape was selected for production and he also submitted one on-glaze transfer pattern for this range called *Nut Tree*. The trade press described the range as 'a fashionable, well designed product which is hard wearing, dishwasher proof and suitable for microwave ovens'.[36] Elaine Williamson, resident designer at Poole 1977-86, designed other patterns such as Springtime and Summer Glory.[37]

Jefferson was a versatile designer who also designed jewellery that was sold in a Bond Street shop in London. In 1969 he designed a 'Dragon' ring, one of a number of official souvenirs for the Investiture of Prince Charles. Jefferson was a proficient artist producing a considerable number of paintings and screen prints; some of his works were exhibited at the Society of Wildlife Artists exhibitions. He also experimented with painting on enamel plaques, creating designs for charity Christmas cards and Nature Trail leaflets. In 1991 Jefferson produced a limited range of figures for Minton.

Few designers were able to work in the diverse disciplines of art and industrial design as Jefferson did. He responded to the many challenges and changes in artistic direction that were demanded over almost forty years, allowing him to make such a significant contribution. During the latter part of 1997 he became ill and died in May 1998, aged sixty-seven. As a tribute to such a versatile and thoughtful designer Margaret Sergeant, of the Royal Doulton International Collectors' Society, recorded that the country had 'lost a distinguished designer and sculptor and we, the collectors here and abroad will mourn his loss'.[38]

CHAPTER 17

PUTTING ART INTO INDUSTRY

Susan Williams-Ellis (b.1918)

407. Susan Williams-Ellis at work in her studio.

Susan Williams-Ellis has made an outstanding artistic contribution to design throughout the last forty years. Few designers have been able to work successfully in textiles, glass, book illustration and pottery. Her original and innovative response to design pushed her to the forefront of the British ceramics industry during the early 1960s. The outstanding *Totem* and *Botanic Garden* ranges are her most important and influential designs.

She was born on 6 June, 1918, into a privileged and artistic family where art and design were deeply rooted and a career in the arts was considered acceptable. Her mother, Amabel Strachey, was a writer and her father was the famous and accomplished architect and designer Sir Clough Williams-Ellis. He is probably best known today for Portmeirion Village that he created in 1925, located in North Wales (Plate 408). Williams-Ellis' formal education was good, although she maintains that her real education was being taken round art galleries by her grandmother every school holiday from an early age. These experiences no doubt prompted her decision, at the age of twelve, to become an artist. She attended various schools during her childhood and later studied for two years at Dartington Hall where she took biology, art and woodwork. She later commented that working with wood was a much better experience than throwing pots, despite being taught

408. A view of the Portmeirion village, North Wales.

by the internationally recognised Bernard Leach and his brother David. Whilst at the Chelsea Polytechnic in London she was taught book illustration by Graham Sutherland and studied modelling, three days a week, with Henry Moore. The latter certainly helped her already marked sense of three-dimensional form. Both teachers encouraged her to develop her sense of colour and form. Williams-Ellis noted that the classes were full of 'giggling society girls not really willing to learn'.[1]

In 1939 Williams-Ellis returned to Dartington Hall to teach art to young children. In order to 'do her bit' for the war effort she secured a post in the RAF at Whitehall in London as a draughtswoman for the Air Ministry. She took lodgings in a rather run-down part of Soho. Whilst working in London she met Euan Cooper-Willis, who shared a room in Cambridge with her brother, Christopher. They married in 1945 and moved to Glasgow as her husband worked for Blackie's Publishers, the family-run business. During this time he learnt about bookbinding and typesetting. After only two years they decided to go to North Wales, to live in a small cottage owned by her father, close to the Portmeirion village. There, they kept pigs and ducks and grew their own vegetables. Whilst Euan worked part time Williams-Ellis undertook some free-lance illustration work, soon realising that it was so badly paid that one had to be either incredibly fast or famous to earn a living from it. One of her first commissions came from a friend, Elizabeth Denby, who needed some decorative tiles for a room setting that she was creating for the 'Britain Can Make It' exhibition held at the Victoria and Albert Museum in London in 1946. The range, entitled *Sea*, featured twelve single motifs of shells, fish and seaweed and was produced by Poole Pottery Ltd., alongside patterns by Edward Bawden and Dora Batty.[2] She also designed and painted four panels that were displayed in the Dome of Discovery at the Festival of Britain in London in 1951.[3]

The prestigious store, Dunbar Hay, commissioned Williams-Ellis to create a seat cover design for dining chairs. Her multi-coloured pattern, *Music*, depicted floaty ladies playing

409. This is a rare example of one Susan Williams-Ellis' textile designs entitled *Music*, produced in two colour variations, about 1951.

different instruments within decorative ovals next to musical instrument motifs (Plate 409). This was produced with a green, gold or pink background. Circular floor mats were made to complement the chair coverings, featuring the musical instruments without the ladies. Her *Granite* carpet design was commissioned by the Wilton Carpet Company.

As early as 1953, Williams-Ellis and her husband became closely involved with Portmeirion Village. Williams-Ellis produced a series of murals, including one depicting Queen Elizabeth, situated outside the Lady Lodge. She also designed a range of items for the Portmeirion Hotel (Plate 410). These included a wool tuft rug featuring aquatic motifs such as crabs, shells and lobsters that retailed for £22 in 1958.[4] Her father, Clough, asked her to run the Portmeirion gift shop, the Ship Shop, situated just off the café terrace, which sold a wide range of English and foreign pottery together with books and small antiques. As the shop became more popular with tourists, Williams-Ellis started to pursue her strong artistic ideas. Her thoughts about what type of giftwares should be sold led her to develop designs for an exclusive range of Portmeirion gifts. During the inter-war period her father had commissioned the Ashstead Pottery to produce a range of items for Portmeirion village.[5] His daughter looked around some of the pottery companies in Stoke-on-Trent, initially approaching Myott, a long established pottery company, to ask if it would be willing to produce wares based on her designs. Unfortunately Myott was not interested in the production of small quantities of giftwares.[6] Determined to introduce her own designs, she sought alternative manufacturers and her father suggested that they should visit the

factory of A.E. Gray and Co. Ltd., founded by Edward Gray in about 1908.[7]

Gray's Pottery, as it was known, came to the forefront of British pottery design during the twenties and thirties by producing popular hand-painted ranges in the current tastes of the period. In particular it was famous for lustreware, developed from the early twenties by both Gordon Forsyth and Susie Cooper. During the post-war years business increased, necessitating a new extension to the factory in 1953.[8] The production of giftwares helped to revive the business. Gray's also produced a wide range of resist lustres, mainly in silver or bronze. Most successful was the Sunderland splatter decorative finish, a reproduction of an early nineteenth century decorative technique. This treatment combined a central black and white print with lustre being applied to the ware. A startling effect was achieved by splashing turpentine on to the lustre, thus creating irregular patches.[9] This popular technique was used chiefly on decorative jugs, loving cups, bowls such as Athena and the Howard jug, the main colours being purple or pink. These pieces were advertised as 'Pottery of Distinction'.

Fortunately a strong connection had already been forged between Edward Gray and Sir Clough Williams-Ellis during the thirties, when they were both members of the Design and Industries Association. For the newly opened Portmeirion Hotel and the Mytton and Mermaid Hotel in Shropshire, Edward Gray had been asked to produce a set of banded dinnerware in his favourite colours, magenta and green.[10] This connection no doubt made it easier for Williams-Ellis, who was not very knowledgeable about the manufacture of industrial pottery, to discuss the production of her giftware with them. She was attracted to the current Gray's wares and was influenced to use antique prints as central motifs combined with the Sunderland splatter decoration. One of the first examples was *Going to Market*, her own design which derived from an old engraving, that was taken to Gray's for production in about 1957 (Plate 411). A lesser-known pattern featuring a mermaid motif, originally designed by Clough Williams-Ellis, was updated by her (Plate 412). The other side of the beaker reads: 'When this you see remember me and bear me in your

411. A souvenir preserve jar and cover decorated with the *Going to Market* pattern with Sunderland splatter decoration. Designed by Susan Williams-Ellis in about 1957-58.

412. The reverse side of an unusual earthenware Mermaid beaker, 1958.

mind. Let all the world say what they will. Speak of me as you find.'[11] Another lesser-known pattern was *Shells*, utilising the same decorative finish but with many different motifs of shells, fish and crabs, designed by Williams-Ellis.

In 1957 Susan Williams-Ellis and her husband opened the Portmeirion shop in Pont Street, London selling antiques, contemporary textiles and her own pottery. It was run by her cousin Sam Beazley, who had previously worked at Asprey's. The popularity of this shop created a demand for more exclusive wares such as the *Portmeirion Dolphin*, introduced in about 1959. This well known pattern was based on an engraving by Williams-Ellis, featuring an architectural frame with a dolphin on each side as heraldic supports. This distinctive design was initially decorated with splatter but was later extended to eight different colourways (Plate 413). The range was developed to include storage jars, rolling pins, jugs and boxed oil and vinegar sets. Both *Going to Market* and *Portmeirion Dolphin* were entered on to the Council for Industrial Design's Design Index in 1960.

With such outstanding success and popularity both in the village and the London shop the demand for new products put a strain on the relationship with Gray's. Both Williams-Ellis and her husband became frustrated with the difficulties they endured to maintain production. In order to resolve these problems they discussed the option of buying Gray's Pottery, which would give them complete control of production. However, for some time Edward Gray had

413. Two earthenware apothecary jars and covers decorated with the *Portmeirion Dolphin* pattern. Designed by Susan Williams-Ellis for Portmeirion Potteries Ltd., about 1961.

hoped that his son Robin, who joined the company in 1923, would continue the business. Unfortunately poor health ruled this out. This setback probably persuaded Edward Gray that the best thing to do would be to sell the firm. The ownership of Gray's passed on to Williams-Ellis on 1 January 1960. For the next two years all her designs were produced under the Gray's backstamp with the additional words PORTMEIRION WARE incorporated. Robin Gray stayed on as Managing Director whilst the company continued to trade as Gray's.[12] Following the purchase of Gray's, the next step was to secure a good Sales and Marketing Director. They acquired the services of Frank Thrower, a young man who sold Swedish glass. Not only was he dynamic and innovative in his post, but he was also an excellent designer. During the first year of his employment Frank Thrower went to Sweden to select a collection of Scandinavian crystal to complement Williams-Ellis' pottery. She learned a lot from Frank Thrower about what would suit the market and many of his later designs reflect the strength and solidity which characterised her shapes.[13] Most importantly, the takeover provided her with the opportunity to promote her belief that gaiety, brightness and good design were successful business as well as good things in themselves. She commented: 'I've always wanted to have a pottery. My husband was slightly horrified at the idea first of all but now he is as keen as I am.'[14]

At the Blackpool Gifts and Fancy Goods Fair in February 1960, Portmeirion exhibited an extensive range of the new *Malachite* pattern on a range of items including tea and coffee wares and fancies, finished with extensive gilding (Plate 414). The design was inspired by the green semi-precious mineral, studied by the designer at the Natural History Museum.[15] The development of this pattern had proved difficult as she wasn't satisfied with the initial reproductions intended for furnishing fabric and carpet for the Portmeirion Hotel. Williams-Ellis declared that it looked like a landlady's chopped cabbage![16] In typical style she had the pattern photographically reduced and had transfer-printed sheets produced to use on earthenware. On the occasion of the launch in 1960 Williams-Ellis declared that this range had a note of restrained opulence! However, *Malachite* was very expensive to produce and therefore costly for the customer. Despite this exciting start, the rearrangements undertaken to improve the running of the factory resulted in a lack of new patterns being developed during 1960.

Meanwhile, Williams-Ellis took the opportunity to develop her free-lance work to help finance the new pottery. At a very early age she decided to go into design rather than fine art, as she felt that contemporary art had almost degraded into a financial state. One of her schoolfriends, an interior decorator, was able to sell one of her textile designs for curtains in the non-stateroom cabins of the *Canberra* for the maiden voyage in May 1961. *Ravenna*, inspired by the mosaic ceilings of Gala Placidia's tomb in Italy, featured stylised circular motifs set against a purple background. She was paid a royalty of sixpence a yard, which amounted to about £200. Within two years replacement curtains were requested after a bad fire on the ship necessitated a refit, and a second fee of £200 was forthcoming. Another design, *African Shields*, came to her in a dream. The pattern, which features strong purple and yellow colours, was put on marquise-shaped coffee tables made out of fibreglass, which had just been made commercially. Unfortunately, little information is available on these patterns.

As business increased for the Portmeirion Pottery it soon became apparent that they should consider building a new site or take over an existing producer of white ware. As a result Kirkham's Ltd., in Stoke, was purchased in January 1961. This firm had been producing its own shapes for many years and also supplied blank wares to several firms including Gray's. Euan Cooper-Willis became Chairman of the firm. Before Portmeirion moved to the new site immediate refurbishment was required, including the installation of new gas and electric kilns. During the takeover Williams-Ellis commented: 'The premises, equipment and environment were no less antiquated than pure Dickensian in decay, but we did have the people and the will and that's where we started.'[17]

Coming from an artistic background, Williams-Ellis tended to create ideas and patterns first, rather than letting the confines and restrictions of the industry impose or limit her creativity. She explained: 'I suppose I am unusual in that I am one of the few really independent designers. In larger firms, everything goes through a sort of committee, all have their own pet ideas, take this out, alter that, and the other, and what comes out of it is the last common denominator. With me, one of my designs will go through exactly as I

see it. I never think now in terms of whether the public will or will not like the thing, when I am working on new designs. When I do that, invariably nobody wants to know about it, but when I follow my custom of doing something that I think is nice, something that I personally like, then it seems to go like a bomb.'[18]

The first full range of patterns was displayed at the Blackpool Fair in February 1961. The

414. A period photograph illustrating the various shapes decorated with the *Malachite* pattern, printed with gold decoration. Designed by Susan Williams-Ellis for Portmeirion Potteries Ltd., about 1960.

415. A period photograph illustrating the lesser known *Moss Agate* range, printed with hand painted decoration. Designed by Susan Williams-Ellis for Portmeirion Potteries Ltd., 1961.

416. A selection of earthenware kitchen items decorated with the *Waterlily* pattern, printed with banded decoration. Designed by Susan Williams-Ellis for Portmeirion Potteries Ltd., 1961.

stand itself created a great deal of interest amongst trade buyers and the press. The buyer for the Harrod's store remarked: 'they are making a real effort'.[19] Attention focused particularly on both *Malachite* and *Moss Agate*. The latter was another new design featuring gold medallion decoration taken from an engraving based on designs in an eighteenth century French geographical book. The pattern was produced mainly on

417. A selection of storage jars, a mixing bowl and other kitchen items decorated with the *Portmeirion Rose* pattern, printed with banded decoration. Designed by Susan Williams-Ellis for Portmeirion Potteries Ltd., 1961.

ornamental wares such as goblets, storage jars, mugs and boxes (Plate 415). Sadly *Moss Agate*, like *Malachite*, proved too expensive to become commercially viable.

Due to this failure Williams-Ellis created commercial wares that were cheaper to produce. Transfer-printed florals provided the solution for the time being and included *Waterlily* (Plate 416) and *Portmeirion Rose* (Plate 417), each available with banding in three alternative colours.[20] Although clearly less sophisticated, they were more practical. One of the most popular patterns was *Tigerlily*, based on the narrowboat style of painting that Williams-Ellis had admired for many years (Plate 418). The designer commissioned a lithographic company to reproduce the pattern from her artwork. The design was rejected by the Design Index as it incorporated overprinting of white. Needless to say, this rejection did not bother Williams-Ellis, neither did it affect the sales.

The production of practical wares did not preclude Williams-Ellis from developing more elaborate patterns such as *Gold Diamond*. This was one of her many designs for coffee wares and was shown at the Blackpool Fair in 1961 (Plate 420). The pattern featured a variety of diamond motifs hand-painted in bronze, platinum and gold. The idea came from her grandmother's eggshell china set, which had assorted colours that went perfectly together. The designer later recalled that customers would often return their tea sets, believing that they didn't match. A more affordable black and white version was produced later; the decoration was initially achieved by applying pen and ink directly on to the ware and then transfer printed from 1963. A series of full colour advertisements was taken out in the trade press to promote these latest designs. The coffee cup and saucers were priced from 23/6 in August of that year.[21]

Williams-Ellis also introduced a range of nursery ware items, based on illustrations by Richard Doyle from the 1840s, later re-issued as Enchanted Garden. One pattern depicted a small girl wrapped in a leaf, printed in sepia. The bowls and plates featured a raised

418. A selection of kitchen wares decorated with the *Tigerlily* pattern, printed with hand-painted and banded decoration. Designed by Susan Williams-Ellis for Portmeirion Potteries Ltd., 1961.

419. A selection of
earthenware nursery items
including the *Hot Air Balloon*
pattern on a plate (centre)
with a raised alphabet on
the border. These patterns
were inspired by illustrations
by Richard Doyle from the
1840s. Designed by Susan
Williams-Ellis for Portmeirion
Potteries Ltd., about 1961.

alphabet border with banded decoration to the edge.[22] Other nursery patterns depicted a hot air balloon against a background of stylised clouds and one of a small boy sitting on a snail shell, both decorated in pinks and blues (Plate 419). An unusual pattern, *Hand and Rose*, depicting a lady's hand holding a rose, was aerographed in pink with sgraffito decoration and produced on a series of shapes and on door furniture for the Portmeirion Hotel.[23]

The new Portmeirion antiques shop at 5a Pont Street in Belgravia was opened in March 1961. The attractive room, painted white over linen paper, featured newly fitted shelves in pine complemented by green vertical wall panels, positioned between the lowest shelves and the floor.[24] Other interior elements included a German 500-day clock, a Victorian armchair upholstered in grey velvet and a charcoal carpet. The *Malachite* pattern featured strongly, with items such as vases, lamp bases and punch sets being displayed alongside the matching Axminster carpet and furnishing material. The pottery was complemented by a range of imported Swedish glass and Danish stoneware, incorporated to extend the business. Portmeirion also found a ready market in kitchen shops for mixing bowls, rolling pins, measuring jugs, spice jar sets, nesting hens and even pestles and mortars. Some years later a game pie dish and a nesting duck were added to the range. The trade press stated: 'Whatever one thought of the wide range of new designs one had to agree that they were refreshingly different, reflecting an unusual and welcomed new approach to pottery decoration.'[25]

During the early sixties a number of unusual items were put in production, but probably for a short period only. These items include a series of ceramic whisky barrels decorated with various patterns such as *Malachite*, *Tigerlily* and *Sailing Ships*, priced £7, £5 and £3 respectively (Plate 421). The *Sailing Ships* pattern was a standard design which had

been used by Gray's in the past. Archive photographs of the period also indicate that several un-catalogued items were produced, including beer pulls decorated with unknown patterns that may have been trial designs (Plate 422), and door furniture (Plate 423). The shapes were probably from the Kirkham's vaults. Patterns such as *Knights*, on an olive ground, from the Gray's Pottery period, and a condiment set called *Little Town*, decorated with drawings of buildings, are extremely rare (Plate 424). In contrast a number of banded designs on more traditional plain tea ware in yellow/grey and purple/turquoise were also

420. A range of cups, saucers and a milk jug decorated with the *Gold Diamond* pattern. Designed by Susan Williams-Ellis for Portmeirion Potteries Ltd., about 1961.

produced. Williams-Ellis also produced two patterns called *Gold Sun* and *Gold Lion*.

From the 1 January 1962, the company was renamed Portmeirion Potteries Limited. Robin Gray resigned soon after and the shareholders, who were mainly the Gray family, were repaid on par.[26] Once all the formalities were dealt with the Gray's site was sold to Royal Doulton. A new standard backstamp, without the words Gray's Pottery, was issued. This basic mark had many variations to it over the next twenty years. With the acquisition of Kirkham's, Williams-Ellis was finally in complete control of both pattern and shape, giving her the staggering opportunity to develop a series of outrageous and innovative designs over the next ten years. At the same time she discovered that this run-down factory had a rich source of prints and old moulds that she could exploit in the creation of her wares. She noted that Kirkham's 'used to make the sort of bed pan that Florence Nightingale had condemned as being insanitary, leech jars, bleeding basins, inks, everything that was becoming obsolete. They had very old machines so my older designs were based on what they could do, such as cylinder forms that became tall coffee pots.'[27]

Williams-Ellis developed a new tall coffee pot shape from an old porous cell, found amongst the moulds. The resultant coffee pot and associated items were called the Cylinder shape. This was much taller than any other coffee pot shape being sold at that time and caused a sensation when viewed by the trade buyers. Moreover, this successful shape was able to take all forms of decoration, including black and white prints such as *Country Life and Sporting Scenes*, based on engravings by Thomas Bewick. Another popular design was *Black Key*, a simple border design taken from an old engraving. *Black Key* proved very popular for many years, produced in many different colourways including *Gold Key* on a black body. Williams-Ellis later commented: 'No one buys one of my coffee pots in

the hope of capital gains.'[28]

As hand-painted decoration was gradually being phased out, attention was placed on more cost-effective ways of decorating pottery. Williams-Ellis turned to silk screen-printing as she was not satisfied with transfer printing, due to the high costs and low quality. One of the first silk-screened patterns was *Talisman*, launched at the Blackpool Gifts and Fancy Goods Fair in February 1962. The pattern consisted of small rectangular and circular motifs, over-printed with one of two colours (Plate 425). The motifs were carefully spaced out to hide failures in register or breaks in the printing. Later on it was produced as a furnishing fabric, the motifs greatly enlarged. A new series called *Medicine Prints*, derived from nineteenth century Patent Medicine Labels, was also in production, initially on old shapes such as dishes and bottles. A typical item featured the words 'Old Wound Cream'. The trade press commented that they were used 'to remedy ailments which today are described more delicately with less clinical accuracy.'[29]

To overcome the need for both transfer-printed and hand-painted decoration Williams-Ellis experimented with incised and raised decoration in the clay. A set of drawings was completed after she found inspiration from a Prattware teapot that she saw in an antique shop, near to the London museums. Using various cutting knives, the designer carved out stylised motifs, working within the mould. From this she created the *Totem* pattern (Plate 426). The embossed abstract symbols resembled those found in primitive art, audaciously decorated on the tall Cylinder shape. To complete the look, the designer used flow glazes that ran thinner over the raised motifs, allowing them to be clearly seen. This design was launched at the Blackpool Gifts and Fancy Goods Fair in 1963. *Totem* really brought the company to the forefront of the trade, earning it a reputation for a creative outlook on

422. A selection of beer pulls decorated with a wide range of patterns such as *Shells, Gold Sun, Knights, Moss Agate* and *Tigerlily* and lesser known designs. Designed by Susan Williams-Ellis for Portmeirion Potteries Ltd., about 1961-62.

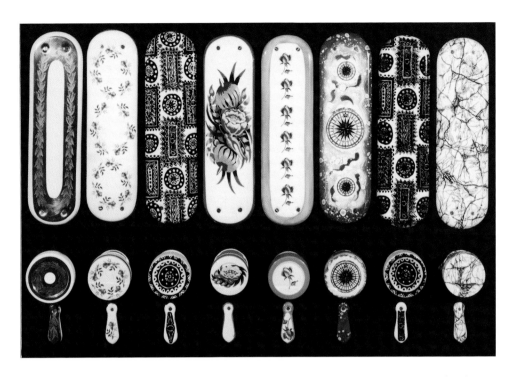

design. There were, however, a few problems, as the taller shapes had to be fired in a different kiln to the smaller items, so matching the glazes was a production nightmare.[30] By the late sixties the range was extended to incorporate dinnerware and associated items such as a cheese dish, sauce boat and cream soup and stand (Plate 427). A new

423. For a limited period a range of door furniture was produced decorated with several patterns such as *Talisman*, *Tigerlily* and *Portmeirion Rose*. Designed by Susan Williams-Ellis for Portmeirion Potteries Ltd., about 1961-62.

424. A rare example of the *Little Town* pattern, decorated on a selection of earthenware shapes. This pattern was probably not put into production. Designed by Susan Williams-Ellis for Portmeirion Potteries Ltd., about 1962-63.

425. An earthenware Cylinder shape coffee pot decorated with the *Talisman* pattern, printed in yellow, orange and black. Designed by Susan Williams-Ellis for Portmeirion Potteries Ltd., about 1962-63.

426. The *Totem* range decorated with various flow glazes. Designed by Susan Williams-Ellis for Portmeirion Potteries Ltd., 1963.

unglazed white version was introduced later. *Totem* made such an impact that many companies copied the style. By 1966 Williams-Ellis counted fifty copies of *Totem* produced by other companies. The flow glazes that she used were commercially available, thus making it easy for others to copy the style, eventually diluting *Totem*'s impact and resulting in the withdrawal of new ranges that were to be produced on a commercial scale.

Williams-Ellis then developed a new shape with a definite Eastern influence, that she called Serif. This bold shape was initially used for a range of patterns in the same style as *Totem*, using the same flow glazes. The *Cypher* pattern, based on her studies at the Museum of Minoan Art in Crete, was produced in various colourways including mustard, grey, rockingham brown and white. The *Jupiter* pattern featured large circular motifs and was available in only two colours, rock and petrol (Plate 428). Williams-Ellis developed further embossed patterns in this range, including the lesser-known *Fortuna*, with zodiac symbols around each item, and *Jewel*. She also developed a startling and extraordinary shape called Volterra. The coffee cups were so tall that the saucers needed a spike in the centre to keep the cups stable![31] Despite the trade press noting that it would be launched in the spring of 1966, the shape didn't go into production, possibly due to high losses in the kiln.

'Those individualists', declared the press on viewing Portmeirion's latest patterns at the

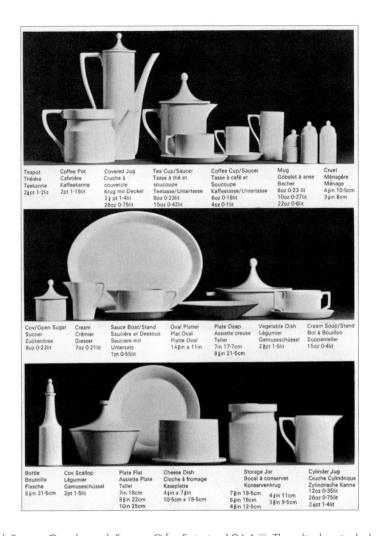

Teapot	Coffee Pot	Covered Jug	Tea Cup/Saucer	Coffee Cup/Saucer	Mug	Cruet
Théière	Cafetière	Cruche à	Tasse à thé et	Tasse à café et	Gobelet à anse	Ménagère
Teekanne	Kaffeekanne	couvercle	soucoupe	Soucoupe	Becher	Ménage
2¼pt 1·2lit	2pt 1·15lit	Krug mit Deckel	Teetasse/Untertasse	Kaffeetasse/Untertasse	8oz 0·23 lit	4¼in 10·5cm
		2¼ pt 1·4lit	8oz 0·23lit	6oz 0·18lit	10oz 0·27lit	3¼in 8cm
		26oz 0·75lit	15oz 0·42lit	4oz 0·1lit	22oz 0·6lit	

Cov/Open Sugar	Cream	Sauce Boat/Stand	Oval Platter	Plate Deep	Vegetable Dish	Cream Soup/Stand
Sucrier	Crémier	Saucière et Dessous	Plat Oval	Assiette creuse	Légumier	Bol à Bouillon
Zuckerdose	Giesser	Sauciere mit	Platte Oval	Teller	Gemuseschüssel	Suppenteller
8oz 0·23lit	7oz 0·21lit	Untersatz	14¾in x 11in	7in 17·7cm	2½pt 1·5lit	15oz 0·4lit
		1pt 0·55lit		8½in 21·5cm		

Bottle	Cov Scallop	Plate Flat	Cheese Dish	Storage Jar	Cylinder Jug
Boutnille	Légumier	Assiette Plate	Cloche à fromage	Bocal à conserves	Cruche Cylindrique
Flasche	Gemuseschüssel	Teller	Kaseplatte	Konservenkrug	12oz 0·35lit
8½in 21·5cm	2pt 1·5lit	7in 18cm	4¼in x 7¾in	7¾in 19·5cm 4½in 11cm	26oz 0·75lit
		8¾in 22cm	10·5cm x 19·5cm	6¼in 16cm 3¾in 9·5cm	2¼pt 1·4lit
		10in 25cm		4¾in 12·5cm	

427. A selection of Cylinder shaped earthenwares decorated with the *Totem* pattern and a coloured flow glaze. Designed by Susan Williams-Ellis for Portmeirion Potteries Ltd., 1963.

Blackpool Fancy Goods and Fancy Gifts Fair in 1964.[32] The display included a new embossed design, *Samarkand*, with some hand-painted detail. Similar decoration was used on mugs and boxes produced to celebrate Shakespeare's bicentenary of that year. Five versions were produced with either a blue, red, brown or olive green glaze, like *Totem*, or a hand-painted version, on a white glaze.[33] A lesser-known design, *Success to the Volunteers*, was first shown at this Fair. It was produced as a set of six one pint tankards for 36/-. The Portmeirion stand, according to the press, was one of the highlights of the show, noting that the firm organised a bistro party with onion soup! During the same year a new showroom was opened at the Portmeirion works that boasted attractive wooden shelves with discreet lighting concealed inside the units in order to throw the ware into silhouette. Another part of the showroom displayed modern Swedish glass. Overseas agents for the firm were listed in Australia, Denmark, Germany, Italy, New Zealand and South Africa.

New transfer-printed designs were developed featuring small abstract motifs within squares and rectangles. These patterns were skilfully designed by Williams-Ellis so that they could be easily cut to fit the various shapes, thus saving costs. Patterns such as *Variations* (Plate 429) and *Tivoli*, both launched in 1964, are typical examples. The latter was inspired by a visit to the Tivoli Gardens in Copenhagen. Originally intending to use a range of bright colours for this pattern, she was persuaded by Frank Thrower to use the

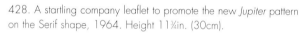

428. A startling company leaflet to promote the new *Jupiter* pattern on the Serif shape, 1964. Height 11¾in. (30cm).

429. A promotional leaflet for the *Variations* pattern. Designed by Susan Williams-Ellis for Portmeirion Potteries Ltd., about 1964.

more fashionable subtle tones. *Monte Sol* was launched two years later (Plate 430). To promote her latest products modern publicity ideas were exploited. One particular double page advertisement featured several photographs presenting the shape ranges, from rolling pins to sifters, from bowls to coffee sets and cheese and butter dishes incorporated under the banner 'Designs by Susan Williams-Ellis' (Plate 431).

During the mid-sixties coffee sets were becoming increasingly popular and an ideal choice for gifts. Williams-Ellis produced a wide range of patterns for coffee sets including *Gold Six*, that encompassed several designs such as *Gold Check*, *Gold Sign* and *Gold Rule* (Plate 432). These were followed by the *Brocade* series encompassing *Aztec Brocade*, *Persian Brocade* and *Coptic Brocade*. Lesser known patterns include *Queen of Carthage* and *Royal Palm*.[34] The mid-sixties was a period of amazing experimentation, allowing her to develop new patterns, some of which went no further than the trial stage. The company's archives have examples of *Volcano/Disaster*, depicting a sailing boat amongst islands with palm trees and a large volcano in the background. This audacious pattern was printed in black on a deep orange ground. The coffee pot depicted a volcano erupting! Other sample patterns include *Lucky Fish*, designed in Libya, featuring symbols of luck and *Sacred Edifice* that used a combination of Christian and Islamic motifs for inspiration.

430. An earthenware beaker decorated with the *Monte Sol* pattern. Designed by Susan Williams-Ellis for Portmeirion Potteries Ltd., about 1965.

357

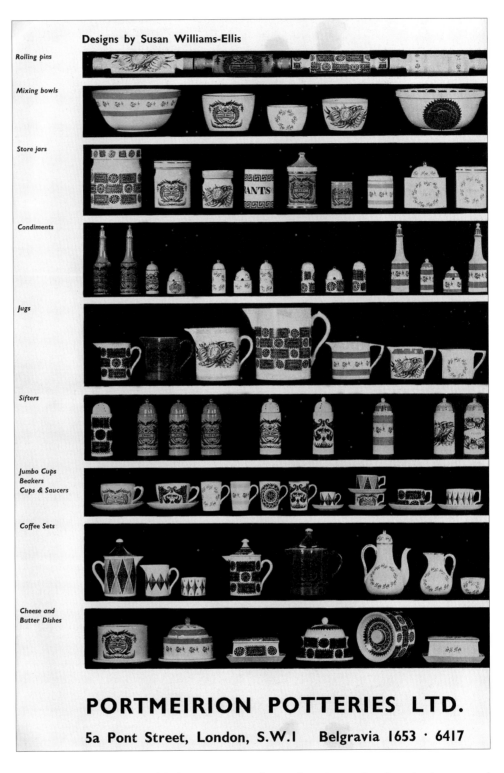

Designs by Susan Williams-Ellis

Rolling pins

Mixing bowls

Store jars

Condiments

Jugs

Sifters

Jumbo Cups
Beakers
Cups & Saucers

Coffee Sets

Cheese and
Butter Dishes

PORTMEIRION POTTERIES LTD.

5a Pont Street, London, S.W.1   Belgravia 1653 · 6417

431. A company advertisement illustrating the current patterns and shapes available, from about 1963.

One of the most successful designs was Williams-Ellis' *Magic City*, launched as part of the Christmas Collection in September 1966. The pattern was inspired by firework displays and classical domes and roofs (Plate 433). A similar design, *Magic Garden* (Plate 434), was launched at the Harrogate Gift Fair in 1970. This pattern was inspired by what the designer felt might resemble a garden on another planet.[35] It proved less successful than

Magic City. In complete contrast she put together a large collection of tablewares and
fancies decorated with black and white prints from a collection of Victorian and Edwardian
engravings that had not been used for over sixty years. Some of these were first shown at
the Blackpool International Gifts Fair in 1966. Williams-Ellis boldly exploited them for
coffee sets, bathroom tumblers, antique frames, ashtrays and mugs. These items included
Penny Plain Pantomime, *Reddington's New Foot Soldiers*, *Favorite Horseman* and *British
Herald* (Plate 435). They proved so popular, particularly on the North American market,
that over the next few years additional patterns such as *Corsets* and a lesser-known design,
The Bottle, that featured Victorian cautionary images, were added.[36] Her *Velocipedes*
pattern, depicting images of Victorians riding cycles, was inspired by an article entitled
'Evolution of Cycles' from *The Strand* newspaper in the 1920s. Some of the drawings were
undertaken by Eve Midwinter.[37]

Williams-Ellis gave the range a new twist by producing several new patterns inspired by
her own collection of vintage postcards and other sources. Patterns such as *Where did you
get that hat?* and *Idols of the Stage* were printed in sepia (Plate 436). They were launched
in 1970 decorated on a wide range of shapes including jumbo cups and saucers, coffee
sets, tankards and other associated items. Unfortunately some of these amusing and
comical patterns, such as *What the Butler Saw*, were a little too advanced for some
customers. This pattern included, amongst others, artistic half-naked modelled ladies and
stocky Victorian wrestlers. Although the Swedish store Ikea showed some interest, they were
not put into production. The local press in Stoke-on-Trent featured some of these patterns in

433. An earthenware coffee set decorated with the *Magic City* pattern, printed on the Serif shape. Designed by Susan Williams-Ellis for Portmeirion Potteries Ltd., about 1966. Height of coffee-pot 9in. (23cm).

an article on Portmeirion. The journalist exclaimed that 'the prospect of a willowy, whale-boned woman with ringletted hair gaping at me from the breakfast coffee pot would be just too much!'[38]

During the latter part of the sixties Williams-Ellis was aided by John Cuffley, who had joined Portmeirion in 1967 as assistant designer. He was responsible for the popular Phoenix pattern for coffee wares and the Zodiac series of mugs, each predicting an interesting forecast. He also designed two limited edition patterns, Apollo II in 1969 and Mayflower in 1970 for Imperial tankards. The former pattern celebrated the first man walking on the moon and was so popular that moonlight shifts were introduced to meet the massive orders. The Houston Space Center later sent a thank-you card to Williams-Ellis for the Apollo II tankards. The Mayflower pattern, produced to celebrate the 350th anniversary of the *Mayflower*, was reproduced on a pint-sized tankard, limited to ten thousand copies only. The A Year to Remember tankards were produced in the same run as the Mayflower, from 1970. The success of this series prompted many different designs for birthdays, sporting events and other such souvenir celebrations. This prompted Portmeirion to purchase a new screen printing machine.

Portmeirion's association with Dartington Glass resulted in the two organisations sharing a new showroom in Holland Park, London, that opened in 1967. The intention to successfully promote both companies' products was made easier by the large floor space for the range of pottery. Typically the interior layout and decoration attracted a great deal of attention and the press remarked it was well ahead of fashion. Portmeirion pottery was displayed in box display fitments in the front showroom, supplemented with table

arrangements. The unique box fitments, made in varying depths, were painted grey on the outside and lined in strident colours, depending on the items displayed. The interior decoration featured charcoal walls, plum carpets and bronze doors, with antique lighting and oil lamps to create a cosy atmosphere. One of the showrooms, originally an ironmonger's shop, featured a translucent greenhouse roof covering whilst the main area boasted a purpose-built balcony.[39]

To keep up with the increasing orders, major expansion and reconstruction of the pottery was undertaken during the early seventies. New machinery, larger warehouse space, a new loading bay and a new factory entrance were all part of these improvements. Simultaneously an electric roller hearth kiln was installed to enable the output to rise. The workforce had reached about 160, with the company's exports now running at 45% of production. By 1970 Portmeirion employed 210 staff, and had a turnover of approximately £350,000.[40] A year later Williams-Ellis was presented with an award by Peter Walker, Secretary of State of the Environment, for winning the household accessories category in the Living Awards for Good Design.

'A Star is Born' declared Portmeirion on the launch of the new Meridian range of coffee mug tankards. This shape evolved as Williams-Ellis began to explore new decorative techniques and shapes that were distinctly different from the Totem range. The shape, based on an antique mug, was glazed in either Terracotta, Saffron, Chocolate Brown or Plover Grey (Plate 437). Unfortunately some difficulties were experienced with oxide specks in the glaze, which were difficult to control. As a result, production was limited.

For some years Williams-Ellis had been sceptical about using transfer-printed designs. She believed that the quality was not up to her exacting standards. She changed her mind following an offer by the representative from a German printer, FX Leipold, who claimed

434. A transfer-printed sheet for the *Magic Garden* meat plate. Designed by Susan Williams-Ellis for Portmeirion Potteries Ltd., 1970.

435. An earthenware leech jar decorated with the *British Herald* pattern. Designed by Susan Williams-Ellis for Portmeirion Potteries Ltd., 1966.

436. A transfer sheet depicting the various motifs from the *Idols of the Stage* range. Designed by Susan Williams-Ellis for Portmeirion Potteries Ltd., 1970.

that his company could produce excellent lithographic images. To test this Williams-Ellis gave him two books of antique prints to reproduce. When they were returned she was very impressed with the detail and colour reproduction achieved and this stimulated her creative ideas for a modern approach for the new decade. For some years she had collected antiquarian books purchased from specialist shops in London. On one occasion she came across a book called *Botanical, Medical and Agricultural Dictionary* by Thomas Green at Weldon and Welsey. This book, containing delicate studies of flowers and plants, gave her the idea to use them for patterns (Plate 438). She later added to the collection by purchasing a copy of *The Moral of Flowers* dated 1835.

For the development of her new range Williams-Ellis modified the Meridian shape. The ridges on the ware were removed and it was renamed the Drum shape. The range was to be compact and multi-functional in recognition of the changing styles in entertaining. The individual floral studies were used as centre motifs, carefully balanced by the addition of small butterfly motifs. To give some cohesion to the various patterns she used a leaf border to link the different motifs together. In 1972 Portmeirion launched the *Botanic Garden* range (Plate 439). The items available were three sizes of plates, a tureen, bowls, cups and saucers, milk jug and a serving platter. The six original plates were decorated with the following motifs: Mexican Lily, Yellow Crown Imperial, Machined Tree, Venus's Fly Trap,

Plover Grey   Photography by Mike Newton   Terracotta   Saffron

Meridian
PORTMEIRION
Meridian
PORTMEIRION
Meridian
PORTMEIRION

African Daisy and Blue Passion Flower. A special backstamp was issued for this range. Doubts were expressed as to whether the buying public would take to a service with multiple motifs but these were soon proved wrong when sales boomed. The designer explained that 'it started as a compact range for people in small flats who didn't have a lot of room, then the Americans wanted their side salad, the Italians pizza plates and it

437. Examples of the lesser known Meridian range, decorated with a speckled glaze. Designed by Susan Williams-Ellis for Portmeirion Potteries Ltd., 1971.

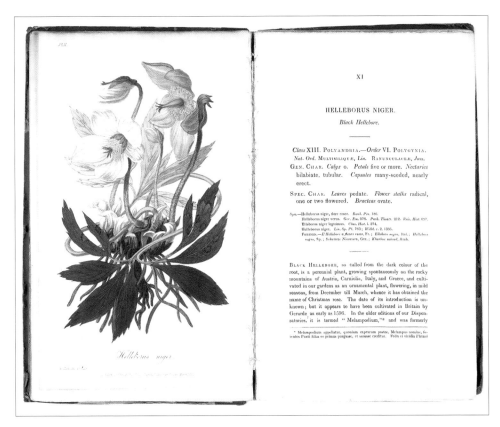

438. An example of the illustrations found in antiquarian books that the designer purchased to develop the *Botanic Garden* range.

439. Plates illustrating two of the earlier patterns from the *Botanic Garden* range.

began to grow and grow'.[41]

Over many years of production, changes have been made to *Botanic Garden*, with some of the original floral motifs being replaced with new ones.[42] In about 1982 a new backstamp incorporating the words 'Dishwasher Proof and Freezer and Microwave Safe' was introduced. The range has also been extended from the original set to incorporate various items such as clocks, matching accessories, pans and other kitchen utensils. By the nineties publicity material boasted that they had in stock over 160 items, including place mats and curtains. The pattern later decorated the new Romantic shape (Plate 440) and this was followed by the introduction of the *Botanic Garden* Bathroom Range comprising a ewer and basin, soap dish, lotion dispenser, wastepaper bin and wall tiles. In 1997 Portmeirion celebrated the twenty-fifth anniversary of *Botanic Garden*; it now takes up at least sixty per cent of total production.[43]

Williams-Ellis further exploited the use of old prints from antiquarian books for her patterns. *Kingdom of the Sea* (Plate 441) features large fish and shells, and was taken from an eighteenth century French book, purchased for a mere £4, as the binding was lost. Within a year of its launch, the pattern was entered on to the Design Council's Index in 1973. More traditional patterns included *Oranges and Lemons* and *Rose and Passion Flower*, based on a Georgian watercolour, from 1975 and 1976 respectively. A new range, the *Birds of Britain* (Plate 442), featured illustrations of birds, taken from the *Natural History of British Birds* by Edward Donovan, published in 1794. The pattern took some time to put together as Williams-Ellis had to wait for nine months before a copy came up at auction. Once purchased, the designer selected forty illustrations from a possible 240. Further delays to the production resulted from her demands to retain the delicacy and subtlety of the pattern. Unfortunately the British public did not take to it, although the range was successful in the United States and Europe. The illustrations of owls were removed following complaints made by Italian buyers – they consider them to be a bad omen. A stylistically similar pattern was *Compleat Angler*, launched in 1981 to appeal to men (Plate 443). She used fish motifs taken from a book by M.J. Lyndon, dated 1879. The designer noted: 'People always say that you can't buy presents for men except a pair of socks or a Porsche.'[44]

One of Williams-Ellis' skills was her ability to interpret the mood of the day. She began to develop a new shape based on natural forms. Inspiration came from two elements – a second century Carthaginian cup that she had seen in a museum in Ibiza and the shape of the seed head of an opium poppy. The Romantic shape was introduced in 1980. The new pattern designed for this shape was *Pomona*, launched in 1982 (Plate 444). Again the motifs were taken from antique books and following the success of *Botanic Garden*, *Pomona* was used on a whole range of kitchen accessories. The Romantic shape was also used for a selection of new floral designs including *Weeping Hearts* and *Queen's Hidden Garden*, the latter successfully utilised drawings by Marjorie Lyon from David Bellamy's book about the gardens of Buckingham Palace, both from 1986.

Williams-Ellis also created a range of crystal that was launched at the Birmingham Spring Show in 1986, manufactured by Kings Lynn Glass.[45] The range was carefully designed to complement her pottery and comprised seventeen items, including stem ware and vases. Each individual piece was named after a famous person or character such as Nelson or the Prince Regent,

440. The *Botanic Garden* pattern decorated on the Romantic shape (introduced in 1980).

441. The lesser known *Kingdom of the Sea* pattern, printed in sepia on an earthenware comport. Designed by Susan Williams-Ellis for Portmeirion Potteries Ltd., 1972.

442. A promotional leaflet to advertise the *Birds of Britain* pattern. Designed by Susan Williams-Ellis for Portmeirion Potteries Ltd., 1978.

443. A selection of items decorated with the *The Compleat Angler* pattern. Designed by Susan Williams-Ellis for Portmeirion Potteries Ltd., 1981.

and was packed in a decorative presentation box (Plate 445).

In 1987 the British Heritage Collection of antique embossed jugs was manufactured from moulds dating from the nineteenth century. Originally attempts had been made to produce these pieces during the sixties but without much success. For this collection a new parian style porcelain was used to reveal the fine details of the modelling.

In a bold step to maximise foreign sales, Portmeirion USA was established in 1986. The aim was to keep in closer touch with the trends of the market and the needs of the customer. The venture was a joint partnership between Naugatuck Triangle Corporation and Portmeirion Potteries Ltd. Part of the showroom on Fifth Avenue in New York was designated for Portmeirion ware. The Portmeirion Sales and Marketing Director, Martin Guliver, explained at the time that the joint venture was decided upon because they didn't know everything about the United States market.[46] In 1988 Portmeirion Potteries Ltd. was floated on the stock market, enabling it to invest in expanding the works to meet the demand for Portmeirion pottery. From 1990 the company became known as Portmeirion Pottery Holdings PLC. During that year the company purchased the Sylvan Works site in Longton, formerly the home of Shaw and Copestake. The site was re-equipped as a casting plant. During the same year the company received the prestigious Queen's Award for Export.

To keep ahead of current trends Portmeirion took the decision to move into the bone china market, producing the new Moonstone range of shapes. This new body contained

444. The *Pomona* pattern, printed on a selection of bone china Romantic shape tea and coffee wares. Designed by Susan Williams-Ellis for Portmeirion Potteries Ltd., 1982.

445. An example of the lesser known range of glasswares designed by Susan Williams-Ellis, 1986.

446. The *Seasons* collection is the most recent range to be released by Portmeirion Potteries Ltd., 1999.

no animal bone and was developed by the Technical Director, Philip White. Moonstone was launched in February 1994 decorated with four new patterns: *Ladies Flower Garden* by Williams-Ellis, *Ancestral Jewels* and *Summer Garland* by Anwyl Cooper-Willis and *Welsh Wild Flowers* by Angharad Menna, her two daughters. Further responsibilities were eventually handed over to Anwyl Cooper-Willis, who was appointed Marketing and Design Director.

At a time when most designers would consider retirement Williams-Ellis is still developing new shapes and patterns, successfully demonstrating her thorough understanding of the tastes and needs of the public, in particular those of the younger generation. In 1998, at the age of eighty, she developed the Mandarin shape with patterns being created by the Portmeirion design team. The *Seasons Collection*, inspired by the moods of nature, was produced in four contemporary colourways, beige, blue, green and lilac (Plate 446). The publicity material emphasised the relaxed approach to dining. A complementary range of accessories including glassware, concrete vases, slate placemats and chunky geometric candles were part of the new range.[47] This was followed by the Dawn to Dusk range, designed by Julie Ingham and Jo Gorman respectively and launched during the new millennium year.

REFERENCES

Introduction

1. For further information on this period see: Stewart, R., *Design and British Industry*, John Murray (Publishers) Ltd., 1987.
2. *The Pottery Gazette and Glass Trade Review*, 1 August 1921, p.1221.
3. Forsyth, G., (Pottery Section) Report on the present Position and Tendencies of the Industrial Arts as indicated at the International Exhibition of Modern Design and Industry, Paris, 1925. Dept. of Overseas Trade, p.129.
4. Ibid., p.128.
5. Pevsner, N., Pottery: Design, Manufacture, Marketing. *Trend in Design*, No. 2, 1936, p.16.
6. *The Pottery Gazette and Glass Trade Review*, 1 August 1921, p.1221.
7. Pevsner, N., Pottery: Design, Manufacture, Marketing. *Trend in Design*, No. 2, 1936, p.14.
8. For further information, see: Sparke, P. (Editor), *Did Britain Make it? British Design in Context 1946-1986*, Design Council, 1986.
9. For further information, see: Jackson, L., *The New Look: Design in the Fifties*, Thames and Hudson, 1991.
10. Reilly, R., Norman Wilson 1902-1988, *Etruria, The Wedgwood International Society*, Vol.3, No.4, p.9.
11. Niblett, K., *Dynamic Design, The British Pottery Industry 1940-1990*, Stoke-on-Trent City Musuems and Art Gallery, 1990, p.23.

Chapter 1 – Daisy Makeig-Jones

1. Fontaines, U. des, *Wedgwood Fairyland Lustre*, Sotheby Parke Bernet, 1975, p.103
2. Anne Makeig-Jones in conversation with the author, August 1997.
3. Fontaines, U. des, *Wedgwood Fairyland Lustre*, Sotheby Parke Bernet, 1975.
4. Anne Makeig-Jones in conversation with the author, August 1997.
5. Information from Martin Chaplin, Wedgwood Museum, January 1999.
6. Fontaines, U. des, 'Fairyland Lustre, The Work of Daisy Makeig-Jones (1881-1945)'. Abridged and edited version of a talk given before the Wedgwood Society on 27 April 1963, *Proceedings of the Wedgwood Society*, No.5, 1963. pp.39-40.
7. For a more detailed account of the history of Josiah Wedgwood and Sons Ltd. see: Batkin, M., *Wedgwood Ceramics 1846-1959 A New Appraisal*, Richard Dennis, 1982.
8. Sharon Gater in conversation with the author, January 1999.
9. For further information see: Fontaines, U. des and Lambourne, L., *Miss Jones and her Fairyland, The work of Daisy Makeig-Jones*, Victoria & Albert Museum, 1990, p.13.
10. Wedgwood bone china was re-introduced in 1876.
11. Buyers' Notes, *The Pottery Gazette*, April 1916.
12. Buyers' Notes, *The Pottery Gazette*, 1 August, 1917, p.765.
13. Quote taken from Fontaines, U. des, 'Fairyland Lustre, The Work of Daisy Makeig-Jones (1881-1945)'. Abridged and edited version of a talk given before the Wedgwood Society on 27 April 1963, *Proceedings of the Wedgwood Society*, No. 5, 1963. p.41.
14. Anne Makeig-Jones in conversation with the author, August 1997.
15. Information from Martin Chaplin, Wedgwood Museum, January 1999.
16. These marks are illustrated in: Fontaines, U. des, *Wedgwood Fairyland Lustre*, Sotheby Parke Bernet, 1975, p.98.
17. Sharon Gater in conversation with the author, January 1999.
18. This sketch is illustrated in: Fontaines, U. des, *Wedgwood Fairyland Lustre*, Sotheby Parke Bernet, 1975, p.34.
19. For further information see: Fontaines, U. des and Lambourne, L., *Miss Jones and her Fairyland, The work of Daisy Makeig-Jones*, Victoria & Albert Museum, 1990, p.15-16.
20. Buyers' Notes, *The Pottery Gazette*, 2 April 1917, p.369.
21. Buyers' Notes, *The Pottery Gazette*, 1 August 1917, p.765.
22. Fontaines, U. des, *Wedgwood Fairyland Lustre*, Sotheby Parke Bernet, 1975, p.97.
23. Information from the Ceramics and Glass Department, Victoria & Albert Museum, London.
24. Fontaines, U. des, *Wedgwood Fairyland Lustre*, Sotheby Parke Bernet, 1975, p.29.
25. Buyers' Notes, *Pottery Gazette and Glass Trade Review*, 1 July 1924, p.194.
26. Gater, S., and Vincent, D., *The Factory in a Garden, Wedgwood from Etruria to Barlaston – the transitional years*, University of Keele, 1988.
27. Anne Makeig-Jones in conversation with the author, August 1997.
28. Information from Joanna Thomas, March 1999.
29. Fairyland Prices, *Financial Times*, 23 October 1976 , p.17.
30. Information from Joanna Thomas, March 1999.

Chapter 2 – Charlotte Rhead

1. Bumpus, B., *Charlotte Rhead, Potter and Designer*, Kevin Francis Publishing, 1987.
2. Watkins, C., Harvey, W., and Senft, R., *Shelley Potteries, The History and Production of a Staffordshire Family of Potters*, Barrie and Jenkins, 1980, pp.26-27.
3. Bumpus, B., *Charlotte Rhead, Potter and Designer*, Kevin Francis Publishing, 1987, p.102.
4. Watkins, C., Harvey, W., and Senft, R., *Shelley Potteries, The History and Production of a Staffordshire Family of Potters*, Barrie and Jenkins, 1980, p.41.
5. Bergesen, V., *Encyclopaedia of British Art Pottery 1870-1920*, Barrie and Jenkins, 1991, p.278.
6. Ibid., p.35.
7. Examples of Charlotte Rhead tile designs are illustrated in: Bumpus, B., *Rhead Artists and Potters 1870-1950*, Geffrye Museum, 1986, p.17.
8. Bumpus, B., *Collecting Rhead Pottery*, Francis Joseph Publications, 1999, p.18.
9. Buyers' Notes, *The Pottery Gazette and Glass Trade Review*, 2 June 1924, p.1012.
10. Information from David V. Williams, September 1999.
11. Bursley Pottery Showroom, *The Pottery and Glass Record*, January 1925, p.97.
12. British Industries Fair, *The Pottery and Glass Record*, March 1926, p.573.
13. For further information on Rhead's designs for Wood's and Bursley *see*: Bumpus, B., *Collecting Rhead Pottery*, Francis Joseph Publications, 1999, pp.24-32.
14. Centenary of Burgess and Leigh 1851-1951, *Pottery and Glass*, November 1951, pp.58-60.
15. Company Advertisement, *The Pottery Gazette and Glass Trade Review*, 1 March 1927, p.375.
16. Information from David V. Williams, September 1999.
17. Buyers' Notes, *The Pottery Gazette and Glass Trade Review*, 1 September 1927, p.1425.
18. Buyers' Notes, *The Pottery Gazette and Glass Trade Review*, 1 September 1928, pp.1415-17.
19. Barry Leigh in conversation with the author, February 1997.
20. Letter from Bernard Bumpus, May 1999.
21. Company Advertisement, *The Pottery Gazette and Glass Trade Review, Directory and Diary*, 1936.
22. Harrods advertisement, *The Sphere*, 19 November 1932, p.317.
23. Shaw, G. and Greysmith, B., Charlotte Rhead, the Clarice Cliff of Crown Ducal, *Collect It*, October 2000.
24. Buyers' Notes, *The Pottery Gazette and Glass Trade Review*, 1 July 1932, p.865.
25. Buyers' Notes, *The Pottery Gazette and Glass Trade Review*, 1 March 1933, p.325.
26. The Crown Ducal pattern books are held at the Potteries Museum, Stoke-on-Trent, Staffordshire.
27. In conversation with Eddie Sambrook, January 1999.
28. Buyers' Notes, *The Pottery Gazette and Glass Trade Review*, 1 February 1934, pp.183-5.
29. Shaw, G. and Greysmith, B., Charlotte Rhead, the Clarice Cliff of Crown Ducal, *Collect It*, October 2000.
30. Buyers' Notes, *The Pottery Gazette and Glass Trade Review*, 1 February 1935, p.199.
31. Company Advertisement, *Pottery Gazette and Glass Trade Review Directory and Diary*, 1937, p.52.
32. Company Advertisement, *The Pottery Gazette and Glass Trade Review*, 1 April 1937, p.468.
33. Miss Charlotte Rhead, Pottery Artist and Designer, *The Pottery and Glass Record*, August 1937, p.220.
34. Britain Can Export, *The Pottery Gazette and Glass Trade Review*, September 1940, p. 847.
35. May Doorbar in conversation with the author, January 2000.
36. Miss Charlotte Rhead, Pottery Artist and Designer, *The Pottery and Glass Record*, August 1937, p.220.
37. Eddie Sambrook in conversation with the author, January 1999.
38. Jessie Tait in conversation with the author, January 1999.
39. Information from Miranda Goodby, Potteries Museum, Stoke-on-Trent, Staffordshire, January 1999.
40. Eddie Sambrook in conversation with the author, January 1999.
41. Company Advertisement, *Pottery Gazette and Glass Trade Review*, March 1949, p.23.
42. Death of Miss C.L.A. Rhead, *Pottery Gazette and Glass Trade Review*, December 1947, p.1012.

43. Company Advertisement, *Pottery Gazette and Glass Trade Review*, February 1960, p.216.

Chapter 3 – Clarice Cliff

1. Alison Wright in conversation with the author, August 1999.
2. 'Clarice Cliff', Brighton Museum and Art Gallery, 15 January to 20 February 1972, p.3.
3. Interview with Clarice Cliff, *Reynolds Illustrated News*, 27 September 1931.
4. 'Clarice Cliff', Brighton Museum and Art Gallery, 15 January to 20 February 1972, p.4.
5. Hopwood, I., and Hopwood, G., *The Shorter Connection*, Richard Dennis, 1992.
6. This story was mentioned by Clarice Cliff during an interview with the *Blackburn Telegraph*, 2 September 1931.
7. Oriflamme sales catalogue, 1910. Stoke-on-Trent City Archives, Hanley Library, Stoke-on-Trent, Staffordshire.
8. Information from Alison Wright, August 1999.
9. 'Clarice Cliff', Brighton Museum and Art Gallery, 15 January to 20 February 1972, p.4.
10. Buyers' Notes, *The Pottery Gazette and Glass Trade Review*, 1 October 1923, p.1619.
11. Ibid., p.1621.
12. Buyers' Notes, *The Pottery Gazette and Glass Trade Review*, 1 September 1924, p.1505.
13. Royal Staffordshire Potteries Showrooms, *The Pottery and Glass Record*, March 1925, p.154.
14. Buyers' Notes, *The Pottery Gazette and Glass Trade Review*, 1 September 1924, p.1507.
15. Royal Staffordshire Potteries Showrooms, *The Pottery and Glass Record*, March 1925, p.154.
16. Interview with Clarice Cliff, *Daily Mirror*, 12 September 1930.
17. 'Clarice Cliff', Brighton Museum and Art Gallery, 15 January to 20 February 1972, p.4.
18. Ibid.
19. Buyers' Notes, *The Pottery Gazette and Glass Trade Review*, 1 March 1928, p.445.
20. 'Clarice Cliff', Brighton Museum and Art Gallery, 15 January to 20 February 1972, p.16.
21. Buyers' Notes, *The Pottery Gazette and Glass Trade Review*, 1 September 1932, p.1122.
22. Buyers' Notes, *The Pottery Gazette and Glass Trade Review*, 1 February 1929, p.252-3.
23. For further information see Griffin, L., Meisel, L.K. and S.P., *Clarice Cliff, The Bizarre Affair*, Thames and Hudson, 1988.
24. For further information see Griffin, L., *Clarice Cliff, The Art of Bizarre*, Pavilion, 1999, pp.117-125.
25. A.J. Wilkinson Ltd and Newport Pottery Collection, Stoke-on-Trent City Archives, Hanley Library, Stoke-on-Trent.
26. Eddie Sambrook in conversation with the author, January 1999.
27. Advertisement, *The Pottery Gazette and Glass Trade Review*, 1 September 1931, p.1171.
28. An Educative Display by Pottery Manufacturers, *The Pottery Gazette and Glass Trade Review*, 1 October 1931, p.1895.
29. Rene Dale in conversation with the author, January 2000.
30. The Biarritz plate was still being advertised as late as 1937. Company advertisement, *The Pottery Gazette and Glass Trade Review*, March 1937.
31. Buyers' Notes, *The Pottery Gazette and Glass Trade Review*, 1 July 1933, p.844.
32. For further information see Pelik, R., 'The Harrods Experiment', *Ceramics*, August 1987, pp.33-41.
33. Design Quiz, *The Pottery Gazette and Glass Trade Review*, April 1951, pp.572-3.
34. 'Clarice Cliff', Brighton Museum and Art Gallery, 15 January to 20 February 1972.
35. Griffin, L., *Clarice Cliff, The Art of Bizarre*, Pavilion, 1999, p.176.
36. Hopwood, I., and Hopwood, G, *The Shorter Connection*, Richard Dennis 1992.
37. Advertisement, *The Pottery Gazette and Glass Trade Review*, July 1946, p.421.
38. Overseas Buyers' Notes, *The Pottery Gazette and Glass Trade Review*, July 1946, p.465.
39. Design Quiz, *The Pottery Gazette and Glass Trade Review*, September 1951, p.1382.
40. Front cover, *British Ceramic News*, June 1951.
41. Buyers' Notes, *Pottery Gazette and Glass Trade Review*, 1 September 1937, p.1201.
42. Advertisement, *New York Times*, 17 June 1956.
43. A.J. Wilkinson Ltd and Newport Pottery Collection, Stoke-on-Trent City Archives, Hanley Library, Stoke-on-Trent, Staffordshire.
44. The Shorter Collection Sale Catalogue, 1st to 2nd May 1973, lot no.356.
45. Information from the A.J. Wilkinson Ltd. and Newport Pottery Collection, Stoke-on-Trent City Archives, Hanley Library, Stoke-on-Trent, Staffordshire.
46. Advertisement, *Pottery Gazette and Glass Trade Review*, January 1955.

47. Advertisement, *Pottery Gazette and Glass Trade Review*, September 1963, p.885.
48. Alison Wright in conversation with the author, August 1999.
49. Information from Stella Beddoe, Brighton Art Gallery and Museum, October 1999.

Chapter 4 – Truda Carter

1. Information from Leslie Hayward, November 1999.
2. The Royal College of Art records for this period were destroyed during the Blitz in the Second World War.
3. Myers, L., *Poole Pottery, The First One Hundred Years, 1873-1973*, Poole Pottery Ltd., 1973, p.23.
4. Information from Leslie Hayward, February 2000.
5. Examples of John Adams' work from this period were exhibited in several museums and art galleries across South Africa in 1991. Information from Leslie Hayward, February 2000.
6. For a more detailed account of the early history of Poole Pottery see Hayward, L., *Poole Pottery, Carter and Company and their Successors 1873-1995*, Richard Dennis, 1995, and Hawkins, J., *The Poole Potteries*, Barrie and Jenkins, 1980.
7. Myers, L., *Poole Pottery, The First One Hundred Years, 1873-1973*, Poole Pottery Ltd., 1973, p.25.
8. An exhibition of Poole Pottery, *The Pottery Gazette and Glass Trade Review*, 1 February 1922, p.245.
9. King, J., 'Truda Carter, René Buthaud, and Surrealism', Unpublished Paper, September 1996, p.2.
10. Modern Pottery of Distinction, *Homes and Gardens*, September 1923, pp.92-3.
11. Hayward, L., *Poole Pottery, Carter and Company and their Successors 1873-1995*, Richard Dennis, 1995, p.50.
12. Ibid, p.49.
13. Forsyth, G., (Pottery Section) Report on the present Position and Tendencies of the Industrial Arts as indicated at the International Exhibition of Modern Design and Industry, Paris 1925. Department of Overseas Trade.
14. King, J., 'Truda Carter, René Buthaud, and Surrealism', Unpublished Paper, September 1996, p.2.
15. Buyers' Notes, *Pottery Gazette and Glass Trade Review*, 1 December 1933, p.1427.
16. Examples of these items are illustrated in: Hayward, L., *Poole Pottery, Carter and Company and their Successors 1873-1995*, Richard Dennis, 1995, pp.74-5.
17. Truda Carter's design for the bathroom is illustrated in: The Craftsman's Portfolio, *Architectural Review*, July to December 1932, p.152.
18. Modernity with Manners, *The Architect and Building News*, 8 January 1932, p.35-41.
19. Buyers' Notes, *The Pottery Gazette and Glass Trade Review*, 1 October 1935, p.1274.
20. Ibid.
21. Buyers' Notes, *The Pottery Gazette and Glass Trade Review*, 1 July 1936, p.927.
22. Information from Leslie Hayward, September 2000.

Chapter 5 – Susie Cooper

1. Eatwell, A., *Susie Cooper Productions*, Victoria & Albert Museum, 1987, p.8.
2. These figures are illustrated in Youds, B., *Susie Cooper, An Elegant Affair*, Thames and Hudson, 1996, p.6 and p.9.
3. For further information on the productions of A.E. Gray and Co. Ltd. see: Niblett, P., *Hand-Painted Gray's Pottery*, City Museum and Art Gallery, Stoke-on-Trent, 1982.
4. Susie Cooper, *Designer*, March 1979.
5. Ibid.
6. 'Business Chief in Three Years', *Daily Mail*, 1 March 1933. Reproduced by kind permission of *Daily Mail* Newspapers Ltd.
7. Susie Cooper, *Designer*, March 1979.
8. Buyers Notes, *The Pottery Gazette and Glass Trade Review*, 1 April 1926, p.602.
9. British Institute of Industrial Art, *The Pottery and Glass Record*, November 1927, p.371.
10. The *Layebands* pattern was often marked with the Heal's logo of a four-poster bed instead of the standard Gray's mark,
11. Report on the British Industries Fair, *The Pottery and Glass Record*, March 1926, p.576.
12. Information taken from an interview with Susie Cooper on the British Forces Broadcasting Service In 1978.
13. These curtains were illustrated in the magazine *Picture House*, Cinema Theatre Association, No.20, Winter 1994/95, p.64.
14. Eatwell, A., *Susie Cooper Productions*, Victoria & Albert Museum, 1987, p.10.
15. Eddie Sambrook in conversation with author, January 1999.
16. Youds, B., *Susie Cooper, An Elegant Affair*, Thames and Hudson, 1996.
17. Company advert, *The Pottery Gazette and Glass Trade Review*, 1 April 1930, p.550.

18. Buyers' Notes, *The Pottery Gazette and Glass Trade Review*, 1 June 1931, p.817.
19. Buyers' Notes, *The Pottery Gazette and Glass Trade Review*, 1 April 1930, p.595.
20. Wakefield, E., 'Top Designer and Innovator for Sixty Years', *Insight on Collectables*, July/August 1985, p.15-16.
21. 'Buyers Notes', *The Pottery Gazette and Glass Trade Review*, 1 June 1931, p.817.
22. Susie Cooper in conversation with the author, June 1990.
23. Eddie Sambrook in conversation with the author, January 1999.
24. The Susie Cooper exhibition stand was illustrated in *The Pottery and Glass Record*, March 1932, p.73.
25. Advertisement, *The Pottery Gazette and Glass Trade Review*, 1 November 1932, p.1337.
26. Some of these patterns were not recorded in the Susie Cooper pattern or description books, although they were thought to have been produced in about 1932.
27. The development of the studio wares necessitated a new prefix Ref. that denoted the shape rather than the pattern. Numbers range from about Ref. 234 to around 575, although all the numbers were not used. The painted studio wares were prefixed with M, thought to denote matt glaze. The pattern numbers ranged from M.60 to M.150.
28. 'Art Pottery that Appeals', *The Industrial World*, October 1932.
29. 'Susan's Red', *The Pottery Gazette and Glass Trade Review*, 1 March 1934, p.341.
30. Susie Cooper in conversation with the author, June 1990.
31. Fondevilles Advertisement, Wedgwood Museum, Josiah Wedgwood and Sons Ltd.
32. 'Susie Cooper', *Designer*, March, 1979.
33. Buyers' Notes, *The Pottery Gazette and Glass Trade Review*, 1 February 1935, p.197.
34. Buyers' Notes, *The Pottery Gazette and Glass Trade Review*, 1 April 1937, p.517.
35. 'Susie Cooper', *Designer*, March, 1979.
36. *Journal of the Royal Society of Arts*, 29 November 1940, p.14.
37. Buyers' Notes, *The Pottery Gazette and Glass Trade Review*, November 1940, p.1029.
38. 'Pottery and Glass at the Britain Can Make It Exhibition', *The Pottery Gazette and Glass Trade Review*, November 1946, p.728-9.
39. Examples of Susie Cooper's textiles are held at the Whitworth Art Gallery, Manchester and the Victoria & Albert Museum, London.
40. Warren, P., 'Susie Cooper, Artist in Pottery', *News Chronicle*, 6 October 1952.
41. R.D.I Reception, *Journal of the Royal Society of Arts*, 17 November 1950, p.545.
42. 'Susie Cooper', *Designer*, March 1979.
43. Portent of a new trend: Exhibition at Harrods, *Pottery and Glass*, November 1956, pp.378-79.
44. Buyers' Notes, *The Pottery Gazette and Glass Trade Review*, February 1957, p.244.
45. 'Fire at Burslem Potteries', *Pottery Gazette and Glass Trade Review*, May 1957, p.676.
46. 'Merger of Plant and Susie Cooper', *Pottery and Glass*, December 1958, p.370.
47. 'Wedgwood takes over china firms', *Pottery Gazette and Glass Trade Review* incorporating *Tableware*, April 1966, p.426.
48. Rose, A., 'Woman whose success came on a plate', *The Times*, 11 July 1984.
49. 'Susie Cooper and William Adams', *Pottery Gazette and Glass Trade Review* incorporating *Tableware*, November 1966, pp.1131-2.
50. 'Princess Alexandra impressed by Burslem potter's designs', *Evening Sentinel*, 27 June 1969, p.11.
51. These are illustrated in: Youds, B., *Susie Cooper, An Elegant Affair*, Thames and Hudson, 1996, p.61.
52. John Ryan in conversation with the author, April 1999.

Chapter 6 – Eric Slater

1. Watkins, C., Harvey, W., and Senft, R., *Shelley Potteries, The History and Production of a Staffordshire Family of Potters*, Barrie and Jenkins, 1980, p.63.
2. Bumpus, B., *Collecting Rhead Pottery*, Francis Joseph Publishing, 1999.
3. Watkins, C., Harvey, W., and Senft, R., *Shelley Potteries, The History and Production of a Staffordshire Family of Potters*, Barrie and Jenkins, 1980, p.73.
4. Terry Corn in conversation with the author, February 2000.
5. Louise Blackwell in conversation with the author, February 2000.
6. Quote taken from the *Shelley Standard*, July 1929.
7. Hill, S., *The Shelley Style: A Collectors Guide*, Jazz Publications, 1990, p.11.
8. For a comprhensive account of Shelley nursery ware see: Watkins, C., Harvey, W., and Senft, R., *Shelley Potteries, The History and Production of a Staffordshire Family of Potters*, Barrie and Jenkins, 1980, pp.79-85.
9. Ibid, p.92.
10. Louise Blackwell in conversation with the author, February 2000.
11. Watkins, C., Harvey, W., and Senft, R., *Shelley Potteries, The History and

Production of a Staffordshire Family of Potters*, Barrie and Jenkins, 1980, p.94.
12. Quote taken from the *Shelley Standard*, July 1929.
13. Buyers' Notes, *The Pottery Gazette and Glass Trade Review*, 2 March 1931, p.381.
14. Watkins, C., Harvey, W., and Senft, R., *Shelley Potteries, The History and Production of a Staffordshire Family of Potters*, Barrie and Jenkins, 1980, p.109.
15. Ibid, pp.104-105.
16. Buyers' Notes, *The Pottery Gazette and Glass Trade Review*, 1 May 1937, p.667.
17. Ibid.
18. Information from Ray Reynolds, Decorating Manager, April 2000.
19. Davenport, C., *Shelley Pottery: The Later Years*, Heather Publications Ltd, 1997, p.3.
20. John Hayward in conversation with the author, February 2000.
21. Davenport, C., *Shelley Pottery: The Later Years*, Heather Publications Ltd, 1997, pp.3-4.
22. These items were illustrated in: *Design '46, A Survey of British Industrial Design as displayed in the Britain Can Make It Exhibition organised by the British Council of Industrial Design*, HMSO, 1946.
23. This item is illustrated in: Watkins, C., Harvey, W., and Senft, R., *Shelley Potteries, The History and Production of a Staffordshire Family of Potters*, Barrie and Jenkins, 1980, p.143.
24. Davenport, C., *Shelley Pottery: The Later Years*, Heather Publications Ltd, 1997, pp.4-5.
25. Information from Michael Roper, September 1999.
26. Information from the Royal College of Art Archives, London.
27. Watkins, C., Harvey, W., and Senft, R., *Shelley Potteries, The History and Production of a Staffordshire Family of Potters*, Barrie and Jenkins, 1980, pp.162-163.
28. John Hayward in conversation with the author, February 2000.

Chapter 7 – Millicent Taplin

1. Lodey, J., 'A flower was picked and a famous pottery design was born', *Six Towns Magazine*, September 1963, p.51.
2. Atterbury, P., and Batkin, M., *The Dictionary of Minton*, Antique Collectors' Club, 1990, revised 1998.
3. Lodey, J., 'A flower was picked and a famous pottery design was born', *Six Towns Magazine*, September 1963, p.51.
4. Buyers' Notes, *Pottery Gazette and Glass Trade Review*, 1 April 1920, p.492.
5. Sharon Gater in conversation with the author, January 2000.
6. Forsyth, G., (Pottery Section) Report on the Present Position and Tendencies of the Industrial Arts as indicated at the International Exhibition of Modern Design and Industry, Paris 1925, Department of Overseas Trade.
7. Information from Cheryl Buckley, September 1999.
8. For more detailed information on marks and pattern codes, see: Batkin, M., *Wedgwood Ceramics, A New Appraisal, 1846-1959*, Richard Dennis, 1982, pp.227-231.
9. Gater, S., and Vincent, D., *The Factory in a Garden, Wedgwood from Etruria to Barlaston – the transitional years*, University of Keele, 1988.
10. Gater, S., Victor Skellern: Wedgwood Art Director 1934-1965, *Journal of the Northern Ceramic Society*, Vol.10, 1993.
11. 'Future Arrangements with Regard to New Designs', 12 December 1933. The Wedgwood Museum.
12. Information from Cheryl Buckley, September 1999.
13. Travellers' Meeting Notes, 17 October 1933. Wedgwood Museum.
14. *Pottery Gazette and Glass Trade Review*, 2 March 1936, p.368.
15. *Pottery Gazette and Glass Trade Review*, 1 July 1933, p.844.
16. Report on the British Art in Industry Exhibition at the Royal Academy, *Pottery Gazette and Glass Trade Review*, 1 February 1935, p.216.
17. Grafton Galleries Exhibition Catalogue, Wedgwood 1936.
18. Information from the Wedgwood Museum, Josiah Wedgwood and Sons Ltd.
19. A Special Wedgwood Display, *Pottery Gazette and Glass Trade Review*, 1 April 1938, p.572.
20. Gater, S., and Vincent, D., *The Factory in a Garden, Wedgwood from Etruria to Barlaston – the transitional years*, University of Keele, 1988.
21. Lodey, J., 'A flower was picked and a famous pottery design was born', *Six Towns Magazine*, September 1963, p.51.
22. Sharon Gater in conversation with the author, January 1999.
23. Expansion of Wedgwood's London Showroom, *Pottery Gazette and Glass Trade Review*, June 1957, pp.784-5.
24. Team Work for Design, *Pottery Gazette and Glass Trade Review*, January 1955, p.101.
25. Spotlight, *Pottery and Glass*, September 1954, p.263.
26. Designs of the Year, *Pottery Gazette and Glass Trade Review*, June 1957, pp.776-7.
27. *Wedgwood Review*, January 1958.
28. A Lifetime in Design, *Wedgwood Review*, September 1962, p.12.
29. Millicent Green in conversation with the author, April 1999.

Chapter 8 – Victor Skellern

1. Ullstein, G., Patrons of Design, Josiah Wedgwood, *Design*, No.35,

November 1951, pp.5-10.
2. Gater, S., Victor Skellern: Wedgwood Art Director 1934-1965, *Journal of the Northern Ceramic Society*, Vol.10, 1993, p.115.
3. Victor Skellern, *Pottery and Glass*, July 1952, p.63.
4. Gater, S., Victor Skellern: Wedgwood Art Director 1934-1965, *Journal of the Northern Ceramic Society*, Vol. 10, 1993, p.115.
5. Ibid.
6. Skellern, V., Design and Decoration, *Pottery Gazette and Glass Trade Review*, February 1953, pp.256-257.
7. Information from the archives of Wedgwood Museum.
8. Rena, M., The English Pottery Industry, *Decorative Art Studio Year Book*, 1936, pp.266-272.
9. Information from the archives of Wedgwood Museum.
10. For more information on these artists see: Batkin, M., *Wedgwood Ceramics, A New Appraisal, 1846-1959*, Richard Dennis, 1982.
11. Gater, S., Victor Skellern: Wedgwood Art Director 1934-1965, *Journal of the Northern Ceramic Society*, Vol. 10, 1993, p.116.
12. These pieces are illustrated in: Reilly, R., *Wedgwood* (Two vols.), Macmillan Publishers Ltd., 1989, p.230.
13. Gater, S., Victor Skellern: Wedgwood Art Director 1934-1965, *Journal of the Northern Ceramic Society*, Vol. 10, 1993, p.118.
14. Skellern, V., Design and Decoration, *Pottery Gazette and Glass Trade Review*, February 1953, pp.256-257.
15. Niblett, K., The Art Directors' Skill, Wedgwood Design 1919-1959, *Antique Collecting*, Vol. 29, May 1994.
16. Gater, S., Victor Skellern: Wedgwood Art Director 1934-1965, *Journal of the Northern Ceramic Society*, Vol. 10, 1993, p.124.
17. Information from the archives of Wedgwood Museum.
18. This item is illustrated in: Reilly, R., *Wedgwood – The New Illustrated Dictionary*, Antique Collectors' Club, 1995, p.122.
19. Buyers' Notes, *Pottery and Glass*, August 1958, p.228.
20. Skellern, V., Design and Decoration, *Pottery Gazette and Glass Trade Review*, February 1953, pp.256-257.
21. Designs of the Year, *Pottery Gazette and Glass Trade Review*, June 1957, pp.776-7.
22. Lyon, P., Growth in the Wedgwood Tradition, *Design* No. 88, April 1956, pp.36-40.
23. *Wigmore Street, Wedgwood In London*, Josiah Wedgwood and Sons Ltd, 1984, p.63.

Chapter 9 – Keith Murray

1. Information from the Ceramics and Glass Department, Victoria & Albert Museum, London.
2. Tyler, L., *Keith Murray in Context* (exhibition cat.), New Zealand, 1996, p.1.
3. Aitken, J., and Lee, S., Who is Keith Murray, New Zealander creates a profession from Architect to Industrial Designer, *New Zealand News*, 25 September 1935.
4. Tyler, L., *Keith Murray in Context* (exhibition cat.), New Zealand, 1996, p.2.
5. Taylor, D., Keith Murray: Architect and Designer for Industry, *Twentieth Century Architecture*, No.1, Summer 1994, pp.45-54.
6. The designer's own copy of the exhibition catalogue indicates that several paintings were sold. Private Collection. Keith Murray was listed in: Dolman, B. (Editor), *A Dictionary of Contemporary British Artists, 1929*, Antique Collectors' Club, 1981, p.329.
7. Murray, K., Some Views of Designer, *Journal of the Society of Glass Technology*, vol.19, 1925.
8. Ibid.
9. Taylor, D., Keith Murray – The Swedish Connection, *The Journal of the Glass Association*, Vol.2, 1987, pp.56-67.
10. Aitken, J., and Lee, S., Who is Keith Murray, New Zealander creates a profession from Architect to Industrial Designer, *New Zealand News*, 25 September 1935.
11. Information from David Redman, March 2000.
12. Murray. K., The Design of Table Glass, *Design for Today*, June 1933, pp.53-56.
13. Information from the Ceramics and Glass Department, Victoria & Albert Museum, London.
14. Ibid.
15. Information from the Royal Brierley Archives.
16. Stevens and Williams Ltd. Advertisement, *The Pottery Gazette and Glass Trade Review*, 1 October 1932, p. 1242.
17. Buyers' Notes, *The Pottery Gazette and Glass Trade Review*, 2 April 1934, p.467.
18. Connolly, C., Household Glass, The Craftsmen Portfolio, *Architectural Review*, February 1933, p.86.
19. Gater, S., Keith Murray at Wedgwood. Architect and Ceramic Designer (1892-1981), *Studio Pottery*, No.22, September, 1996, pp.25-32.
20. Information from the Murray family, February 2000.
21. These pieces were illustrated in the *Decorative Art Studio Year Book* of 1932, p.97.
22. Information from the Ceramics and Glass Department, Victoria & Albert Museum, London.
23. Buyers' Notes, *The Pottery Gazette and Glass Trade Review*, 1 August

1933 p.973.
24. Information from the Wedgwood Archives.
25. Information from the Ceramics and Glass Department, Victoria & Albert Museum, London.
26. Minutes from Travellers Meetings, 4 October 1933, Wedgwood Museum.
27. Letter from Josiah Wedgwood to Keith Murray, dated 8 October 1933, Wedgwood Museum.
28. Minutes from Travellers Meetings, 24 April 1934, Wedgwood Museum.
29. Information from the Ceramics and Glass Department, Victoria & Albert Museum, London.
30. Information taken from *Wedgwood in London, 225th Anniversary Exhibition 1759-1985*, Josiah Wedgwood and Sons Ltd, p.58.
31. Buyers' Notes, *The Pottery Gazette and Glass Trade Review*, 1 February 1935, p.221.
32. A Great Designer, *New Zealand News*, 25 June 1935.
33. Buyers' Notes, *The Pottery Gazette and Glass Trade Review*, 1 June 1936, p.791.
34. Buyers' Notes, *The Pottery Gazette and Glass Trade Review*, 1 October 1936, p.1371 and p.1376.
35. This piece is illustrated in *British Art and Design 1900-1960*, Victoria & Albert Museum, 1983, pp.154-155.
36. Gater, S., Keith Murray at Wedgwood, Architect and Ceramic Designer (1892-1981), *Studio Pottery*, No.22, p.30.
37. Buyers' Notes, The Pottery Gazette and Glass Trade Review, 1 October 1936, p.1376.
38. Information from The World of Keith Murray: Surface Patterns, *Etruria*, The Wedgwood International Society, Vol.3, No.4, pp.14-15.
39. Information from the Royal Society of Arts, London, February 2000.
40. *The Pottery Gazette and Glass Trade Review*, 1 October 1936, p.1376.
41. Wilson, N., Tribute to architect of Barlaston and his ceramic designs, *Wedgwood Review*, September 1981, p.10.
42. Crossingham-Bell, G., Pottery Pure and Simple, *Art and Antiques*, 22 May 1976, pp.25-27.
43. Design Casebook, *Pottery and Glass*, October 1948, pp.41-42.
44. Expansion of Wedgwood's London Showroom, *Pottery Gazette and Glass Trade Review*, June 1957, pp.784-785.
45. Information from the Murray family, February 2000.
46. Obituary: Mary Beatrice De Carteret Murray, *The Times*, 14 October 1995.
47. Prestressed Concrete Hangars at London Airport, *The Builder*, 7 November 1952, pp.650-651.
48. Buildings in Oxford, *Architectural Review*, Vol.127, January 1960, p.275.
49. Information from the Murray family, February 2000.
50. Wilson, N., Tribute to architect of Barlaston and his ceramic designs, *Wedgwood Review*, September 1981, p.10.
51. Ibid.

Chapter 10 – Eric Ravilious

1. For a more thorough account of Eric Ravilious' upbringing see: Binyon, H., *Eric Ravilious: Memoir of an Artist*, Lutterworth Press, 1983.
2. Information taken from: *Eric Ravilious*, The Minories, January to February 1972, exhibition catalogue.
3. Ibid.
4. Binyon, H., *Eric Ravilious: Memoir of an Artist*, Lutterworth Press, 1983, p.33.
5. Ibid, p.35.
6. Rothenstein, J., The Mural Decorations at Morley College, *The Studio*, 1930, pp. 429-432.
7. These murals are illustrated in: Binyon, H., *Eric Ravilious, Memoir of an Artist*, Lutterworth Press, 1983, p.55.
8. For further information on the glass designs by Eric Ravilious see : Dodsworth, R., *Glass between the Wars*, Dudley Leisure Services, 1987.
9. Gater, S., Eric Ravilious – A Designer Ahead of his Time, *Studio Pottery*, No.24, Dec. 1996/Jan., 1997.
10. Letter from Eric Ravilious to Helen Binyon, 10 July 1936.
11. Letter from Eric Ravilious to Helen Binyon, 19 August 1936.
12. Gater, S., Eric Ravilious – A Designer Ahead of his Time, *Studio Pottery*, No.24, Dec. 1996/Jan., 1997.
13. Binyon, H., *Eric Ravilious: Memoir of an Artist*, Lutterworth Press, 1983, p.88.
14. Skellern, V., *lectures on Wedgwood*, unpublished 1957, Wedgwood Museum, Barlaston.
15. Information from the Ravilious family, January 2000.
16. Advertisement, *Decorative Art Studio Year Book* 1939.
17. Information from the Wedgwood Museum, Josiah Wedgwood and Sons Ltd., Barlaston, Stoke-on-Trent.
18. Letter to Eric Ravilious from Josiah Wedgwood V, 1 June 1937, p.1.
19. Ibid.
20. Ibid.
21. Letter to Eric Ravilious from Victor Skellern, 11 November 1938.
22. Information from *Ravilious and Wedgwood: The Complete Wedgwood Designs of Eric Ravilious*, Dalrymple Press, 1986, p.48.
23. Letter to Eric Ravilious from Josiah Wedgwood V, 1 June 1937, p.1.
24. Letter to Eric Ravilious from Tom Wedgwood V, June 1938.
25. Letter to Eric Ravilious from Victor Skellern, 11 October 1938.

26. The artwork for this pattern is illustrated in *Ravilious and Wedgwood: The Complete Wedgwood Designs of Eric Ravilious*, Dalrymple Press, 1986, pp.36-37.
27. Information from the Wedgwood Museum, Josiah Wedgwood and Sons Ltd., Barlaston, Stoke-on-Trent.

Chapter 11 – A.B. Read

1. Hawkins, J., *The Poole Potteries*, Barrie and Jenkins, 1980, p.155.
2. Decoration, Architectural Supplement, *Architectural Review*, Jan/June 1935, pp.33-36.
3. Obituary: Mr. A. B. Read, Lighting Design Pioneer, *The Times*, 17 October 1973, p.23.
4. Ibid, pp.18-19.
5. Information from the archives of the Ceramics and Glass Department, Victoria & Albert Museum, London, February 2000.
6. Gloag, J., Modernity with Manners, *The Architect and Building News*, 8 January 1932.
7. Holland, R., Developments at Poole Pottery, *Ceramics*, September 1962.
8. Atterbury, P., *Poole in the Fifties* (exhib. cat.), Richard Dennis, 1997, p.6.
9. These items are illustrated in: Hayward, L., *Poole Pottery: Carter and Company and their Successors 1873-1995*, Richard Dennis, 1995, p.99.
10. Design Overseas, *Design*, No.34, October 1951, p.25.
11. These are illustrated in Hayward, L., *Poole Pottery: Carter and Company and their Successors 1873-1995*, Richard Dennis, 1995, p.109.
12. Information taken from a presentation by David Queensberry to the Poole Collectors' Club, 28 September 1996, p.5. Information from Leslie Hayward.
13. Poole Ware in Pitt-Rivers Museum, *The Western Gazette*, 1 October 1954.
14. Atterbury, P., *Poole in the Fifties* (exhib. cat.) Richard Dennis, 1997, p.7.
15. For further information on the work of Ann Read and Ruth Pavely see: Hayward, L., *Poole Pottery: Carter and Company and their Successors 1873-1995*, Richard Dennis, 1995, pp.105-109.
16. Obituary: Mr. A.B. Read, Lighting Design Pioneer, *The Times*, 17 October 1973, p.23.
17. Information taken from a presentation by David Queensberry to the Poole Collectors' Club, 28 September 1996, p.5. Information from Leslie Hayward.

Chapter 12 – Jessie Tait

1. Jessie Tait in conversation with the author, January 1999.
2. Forty Years of Expansion, W.R. Midwinter Ltd, *Pottery and Glass*, October 1952, p.66.
3. Buyers' Notes, *Pottery Gazette and Glass Trade Review*, 1 October 1928, p.1595.
4. A Notable Burslem Potter, *Pottery Gazette and Glass Trade Review*, March 1952, p.422.
5. Recording of interview with Roy Midwinter by Ann Eatwell, 1984.
6. Welcome to British Coupe Ware, *Pottery Gazette and Glass Trade Review*, February 1953, p.252.
7. Problems of Pioneering Pottery, *Pottery Gazette and Glass Trade Review*, April 1964, p.456.
8. Recording of interview with Roy Midwinter by Ann Eatwell, 1984.
9. Jessie Tait in conversation with the author, January 1999.
10. Welcome to British Coupe Ware, *Pottery Gazette and Glass Trade Review*, February 1953, p.253.
11. Recording of interview with Roy Midwinter by Ann Eatwell, 1984.
12. Welcome to British Coupe Ware, *Pottery Gazette and Glass Trade Review*, February 1953, p.253.
13. A Studio Pottery in Hanley, *Pottery Gazette and Glass Trade Review*, October 1953, pp.1494-6.
14. Examples are illustrated in: Jenkins, S., *Midwinter Modern: A Revolution in Tableware*, Richard Dennis, 1997, p.49.
15. Keeping Ahead with Contemporary Designs: New Midwinter range for home and export, *Pottery Gazette and Glass Trade Review*, June 1955, p.913.
16. A Potter at Home: A visit to Woodville, Oulton, Staffs., *Pottery Gazette and Glass Trade Review*, August 1958, pp.971-2.
17. Company advertisement, *Decorative Art Studio Year Book*, 1957-1958.
18. Harmony and Contrast, *Pottery Gazette and Glass Trade Review*, July 1956.
19. These are illustrated in: Jenkins, S., *Midwinter Modern: A Revolution in Tableware*, Richard Dennis, 1997, p.16 and p.59.
20. Queensberry Range by Midwinter: A New Tableware for Modern Tastes, *Pottery Gazette and Glass Trade Review*, August 1962, pp.945-9.
21. Midwinter's Accent, *Tableware International*, April 1972, p.30.
22. Midwinter's New China Shape, *The Gift Buyer*, 1962, pp.17-20.
23. Midwinter's Accent, *Tableware International*, April 1972, p.30.
24. Problems of Pioneering Pottery, *Pottery Gazette and Glass Trade Review*, April 1964, p.456.
25. Midwinter's Accent, *Tableware International*, April 1972, p.30.
26. Letter from Dick Fletcher, December 1998.
27. Introducing MQ2 by Midwinter, *Pottery Gazette and Glass Trade Review*, September 1967, p.875.
28. J. & G. Meakin Ltd. Press Release, October 1967. Information from the Wedgwood Museum, Josiah Wedgwood and Sons Ltd., Barlaston, Stoke-on-Trent.
29. Letter from Dick Fletcher, December 1998.

30. Blackpool Fair 21, *Pottery Gazette and Glass Trade Review* incorporating *Tableware*, February 1970, p.86.
31. Make the Meal Time Breakthrough, Advertising leaflet produced by J. & G. Meakin, 1972.
32. Wedgwood to acquire Meakin and Midwinter (Holdings), *Pottery Gazette and Glass Trade Review* incorporating *Tableware*, April 1970, p.39.
33. Midwinter's Accent, *Tableware International*, April 1972, p.30.
34. Jessie Tait in conversation with the author, September 1999.
35. David Johnson in conversation with the author, August 1999.
36. Johnson Originals: Casual Elegance at a reasonable price, *Tableware International*, September 1976, p.20.
37. Ibid.
38. Jessie Tait in conversation with the author, September 1998.
39. Niblett, K., *Dynamic Design, The British Pottery Industry 1940-1990*, Stoke-on-Trent City Museum and Art Gallery, 1990.
40. The Story of Johnson Brothers, Press Release, May 1983. Information from the Wedgwood Museum, Josiah Wedgwood and Sons Ltd., Barlaston, Stoke-on-Trent.
41. Information from Jessie Tait, August 1998.
42. Cover Story, *Housewares*, March 1992, p.3.

Chapter 13 – Kathie Winkle

1. Hopwood, I., and Hopwood, G., *The Shorter Connection*, Richard Dennis, 1992.
2. Letter from Kathie Winkle, March 1998.
3. Transformation at Broadhursts, *Pottery Gazette and Glass Trade Review*, November 1956, pp.1607-1610.
4. For a more detailed account of the company's history see Hampson, R., *Churchill China: Great British Potters 1795*, University of Keele, 1994.
5. James Broadhurst New Showroom, *Pottery Gazette and Glass Trade Review*, February 1957, p.272.
6. Letter from Kathie Winkle, March 1998.
7. Letter from Michael Roper, March 1998.
8. Advertisement, *Pottery Gazette and Glass Trade Review*, January 1958, p.41.
9. Company Advertisement, *Pottery Gazette and Glass Trade Review*, February 1963, p.122.
10. Company Advertisement, *Pottery Gazette and Glass Trade Review*, February 1964, p.1277.
11. Letter from Kathie Winkle, March 1998.
12. Diary, *Pottery Gazette and Glass Trade Review*, February 1964, p.246.
13. Diary, *Pottery Gazette and Glass Trade Review*, July 1964, p.752.
14. Letter from Kathie Winkle, March 1998.
15. Company Advertisement, *Pottery Gazette Reference Book 1964*, p.159.
16. Company Advertisement, *Pottery Gazette and Glass Trade Review*, April 1965, p.468.
17. Letter from Kathie Winkle, March 1998.
18. Broadhurst Export activities, *Pottery Gazette and Glass Trade Review* incorporating *Tableware*, February 1969, p.228.
19. Topical Tableware and Gifts, *Pottery Gazette and Glass Trade Review*, March 1968, p.304.
20. Trade and Industry, *Tableware International*, August 1972, p.66.
21. Healacraft and British Pottery, *Pottery Gazette and Glass Trade Review* incorporating *Tableware*, March 1969, p.295.
22. Company advertisement, *Pottery Gazette and Glass Trade Review* incorporating *Tableware Reference Book*, December 1969, p.30.
23. Company advertisement from the archives of Churchill Ltd.
24. Letter from Kathie Winkle, September 1997.
25. *Tableware International*, February 1973, p.115.
26. Hampson, R., *Churchill China: Great British Potters since 1795*, University of Keele, 1994, p.111.
27. Letter from Kathie Winkle, March 1998.

Chapter 14 – John Clappison

1. Information from Dr. J.E.S. Walker, Hornsea Museum, December 1999.
2. For further information on the history of the Hornsea Pottery: Heckford, B., *Hornsea Pottery 1949-1989 – Its People, Processes and Products*, Hornsea Pottery Collectors and Research Society, 1998.
3. Information from Dr. J.E.S. Walker, Hornsea Museum, December 1999.
4. John Clappison in conversation with the author, January 2000.
5. Highlights of Blackpool, *Pottery and Glass*, March 1957, p.89.
6. Blackpool Fair, *Pottery and Glass*, January 1958, p.11.
7. Information from John Clappison, April 2000.
8. Advertisement, *Pottery Gazette and Glass Trade Review*, January 1958, p.43.
9. John Clappison in conversation with the author, January 2000.
10. Michael Walker in conversation with the author, December 1999.
11. Information from John Clappison, March 2000.
12. New to Design Centre, *Pottery and Glass*, January 1962, p.61.
13. Design at Hornsea, *Pottery Gazette and Glass Trade Review*, July 1963, pp.763-766.
14. Michael Walker in conversation with the author, December 1999.
15. Information from Dr. J.E.S. Walker, Hornsea Museum, December 1999.

16. Hornsea installs automatic glazing, *Ceramics*, May 1968, pp.26-27.
17. Party trips boost pottery sales, *Pottery Gazette and Glass Trade Review* incorporating *Tableware*, August 1970, pp.20-21.
18. Information from John Clappison, March 2000.
19. John and his Magic Box, *Ravenhead News*, No.3, September 1974.
20. Information from John Clappison, March 2000.
21. Ibid.

Chapter 15 – Eve Midwinter

1. Eve Midwinter in conversation with the author, August 1997.
2. Letter from Dick Fletcher, December 1998.
3. Norman Tempest in conversation with the author, March 1999.
4. Eve Midwinter in conversation with the author, March 1997.
5. Jenkins, S., *Midwinter Modern: A Revolution in British Tableware*, Richard Dennis 1997, p. 59.
6. Letter from Norman Tempest, March 1999.
7. Eve Midwinter in conversation with the author, January 1999.
8. Letter from Norman Tempest, March 1999.
9. The J. & G. Meakin Ltd. pattern books are held at the Wedgwood Museum, Josiah Wedgwood and Sons Ltd.
10. Eve Midwinter in conversation with the author, August 1997.
11. Norman Tempest in conversation with the author, April 1999.
12. *Design* magazine, September 1972, No. 285, p.78.
13. Midwinter leaflet, Wedgwood Museum, Josiah Wedgwood and Sons Ltd.
14. These patterns are illustrated in Jenkins, S., *Midwinter Modern: A Revolution in British Tableware*, Richard Dennis 1997, pp.68-69.
15. Midwinter advertisement, *Tableware International*, February 1976, p.121.
16. Robin Welch in conversation with the author, March 1997.
17. Midwinter's Ascent, *Tableware International*, April 1972, p.30.
18. Robin Welch in conversation with the author, March 1997.
19. John Ryan in conversation with the author, April 1998.
20. Stoneware: The Body Beautiful, *Tableware International*, May 1981, p.17.
21. Elizabeth Benn, All Fresh for a new look at tableware, *The Daily Telegraph*, 23 August 1983.
22. Style leaflet, Wedgwood Museum, Josiah Wedgwood & Sons Ltd.
23. Eve Midwinter in conversation with the author, August 1997.
24. Midwinter, The Bizarre Collection : Clarice Cliff leaflet, 1985.
25. Lynn Boyd in conversation with the author, July 1999.
26. John Ryan in conversation with the author, January 1999.
27. Eve Midwinter in conversation with the author, August 1997.
28. Lynn Boyd in conversation with the author, July 1999.
29. Bergesen, V., *Encyclopaedia of British Art Pottery*, Barrie and Jenkins, 1991.
30. Eve Midwinter in conversation with the author, August 1998.
31. Norman Tempest in conversation with the author, January 1999.
32. Information from Julie Pople, May 1999.
33. Margaret Brindley in conversation with the author, February 1997.

Chapter 16 – Robert Jefferson

1. Information from: Lyons, H., and Boston, N., Exhibition of Poole Pottery Studio in the Sixties, February 1993, New Century, 69 Kensington Church Street, London, p.9.
2. RCA designs on show, *Design*, October 1952, pp.22-23.
3. RCA designs on show, *Design*, August 1953, p.32.
4. Information from the Royal College of Art Archives.
5. Information from: Lyons, H., and Boston, N., Exhibition of Poole Pottery Studio in the Sixties, February 1993, New Century, 69 Kensington Church Street, London, p.9.
6. News, Nautical Pottery, *Design*, November 1954, p.42.
7. Information from Rena Jefferson, March 2000.
8. Jefferson, R., Problems facing the Pottery Designer, *Pottery and Glass*, December 1957, pp.398-399.
9. Ibid, p.398.
10. Information from Rena Jefferson, March 2000.
11. Adams., J., Potters Parade, *Pottery and Glass*, July 1951, p.72.
12. Information from Leslie Hayward, March 2000.
13. Tableware Designers: Bob Jefferson, *Tableware*, May 1963, pp.375-383.
14. Robert Jefferson, Designer at Poole, *Euro-Ceramic*, Germany, 12 August 1964.
15. Decorated Ovenware by Poole, *Pottery and Glass*, July 1962, p.545.
16. Good, E., Plain or Fancy, *The Sunday Times*, 14 April 1963.
17. Potters look to their Packaging, *Pottery and Glass*, September 1962, p.727.
18. Information taken from: Hayward, L., Delphis Development 1963-1966, unpublished paper.
19. Ibid.
20. Adams, J., Potters Parade, *Pottery and Glass*, October 1950.
21. Delphis Collection, *Tableware*, November 1963, p.786.
22. Information from Leslie Hayward, April 2000.
23. Poole Pottery press release, October 1963.
24. Ibid.
25. Ibid.
26. Poole Pottery sales catalogue, 1964.
27. Ibid.

28. Tate, C., Delphis Production 1964-1970, *Poole Pottery Collectors Club Magazine*, Winter 1995, p.10.
29. Robert Jefferson, Designer at Poole, *Euro-Ceramic*, Germany, 12 August 1964.
30. For further information on this period see: Hayward, L., *Poole Pottery and their Successors, 1873-1995*, Richard Dennis, 1995.
31. Information from Peter Barnes, Purbeck Pottery Ltd., March 2000.
32. Philip Barnes in conversation with the author, March 2000.
33. Purbeck Pottery gets into production, *Pottery Gazette and Glass Trade Review* incorporating *Tableware*, March 1967, pp.329-331.
34. Information from Peter Barnes, March 2000.
35. Sergeant, M., A Tribute to Robert Jefferson, Royal Doulton International Collectors' Society, Autumn 1998.
36. Style for Catering, *Tableware International*, May 1980.
37. Information from Leslie Hayward, March 2000.
38. Sergeant, M., A Tribute to Robert Jefferson, Royal Doulton International Collectors' Society, Autumn 1998.

Chapter 17 – Susan Williams-Ellis

1. Information from the Portmeirion Potteries Ltd. archive.
2. Hayward, L., *Poole Pottery, Carter & Company and their Successors 1873-1995*, Richard Dennis Ltd., p.169.
3. Jenkins, S., and McKay, S., *Portmeirion Pottery*, Richard Dennis, 2000, p.11.
4. This rug is illustrated in *Design* magazine, January 1958, No.109, p.59.
5. These items are illustrated in: Jenkins, S., and McKay, S., *Portmeirion Pottery*, Richard Dennis, 2000, p.33.
6. Information from the Portmeirion Potteries Ltd. archive.
7. Ibid.
8. The House of Gray, *Pottery Gazette and Glass Trade Review*, May 1953, pp.732-733.
9. Lustre, *Pottery and Glass*, July 1956, pp.220-223.
10. Information from Anwyl Cooper-Willis, February 1999.
11. Information from Stephen McKay, February 1998.
12. Letter from Ronald Bailey, September 1997.
13. Letter from Euan Cooper-Willis, February 1999.
14. The New Gray's Pottery, *Pottery and Glass*, June 1961, p.494.
15. Malachite Pottery by Portmeirion, *Pottery Gazette and Glass Trade Review*, June 1960, p.784.
16. Information from the Portmeirion Potteries Ltd. archive.
17. Room of My Own: Susan Williams-Ellis, *Sunday Observer*, 23 September 1990.
18. Roberts, C., A Woman among the Potters, *Six Towns Magazine*, June 1965, p.31.
19. Buyers' Guide, *Pottery and Glass*, March 1961, p.232.
20. Gray's Pottery advertisement, *Pottery and Glass*, August 1961, p.605-607.
21. Ibid.
22. A special boxed set was illustrated in: *Pottery and Glass*, February 1961, p.147.
23. This pattern is illustrated in Jenkins, S., and McKay, S., *Portmeirion Pottery*, Richard Dennis, 2000, p.11.
24. A.E. Gray and Co. Ltd., Knightsbridge Showroom, *Pottery Gazette and Glass Trade Review*, March 1961, p.386.
25. The New Gray's Pottery, *Pottery and Glass*, June 1961, pp.492-494.
26. Letter from Ronald Bailey, September 1997.
27. Room of My Own: Susan Williams-Ellis, *Sunday Observer*, 23 September 1990, *The Guardian* ©
28. Reflections on Blackpool, *Pottery and Glass*, March 1962, p.241.
29. Buyers' Guide, *Pottery and Glass*, March 1962.
30. Eve Midwinter in conversation with the author, August 1998.
31. Euan Cooper-Willis in conversation with the author, August 1997.
32. Blackpool Fair, *Pottery and Glass*, March 1964.
33. Born April 23, 1564, *Pottery Gazette and Glass Trade Review*, April 1964, p.430.
34. These patterns are illustrated in: Jenkins, S., and McKay, S., *Portmeirion Pottery*, Richard Dennis, 2000, p.47.
35. Information from Stephen McKay, April 2000.
36. Gifts, *Pottery Gazette and Glass Trade Review* incorporating *Tableware*, September 1967, p. 863.
37. Information from Eve Midwinter, August 1998.
38. Roberts, C., A Woman among the Potters, *Six Towns Magazine*, June 1965, p.30.
39. Holland Park Showroom, Portmeirion and Dartington, *Pottery Gazette and Glass Trade Review* incorporating *Tableware*, October 1967, pp.974-975.
40. Definitely Different at Portmeirion Potteries, *Pottery Gazette and Glass Trade Review* incorporating *Tableware*, October 1969, p.816.
41. Room of My Own: Susan Williams-Ellis, *Sunday Observer*, 23 September 1990, *The Guardian* ©
42. For further information on *Botanic Garden* see: Jenkins, S., and McKay, S., *Portmeirion Pottery*, Richard Dennis, 2000.
43. Susan Williams-Ellis in conversation with the author, August 1997.
44. *Portmeirion Collectors' Club News*, Vol. 2, No.2, September 1994.
45. Information from Anwyl Cooper-Willis, August 1999.
46. Portmeirion Expands Stateside, *Tableware International*, February 1985, p.146-147.
47. Retailers leaflet, Portmeirion Potteries Ltd.

DIRECTORY OF DESIGNERS

ADAMS, John (1882-1953)

Adams was born in the Stoke-on-Trent area. He studied at the Stoke School of Art, later working at a tile works and then joining the studio of the potter Bernard Moore. In 1909 he gained one of ten scholarships to study at the Royal College of Art. Between 1912-14 he taught at the RCA where he met and married Truda Sharp (Carter). In 1914 he took the position as Head of School of Art at Durban Technical College in South Africa. In 1921 he returned to Britain to form a business partnership with Harold Stabler and Cyril Carter, called Carter, Stabler and Adams. During the twenties and thirties he produced a wide range of shapes, patterns and glazes for the company, including the *Streamline* tableware in 1936. During the early fifties he contributed several articles to the trade press on pottery design and production.

See: Hayward, L., *Poole Pottery, Carter & Company and their Successors, 1873-1995*, Richard Dennis (1995).

ARNOLD, Tom, RCA, MSIA

Arnold studied industrial ceramics at the Royal College of Art. In 1953 he joined Booth and Colcloughs, part of the Ridgway Group, where he produced patterns for bone china shapes, including *Bluebells*, and in 1953 modelled a figure of Queen Elizabeth II that was decorated by the designer Enid Seeney. They also collaborated on a contemporary ceramic chess set, however neither of these items went into production. Following a trip to North America he was inspired to design the Sapphire shape range. This shape was later made on earthenware and renamed Metro. Arnold became Art Director when the branches of the company were brought together. He left Ridgway's in 1960 to join Empire Porcelain Co., based in Shelton, Stoke-on-Trent, where he designed a range of contemporary patterns including *Mirage* and an oven-to-tableware range called *Caldor*. Arnold also acted as design consultant to several pottery companies, including Gibson & Sons Ltd. For this company he designed the Roulette tableware shapes in about 1965. In 1963 he joined the Council of Industrial Design Committee. During the sixties he worked for a number of companies, including T.G. Green and Royal Crown Derby. In 1960 he became Deputy Head of Wolverhampton College of Art. He also designed a number of new shapes and patterns for the Armed Forces. Hostess shape 1967.

See: Moss, S., *Homemaker: A 1950's Design Classic*, Cameron and Hollis (1997) and Tom Arnold, *Tableware*, April 1962, p.301.

BAWDEN, Edward, CBE, RA, RDI (1903-1989)

Born in Braintree, Essex. He studied at the Cambridge School of Art from 1919 and then at the Royal College of Art between 1922-25. He was a prolific artist, illustrator and designer for book illustration, posters for London Passenger Transport Board, wallpaper designs for Cole & Son and a textile designer. From 1930-40 he taught at the Royal Academy of Art. Bawden was also a war artist. He undertook design work for Josiah Wedgwood and Sons Ltd. from about 1946. From a range of trials one of his patterns was selected for the New Zealand Shipping Line. This was followed in 1952 with Bawden's *Heartsease* pattern for the Orient Shipping Line. In 1948 he was made a Royal Designer for Industry.

See: McCarthy, F., and Nuttgens, P., *Eye for Industry: Royal Designers for Industry 1936-1986*, Lund Humphries (1986) and Batkin, M., *Wedgwood Ceramics 1846-1959*, Richard Dennis (1982).

BEARDMORE, Freda (fl.1930-40s)

Beardmore was probably born and raised in the Stoke-on-Trent area. She studied on a full time basis at the Burslem School of Art from 1926. Two years later she joined Josiah Wedgwood and Sons Ltd. as a trainee paintress. In 1930 she joined Maddox in Burslem for a short period and then took a position as designer at E. Brain and Co. Ltd. During the thirties she designed a wide range of modern patterns including *Oakleaf* and *Harebell*. Beardmore co-ordinated the submission of designs by outside artists such as Henry Moore, Graham Sutherland and Vanessa Bell for the experimental project of artists in industry. These ranges, in bone china, alongside those co-ordinated by Clarice Cliff, were exhibited at the Modern Art for the Table exhibition in 1934. Beardmore showed her work alongside that of *Sherwood, Feathers and Carillon*. Beardmore submitted a number of her own designs for this exhibition. In 1935 she was commissioned by the London store Selfridges to design a range of nursery wares. Beardmore continued to work for E. Brain and Co. Ltd. until after the War. In 1947 she decided to retire to look after her new family and later turned to teaching.

See: Buckley, C., *Potters and Paintresses, Women Designers in the Pottery Industry 1870-1955*, Women's Press (1990).

BRANGYWN, Sir Frank, RA (1867-1956)

Throughout his life Brangwyn was an accomplished painter and muralist. During the 1880s he was employed by William Morris designing tapestries. His paintings were exhibited widely and received considerable acclaim. He first exhibited at the Royal Academy in 1885 and in 1904 became an Associate of the RA. During that year he started to develop mural panels for Skinners Hall that took five years to complete. In 1926 he produced murals for the House of Lords and in 1932 murals for the Rockefeller Center in New York City. By the early thirties he was also distinguished for his work in stained glass, designs for furniture, chenille carpets and textiles. Examples of these were exhibited at E. Pollard and Co. Ltd. From about 1930 he designed a number of tablewares for Royal Doulton. His patterns and shapes, including vases, ashtrays, tea and coffee services, plaques, covered boxes and lamp bases, were marketed under the name Brangwyn Ware. His most popular pattern was *Harvest*, a subtle design depicting stylised fruits. A tea set for twelve retailed for £3 3s 0d in about 1930. Of particular note was the series of plaques that he designed for the Modern Art for the Table Exhibition at Harrods in 1934. The complex patterns submitted were originally intended for a scheme to decorate the Royal Gallery of the House of Lords in London in 1925. Unfortunately these were rejected by the Royal Fine Art Commission but they were later used for a new Guildhall in Wales in 1934. These plaques, produced by A.J. Wilkinson Ltd., required great skill to produce and therefore proved expensive, so few were sold. A Brangywn Museum opened in Bruges in 1936. Five years later he was knighted. This was followed a year later by a retrospective exhibition at the Royal Academy and in 1967 a Centenary exhibition at the National

Museum of Wales.
See: *Thirties, British Art and Design before the War*, Hayward Gallery, exhibition catalogue (1979) and Griffin, L., Louis, K., and Meisel, S., *Clarice Cliff: The Bizarre Affair*, Thames and Hudson (1988).

BUTLER, John (1866-1935)
Little is known about John Butler. He is closely associated with the range of art wares produced by A.J. Wilkinson Ltd. during the early part of the century. He was Art Director for the firm and worked closely with Fred Ridgway. During the early part of the twentieth century he developed outstanding ranges that included *Tibetan* and *Oriflamme*, the latter dating from 1910. The progression of Clarice Cliff resulted in the production of the commercially successful Bizarre range by Clarice Cliff in 1928. Possibly in response to her success Butler produced his own range of modern wares that included *Aquatic* and *Tahiti*. As Clarice Cliff rose to prominence Butler left the company to take up a position as Art Director at Wood and Sons Ltd in 1930. He is thought to have designed tube-lined patterns for the company. He was tragically killed in 1935.
See: Griffin, L., *Clarice Cliff, The Art of Bizarre*, Pavilion Books (1999).

CASSON, Sir Hugh, CH, KCVO, RA (1910-1999)
Casson was trained at Eastbourne College and later at St. John's College in Cambridge. He attended the British School in Athens. In 1937 he was appointed as an architect, later becoming the Director of Architecture for the Festival of Britain in 1951. During that year Casson was elected to the faculty of the Royal Society of Arts. In 1952 he was knighted. During the fifties he was asked by Roy Midwinter, who had seen some of Casson's sketches for the Coronation route, to submit a pattern for the Midwinter range. Casson produced several sketches whilst on holiday in the south of France which formed the basis of his *Riviera* pattern on the Stylecraft shape, launched in 1953. The pattern proved so popular that it was later reproduced on the Fashion shape but renamed *Cannes*. In 1975 he was awarded an Honorary Doctorate from the Royal College of Art.
See: Peat, A., *Midwinter – A Collector's Guide*, Cameron and Hollis (1992).

COLLIDGE, Glynn (b.1922)
Collidge was born in Kilburn, London in July 1922. He was educated at Swanwick Hall Grammar School and then studied at the Burslem School of Art. In July 1938 he joined his father at Denby, a pottery company based in Derbyshire. During the Second World War he joined the Royal Air Force, afterwards returning to work for Denby. In 1956 he produced the Cheviot range of vases. A number of hand painted decorated vases and similar shapes were marketed as 'Glynn Ware'. He designed several patterns including *Hazelwood*, *Tapestry*, *Ferndale* and *Burlington*, from about 1960. He retired in 1983.
See: Hopwood, I., and Hopwood, G., *Denby Pottery*, Richard Dennis (1998).

CONRAN, Sir Terence (b.1931)
Conran was educated at Bryanston School and then at the Central School of Art and Design from 1947, studying textile design. During the fifties he undertook a number of important design commissions for fabrics, furniture and ceramics. For David Whitehead Ltd. he designed several textile patterns, including *Chequers* from 1951 and *Black Goblet* from 1953. He was invited to submit patterns for ceramics for W.R. Midwinter Ltd. These included *Nature Study* and *Chequers* from 1955, *Plant Life* from 1956 and *Melody* from 1958, all on the Fashion shape. During that year Conran and Roy Midwinter produced a range of saladware shapes that included a 'celery nest', a boomerang tray and a giant condiment set. He also designed a series of small trays printed with various motifs of aeroplanes, liners, trains and buses. In 1956 Conran redesigned the Midwinter showrooms. He also designed patterns for his own company, Conran Ceramics, including a range decorated with air balloons. In 1964 he formed Habitat, selling everything for the modern home. This venture proved so popular that several stores opened across the country. He also started to teach at the Royal College of Art. By 1971 he was the Chairman of the Conran Design Group. He was knighted in 1983 for his achievements in design and retailing.
See: Jenkins, S., *Midwinter Pottery – A Revolution in British Tableware*, Richard Dennis (1997).

DAVIES (*née* GIBBONS), Peggy (1923-1989)
Born in the Potteries area. At the age of twelve she took up a scholarship to attend the Burslem School of Art. In 1935, at the age of fourteen, she joined A.J. Wilkinson Ltd. as an assistant modeller to Clarice Cliff at the Newport Pottery, undertaking a wide range of work including modelling face masks. At the same time she continued her evening classes at the local schools of art. Davies later worked for about a year at W.R. Midwinter Ltd. producing a range of Nursery Wares. From 1938 she was designer for Royal Doulton Ltd. She modelled birds and animals and later, after the War, produced over 200 figures including *Home Again* from 1956 and *Bunny* from 1960. From 1945 she worked as a free-lance designer. Davies was also an accomplished portrait painter.
See: Buckley, C., *Potters and Paintresses, Women Designers in the Pottery Industry 1870-1955*, Women's Press (1990).

DAY, Lucienne, RDI (b.1917)
Day was born in Croydon. Following her training at the Croydon School of Art she studied at the Royal College of Art from 1937-40. For a brief period she taught at the Beckenham School of Art. Whilst at the RCA she met, and later married, Robin Day. She made an outstanding and influential contribution to textile design during the immediate post-war period and throughout the sixties. Her well known *Calyx* design for Heal's is now considered to be a design classic as are a number of her other patterns including *Spectators*, *Graphica* and *Herb Anthony*. Day also worked for the Edinburgh Weavers, John Lewis, John Line and other companies in Britain. She also designed carpets, wallpapers and tea cloths. Her international reputation led to a number of commissions from European companies such as Gebr. Rasch & Co. for wallpaper designs. Most important was the work she produced for Rosenthal Porzellan AG, based in Bavaria. Over a twelve year period she designed a number of stylised patterns on the Studio Line shape. Her patterns, echoing her textile designs, included *Bond Street*, *Regent Street*, *Odyssey* and *Four Seasons*. Day also produced patterns for flower blocks. In 1962 she was made a Royal Designer for Industry.
See: Harris, J., *Lucienne Day – A Career in Design*, Whitworth Art Gallery (1993).

FORSYTH, Gordon Mitchell, RI, ARCA, FRSA (1879-1952)
Forsyth was born in Fraserburgh, Aberdeenshire. He studied at the Robert Gordon's College and the Gray's School of Art, Aberdeen, then for three years at the Royal College of Art in London, gaining a Travelling Scholarship in Design to Italy in 1902. In 1905 he was appointed as Art Director at Minton, Hollins and Co., based in Manchester. In 1915 Forsyth became Art Director for Pilkington's Tile and Pottery Co., where he produced an outstanding range of lustre decorated vases, bowls

and other decorative wares. A number of these featured heraldic motifs. During the First World War Forsyth served with the Royal Air Force. In 1920 he became Superintendent of Art Education in the Potteries. During the early twenties he produced a number of lustre wares for A.E. Gray and Co. Ltd. under the Gloria Lustre range. These were exhibited in some of the most important expositions of the period, including the British Empire Exhibition in 1924. Forsyth was Art Adviser British Pottery Manufacturers' Federation. His publications included, '20th Century Ceramics' (1936) and a wide range of articles and industrial reports.
See: *Thirties, British Art and Design before the War*, Hayward Gallery, exhibition catalogue (1979) and Spours, J., *Art Deco Tableware*, Ward Lock (1988).

GOODEN, Robert York, RDI, ARIBA, FSIA (b.1909)

Born in Dorset, he was educated at Harrow School and then at the Architectural Association from 1926 to 1931. He travelled in Italy, Holland and Scandinavia. He was appointed assistant designer to Gordon Russell Ltd. in 1932. For many years he worked for a private architectural practice whilst working on a freelance basis for a number of companies. Gooden was a specialist in several areas of industrial and decorative arts including architecture, ceramics, glass and wallpaper. He designed domestic pressed glass for Chance Brothers Ltd., from 1934, and silverware for Wakeley and Wheeler Ltd. In 1940 he designed a number of vases and beakers, with a ribbed surface, for A.J. Wilkinson Ltd. under the direction of Clarice Cliff. Unlike the other designers and artists brought in to work for the company, his name was impressed into the ware. With the advent of the Second World War this range was not marketed until the first British Industries Fair in 1947. Gooden was consulting designer for this event. He was a Member of the Board of Trade Utility Furniture Design Panel 1945-47. In 1946 he designed the Sports Section for the Britain Can Make It exhibition and then the Unicorn Building, with R.D. Russell, for the Festival of Britain in 1951. Between 1948-74 he was Professor of Silversmithing and Jewellery at the Royal College of Art. In 1959 he was commissioned to design a pattern for a commemorative mug for Josiah Wedgwood and Sons Ltd. to celebrate the bicentenary of the company. In 1960 he designed the tableware for the first class restaurant for the P & O liner SS *Oriana*, manufactured by Wedgwood.
See: *Thirties, British Art and Design before the War*, Hayward Gallery, exhibition catalogue (1979). McCarthy, F., and Nuttgens, P., *Eye for Industry: Royal Designers for Industry 1936-1986*, Lund Humphries (1986).

GOODWIN, John (1867-1949)

Goodwin was the Art Director for Josiah Wedgwood and Sons Ltd. from 1904. Throughout his prestigious career with the company he produced many successful patterns and shapes. His outstanding range of shapes includes Colonial, Osier, Patrician and Edme. The latter shape, from 1908, is still in production. He inspired and assisted Daisy Makeig-Jones with the development of lustre wares. During the early thirties he developed, with Tom Wedgwood, the Annular shape. He designed many successful patterns during the thirties, including *Montreal* and *Ruby Tonquin*. He retired in 1934.
See: Reilly, R., *Wedgwood – The New Illustrated Dictionary*, Antique Collectors' Club Ltd. (1995).

HAGGAR, Reginald, ARCA, MSIA, FRSA (1905-1988)

Haggar was a well respected man in the pottery industry. He was born in Ipswich, Suffolk in 1905 and studied under Leonard Squirrel at the Ipswich School of Art. In 1929 he joined Minton, becoming assistant designer within six weeks and in 1935 the

Art Director. He produced an outstanding range of art deco vases, Les Vases Modernes, as well as a range of standard patterns such as *Alpha*, *Noah's Ark* and *Landscape*. The latter was exhibited at the British Art in Industry at the Royal Academy in 1935. Haggar left the company during that year. He was also an outstanding painter, showing at the Royal Academy in 1935, and produced hundreds of studies of the Potteries area including old pot banks and local places of interest over a number of years. He later designed a number of patterns for Johnson Brothers, including *A Country Scene* in 1947. He was also a consultant for the Campbell Tile Company. He retired in 1945 to teach full time.
See: Spours, J., *Art Deco Tableware*, Ward Lock (1988).

HASSALL, Thomas (1878-1940)

Hassall trained at the Burslem School of Art. In 1892 he joined Spode, at the age of fourteen. He became the Art Director in 1910. During the thirties he designed a number of successful patterns, many of these were simple banded borders in two colours. Some of his popular patterns included *Polka Dot* (1935), *Request*, *Mimosa*, *Wineberry* and *Kymono*. In 1939 he designed a fish hors d'oeuvres set.
See: Spours, J., *Art Deco Tableware*, Ward Lock (1988).

HOLDCROFT, Harold, FRSA, MSIAD (fl.1920-1960s)

Trained at the Burslem School of Art, later teaching there and also at Longton School of Art, on a part time basis. From 1920 he held the position as assistant to the Designer, becoming Design Director in 1929. Holdcroft joined Royal Albert, based in Longton and was appointed as works designer in 1934 with responsibility for introducing several successful patterns and some shape ranges. In 1962 he designed the well known *Old Country Roses* pattern, which has proved to be an enduring success.
See: Niblett, P., *Dynamic Designers – The British Pottery Industry 1940-1990*, City Museum and Art Gallery, Stoke-on-Trent (1990).

HOLDWAY, Harold (b.1913)

Holdway was born in Stoke-on-Trent. He studied at the Burslem School of Art from 1926, under Gordon Forsyth. He joined Spode in about 1933-34 as assistant to Tom Hassell. His range of patterns during the thirties included *Reindeer*, *Christmas Tree* and *Queen's Bird*. He also taught art evening classes at the local school of art. In 1940 he became the company's Art Director when Tom Hassall died. During the fifties he produced a wide range of contemporary patterns including *Oklahoma* on a modern coupe shape and *Strathmere*, a more traditional design influenced by Chinese art. During the fifties he produced the new Lincoln shape decorated with the *Gail* pattern specifically for the North American market. He also produced a wide range of fluted vases and small giftwares under the name Fortuna, that proved very popular. In 1976 Holdway became Art Director for Royal Worcester Spode Ltd., retiring in 1978.
See: Harold Holdway – Inspiration from China, *Pottery and Glass*, April 1957. Spours, J., *Art Deco Tableware*, Ward Lock (1988).

KNIGHT, Dame Laura, DBE, RA (1877-1970)

Born Laura Johnson in Long Eaton, Nottinghamshire, she trained at the Nottingham School of Art from 1892. In 1903 she married the painter, Harold Knight. She was a very accomplished painter and exhibited at the Royal Academy for many years, from 1903. In 1936 she became the first female Academician. Knight produced several posters for the London Underground between 1921 and 1957. She is well known for

her paintings of ballerinas and circus themes. During the thirties she designed patterns for glass for Stuart and Sons Ltd. In 1936 Josiah Wedgwood and Sons Ltd. commissioned her to design a loving cup for the Coronation of Edward VIII; this was quickly adapted for the Coronation of George VI for the following year. However her main work in ceramics was for the Exhibition of Contemporary Art for the Table at Harrods in 1934. She designed several patterns, including a notable dinner service, *Circus*, that depicted the various acts against a detailed border. The British film star Gracie Fields bought a complete dinner service during this period; this is now in the collection of Manchester City Art Gallery. Other designs for this project included *Cupids*, *Plumes* and *White Dove*. During the Second World War she was an Official War Artist. In 1965 the Royal Academy staged a retrospective exhibition of her work.
See: *Thirties, British Art and Design before the War*, Hayward Gallery, exhibition catalogue (1979). Green, O., *Underground Art, London Transport Posters 1908 to Present Day*, Studio Vista (1990).

LEDGER, Joseph W., ARCA (b.1926)
Ledger studied at the Royal College of Art, specialising in mural painting. After gaining a travel scholarship he studied at the Beaux Arts in Paris, becoming interested in Romanesque painting and stained glass. He later taught mural painting at the Brighton College of Art and then Design at the Kensington Art School. From the early fifties he undertook design commissions for Carter & Co. Ltd., based in Dorset. He produced the outstanding faience panel *Europa and the Bull* for the Building Trades Exhibition in 1953. In 1955 he completed a mural for the Poole Pottery depicting the various important aspects in the production of decorated pottery. From 1955 until 1989 he was Design Director at Royal Doulton Ltd. He produced a range of contemporary figures, including several teenage girls that were stylistically different from the company's previous styles and were known as 'The Ledger Ladies'. He worked closely with Robert Jefferson during this period. From 1989 he was a consultant designer to Royal Crown Derby Ltd.
See: Dennis, R., *Jo Ledger at Poole Pottery*, Poole Collectors' Club Newsletter, Spring, 1996.

LEIGH, Mabel (1915-1996)
Born in January 1915, she trained at the Burslem School of Art. She then worked at Royal Cauldon Pottery where she completed her apprenticeship under the designer Jack Price. When Cauldon closed down she was offered a position as designer at Shorter and Sons Ltd. At the age of eighteen she was given her own studio to work on designs in 1933. She produced many original patterns advertised as Period Pottery. For inspiration she looked to the Middle East, Africa and Central America. Her patterns included *Medina*, *Moresque*, *Algerian*, *Espanol* and *Samarkand*. Furthermore she had the opportunity of designing shapes for her patterns. However after only two or three years she left the company to work with Charlotte Rhead at Crown Ducal Ltd. After the Second World War she worked for Royal Winton. She retired in 1964.
See: Hopwood, I., and Hopwood, G., *The Shorter Connection*, Richard Dennis (1992) and Hopwood, I., and Hopwood, G., Fired with Enthusiasm (Obituary), *The Guardian*, 7 February (1996).

MACHIN, Arnold, OBE, RA (b.1911)
Born in Stoke-on-Trent, he joined Minton as an apprentice painter. He studied under Eric Owen at the Stoke School of Art. For a period he worked for Royal Crown Derby as a decorator. Following a full time course at Derby School of Art he gained a

scholarship to attend the Royal College of Art from 1937. From 1940 he was employed as a full time modeller for Josiah Wedgwood and Sons Ltd. His range included *Taurus the Bull*, *Sea Nymph*, *Ferdinand the Bull* and *Bridal Group*. He also produced a range of pottery figures that included *The Placer* and *The Thrower*. During the fifties he taught at the local schools of art. In the 1960s he designed the new coinage. He became an OBE in 1964.
See: Reilly, R., *Wedgwood – The New Illustrated Dictionary*, Antique Collectors' Club Ltd. (1995).

MELBOURNE, Colin (fl.1978-94)
Studied at the Burslem School of Art. He won a scholarship to attend the Royal College of Art. During the fifties he designed a a range of modelled figures for W.R. Midwinter Ltd. He also designed for John Beswick Ltd. In particular he produced a range of stylised vases and figures of animals under the banner CM. During the sixties he became a consultant for Crown Devon Ltd. He designed a number of shapes for them including the outstanding Memphis range. Between 1958 and 1986 he was Head of Ceramics at Stoke-on-Trent College of Art. In 1978 he modelled *The Hands of the Potter* in a limited edition of 500 for Josiah Wedgwood and Sons Ltd. From 1986 he was Head of the new Sir Henry Doulton Sculpture School in Fenton, Stoke-on-Trent.
See: Niblett, K., *Dynamic Designers – The British Pottery Industry 1940-1990*, City Museum and Art Gallery, Stoke-on-Trent (1990).

MINKIN, Robert, Des. RCA, FSIAD (b.1928)
Minkin trained at the Wimbledon College of Art followed by three years at the Royal College of Art. In 1955 he joined Josiah Wedgwood and Sons Ltd., becoming Wedgwood Senior Designer in 1966 and Design Director in 1979. He produced several successful patterns such as *Ice Rose*, *Sunflower*, *Summer Rose*, *Box Hill* and an outstanding black basalt coffee set in 1963. During the same year he collaborated with Peter Wall on the 'Design 63' project. Both designers were given freedom to create highly individual works. He collaborated with Peter Wall again on the 'Design for Today' project in 1967. A year later Minkin designed the Orbit shape. He left Wedgwood in 1988 and was later made an Honorary Fellow of the Royal College of Art.
See: Reilly, R., *Wedgwood – The New Illustrated Dictionary*, Antique Collectors' Club Ltd. (1995).

MORRIS, Tony (b.1942)
Morris was educated at Newport School of Art. He joined the Poole Pottery Ltd. in 1963, working closely with Robert Jefferson on the experimental range that formed the Delphis Studio collection. During the early seventies Morris produced a number of outstanding patterns as part of the Delphis range, including *Sun Face* from 1963-64. During the late sixties he worked with Guy Sydenham to develop a new range of shapes. In 1972 he launched a series of Calendar plates, designed in the traditional stained glass window technique. These were produced in a limited edition of one thousand, as was a set of Cathedral plates issued in about 1975. He later went on to design a successful series of embossed trays and then a selection of wicker effect pots decorated with a snow white glaze, in 1980. Morris left Poole during the early eighties but returned some years later. In the spring of 2000 he launched a number of outstanding plaques that he designed for Poole Pottery, featuring a living glaze.
See: Hayward, L., *Poole Pottery, Carter and Company and their Successors, 1873-1995*, Richard Dennis (1995).

NOKE, Cecil 'Jack', NRD (fl.1930s)

Born in the Stoke-on-Trent area. He was the son of C.J. Noke, the Art Director for Royal Doulton. His father had made a significant contribution to the company, not least for re-establishing Doulton's reputation as figure-makers. Noke was educated at Newcastle High School. After leaving school in 1910 he was apprenticed to an architect and at the same time attended evening classes at the Stoke School of Art and then in Burslem. From 1914 he served with the Fifth North Staffords in France. After being demobilised in 1920 he joined Royal Doulton. During his training he worked in several sections of the company. In 1926, after his training was completed, he joined his father. In 1936 he became Art Director. During the thirties he produced several modern patterns on his new Casino shape, in both bone china and earthenware, alongside more traditional patterns such as *Poppy* and *Leonora*. Noke continued to create new and innovative designs throughout the thirties.
See: Spours, J., *Art Deco Tableware*, Ward Lock (1988) and British Designers: Cecil J. Noke NRD of Doulton and Co. Ltd, *Pottery and Glass*, November 1948.

POWELL, Alfred (1865-1960)

Born near Marlow, later studying in Uppingham. He trained as an architect at the Slade School of Art. In 1887 he joined the offices of architect J. Sedding. In 1901 he set up a small craft pottery in Gloucestershire. Subsequently some of his designs for pottery were shown to Josiah Wedgwood and Sons Ltd. In 1905 the first exhibition of his hand-painted designs for Wedgwood was held in London. A formal agreement was made with the company and a studio was set up in London. In 1906 he married Louise Lessore. The couple spent some time at the Wedgwood factory working on new lines and training the hand paintresses. Powell designed a selection of patterns for large plaques with his work continually illustrated in the *Decorative Art Studio Year Books*. During the First World War he was a member of the Society of Friends War Relief Committee and spent some time teaching crafts in Belgium. The relationship with Wedgwood ended during the thirties.
See: Batkin, M., *Wedgwood Ceramics 1846-1959: A New Appraisal*, Richard Dennis (1982).

POWELL, Louise (née LESSORE) (1882-1956)

From a prestigious artistic family, she trained at the Central School of Art where she specialised in illumination and calligraphy. Powell was involved with the Arts and Crafts Exhibition Society. She worked extensively with her husband, producing many patterns for Josiah Wedgwood and Sons Ltd. and is also credited with the suggestion that the management should re-introduce some of the patterns from the early pattern books. In 1930 she designed the commemorative vase to celebrate the bicentenary of the birth of the company founder.
See: Batkin, M., *Wedgwood Ceramics 1846-1959*, Richard Dennis (1982) and Buckley, C., *Potters and Paintresses, Women Designers in the Pottery Industry 1870-1955*, Women's Press (1990).

QUEENSBERRY, David, MSIA HON, Des.RCA (b.1929)

After studying at the Central School of Arts and Crafts in London, the 12th Marquess of Queensberry worked for a number of years at Midwinter. Following a period of study at the North Staffordshire College of Technology he formed a design consultancy with Colin Melbourne in 1954, called Drumlanrig Melbourne. From 1959 to 1983 he was Professor of Ceramics and Glass at the Royal College of Art. In the late fifties he worked for Crown Staffordshire producing a range of patterns, including a series of vases. During the 1960s he designed shapes and one pattern for W.R. Midwinter Ltd. In 1966 he founded the Queensberry/Hunt Design Group with Martin Hunt. His design company undertook many important commissions, including the production of the Concept range for Hornsea Pottery Ltd. during the 1980s.
See: Dormer, P., China Syndrome, *Design Week*, 12 December 1986.

SEENEY, Enid

Seeney studied at Slepe Hall, St. Ives in Huntingdonshire and later at the Burslem School of Art. She started work at Spode-Copeland where she stayed for three years. In 1951 she joined Booth and Colclough. During 1954 Seeney spent a year at the Royal College of Art and at the same time visited many important exhibitions. She designed several patterns such as *English Garden*, *Samoa*, *Bamboo* and *Pavan*. However she is better known for her *Homemaker* pattern, a design classic of the late fifties and early sixties, sold in Woolworths from 1958-67. Seeney left the company in 1958.
See: Moss, S., *Homemaker – A 1950's Design Classic*, Cameron and Hollis (1997).

SKEAPING, John, RA (1901-1980)

Skeaping was born in South Woodford, Essex. He studied at the Blackheath School of Art, then at Goldsmiths' College in London and later won a scholarship to study at the Royal College of Art. In 1924 he won the Prix de Rome and studied for three years in Italy, being taught to carve marble. He married the sculptor Barbara Hepworth in 1924. In 1926 Josiah Wedgwood and Sons Ltd. commissioned him to produce a range of figures, including *Fallow Deer*, *Polar Bear*, *Sea Lion* and *Duiker*. During the thirties these items were publicised alongside the work of Keith Murray. Skeaping was Professor of Sculpture at the Royal College of Art during the fifties. He was appointed an Academician in 1959.
See: Batkin, M., *Wedgwood Ceramics 1846-1959: A New Appraisal*, Richard Dennis (1982) and Reilly, R., *Wedgwood – The New Illustrated Dictionary*, Antique Collectors' Club Ltd. (1995).

SYDENHAM, Guy (b.1916)

Sydenham joined Carter, Stabler and Adams Ltd. in 1931. He worked as a thrower. From 1949-51 he was foreman in the clay shape department. He worked closely with Alfred B. Read and Robert Jefferson. From the mid-sixties he worked as a designer and studio potter, producing many outstanding items for the Atlantis range, 1966-67. During 1972 he developed an outstanding range of red earthenware lamps that were hand-thrown and carved. He retired in 1977.
See: Hayward, L., *Poole Pottery, Carter & Company and their Successors, 1873-1995*, Richard Dennis (1995).

TALBOT, Sam (fl.1920s-1950s)

Little is known about Sam Talbot. He joined A.E. Gray and Co. Ltd. in about 1925. He later became Art Director during the thirties following the departure of Dorothy Toomes. In the thirties he produced a range of stylish and attractive patterns. During the late forties he produced a number of print and enamel designs, some of which were illustrated in the trade press of the period, including *Magnolia* and *Ludlow*. In the fifties he introduced several modern patterns such as *Tudor*, and a range of resist patterns including *Carnation*, from 1951. For the 1953 Coronation Talbot designed several items. He left Gray's in 1959 to join Lancaster and Sandland. Soon afterwards, he was appointed Managing Director of the company.
See: Niblett, P., *Hand-Painted Gray's Pottery*, City Museum and Art Gallery, Stoke-on-Trent (1982).

WADSWORTH, John (1879-1955)

His father was a cabinetmaker. Wadsworth had originally intended to take a career as a silk designer. He was born in Macclesfield and trained at the Stockport School of Art, later studying at the Royal College of Art in 1898. He joined Minton's in 1901, working closely with Léon Solon. When Solon left the company Wadsworth became Art Director from 1905 until 1915. On leaving Minton's he was appointed Art Director at the Royal Worcester Porcelain Company. A number of his patterns were shown at the British Art in Industry Exhibition at the Royal Academy in 1935. He later returned to Minton in about 1935 and in 1937 he designed the Solano Ware range, that featured stencilled style floral motifs. This was followed by the Byzantine range a year later. He also designed several border patterns alongside bone china vases. In 1949 Minton launched *Haddon Hall*, designed by Wadsworth, which was one of the company's best-selling patterns. He designed a vase for the Queen's Coronation in 1953.

See: Muter, G., *Léon Solon and John Wadsworth: Joint Designers of Minton's Secessionist Ware*, The Journal of the Decorative Arts Society, 1850 to the Present Day, No. 9, 1985.

WALL, Peter, ARCA, Des.ARCA, MSIA (b.1926)

Following his training at the Burslem School of Art, Wall studied at the Wimbledon School of Art. He attended the Royal College of Art between 1947-51. In 1951 he gained a silver medal for his designs that were exhibited at the Festival of Britain. A year later he joined Josiah Wedgwood and Sons Ltd. for a period of sixteen years; he was appointed to the position of Deputy Art Director in 1954. He later became Design Manager. Wall designed a range of patterns for both bone china and earthenware. Notable examples include *Woodbury* and *Penhurst*, both lithograph patterns, on the Barlaston shape from 1955-56. His *Hathaway Rose* and *Beaconsfield* patterns for bone china are typical examples. He also produced a limited range of nurseryware including *Big Top* in 1959. In 1961 Wedgwood launched his *Hereford* pattern on Queen's ware. He collaborated with Robert Minkin for the 'Design 63' project, creating the *Beehive* and *Circle and Star* patterns for tea caddies. For the 'Design for Today' project Wall introduced a Black Basalt vase and several other items. He left Wedgwood in 1968 to become Head of the School of Ceramics at Birmingham Polytechnic. He retired in 1988.

See: Reilly, R., *Wedgwood – The New Illustrated Dictionary*, Antique Collectors' Club Ltd. (1995).

WEDGWOOD, Star (1904-1995)

Cecily Stella Wedgwood was the daughter of Major Frank Wedgwood. She became interested in pottery design after various trips abroad, particularly to Florence. She studied pottery decoration at the Burslem School of Art and spent one term at the Royal College of Art in 1923, where she studied drawing, lettering and heraldry, amongst other subjects. This was followed by a period of study at the Central School of Art and Design. At Wedgwood she trained under Alfred and Louise Powell. During the late twenties and thirties she designed several patterns for both bone china and earthenware. Notable examples include *Lady Jane Grey*, *Coronation* and *Eurydice*. Her *Turkey Oak* pattern was produced on Cane ware. Following her marriage in 1937 she retired from design.

See: Buckley, C., *Potters and Paintresses, Women Designers in the Pottery Industry 1870-1955*, The Women's Press (1990).

WILSON, Norman (1902-1988)

Wilson was the son of a china manufacturer. During the early 1920s he studied at Ellesmere College and later at North Staffordshire Technical College, where he graduated as a Silver Medallist in 1923. At the age of twenty-three he emigrated to Canada, earning his living by breaking-in ponies. In 1927 he became Works Manager for Josiah Wedgwood and Sons Ltd. During his significant career he introduced a number of new glazes such as *Alpine Pink*, first shown in 1936, and the matt glazes used on the Keith Murray range. He also designed a number of shapes. In 1932 Wilson introduced new glazes for the Veronese range, decorated with stylised floral motifs in silver lustre. During the Second World War he served with the Royal Artillery. He returned to Wedgwood in 1946, to the post of production manager. In the late fifties he introduced *Summer Sky* and *Havanna*, two-coloured earthenware, on the Barlaston shape, designed in 1955. He designed the Leigh shape in 1960. Of particular note was his range of vases, bowls and other small items decorated with various experimental glazes known as Unique Ware. Throughout his career he worked with a number of designers, including Millicent Taplin and Keith Murray. In 1961 he became joint Managing Director with F. Maitland Wright. He retired in 1963.

See: Reilly, R., *Norman Wilson (1902-88)*, Etruria, The Wedgwood International Society, Vol.3, No.4, pp8-11.

BIBLIOGRAPHY

General

Anscombe, I., *A Woman's Touch, Women in Design from 1860 to the Present Day*, Phaidon, 1985.

Atterbury, P., and Batkin, M., *The Dictionary of Minton*, Antique Collectors' Club Ltd., 1990.

Atterbury, P., Batkin, M., Paul Denker, E., *Twentieth Century Ceramics, A Collectors' Guide to British and North American Factory Produced Ceramics*, Millers, 1999.

Banham, M., and Hillier, B., *Tonic to the Nation, Festival of Britain 1951*, Thames and Hudson, 1971.

Batkin, B., *Wedgwood Ceramics 1846-1959 A New Appraisal*, Richard Dennis, 1982.

Bergesen, V., *Encyclopedia of British Art Pottery*, Barrie and Jenkins, 1991.

Buckley, C., *Potters and Paintresses, Women Designers in the Pottery Industry 1870-1955*, The Women's Press, 1990.

Chamberlain, R., Rayner, G., and Stapleton, A., *Austerity to Affluence, British Art and Design 1945-1962*, Merrell Holberton, 1997.

Cross, R., *The Silver Lining, Britain in Colour 1945-1952*, Sidgwick and Jackson, 1985.

Forsyth, G., *Twentieth Century Ceramics*, The Studio Ltd., 1936.

Hannah, F., *Ceramics, Twentieth Century Design*, Bell and Hyman, 1986.

Hawkins, J., and Hollis, M. (eds.), *Thirties: British Art and Design before the War*, Arts Council of Great Britain and Lund Humphries, 1979.

Hillier, B., *The Style of the Century 1900-1980*, The Herbert Press, 1983.

Hollowood, B., *The Things We See No. 4: Pottery and Glass*, Penguin Books, 1947.

Honey, W.B., *Wedgwood Ware*, Faber and Faber, 1948.

Jackson, L., *The New Look, Design of the Fifties*, Thames and Hudson, 1991.

McCarthy, F., *A History of British Design, 1830-1970*, Allen and Unwin, 1979.

McCarthy, F., and Nuttgens, P., *An Eye for Industry: Royal Designers for Industry 1936-1986*, Lund Humphries, 1986.

McCready, K., *Art Deco and Modernist Ceramics*, Thames and Hudson, 1995.

McLaren, G., *Ceramics of the 1950s*, Shire Books, 1997.

Niblett, P., *Dynamic Designers* (exhibition catalogue), City Museum and Art Gallery, Stoke-on-Trent 1990.

Reilly, R., *Wedgwood: The New Illustrated Dictionary*, Antique Collectors' Club Ltd., 1996.

Sparke, P., *Design in Context*, Guild Publishing, 1988.

Spours, J., *Art Deco Tableware*, Ward Lock, 1988.

Stevenson, G., *Art Deco Ceramics*, Shire Books, 1998.

Stewart, R., *Design and British Industry*, John Murray Ltd, 1987.

Periodicals, Journals and Year Books

Architectural Review
Decorative Art, The Studio Year Book
Design
Design for Today
The Pottery Gazette and Glass Trade Review
The Pottery Gazette and Glass Trade Review Diary and Directory
Pottery and Glass Record
Journal of the Royal Society of Arts
The Studio Year Book
Society of Industrial Artists, Designers in Britain. Review of work of Members, 1947, 1949, 1953, 1957, 1964, 1971
Tableware International
Twentieth Century British Decorative Arts (Sales Catalogues) Christies, South Kensington, London
The Wedgwood Review

Works of reference on individual designers

Truda Carter

Hawkins, J., *The Poole Potteries*, Barrie and Jenkins, 1980.

Hayward, L., *Poole Pottery, Carter and Company and their Successors 1873-1995*, Richard Dennis, 1995.

Myers, L., *The First One Hundred Years 1873-1973*, Poole Pottery Ltd., 1973.

Articles:

Adams, J., Potters' Parade, *Pottery and Glass*, October 1950.

Crossingam-Gower, G., The Potters of Poole, *Art and Antiques*, 22 March 1975.

Hawkins, J., The Poole Potteries, *Antique Collectors' Guide*, February 1978.

King, J., Truda Carter, René Buthaud, and Surrealism, Unpublished Paper, September 1996.

Modern Pottery of Distinction, *House and Garden*, September 1923.

Modernity with Manners, *Architect and Building News*, 8 January 1932.

John Clappison

Heckford, B., *Hornsea Pottery 1949-1989 – Its People, Processes and Products*, Hornsea Pottery Collectors' Club and Research Society, 1998.

Articles:

Highlights of Blackpool, *Pottery and Glass*, March 1957.

New to Design Centre, *Pottery and Glass*, January 1962.

Design at Hornsea, *Pottery Gazette and Glass Trade Review*, July 1963.

Party Trips boost Pottery, *Pottery Gazette and Glass Trade Review incorporating Tableware*, August 1970.

John and his Magic Box, *Ravenhead News*, No. 3, September 1974.

Hornsea Pottery – From A Holiday Island, *Tableware International*, September 1980.

Clarice Cliff

Griffin, L., Meisel. L. K. and S.P., *The Bizarre Affair*, Thames and Hudson, 1988.

Griffin, L., *Taking Tea with Clarice Cliff*, Pavilion, 1996.

Griffin, L., *Fantastic Flowers of Clarice Cliff*, Pavilion 1997.

Griffin, L., *Clarice Cliff – The Art of Bizarre*, Pavilion, 1999.

Hopwood, I., and Hopwood, G., *The Shorter Connection*, Richard Dennis, 1992.

Jones, D., and Green, R., *Rich Designs of Clarice Cliff*, Rich Designs, 1995.

Wentworth-Shields, P., and Johnson, K., *Clarice Cliff*, L'Odéon,

1976.

Articles:

Gosling, K., Revival of Art Deco, *Evening Sentinel*, 24 May 1976.

Stevenson, G., Better than Bizarre, *Things*, Winter 1997-98.

Design Quiz No.2, *The Pottery Gazette and Glass Trade Review*, April 1951.

Brighton Museum and Art Gallery exhibition catalogue, 15 January to 20 February 1972.

The Bizarre World of Clarice Cliff, *Homes and Antiques*, October 1998.

Susie Cooper

Casey, A., *Susie Cooper Ceramics – A Collectors' Guide*, Jazz Publications, 1992.

Eatwell, A., *Susie Cooper Productions*, Victoria & Albert Museum, 1987.

Niblett, P., *Hand-Painted Gray's Pottery*, City Museum and Art Gallery, Stoke-on-Trent, 1982.

Woodhouse, A., *Elegance with Utility, The Work of Susie Cooper 1924-1978*, Arthur Sanderson & Sons, 1978.

Woodhouse, A., *Susie Cooper*, Trilby Books, 1992.

Youds, B., *An Elegant Affair*, Thames and Hudson, 1996.

Articles:

Ades, J., Designs for many markets, *The Illustrated London News*, 1 February 1969.

Benn, E., Why Susie is top of the table, *The Daily Telegraph*, Saturday 27 May 1978.

Benn, E., All Set for a Fresh Look at Tableware, *The Daily Telegraph*, 23 August 1983.

Casey, A., Dynamic Designer: A Tribute to Susie Cooper OBE, RDI, *Antique Collecting*, November 1995.

Critchlow, D., Susie Cooper, an artist who brings beauty to many homes, *The Manchester Evening News*, Wednesday, 1 March 1933.

Dale, S., Designed for Elegance and Utility, *The Antique Collector*, November 1990.

Eatwell, A., Susie Cooper: Her Pre-war Productions 1922-1939, *V & A Album*, 1986.

Fletcher, N., Sixty Glorious Years – The Work of Susie Cooper, OBE, *Antique Collecting*, October 1984.

Levin, A., At Home with the Queen of Ceramics, *The Mail on Sunday*, 26 June 1983.

Marsh, M., If you knew Susie, *The Independent on Sunday*, 8 November 1992.

Rose, A., Woman whose success came on a plate, *The Times*, 11 July 1984.

Scott, M., Susie Cooper, *The Gazette*, 6 March 1993.

Silver, R., Susie Cooper: Ceramic Designer 1902-1995, *Studio Pottery Magazine*, November/December 1995.

Taylor, M., Susie Cooper, *Period Living*, March 1993.

Youds, B., Susie Cooper OBE, RDI, *Royal Society of Arts Journal*, March 1997.

Robert Jefferson

Atterbury, P., *Poole in the Fifties* (exhibition catalogue), Richard Dennis, 1997.

Hayward, L., *Poole Pottery and their Successors 1873-1995*, Richard Dennis, 1995.

Lyons, H. and Boston, N., *Exhibition of Poole Pottery Studio in the Sixties* (exhibition catalogue), New Century, London, 1993.

Articles:

Donaldson, A., Pottery from Poole, *The Glasgow Herald*, 16 May 1964.

Good, E., Plain or Fancy, *The Sunday Times*, 14 April 1963.

Holland, R.T., Developments at Poole Pottery, *Ceramics*, September 1963.

McCarthy, F., Crafts Council, *The Guardian*, 29 August 1964.

Eyes are on a new designer, *Poole and Dorset Herald*, 8 January 1958.

Robert Jefferson: Designer, *Euro-Ceramics*, 12 August 1964.

Purbeck Pottery, *Pottery Gazette and Glass Trade Review* incorporating *Tableware*, March 1967.

Daisy Makeig-Jones

Fontaines, U. des, *Wedgwood Fairyland Lustre*, Sotheby Parke Bernet, 1975.

Fontaines, U. des, and Lambourne, L., *Miss Jones and her Fairyland*, Victoria & Albert Museum, 1990.

Articles:

Fontaines, U. des, Fairyland Lustre: The work of Daisy Makeig-Jones (1881-1945), abridged and edited from a talk given before the Wedgwood Society on 27 April 1963. *Proceedings of the Wedgwood Society*, 1963.

Langella, J., A Fairyland Lustre Cup and Saucer, *The Wedgwoodian*, November 1978.

Makeig-Jones, D., *Some Glimpses of Fairyland*, Josiah Wedgwood and Sons Ltd., 1921.

Mones, J., Celtic Designs on Wedgwood Wares, *The Wedgwoodian*, November 1991.

Ronald, J., Fairyland Lustre, *Antique Collector*, December 1979.

Fairyland Prices, *Financial Times*, 23 October 1976.

Eve Midwinter

Jenkins, S., *Midwinter Modern: A Revolution in British Tableware*, Richard Dennis, 1997.

Peat, A., *Midwinter – A Collectors' Guide*, Cameron and Hollis, 1992.

Articles:

Benn, E., All Set for a Fresh Look at Tableware, *The Daily Telegraph*, 23 August 1983.

Fokscahner, S., A Midwinter's Tale, *Homes and Antiques*, May 1994.

Midwinter's Accent, *Tableware International*, April 1972.

The New Stonehenge, *Tableware International*, January 1972.

Why Midwinter developed its new shape in Stoneware, *Tableware International*, May 1979.

Stoneware, The Body Beautiful, *Tableware International*, May 1980.

Stoneware, *Tableware International*, May 1981.

Keith Murray

Beard, G., *International Modern Glass*, Barrie and Jenkins, 1976.

Dodsworth, R. (ed.), *British Glass Between the Wars*, Dudley Leisure Services, 1987.

Hawkins, J., *Keith Murray* (exhibition catalogue), Victoria & Albert Museum, HMSO, 1987.

Tyler, L., *Keith Murray in Context* (exhibition catalogue), New Zealand, 1996.

Articles:

Aitken, J. and Lee, S., Who is Keith Murray, New Zealander creates a Profession from Architect to Industrial Designer, *New Zealand News*, September 1935.

Gater, S., Keith Murray at Wedgwood, Architect and Designer (1892-1981), *Studio Pottery*, No.22, September 1996.

Murray, K., Some Views of a Designer, *Journal of the Society of Glass Technology*, Vol.19, 1925.

Murray, K., The Design of Table Glass, *Design for Today*, June 1933.

Murray, K., The Designer in Industry; What is the Prospect, *The Journal of Careers*, January 1935.

Murray, K., The Designer and his Problem II, *The Journal of Careers*, January 1935.

Murray, K., Prestressed Concrete Hangars at London Airport, *The Builder*, 7 November 1952.

Taylor, D., Designs of the Times: Keith Murray, Designer in Glass, Ceramics and Silver, *Antique Collecting*, Vol.21, No.11, April 1987.

Taylor, D., Keith Murray – The Swedish Connection, *The Journal of the Glass Association*, Vol.2, 1987.

Taylor, D., Keith Murray: A Modernist Designer in Glass, Ceramics and Metal, *Studies in the Decorative Arts*, Spring 1994.

Taylor, D., Keith Murray: Architect and Designer for Industry, *Twentieth Century Architecture*, No.1 (Summer 1994).

Wilson, N., Tribute to architect of Barlaston and his ceramic designs, *Wedgwood Review*, September 1981.

New factory at Barlaston, Staffs. for Josiah Wedgwood and Sons Ltd., *The Architectural and Building News*, 25 June 1943.

Buildings in Oxford, *Architectural Review*, January 1960.

Eric Ravilious

Binyon, H., *Eric Ravilious: Memoir of an Artist*, Lutterworth Press, 1983.

Constable, F., *The England of Eric Ravilious*, Scholar Press, 1982.

Dalrymple, R., and Batkin, M., *Ravilious and Wedgwood: The Complete Wedgwood Designs of Eric Ravilious*, Dalrymple Press, 1986.

Articles:

Bury, H., Designs for Glass by Eight British Artists, 1934, *The Journal of the Decorative Arts Society 1890-1940* (No.2), 1978.

Gater, S., Eric Ravilious – A Designer ahead of his time, *Studio Pottery*, No,.24, December 1996/January 1997.

Gooden, R.Y., Eric Ravilious as a designer, *Architectural Review*, December 1943.

Hamilton, W., Ravilious Revealed, *Art and Antiques*, February 1993.

The Mural Decorations at Morley College, *The Studio Year Book*, 1930.

Eric Ravilious, 1903-1942 (exhibition catalogue), The Minories, Colchester, 1972.

Eric Ravilious, 1903-1942: A Commemorative Exhibition (exhibition catalogue), Towner Art Gallery, 1992.

Alfred Burgess Read

Atterbury, P., *Poole in the Fifties* (exhibition catalogue), Richard Dennis, 1997.

Hayward, L., *Poole Pottery: Carter and Company and their Successors 1873-1995*, Richard Dennis, 1995.

Articles:

Read, A., Versatility in Lighting, *Design*, No. 34, October 1951.

Poole Ware in Pitt-Rivers Museum, *The Western Gazette*, 1 October 1954.

Mr. A.B. Read, Lighting Design Pioneer, *The Times*, Obituary, 17 October 1973.

Charlotte Rhead

Batkin, M., *Good Gifts for Good Children*, Richard Dennis, 1996.

Bumpus, B., *Rhead Artists and Potters 1870-1950* (exhibition catalogue), Geffrye Museum, London, 1986.

Bumpus, B., *Charlotte Rhead, Potter and Designer*, Kevin Francis Publishing, 1987.

Bumpus, B. *Collecting Rhead Pottery*, Francis Joseph Publications, 1999.

Rhead, G.W. and Rhead, F.A., *Staffordshire Pots and Potters*, Hutchinson, 1906.

Articles:

Bumpus, B., Pottery designed by Charlotte Rhead, *The Antique Collector*, January 1983.

Bumpus. B., Tube-Line Variations, *The Antique Collector*, December 1985.

Bumpus, B, Cheerful Charlotte Rhead, *Antique Dealers and Collectors Guide*, August 1988.

Bumpus, B., The Rheads as Art Educators, *The Journal of the Decorative Arts Society*, No.13.

Shaw, G. and Greysmith, B., Charlotte Rhead, the Clarice Cliff of Crown Ducal, *Collect It*, October 2000.

Watson, P., Charlotte Rhead – A Gentle Genius, *Antiques Bulletin*, 14 November 1992.

Miss Charlotte Rhead, Pottery Artist and Designer, *The Pottery and Glass Record*, August 1937.

Centenary of Burgess and Leigh, *Pottery and Glass*, November 1951.

Lottie and her decorative wares, *Staffordshire Life*, 1989.

Victor Skellern

Articles:

Gater, S., Victor Skellern: Wedgwood Art Director 1934-65, *Journal of the Northern Ceramic Society*, Vol. 10, 1993.

Skellern, V., Design and Decoration, *Pottery Gazette and Glass Trade Review*, February 1953.

Victor Skellern, *Pottery and Glass*, July 1952.

Eric Slater

Davenport, C., *Shelley: The Later Years*, Heather Publications Ltd., 1997.

Hill, S., *The Shelley Style*, Jazz Publications, 1990.

Watkins, C., Harvey, W., and Senft, R., *Shelley Potteries, The History and Production of a Staffordshire Family of Potters*, Barrie and Jenkins, 1980.

Jessie Tait

Hollowood, B., *The Story of J & G Meakin 1851-1951*, Bemrose Publicity, 1951.

Jenkins, S., *Midwinter Modern: A Revolution in British Tableware*, Richard Dennis, 1997.

Peat, A., *Midwinter – A Collectors' Guide*, Cameron and Hollis, 1992.

Articles:

Peat, A., Midwinter 1950's Tableware: A Radical Departure from Tradition, *Antique Collector*, 1992.

Forty Years of Expansion, W.R. Midwinter Ltd., *Pottery and Glass*, October 1952.

A Notable Burslem Potter, *Pottery Gazette and Glass Trade Review*, March 1952.

Welcome to British Coupe Ware, *Pottery Gazette and Glass Trade Review*, February 1953.

A Studio Pottery in Hanley, *Pottery Gazette and Glass Trade Review*, October 1953.

Keeping ahead with Contemporary Designs:, New Midwinter range for home and export, *Pottery Gazette and Glass Trade Review*, June 1953.

Queensberry range by Midwinter: A New Tableware for Modern Tastes, *Pottery Gazette and Glass Trade Review*, August 1962.

Reflections on Blackpool, *Pottery and Glass*, March 1962.

Problems of Pioneering Pottery, *Pottery Gazette and Glass Trade Review*, April 1964.

Introducing MQ2 by Midwinter, *Pottery Gazette and Glass Trade Review*, September 1967.

Modernisation at J & G Meakin Ltd., *Pottery Gazette and Glass Trade Review*, April 1969.

Johnson Originals: Casual Elegance at a Reasonable Price, *Tableware International*, September 1976.

Johnson Brothers: Around the World in Eighty Days, *Evening Sentinel*, 16 October 1991.

Millicent Taplin

Attfield, J. and Kirkham, P., *A View from the Interior. Feminism, Women and Design*, The Women's Press, 1989.

Catalogue of bodies, shapes and glazes. Current for 1940-1950, Josiah Wedgwood and Sons Ltd., 1940.

Gater. S., and Vincent, D., *Wedgwood from Etruria to Barlaston – the transitional years*, University of Keele, 1988.

Articles:

Gater, S., Victor Skellern: Wedgwood Art Director 1934-1965, *Journal of the Northern Ceramic Society*, Vol. 10, 1993.

Lodey, J., A flower was picked and a famous pottery design was born, *Six Towns Magazine*, September 1963.

A Special Wedgwood Display, *The Pottery Gazette and Glass Trade Review*, 1 April 1938.

Overseas trade in Wedgwood Ware, *The Pottery Gazette and Glass Trade Review*, February 1940.

Team work for Design, *The Pottery Gazette and Glass Trade Review*, January 1955.

Designs of the Year, *Pottery Gazette and Glass Trade Review*, June 1957.

A Lifetime in Design, *Wedgwood Review*, September 1962.

Susan Williams-Ellis

Cooper-Willis, E., and Stanton, V., *The Story of Portmeirion Potteries, 1960-1995 – A Collectors' Guide*, Portmeirion Potteries Ltd., 1995.

Jenkins, S., and McKay, S., *Portmeirion Pottery*, Richard Dennis, 2000.

Niblett, P., *Hand-Painted Grays Pottery*, City Museum and Art Gallery, Stoke-on-Trent, 1982.

Portmeirion, The World of Botanic Garden 1972-1997, Portmeirion Potteries Ltd., 1997.

Articles:

Casey, A., Putting Art into Industry, *Antique Collecting*, March 1999.

McKay, S., *Portmeiriana* newsletters, 1997 to 1998.

Marshall-Jones, M., Portmeirion Pottery, *Homes and Antiques*, February 1998.

The House of Gray, *Pottery Gazette and Glass Trade Review*, May 1953.

Roberts, C., A Woman Amongst the Potters, *Six Towns Magazine*, June 1965.

Lustre wares, *Pottery and Glass*, July 1956.

The New Gray's Pottery, *Pottery and Glass Record*, June 1961.

Definitely Different at Portmeirion Potteries, *Pottery Gazette and Glass Trade Review* incorporating *Tableware International*, October 1969.

Susan Williams-Ellis: Room of my Own, *Sunday Observer*, 23 September 1990.

Kathie Winkle

Hampson, R., *Churchill China: Great British Potters since 1795*, University of Keele, 1994.

Leith, P., *The Designs of Kathie Winkle*, Richard Dennis, 1999.

Articles:

Marshall-Jones, M., Innovative Designs, *Collect It*, July 1999.

Rimmer, P., Kathie Winkle: Post-War Designer, *Antique Collecting*, November 1995.

Transformation at Broadhurst's, *Pottery Gazette and Glass Trade Review*, November 1956.

So this is James Broadhurst, *Tableware International*, February 1982.

PICTURE CREDITS

INDEX